Bodies of Difference

Hand-crank tricycles mark a gathering of the Beijing Disabled Youths Club at the home of a former club member, mid-1980s. Anonymous photo.

Bodies of Difference

*Experiences of Disability and Institutional
Advocacy in the Making of Modern China*

Matthew Kohrman

UNIVERSITY OF CALIFORNIA PRESS
Berkeley   Los Angeles   London

University of California Press
Berkeley and Los Angeles, California

University of California Press, Ltd.
London, England

Library of Congress Cataloging-in-Publication Data

Kohrman, Matthew, 1964–.
  Bodies of difference : experiences of disability and institutional
advocacy in the making of modern China / Matthew Kohrman.
      p.   cm.
  Includes bibliographical references and index.
  ISBN 0-520-22644-5 (cloth : alk. paper) —ISBN 0-520-22645-3
(pbk. : alk. paper)
    1. People with disabilities—China.   2. Biopolitics—China.
I. Title.

HV1559.C6K64   2005
362.4'0951—dc22   2004005279

Manufactured in the United States of America
13   12   11   10   09   08   07   06   05
10   9   8   7   6   5   4   3   2   1

Printed on Ecobook 50 containing a minimum 50% post-consumer
waste, processed chlorine free. The balance contains virgin pulp,
including 25% Forest Stewardship Council Certified for no old
growth tree cutting, processed either TCF or ECF. The sheet is
acid-free and meets the minimum requirements of ANSI/NISO
Z39.48–1992 (R 1997) (Permanence of Paper).♾

For Asa and Ezra

CONTENTS

ILLUSTRATIONS

PREFACE

In the summer of 1998 I spent a week in Beijing. The highlight of that warm-weather visit was not the anthropological conference I was attending at Beijing University, nor the interview that I conducted with an official from whom I had long sought an audience. The most meaningful aspect of the week, for me, was the lunch I had with a dozen people, mostly men, whom I had befriended in the mid-1990s, when I had conducted the major portion of the research for this book.

One of these friends was Hai Jun.[1] Hai had picked me up at the Beijing Drum Tower subway station, and once we had cleared the tangle of bicycles parked around the tower, we motored for about a mile to our destination, a Shandong restaurant, weaving through back streets filled with sundry vehicles, potholes, and pedestrians. Two years had passed since I had last been in Hai Jun's city, or upon his motorcycle, and it seemed to me that the few pedestrians who bothered to even look up as we drove past were far less attentive to the sight of us. Have things changed that much in my absence? I wondered. When I had first visited China in the 1980s, my tall, Euro-American persona had frequently been the object of significant stares, even in cosmopolitan centers like Beijing. And when Hai had begun giving me rides through the capital city in 1994, many people would gawk at the sight of two men riding on a three-wheeled motorcycle, one of them an obvious polio survivor and the other an obvious foreigner. It was the odd combination of our *alterity* (sociopolitically mediated otherness) and our *bodiliness* (sociopolitically mediated body-self) that no doubt had caused many to stop and stare. But on this day in 1998 it seemed to me that we hardly attracted attention at all.

Hai parked in front of the restaurant next to a group of similarly designed motorized tricycles and then he quipped over his shoulder, "Looks like everyone else is here." After being seated in a pre-reserved dining room, we all settled into our table activities, slowly eating an array of meats, vegetables, and grains, commenting on the dishes one by one, and chatting about a variety of topics, some humorous, some more disturbing.

Hai Jun briefly discussed a weightlifting class he was contemplating taking. The woman to my right described recent battles she and her "crippled" business partner, as she referred to him, had been having with the tax collectors. I reported on recent events in my own life and received a fair amount of teasing about still not having completed this book despite being so seemingly "able-bodied" *(jianquan)*, as one friend noted. Two dining companions regaled the rest of us with wry details about a karaoke party they had attended that had been sponsored by China's nationwide disability advocacy organization, the Disabled Persons' Federation. And the man seated across from me, an employee of the Federation for the previous six years, talked with biting wit about changes in policies and personnel within the institution.

Shortly before the meal's end, I mentioned my earlier surprise at the fact that Hai and I had elicited so little attention as we had zigzagged our way to the restaurant. Several minutes of discussion ensued, and then, being that he was our host, Hai took it upon himself to sum up what he understood to be the group's overall view:

> Yes, you could say, in recent years here in Beijing, people like us have experienced transformations similar to *dabizi* ["longnoses," a Mandarin Chinese term used to code people of Euro-American descent, who are not citizens of the People's Republic of China]. Just think of what life was like during the first decade after the Cultural Revolution. Foreigners were still a rarity outside of the diplomatic and university districts, and most of us around this table spent nearly all our time as hermits cooped up at home. We *quezi* [crippled] were invisible because we hid ourselves away. That's no longer the case. We're out on the streets going where we want to go. The world is talking about the disabled now. And the Federation has been telling everyone about us. So, now we've become known. We're *canji ren*. In that way, like foreigners over the last few years, we've become a part of modern life here in Beijing. Now, most Beijingers expect to see and hear about people like you and me, about foreigners and *canji*. That means they have come to develop expectations about what we do, what we say. It also means, oddly, that we've become somewhat invisible again. That's particularly the case with us *canji* because most people in this city prefer not to think about us. Doing so makes them feel guilty for how terribly we're treated and it frightens them that, they too, could have bodies like us.[2]

This book pertains to bodiliness, alterity, and the lives of a large number of people who reside in the People's Republic of China (PRC). While self-reflexivity has become a valuable part of my scholarly discipline, anthropology, and while aspects of my own positionality have been important for the production of this book, the alterity that primarily animates this study is not that of "foreigner" *(waiguo ren)*. Rather, it is a different otherness, a different piece in modernity's order of things—one certainly shaped by processes defining foreignness in recent years across China, but one that has come to carry very different meanings and significance—that is of central concern here.

This book discusses an embodied form of otherness that, over the last two decades, has become increasingly important to many people in China and that, over this period, has become a subject of increasing public attention. The otherness that comprises the focus in this text is what Mandarin speakers in China increasingly refer to as *canji* [pronounced "tsan-jee"] and what more and more English speakers around the world refer to as "disability."

Several questions about *canji* are attended to here. On a relatively broad level, these questions include: In 1980s and 1990s China, how did people become subject to new kinds of knowledge production and distinctive identification having to do with *canji*? Why did *canji*, a hitherto rarely used term in China, get mapped onto the English category "disability" and emerge in the PRC as a topic of significant meaning-making at the end of the twentieth century, something about which books were published, articles written, films produced, and professional disciplines established? Why, in the 1990s, did groups of people—people like Hai Jun and several of the other male dining partners at the Shandong eatery—begin to self-identify as *canji* and to spend a considerable amount of time together, thereby creating for themselves new social spaces? Why, in some cities, were men who had difficulty in walking particularly inclined to develop what they sometimes called "disability circles" and "disability brotherhoods"—associations that afforded their members everything from audiences for storytelling, to trusted shoulders upon which to lean, introductions for sexual encounters, partnerships for businesses, to collaborators for acts of public defiance, and interpersonal intimacy that promoted greater self-understanding?

In addressing these questions, this book is designed to draw our attention to the ways that *canji* has been emerging and metamorphosing in China as a social, political, and somatic sphere of existence in recent decades. However, it must be emphasized that this book is about more than how a specific social category, *canji*, was constructed in late-twentieth-century China, or how a sizable number of men used the term *canji* to map their own suffering, palliation, sociality, and self-making.

This book is also about the production of a new state bureaucracy within a national and international context. In particular, it is about the production of the specific bureaucracy that my dining companions and I discussed on that summer afternoon as we enjoyed the flavors so distinctive to Shandong cuisine. Throughout this book, I focus extensively on the formation of that organization, an institution which, within only a decade, became a vice-ministry in the People's Republic's governmental apparatus. This is the China Disabled Persons' Federation *(zhongguo canjiren lianhehui)*. Founded in March 1988 with great fanfare by the Chinese and international media, the China Disabled Persons' Federation has three formal objectives: to represent the common interests of all Chinese citizens with disabilities, to protect their legal rights and interests, and to mobilize social forces to serve them.

How and why did an institution like the Federation surface just as China was emerging from three decades of Maoism? How, in the rapidly changing nation-state that was late-twentieth-century China—a country ruled by communist imprimatur yet increasingly engaged with the forces of transnationalism and neoliberal economics—were resources marshaled and directed into the development of a governmental disability-advocacy organization? Why, at the end of the 1980s, did China's party-state launch an organization that was specifically devoted to helping those citizens it identified as disadvantaged by virtue of the conflict between the demands of everyday life, morally infused perceptions of normality, and biomedically defined dysfunctional bodies? Why, in the 1980s and 1990s, when China's government was in the midst of dismantling many of its erstwhile socialist guarantees, would the party-state choose to foster an institution for the disabled, one charged with creating welfare mechanisms, social service personnel, laws, media, and medical interventions? Moreover, how did the Federation grow so quickly? How is it that by the late 1990s, a decade after its founding, the Federation had offices located in tens of thousands of China's townships, county seats, and city neighborhoods?

By raising these questions here, in the book's Preface, I wish to emphasize, as already noted, that this book is as much about the formation of state bureaucracy (the creation of the Federation) as it is about the formation of embodied otherness (the framing of *canji* as lived experience).

How are we to examine these two domains of sociopolitical formation? How are we to analyze, on the one hand, the development of a new governmental agency and, on the other hand, a transforming and expanding sphere of difference? Should our method be that of a compartmentalizing clinician, wherein we analyze one of these limbs first, then move on to dissect its opposite member, making believe that at any given moment one appendage is missing or that its prosthetic is out for repair?

A central tenet of this book is that these two aspects of sociopolitical formation need not be investigated separately and that, in fact, there is much to be learned by examining how the two interact—or to extend the somatic metaphor further, how they work hand-in-hand. Indeed, a central argument of this book is that there is a great deal to be gained, analytically, and to a certain degree, sociopolitically, by examining how and why governmental bureaucracies and alterity may be mutually constitutive within and across social and historical contexts.

Toward these ends, the lines of inquiry persistently present in this text are purposely designed to fuse many of the questions already posed above. These integrated lines of inquiry can be articulated as follows: How is it that, at the end of the twentieth century, some people's bodies in the PRC became the loci for sizable sociopolitical formation, both governmental and experiential? In the 1980s and 1990s, how were such people central to the development of China's Disabled Persons' Federation and, by extension, to China's party-state? Conversely, how did this newly emerging branch of the party-state, the Federation, help define *canji* as a biomedically grounded state of existence, how did it influence how people responded to *canji* within community contexts, and how did it shape the ways, for some, *canji* would be lived? In what ways did the overlap of these two spheres of sociopolitical formation become dependent upon and disruptive to the historical trajectory of more overarching modes of organization in China (e.g., state control, patriarchy, and ableism)? And, finally, how were these spheres of sociopolitical formation especially contingent upon the interplay of additional founts of modernism at the end of the twentieth century, like humanitarian internationalism, empiricism, and capital expansion?

This is a unique menu, no doubt one that will satisfy the palates of some readers while leaving others less sated. At the end of the Shandong lunch that Hai Jun hosted, the sole woman at the table, Wang Xiaoping, teased Hai Jun about the array of dishes he had ordered, which, while adequate in number, she said, were somewhat lacking since the balance between meats, vegetables, and grains did not follow common banqueting convention. And then she quipped, "Hai, you're such a capable *canji*, but still you don't know how to order at a restaurant. Maybe, instead of taking that weightlifting course, instead of trying to become a more modern man, you could convince the Federation to provide you a rehabilitation course in banqueting." Hai retorted:

> Wha! I don't need anything more to be a modern man [*xiandai nanzihan*]. Maoism has faded and the Federation has become my big uncle [*dashushu*]. I'm quite the modern man now. I've had corrective polio surgery three times. I've launched my own *canji* business. I may even go to Australia next year as a member of a Federation delegation. If you wanted a conventional menu today, you should have provided me a more conventional set of companions. What's conventional about you and everyone else here—a foreign anthropologist and a bunch of disabled men like me? Give me a more conventional guest list, and I'll provide a more conventional array of dishes.

In order to disentangle some of the unique processes underlying my "unconventional" dining companions' barbs, I hope you will recognize the need for this book to provide a likewise distinctive if not unconventional anthropological feast.

ACKNOWLEDGMENTS

There is an insight about sentience that I first heard described a few years ago. It has to do with pain. It goes like this. You can share a space with one or more people, sit only inches away from them, even listen to them talk about topics in great detail, and be unaware that any one of them is in a state of utter agony.

Cannot the same be said about other forms of sentience, though? For instance, cannot the same be said for gratitude?

Before you become absorbed in the topics of this book in any great detail, before you become rooted in the textual spaces that comprise this volume, I would like to divulge something about the sentiments that animate what you will be reading here. This admission is not that my ethnography arises in part from the suffering of people with whom I have carried out research over the last decade. That is obvious, or will be soon enough. Rather I want to make it clear that this book's every line is underlain by debt and appreciation.

And toward that end, there is a dizzying array of friends and allies who deserve acknowledgment. To all those who helped me in China during my fieldwork, *duo xie* (many thanks)! Thank you for assisting me, thank you for sheltering me, and thank you for putting up with my inquiries over the years. Some of you who deserve special recognition here and who I can identify by name (alas, many I cannot because of the need for anonymity) are Gao Xiaorui, Wei Maoguo, Li Qiang, Chen Wen, Lin Daodan, Geng Jun, Willie Brent, Susan Lawrence, and Chen Yu, as well as Michael Phillips, Sing Lee, Veronica Pearson, Han Feng, and Li Shizhuo. My deepest appreciation and affection goes out to everyone in Min Song, particularly the Chen family for welcoming me into their home, taking me for starlit canoe rides, and teaching me so much about the intimacies of everyday life.

Here in the United States, there are three mentors and friends who are due special acknowledgement. These are James L. Watson, Arthur Kleinman, and Michael Herzfeld. Without their support, attention to detail, and astute advice, this book may never have been produced. For sure, it would not have developed into its current form. Others who helped inform key conceptual foundations of this ethnography over the years are current and former participants in Harvard's Friday morning medical anthropology seminar and members of Harvard's Department of Social Medicine. Especially notable people in this regard are Mary-Jo DelVechio Good, Joe Dumit, Byron Good, Karen-Sue Taussig, João Biel, Jean Jackson, Cheryl Mattingly, Paul Farmer, and Bob Desjarlais.

Many more friends and colleagues—whether now living in the U.S., China, or elsewhere—are likewise owed words of gratitude for peppering me not simply with keen suggestions and critique on segments of this study, but also, just as importantly, encouragement and good humor. These include many of my former doctoral classmates, like Lida Junghans, Jing Jun, Julie Goldman, Jeanne Shea, Maris Gillette, Maya Todeschini, Matthew McGuire, Lindsay French, Fuji Lozada, Yan Yunxiang, John Fox, Lawrence Cohen, Narquis Barak, John Gerry, and Komatra Chuengsatiansup.

Also to be mentioned are Suzanne Gottschang, Liu Xin, Lisa Rofel, Gail Hershatter, Ken George, Sandra Hyde, Judith Farquhar, Susan Greenhalgh, Hugh Gusterson, Tanya Luhrmann, Adriana Petryna, Paul Longmore, Zhang Li, Emily Martin, Myron Cohen, Benedicte Ingstad, Linda Mitteness, Andrew Walder, Susan Brownell, Rayna Rapp, Ezra Vogel, Jean Oi, Begonia Aretxaga, Philippe Bourgois, Jay Dautcher, Ann Anagnost, Russell Shuttleworth, Vincanne Adams, Nancy Chen, and Rubie Watson. Thank you all for responding to sections of this study, providing feedback to materials presented at conferences, or simply pausing in the midst of your busy lives to buoy my confidence about this project.

Margery and Lee Kohrman are due my most heartfelt appreciation for providing me the encouragement, nurturance, and nerve to drift off through scholarly lands. Many thanks go out to my colleagues in CASA—the Department of Cultural and Social Anthropology at Stanford—for extending their warmth, for creating such a vibrant intellectual space here in California, and for helping me find my footing in recent years on this sometimes shaky edge of the Pacific. I would also like to express special thanks to current and former graduate students at Stanford working in the terrains of medical anthropology and cultural studies of science, with whom I have had the good fortune to interact and who have repeatedly contributed to my thinking. These include Mei Zhan, Jennifer Chertow, Julia Carpenter, Miriam Ticktin, Tiffany Romain, and Sarah Ramirez.

Financial support for this project was provided by grants from the Committee on Scholarly Communication with China, Harvard University's

Sinclair Kennedy Traveling Fellowship, the National Institute of Mental Health, the Chiang Ching Kuo Foundation, the Mellon Foundation, the Hoberman Fund, and the Foreign Language and Area Studies Program.

Gratitude is duly owed Ravneet Kar for proofreading sections of this book as they neared final stages of completion. Some materials of this book have appeared in four journals: *Medical Anthropology Quarterly, Cultural Anthropology, American Ethnologist,* and *Culture, Medicine, and Psychiatry.* My thanks to the editors of those journals and to their anonymous readers for pushing me to clarify my ideas. I am also grateful to all those at University of California Press who have worked on this text and repeatedly awed me with their patience and professionalism, most notably Sheila Levine, Reed Malcolm, and Ruth Steinberg.

More than anyone else, though, I wish to express my ongoing appreciation to Amy Kohrman. Since that blustery December day we met in a garage along the northern bank of the Charles River, you have provided me the confidence to weather long periods of intellectual doubt. You have helped discipline my disheveled prose. And you have embraced me with your unmatched love and levity.

Introduction

One day in the spring of 1968, a body dropped from a third-floor window at Beijing University. On the way down, it bounced off a steel guide wire, flipped, and thudded to the ground. A crowd of people quickly congregated. At first, no one did anything except look at the young man and point toward the window of the physics building from where he fell. Moments later, the twenty-four-year-old man regained consciousness and began to call to those around him for medical treatment. Still, nobody came to the man's aid. As is the case in many urban settings around the world, indifference to the plight of strangers has and continues to occur in the cities of China, but in this instance nearly everybody knew the injured man. He was a classmate.

Eventually, some people stepped forward. They carried the student, who was in acute pain and experiencing complete paralysis in his lower extremities, to the university clinic. Medical personnel blocked them from carrying the man into the clinic, however. The rescuers then decided to transport the student off campus to the emergency ward of the nearby Beijing Medical College (BMC) hospital. Again, doctors refused to treat the student. After failing twice to get him medical care, the rescuers opted to leave the young man lying in a BMC hallway and, when nobody was looking, ran away. The paralyzed student remained there in the hallway, unattended until nightfall, at which time BMC officials ordered an ambulance to return him to the Beijing University clinic. Upon reaching campus, the ambulance crew left their paralyzed charge on the ground alongside the clinic's front door and then sped off. The student lay there alone until morning (Qin 1997, 190, 198–99).

SOCIOPOLITICAL FORMATION AND BIOBUREAUCRACY

In the pages that follow, I tell the stories of a wide variety of people. Or it might seem like a wide variety, given the received ways of apprehending one another shared by many of this book's likely readers. For instance, some stories in this volume are of social scientists trained in early-twentieth-century London and New York City. Some are of people born several decades ago who now struggle to walk because of polio epidemics. Some are of figures who currently hold the formal rank of cadre *(ganbu)*, a designation of authority and employment within China's contemporary party-state. And still other stories are of Ohio children maimed in a train crash, functionaries of the United Nations, and residents of a sand-strewn village near Vietnam.

There is one person, however, who receives regular mention throughout this book. A piece of his story—an episode from late-1960s Beijing, a vignette of acute calamity and suffering—is synopsized above. The man at the center of that anecdote is Deng Pufang.[1] The appearance and reappearance of Deng Pufang in many pages of this text, in part, stems from his unique pedigree. Deng Pufang is the oldest son of Deng Xiaoping, China's top government official from the late 1970s to the mid-1990s. Pufang regularly surfaces in this text even more because of what is widely recognized as his overarching pertinence to this book's main descriptive agenda.

The main ethnographic aim here is to examine the sociopolitical formation of a new bureaucracy within the People's Republic of China and its relationship to a specific category of alterity. By sociopolitical formation, I mean the processes by which people craft, regulate, symbolize, and experience facets of everyday life—ranging from modes of work, aspects of kinship, or other forms of distinction (like class, gender, or ethnicity), to administrative structures, aesthetic norms, notions of self, or religious and scientific practices and doctrines. These processes merit the suffix "political" as much as the prefix "socio" because they are always complicit with, constitutive of, and/or in conflict with structures of domination. Moreover, while often seemingly hermetic when viewed from certain scholarly perspectives, sociopolitical processes are usually much messier, as I understand them. They overlap and often contradict each other. They are the ongoing products of long, complicated, and contested histories. They are always being, at once, reproduced, redirected, and challenged. And they are always somewhat circular, in that the people who fuel them are always themselves greatly enmeshed and directed by the processes.

The bureaucracy whose sociopolitical formation sits at the center of this book goes by the name Zhongguo Canjiren Lianhehui and gives itself the English-language name China Disabled Persons' Federation. The main publicly stated mission of this organization is to help Chinese citizens who are *canji* or, in English, "disabled." Guided by this mission, Federation staff have labored on several fronts: most notably, developing a range of biomedical services, loosely termed rehabilitation medicine *(kangfu yiliao)*, extending those and other recuperative services to millions of people, and producing media aimed at destigmatizing the disabled body.

The China Disabled Persons' Federation is an appendage of two much larger institutional webs, each of which continues to be entangled in multileveled streams of sociopolitical formation. The first web comprises the formal government structures of the nation-state founded in 1949 and known as the People's Republic of China. The second institutional web is much bigger, more loosely coordinated, and somewhat more difficult to outline. A key hallmark of this latter web is that its innumerable institutions share the conceptual and practical orientation of advancing the health and well-being of people understood to have bodies which are either damaged, sickly, or otherwise different, based on local or translocal norms of existence. I refer to these institutions by a neologism, bant bioburcaucracy, in order to highlight the degree to which they are integrally undergirded by what has been, for decades, an accelerating proliferation worldwide of the biological and biomedical sciences, a set of patterned ways for conceiving of and responding to normalcy and abnormality, health and pathology. As I understand them, bioburcaucracies today may be transnational in their organization, like Doctors Without Borders or large pharmaceutical corporations. They may be highly internationalist, such as the World Health Organization. They may be community and/or religiously based, like a local temple-sponsored clinic. They may be an integral piece of a nation-state, for instance, a veterans' medical administration. Or they may be, as often is the case, a blend of any number of these forms.

In this volume I examine the China Disabled Persons' Federation with one time frame and one set of issues in mind, although the complexity of sociopolitical formation demands that such singularities must often be transgressed. What concerns me most here is how people came to fashion and be fashioned by the Federation's development at the close of the last century.

EMBODYING BIOBUREAUCRACY

Of the many people involved with the Federation since its founding in the late 1980s, no one is more widely recognized as vital for its fashioning than the man who in 1968 leapt from the third story of the physics building at Beijing University, Deng Pufang. Deng Pufang is generally attributed as the most influential champion for the Disabled Persons' Federation, at once its most prominent leader, spokesperson, and lobbyist. He is also widely viewed as the person, more than any other in memory, who has drawn public attention to the needs of China's *canji*. For instance, he is generally acknowledged to be the figure most decisive in prompting branches of China's central government to declare in the late 1980s that the People's Republic possessed within its midst a long-ignored, maltreated, "special population" of disabled people numbering more than fifty million.

Given Deng Pufang's centrality for the Federation, it should be of little surprise then that this introductory chapter starts with an account of a significant moment in his life. Yet placing Deng Pufang's paralysis-inducing fall, the shattering of his spine and his life, at the start of this introduction is not simply a literary device. As effective as it may be for spurring some readers to sit up and take note of a person who has worked much of his adult life on behalf of the Federation's, Deng's fall is foregrounded here for another reason. It is a touchstone for an analytical and existential matter— the body—that is deeply linked to this volume's descriptive agenda in a multiplicity of ways.

Deng Pufang's fall confronts us with a key moment in the making of an exceedingly unique and highly recognized body, one that, according to many across China, has been indispensable for the Federation's formation. Deng Pufang's fall directs us to a tale about a person whose body is understood to have been decisive for how the Chinese nation-state made the category "disability" a catalyst for new institutional action, meaning-making, and identity-formation within the Chinese polity. His fall places us on the most pivotal page in a narrative about bodily maturation and breakdown during China's tumultuous twentieth century, a narrative that many in the People's Republic and beyond understand as having enabled the term *canji*, previously relatively little used, to be fused to modernist discourses and practices pertaining to health, social provision, institution-building, and nation-making. The fall connects us viscerally and symbolically with what Deng Pufang and others have come to represent as his unique *canji*, a distinctive case of elite corporality which they have used during the 1980s and 1990s to focus public attention on improving the lives of what the Chinese government was then beginning to call China's "disabled population." And, equally significant, the fall directs us to well-publicized bodily traumas which are viewed within China today as having been not just important for spurring many people at the end of the last century to start paying attention to *canji*, but also influential in how numerous people then actually experienced being *canji ren*.[2]

What is the body? How are bodies made knowable and lived in different spatial and temporal contexts? What roles can they play in the ways people craft, regulate, symbolize, and experience aspects of everyday life?

While a key descriptive goal of this book is to chronicle the development of the Disabled Persons' Federation—and thereby to detail something about sociopolitical formation of and within the Chinese nation-state—

much of this text's analytical agenda revolves around bodies. In its broadest strokes, the overarching analytical aim of this book is to examine how bodies, locally and translocally understood, may be instrumental for the sociopolitical formation of biobureaucracy and alterity. And many of the analytical arguments developed in this text are built upon ideas about bodiliness or embodiment—the intersection of the sociopolitical, somatic, and personal—ideas first articulated some seventy years ago by Marcel Mauss.

Mauss expressed these ideas in his essay "Les Techniques du Corps" ([1935] 1979), in which he argued that anthropologists and sociologists needed to inject the body into their inquiries for at least two reasons. First, Mauss argued, for too long the academy had promoted a myopic view that corporeality is asocial and acultural. Bodies are, in fact, "physio-psycho-sociological assemblages" (120). This, Mauss wrote, is witnessed at the most basic level by the penchants for people to be identified and grouped, one from the other, by the ways in which bodies do things (e.g., swim, sit, or give birth) in distinctive ways. Second, bodies must be placed at the center of inquiry because of their pivotal and polymorphous position in all people's lives, because they hold the unique status of being simultaneously objects, means, and subjective sources of sociopolitical formation. As we go about our daily activities, we act upon bodies, we use bodies, and we come to know ourselves and others through our corporeality (104).

Until one or two decades ago, most social scientists and humanists overlooked not only Mauss's insights, but nearly all aspects of the somatic as topics of sociopolitical analysis. Now, however, bodies sit at the center of sociopolitical investigation, a portion of which directly references Mauss, in a vast English-language literature that is plainly visible in any well-stocked university library (e.g., Bourdieu 1977; Csordas 1994b; Lock and Scheper-Hughes 1996). There are several explanations for why, within only two or three decades, bodies have been catapulted from ciphers to celebrities in the non-biological branches of the academy (see Farnell 1999; Frank 1991; Martin 1992; Strathern 1996; B. Turner 1992; T. Turner 1995). Certainly, one of the most widely recognized explanations is that political turns outside the academy in the late twentieth century stimulated numerous scholars to recognize that bodies have long been loci for the production of socially celebrated and socially discredited identities; that corporeality has long been central to the fixing of normalcy and alterity and thus pivotal for modes of domination and marginalization, like racism, sexism, and colonialism (see, e.g., Comaroff 1985; Grosz 1994; McClintock 1994; Stoler 2002; Young 1990). Another reason is that numerous scholars have become disenchanted with positivist metanarratives, built upon Cartesianism, which depict bodies as asocial and acultural, and which thereby preclude phenomenological explorations into such key topics of social analysis as agency, personhood, and social reproduction (see, e.g., Bourdieu 1990; Connerton

1989; Desjarlais 1992; Jackson 1989). Yet, it is likely that equal credit for the body's rising stature should be given to one basic component of modernity, one overlooked by Mauss and most others of his generation but well illuminated by Michel Foucault (1971; 1973). And that is that the category of the "body" itself has taken on expanding existential, symbolic, and politico-economic significance in large part because of the ongoing proliferation of the biological and biomedical sciences and their expanding linkages to other fields (e.g., politics, law, pedagogy, economics). In other words, one reason bodies are now important loci for analytical inquiry is that people around the world are enmeshed not just in the overlapping processes of sociopolitical formation but more and more in the overlapping processes of biopolitics, what we might parse more finely as everything from biolegalism, bioeducation, and bioeconomics, to biosexuality, biobeautification, bioaging, and biosociality (Franklin 1995; Cohen 1998; Harvey 1990; Martin 1994; Rabinow 1996; Rapp 1999).

MEDICALIZATION ON THE MOVE

The expansion of these processes is often referred to as "medicalization." One way medicalization increasingly touches upon nearly all aspects of life is by configuring it in terms of highly materialist entities (e.g., bones, muscles, viruses, hormones, T-cells, neurotransmitters, genes). But medicalization involves more than the encroachment of biological reductionism. It also involves a fusion of the biological sciences with the political, moral, and existential. Such biopolitics plays out differently from place to place and is never static. Invariably, though, it works to differentiate both individuated selves and group distinctiveness. And it regularly does so along a continuum that extends from "the healthy," "the high-functioning," and "the stable," at one end, to "the sickly," "the unsound," and "the dangerous" at the other. Medicalization involves the mapping of what constitutes a "desirable," "healthy," and "normal" person, and, by contrast, what constitutes a "dysfunctional," "needy," "contagious," and, more euphemistically, "special" and/or "different" individual. Likewise, medicalization entails the demarcation of collectivities along such modernist-informed spectrums as "advanced," "sanitary," and "safe," on the one hand, and "backward," "unhygienic," and "high risk," on the other.

In East Asia the fusion of the biological sciences with the moral, existential, and political has been occurring over the last century or more. In China, a categorical locus of much medicalization, disability included, has been the term *shen*. Chinese–English dictionaries usually proffer the term "body" as the main equivalent for *shen*. For a number of reasons, this is a problematical gloss, most importantly because *shen* and "body" have had such distinct trajectories over previous centuries (see Ames 1993; Elvin

1989; Kuriyama 1999; Sivin 1995; Zito 1997). That noted, there are important parallels between the two terms that should not be overlooked. One is polyvalence. As is the case with the idiomatic use of "body" among many English speakers in the world today, *shen* has multiple applications for people in contemporary China, and many of these convey an underlying and highly robust non-Cartesian, non-materialist vision of the integration of the somatic, the symbolic, the spiritual, and the social.[3] Another similarity, one that somewhat contravenes the first, is the ongoing transformation of language. Like "body," the term *shen* has not been stable over time; it has been subject to some very significant changes in meaning, particularly in the last century. As Thomas Ots explains, two thousand years ago, *shen* denoted a sense of existence or self-presence that is nearly entirely "undifferentiated" by what in the English language today is often conveyed by the terms "anatomy" and "physicality"; in twentieth-century China, however, owing to an increasing dichotomization between mind and matter, formal articulations of *shen,* in many contexts, have given way to more Cartesian, more materialist definitions of "bodiliness" (1994, 117).

As I discuss further below and as several other authors have more fully chronicled, the materialization and medicalization of *shen* started some time ago, certainly well before Deng Pufang and others founded the China Disabled Persons' Federation in the 1980s. In the late nineteenth century, colonialism prompted a set of biologically informed methods for seeing and acting in the world—for example, biomedicine, public health, athletics, eugenics, sociobiology, epidemiology—to trickle into and help define the Chinese polity. In the intervening years, in fits and starts, in innumerable ways, and at different levels of intensity, these biologically informed methods became institutionalized within China in various forms (e.g., clinics, medical schools, pharmaceutical manufacturers, government administrations), injected into the everyday lives of people across the country and varyingly placed alongside, incorporated into, and often taking precedence over other techniques for making sense of and responding to existence, otherness, and misfortune (e.g., humoral medicine, herbal treatments, accupressure/acupuncture therapies, spirit healing).[4]

STATES OF BODILINESS

Despite rising popular and academic attention to the body, and despite recognition that proliferation of biobureaucracies in China and elsewhere has been central to how we know and experience the body, academic inquiry into the relationship between the emergence of these structures and embodiment remains underdeveloped. To be sure, that is not to say that the relationship has been ignored altogether. While relatively few academics have studied bureaucracies that are linked to the rubric of disability

(Albrecht 1992; Skocpol 1992; Stone 1984), many of them, from a variety of disciplines, have provided historical accounts of biobureaucratic formation. And they have all paid attention to bodiliness, some implicitly, some explicitly. That noted, such scholarship has usually avoided the adoption of a robust vision of bodiliness, such as that offered by Mauss's most well-known contemporary interpreter, Pierre Bourdieu, under his concept of "habitus."[5] Rather, chroniclers of biobureaucratic formation have tended to rely on two visions of the body. The first perspective is highly biomedical in orientation, wherein the body is a biological entity that is prone to break down and is thus in need of the healing effects of biomedical institutions. The second perspective is far more novel and sociopolitically oriented, but also limiting. In it, the body is primarily an emergent object of cross-cutting modes of authority. Such authority, in order to expand and legitimate itself, works to define, manage, and heal populations and the constituents of those populations. It promotes an institutionalization of discourses and practices—that is, biomedical sciences—that are designed to know bodies, to distinguish bodies in terms of set systems of health and pathology, and to draw bodies into the curative scope of the health care professions.

This latter perspective, as with much medicalization theory, significantly stems from the work of Michel Foucault, particularly his early writings. As is well known, in several of his early books (1965; 1973; 1977), Foucault described at length the overlapping emergence in Western Europe of biobureaucratic institutions (e.g., clinics, psychiatric hospitals, welfare homes) and what he calls normalizing discourses (modernist forms of apprehension—such as biomedicine, public health, demography, and psychiatry). Foucault states that the overlapping emergence of these institutions and discourses manifested a new and unprecedented regime of authority, something that he came to call "biopower."

Among its many characteristics, biopower promotes (1) the signification of populations and individuals, (2) the identification of differences among and between populations and individuals (differences running along spectrums from normal to abnormal, healthy to pathological), (3) the management of such populations' problematical bodies, those reputedly sitting outside the range of the normal (i.e., the diseased, the mad, or the otherwise deviant), and (4) the configuration of what is life, personal fulfillment, and successful individuality in terms of a bourgeois modernist telos of efficiency, progress, and economic expansion.

Over time, as its institutions proliferated across Europe and its discourses leached into nearly every social domain, biopower became ubiquitous and naturalized within the local populace, Foucault asserts. Everyone's existence came to be constrained by and dependent upon what biopower's key institutions and discourses ordained as the normal, healthy, competent, well-individuated, non-deviant man, woman, or child.

Other features of biopower, which Foucault argues make it unprecedented, pertain to the State. Although in previous epochs authority was often tightly tied to state sovereignty and acts of state repression, that has not generally been the case with biopower, Foucault explains. Unlike erstwhile modes of authority, biopower is far more expansive and productive, and it springs from numerous domains of everyday life: "Relations of power, and hence the analysis that must be made of them, necessarily extend beyond the limits of the state." When it comes to the age of biopolitics, "the state is superstructural in relation to a whole series of power networks that invest the body" (1980a, 122). However, Foucault did not just qualify the state's role in making and maintaining biopower. In his famous essay, "Governmentality," he argued, "The state is no more than a composite reality and a mythicized abstraction" (1991, 102).[6]

Foucault's work, particularly his early books, has been subject to innumerable reviews (see Smart 1994), which are too numerous and complex to describe thoroughly here. That noted, two of the more important critiques to emerge from the reviews need to be highlighted. The first is that, in his early books, Foucault's orientation was so focused on representation that it rendered bodiliness largely non-sentient and inert (Fox 1997; Hacking 1986; T. Turner 1994). The second is that, over much of his career, Foucault was so interested in demonstrating that authority was always relational and diffuse that he overplayed the state's insignificance as a sphere of sociopolitical formation (Agamben 1998; Hall 1985).

This book is an ethnography of institutionalization and alterity. And it is designed to be in dialogue with and to extend the literature pertinent to those topics. As such, I develop two arguments vis-à-vis Foucault's oeuvre, by tapping into several sources—including the insights about embodiment formulated by Mauss, ideas developed by a variety of more recent scholars, and even reformulations made by Foucault at the end of his life. The first of my arguments is that, in our ongoing epoch of "the bios," corporeality is always fashioned by a fusion of history, knowledge, power, and other factors, yet the body's role in sociopolitical formation is always far more than that of docile discursive object. In any given context, sociopolitical formation occurs for many reasons, but always because historically situated persons act not just upon, but also through and in response to what they understand to be their and others' corporeality. The second argument is that, when studying how the processes of "the bios" unfold—everything from biopolitics, biolegalism, and bioeducation, to biosexuality, biobeautification, bioeconomics, and biosociality—one must be attentive to the fact that, in any given setting there may be several domains that are immensely important, and that the inner workings of states (particularly nation-states) may be as important, if not more important, than any other.

In developing these two arguments, I hold fast to the view that an analysis of bodies cannot and should not end with reductionism, whether material, symbolic, or otherwise.[7] No matter how much bodies are animated by material facticity and meanings, and no matter how dependent we are on those very same modalities to know about others' existence, academic analysis must strive to examine how people's corporeality is always an irreducible sphere, one that is always more than mere object (e.g., biomedical, statistical, humoral, politico-economic, discursive). To do so, we must endeavor to examine the multiple ways by which, not simply corporeality, but more specifically the lived body (that which exists in everyday action), both influence and are influenced by domains of sociopolitical formation. We must strive to understand how the quotidian aspects of people's bodiliness—for example, how people move through space, how they identify themselves as part of the larger body politic, how they act upon the built and imagined world—are implicated in specific processes of sociopolitical formation, such as the making of institutions and alterity.

Also, I hold fast to the position that, in any spatial and temporal setting, there are always distinct terrains of authority that are particularly important to new areas of not just sociopolitical formation but biopolitical and biosocial formation. In other words, such formation is not the same everywhere. And its most important wellsprings and spheres of influence are not the same or as strong from setting to setting. In any large geographical context, some overlapping "nodes" of power are always particularly pertinent to people, yet they vary in their saliency from moment to moment and from locality to locality. When it comes to the study of *canji* in late-twentieth-century China, there are three specific nodes of power that seem to be most important. These are gender, modernity, and, yes, the nation-state.

ENGENDERING A PROJECT

In light of the academy's growing fascination with embodiment, it is understandable that, after beginning doctoral studies in anthropology a decade ago I developed an interest in the body. What still strikes me as somewhat surprising, however, is that this volume has developed as an effort to enhance anthropological understanding of the body by focusing on both a specific biobureaucratic offshoot of China's party-state—the Federation—and on that agency's engagement with the somatosocial realm of disability.

For, in the early 1990s, when I began organizing the research upon which this book is based, neither the topic of governmental bureaucracy nor that of disability was of much concern to anthropology. Despite anthropologists' long-standing conviction that social organization is central to ethnographic inquiry, until recently most were content to treat the topic of bureaucracy (State or otherwise) as the domain of sociologists, political scientists, and historians (see Heper 1985; Heyman 1995). Similarly, despite an early recognition that illness and disease are vital areas of ethnographic inquiry, until a few years ago, anthropologists generally saw "disability" as being a research topic for biomedical practitioners and rehabilitation specialists.[8]

Blinkered by such academic partitions and animated by different concerns, when I began organizing the research upon which this book is grounded, my ethnographic lens was directed elsewhere. In general, I wanted to learn something of how, in relation to China's post-Mao (after 1978) reforms, people in varying Chinese communities conceived of and responded to chronic illness and bodily abnormality among men. My interest in bodily breakdown and men stemmed, in part, from my ongoing desire to create scholarship that would be pertinent to both palliation and to the main specialties for which I was then receiving training: China Studies and the Social Anthropology of Medicine. Those specialties had been making important contributions to theorizing the body's role in sociopolitical processes. One mode of inquiry that was proving particularly promising at that time involved an investigation of how the crafting, regulating, signifying, and experiencing of the female body-politic undergirded not just social inequality but additional domains, including national identity, self, ethnicity, and kinship (see, e.g., Kondo 1990; Yanagisako and Collier 1987; Martin 1987; Singer et al. 1988; Strathern 1988). Like others in the Euro-American academy at that time, I began to wonder how similar perspectives might be applied to men. What might be learned if the same kind of attention were given to male embodiment? In the past, anthropologists working in my geographical region of interest, China, and most elsewhere in the world had carried out extensive research "among" men, teaching us a great deal about innumerable facets of sociopolitical life. But until a decade or two ago, rarely had anthropologists directly analyzed the gendered and, in broader terms, bodily positioning of their male informants. Instead, they had generally treated their informants as ungendered, unbodied representatives of either society writ large or of segments within society (e.g., villages, ethnicities, class groupings).[9]

As my preliminary research was unfolding, and as I began conducting brief field trips in post-Mao China, I hoped that my investigations would provide some local context for what happens when men's lives are threatened and marginalized by illness, accident, or various kinds of locally understood "abnormalities," thus shedding light on unnoticed workings of gender and the body.

HAINAN HAPPENINGS

How did this initial interest in gender and bodily breakdown lead me to a study of the bureaucratization of disability-advocacy in late-twentieth-century China?

In the early 1990s, one of the first places that my ethnographic curiosities took me—partially by happenstance, partially by design—was a Chinese region largely unfamiliar to me and, for that matter, to many others in the world. Hainan Province, which I visited during the summers of 1991 and 1992, is located at some distance from famed Chinese metropolises like Shanghai or Beijing, but it was subject to many of the sociopolitical changes then affecting those cities. Situated in the South China Sea near Vietnam, Hainan is an island about the size of Taiwan, although far less populated. Among non-Chinese speakers, the province has recently became more known because, on April 1, 2001, a U.S. spy plane and a Chinese fighter jet collided off of Hainan's southern coast. The Chinese pilot died, and the U.S. crew made an unplanned landing on the island.

A decade before that high-profile geopolitical clash, during my first two stays in Hainan, I visited a number of the province's county seats, towns, and villages. Much of my time over those summers was also spent in Haikou, the province's capital city. There, I lived at Hainan University (Haida). When not studying the local dialect with university tutors, I often occupied myself by chatting in Mandarin with city residents.[10] And whenever convenient, I attempted to steer those conversations into discussions about what life was like in Haikou for the men and women living there who suffered from long-term forms of ill health. Quite often, such conversations resulted in residents directing me to Zhu Wenping.

Zhu operated a small convenience store near Haida, not far from its south gate. He had opened the store in the late 1980s at the age of twenty-eight, with the financial and emotional support of his older brother and sister-in-law, both university employees. When we met, Zhu was spending nearly every hour of every week in his store. He usually hovered on a stool behind a small counter until 10 or 11 at night, and then slept on a small platform above the counter. Wedged between a bicycle repair shop and another convenience store, Zhu's shop provided customers with a familiar array of items, everything from toothpaste, beer, and ice cream, to cigarettes, nail clippers, and notebooks. Why did acquaintances direct me to Zhu? In part, they did so for the reason that so many people I met in Haikou disparagingly called him "camel-back." In infancy, an ache had developed between Zhu's shoulder blades, and over the years, around the ache, had grown a highly discernable hunch, which had left Zhu with an especially diminutive stature. Just as importantly, though, acquaintances pointed me to Zhu because his convenience store—as a plaque hanging across from the cash register pronounced—was a formally registered *canji* enterprise, a governmental designation that allowed Zhu to claim certain tax exemptions.

Whenever I would linger near his store, before or after making a purchase, Zhu never seemed particularly inclined to talk with anyone, unlike many of the small-business owners nearby. One day, when the proprietress of the bike shop saw that Zhu was out of earshot, she began to talk to me about Zhu. She emphasized how significantly Zhu's life had been redirected in recent years and how those changes were closely linked to Zhu's body, to the Disabled Persons' Federation, and to major shifts underway in China's political economy.

> With such a screwed-up body, Zhu's been struggling for a long time. But in recent years, his condition has changed quite a bit. After the [post-Mao] reforms were launched, Zhu showed up in Haikou, went to Deng Pufang's Federation for a medical checkup, got his tax exemptions, and began his business here. Without that exemption, he'd have gone bust a long time ago and had to run back to his village. Now he's making money and chasing after girls for marriage. One of the local newspapers has even written Zhu up as a model *canji* businessman. That's right, he's become quite the real man [*nanzihan*].

As might be expected, comments like this began to pique my interest in what the repair shop owner called "Deng Pufang's Federation." What was this government bureaucracy? How was its presence related to the Chinese nation-state, particularly its move away from governance characterized by heavy-handed socialist control and toward governance structured by more market-driven imperatives? And how was the Federation mediating the ways in which men's bodily sufferings were locally known, experienced, and responded to by people at various levels and in various regions of the PRC?

Well before my first trip to Hainan, I was aware of the China Disabled Persons' Federation and of Deng Pufang. I had learned of them initially, perhaps, in the late 1980s, when for two years I was a language student in Beijing. But not until I began interacting with Zhu and his neighbors did I have reason to think about the Federation or Deng Pufang carefully.

FEDERATION FORAY

It was a summer morning in 1992, and it was my first time up or down Qiong Yuan Street. My taxi driver that morning had plied it several times in the past, though. Most people who lived in Haikou for any length of time, I later learned, were familiar with the small but bustling thoroughfare. Set in the heart of the city, the street ran along the edge of Hainan's provincial government compound. At one end, across its T-junction with People's Boulevard, was Hainan province's Bureau of Public Health. At the other end of the street was the headquarters of the province's police apparatus, the Public Security Bureau. In between was a string of medium-sized office and residential buildings. Small shops and restaurants occupied the ground floors of the buildings, many with pop music wafting out into the summer air.

The building that the cabbie and I sought, as it turned out, was a nondescript six-to-eight story concrete edifice, most likely built five to ten years prior. On its ground floor was an outpatient clinic specializing in a form of medicine I had not come across in China before: *kangfu yiliao* (rehabilitation medicine). I paid my taxi fare and then one of the clinic's white-coat-clad staff directed me to an unmarked doorway around the back, which led to the building's only mode of ascent, a poorly lit flight of concrete stairs. After pausing to examine an old wooden placard that rested upturned on the first landing and stated, in English and Chinese, "The Disability Welfare Fund of Hainan Island," I continued up to the fourth floor, wondering how anyone without the use of two legs could make this ascent.

Ma Zoufu was not surprised to see me. An acquaintance had scheduled our meeting and provided information on my background. When I appeared outside a doorway near his desk, Ma put down his copy of the *Hainan Daily*, rose, and extended a hand, warmly welcoming me to Hainan's provincial headquarters of the China Disabled Persons' Federation.

Over the ensuing years, I sought out and spent a great deal of time with Federation employees like Ma. Some of that time was spent in Federation offices. Often it was spent in less formal contexts.[11] During our initial meeting that morning, Ma escorted me through the Hainan Federation's drab administrative offices and introduced me to his fellow functionaries, nearly all men between the ages of thirty and fifty. He sat the two of us down on wooden chairs on either side of his utilitarian wooden desk, a staffer gave me a hot cup of jasmine tea, and then Ma graciously offered to answer any questions I might have. Since this was my first formal encounter with the Disabled Persons' Federation, I avoided asking Ma any particularly pointed questions that were on my mind, like why my Haikou acquaintances had been mostly directing me to male entrepreneurs they called *canji*, why most of the people in Ma's office were men, or why all the people in his office that morning struck me as so stereotypically "able-bodied," that is, unmarked by any of the conditions my Hainan friends were referring to as *canji*. Rather, I decided to simply ask Ma if he could spend a few minutes explaining why the Federation had developed over the previous few years and how it was organized.

Blithely making that inquiry a decade ago, I had no sense that it would become such a big part of my work. I had no notion that the Federation's early formation would become one of the overarching processes that I would examine and write about for years thereafter. Following my conversation with Ma, at the end of which he enthusiastically offered to assist with my future fieldwork arrangements, what I gleaned was that it might be interesting and productive for me to link my broad research agenda to *canji*, a term I was increasingly encountering in China. Based on my meeting with Ma as well as others I had with acquaintances during that summer, I thought it would be worthwhile to hang my analytical curiosities pertaining to bodily breakdown and gender on this categorization of "disability."

The fact that much of the substance of this book came to revolve as much, if not more, around better understanding the Federation's founding as it did around better understanding the term *canji* directly relates to what, a year later, I began to hear—and not hear. My examination of the Federation was born to a large degree out of my attempts, sometimes confounding, to converse with people in China about *canji* during the first of two lengthy fieldwork stints.[12]

CANJI CONTRASTS

These fieldwork stints were set in two very different parts of the country. One site was Beijing. There, in the PRC's capital, people often were eager to talk with me about *canji*, particularly about what they saw as *canji*'s recent genealogy.

As they frequently explained to me, until the latter part of the 1900s, that is, until shortly before the Federation's founding in the late 1980s and its fast-paced growth, *canji* was something that few capital-city residents voiced in daily life or saw in print. Yet in a relatively short amount of time, about two decades, *canji* had become deeply enmeshed in many Beijingers' daily lexicon and mode of apprehending existence.

Han Meifu, a sixty-five-year-old former language instructor of mine from my undergraduate days in China's capital, was one of the first people to describe this change to me when she and I chatted in 1994:

> It sure seems like, with the Federation's founding, *canji ren* have drawn a lot of attention. I didn't hear much about *canji* before liberation [in 1949]. Nobody used the term. Since the 1980s, though, newspaper articles, movies, books, sporting events and even art shows about *canji ren* have appeared. If you want to meet some *canji ren*, I'd be happy to help. I know several. There're some shop owners in my neighborhood who are lame . . . you know . . . guys who caught polio when they were young. They're a lot like Deng Pufang. You've heard of Pufang, right? He's China's most famous *canji*. He founded the Federation. Before him and the Federation, you never saw anything in the newspapers about *canji*, you rarely heard anyone talking about helping the *canji*.

In addition to statements like this, there is another, more specific form of dialogue which helps highlight how, as I began researching the topic in the 1990s, the category of *canji* was very much undergoing significant transformation in Beijing.

When new and long-standing Beijing acquaintances heard I was researching *canji*, they often redirected our conversations to the Federation and the question, "What is *canji*?" And frequently, in quick order, they transformed themselves from everyday conversationalists into speculative cataloguers of bodies and alterity. An example of this cataloguing and its accompanying commentary was provided to me one afternoon over lunch in Beijing by a longtime friend, Xu Luping:

> Wha! *Canji.* Now there's a term we've been hearing a lot lately. The government sure has been making noise about *canji* since the reforms began. They sure have been making noise about how the Federation helps *canji ren* become modern, how it helps *canji ren* contribute to China's new market economy. And in recent years, all kinds of Federation offices have been created in Beijing to coordinate this work.
>
> In English, what do you call *canji?* . . . "Disability," right? Heaven knows what is *canji.* So many people seem to say they're *canji ren* now. But who's really *canji,* who's got that kind of fundamental biology? I guess the only way to figure that out is to go over to a Federation office or maybe a hospital and have staff there tell us.
>
> If you ask me, though, there are many kinds [of people] that should count as *canji ren.* There are many that should receive social assistance [*shehui bang-zhu*] because of how the designs of our society makes life so different for them and makes it hard for them to join in on China's economic development.
>
> Like who? *Canji ren* should include all those people who are lame [*que*], you know the people who are unable to do things because they're missing an arm or have a crippled leg, people like Deng Pufang, or people like my brother, who was injured in the army. In addition to them . . . well . . . I guess *canji* should also cover the blind . . . and the deaf. I guess dwarves should also be tossed in. Oh, also the dumb [*sha*], those who only have the ability [*nengli*] of children all their lives. They should definitely be included and helped. They and their families have such difficult lives. Still, to know, to really know what's *canji,* you got to ask someone who works at the Federation or a doctor familiar with the Federation's standards.

Ma Ping's monologue, as much as any other I have heard in Beijing, articulates a set of broad, sweeping, and sometimes contradictory presuppositions about what, by the 1990s, *canji* had come to signify for many people in China's capital. These presuppositions include:

- *canji* is part and parcel of a broader phenomenon of difference/otherness/alterity known in English as "disability";
- *canji* is a conceptual umbrella of otherness, under which an array of knowable alterities may be aggregated;
- *canji*'s definitional boundaries are subject to interpretation and questioning, whether by bureaucrats, clinicians, or other kinds of community members;
- *canji* is formally a matter of clinical and governmental facticity, something which biomedical practitioners and government bureaucrats work to define biologically;
- *canji* is a matter of dissonance between biology and socially structured

normativity (the latter often measured in terms of expected levels of ability but always framed by how the built world is designed);

· *canji* is not simply a source of suffering but also one of self-making (for the *canji* individual, as well as for his or her family, neighbors, etc.);

· *canji* is a moral claim whereby a person with *canji*, because of his or her "difference," is justly owed something, from empathy or pity to forms of institutional and regulatory accommodation;

· *canji* is an existence any one of us could potentially live;

· *canji* is something associated with men more than women, and particularly with one man, Deng Pufang;

· *canji* is a concept promoted by the party-state as a way to help people adapt to China's new market economy;

· *canji* is closely linked to the Federation.

Quite a number of these presuppositions, I would imagine, will seem familiar to those who read this book. For, as Ma identified, most of these tenets have been strongly present in English-speaking settings for decades, under the heading of "disability." They certainly were present where I matured into adulthood, in northern Ohio, and in the U.S. cities where I have spent most of my life since. But there are other presuppositions here that may seem less intuitive to readers. Notably among them are that disability in China is deeply linked to a specific branch of the party-state; that disability is closely associated with men, most often Deng Pufang; and that it has been intertwined with the government's complex management of China's "modernization," more specifically, with efforts to sustain the party-state's preeminence while shifting China to a more market-based political economy.

Yet not everyone I met while conducting research in China for this book shared all of the presuppositions listed above or shared them to the same degree. Nor has everyone been particularly inclined to chat about *canji*. Indeed, in the other venue where I spent a considerable amount of time conducting research in the mid-1990s, I was initially taken aback by the degree to which *canji* seemed to be something of a conversational barrier. Often, even the most basic inquires I posed about *canji* produced an awkward silence or a struggled response. For instance, when I would ask, "What is *canji*?" or "Who in your community is *canji*?" I would rarely receive an answer let alone a typology of the term. Instead, those questions would often elicit blank stares. Or the questions would sometimes elicit answers like the ones provided by a sixty-year-old woman, Zeng Liping, and her middle-aged son and daughter-in-law:

> *Zeng:* Canji . . . canji . . . never heard of it.
>
> *Son:* Yeah, what's that?
>
> *Daughter-in-law:* Whatever it is, there's no one here who's *canji*.

> *Son:* *Canji* . . . is that what they call Deng . . . Deng Pufang . . . that crippled guy.
>
> *Zeng:* Deng Pufang, who's he? I've lived here all my life, and I can tell you for certain, we don't have anyone living in this area by that name.
>
> *Son:* If you mean someone like Deng Xiaoping's son, I guess Ah Bo might be what you're looking for. He lives over there near the rice-thrashing machine. He's been unable to walk since he was a little boy. He runs a nice little coconut enterprise right now.

Zeng Liping and her family lived a long way from Beijing, about as far away as possible in the People's Republic. They resided in eastern Hainan, in a setting where mangrove and palm trees jostle with rice fields for control of the landscape. They lived in Min Song Village, Wenchang County, an agricultural community where plastic sandals are the preferred footwear, where eight months out of the year the sun will easily redden your complexion, where people are far more likely to worry about the monsoons than the shifting political climate, and where specialized government offices like the Federation are seemingly a distant urban phenomenon.

Considering the suffering that had enveloped Zeng over the previous decades, one might expect that she and her family would have identified with *canji*. When we met, Zeng had already been afflicted with severe joint pain for more than twenty years. Diagnosed by local clinicians as acute rheumatoid arthritis, the pain had forced Zeng to spend nearly all of the 1980s and 1990s bedridden. During that time, she had become dependent on her family for nearly everything: to be turned over, to eat, to bathe, and to acquire costly painkillers, which for a few days each month relieved her agony. Compounding these realities, Zeng and her family were immensely frustrated by what they saw as her inability to fulfill her duties as grandmother and contributor to the family labor force.

Nonetheless, *canji* (pronounced "tsan-jeet" in the local Wenchang dialect) held little salience for Zeng or other residents of Min Song. Zeng's son possessed a few associations for *canji* (largely connected to Deng Pufang and one man in Min Song, Ah Bo, who had difficulty walking). But for Zeng and most others in the village in the mid-1990s, *canji* was not a familiar term. *Canji* was not something especially meaningful for apprehending, aggregating, or responding to an array of bodily conditions. It was also not something especially significant for making sense of broader political matters like national development.

That Min Song residents made so little of *canji*—except for a small number who tended to apply it to Deng Pufang or to a few men in the community—initially left me somewhat confused. As to be expected, given my training in anthropology, when starting my project I assumed that there would be sizable "cultural variation" at play during my fieldwork and that people across China might define *canji* in radically different ways. I was not prepared, however, for the possibility that the category and subject position of disability might be nearly meaningless for acquaintances in rural Hainan, especially for those struggling with what they and their families experienced as severe forms of long-term incapacitation. Nor, for that matter, had my earlier readings about disability prepared me to make sense of *canji* as a sphere of existence more meaningful for men.

Looking back, I can see that my confusion had been amplified by epidemiological data that I had drawn upon not long after my first trip to Hainan, when I was deciding where in the province's countryside I should live. The data had been provided by my host institution in Hainan, the provincial Bureau of Public Health, and were the results of a 1991 survey that had been conducted by statisticians, township doctors, and village cadres at the behest of the provincial office of Hainan's Disabled Persons' Federation. According to the data, significant numbers of residents in Min Song village and surrounding environs were *canji*. More specifically, the data had indicated that fifty-one men and seventy-four women in Min Song were *canji*, and that, on average, one out of every five households in the village contained someone *canji*. The latter figure had been particularly important to me as my Hainan research was getting underway, since it corresponded to a countrywide prevalence rate for *canji* that had been established in 1987 by a large-scale government survey.

During my first few months in Min Song, one way I initially tried to quell my mounting confusion was by dismissing the discrepancies I encountered as temporary and of my own making. I earnestly assumed that the discrepancy between what numerous Min Song residents were telling me (i.e., that there were no disabled people in Min Song save for a few men) and what the epidemiological data indicated stemmed from my own gendered, "outsider" status—from my North American male visage. Min Song community members were reluctant to ascribe to one another any mark of difference or abjection in my presence, I conjectured, because of my decided foreignness and maleness. That did not prove to be the case, however, at least not significantly so. As time passed and our relationships in the community multiplied and deepened, my research assistant (a local woman in her thirties) and I frequently watched and listened (sometimes together, sometimes apart) as those around us, male and female, would apply a wide variety of descriptors to one another. Many of these descriptors were extremely demeaning, so much so that Min Song residents often expressed great anger and hurt when they heard how they had been described. The term *canji,* however, was just not part of the vocabulary that most residents drew upon to make sense of their and their neighbors' lives, with the exception, on rare occasions, of a few male community members.

How is it possible that, in the 1990s, people in this small community of the PRC—some of whom suffered intense incapacitation and many of whom statisticians, clinicians, and local officials had characterized as *canji*— were disinclined to apply the term to themselves or to recognize it as a distinctive sphere of alterity?

Of course, this question is a variation on a line of inquiry that anthropologists (e.g., Evans-Pritchard 1937) and other scholars began pursuing long ago: Why do people in a particular time and place, often rural and at great distance from Euro-American settings, not recognize and apply a reputedly universal conceptual framework?

Under different circumstances, I might have utilized this approach. If I had only conducted my research in a Hainan village and had not spent much time in a major city like Beijing, if my fieldwork had occurred during an earlier era of anthropological inquiry, and if I had not retained my interest in how embodiment can be generative for the nation-state, I quite likely would have walked down that analytical path, making it the centerpiece of this book.

But as has been acknowledged across much of the academy in recent decades when confronting a matter of "universality gone missing," often the most interesting as well as ethical modus operandi is not asking, "Why do informants 'fail' to recognize the reputedly universal framework?" Or, "What hampers them from experiencing its obvious saliency?" Rather than focusing on absence, the more appropriate line of inquiry centers on broader matters of sociopolitical production. This latter approach pivots on such questions as: Why does anyone recognize the framework under scrutiny? From whence does the framework's reputedly universal referentiality emerge? In what ways does the framework gradually become commonplace (i.e., naturalized and normalized) within and across sociopolitical, spatial, and temporal contexts? How does it gather authority enough so that it is something about which people—whether they are government officials, statisticians, clinicians, journalists, or academics—want to effect action and generate greater knowledge? Who and what are served by such a framework's global proliferation and local reification? And what are some of the ways people embrace or resist its integration into their lives, as ways for crafting, regulating, symbolizing, and experiencing each other?

VIEWS FROM OTHER VENUES

Over the last several decades, a growing number of books and journals have been produced in which scholars explore disability as an aspect of modernist sociopolitical formation. As already mentioned, contributors to these texts come from a variety of disciplines and their work has increasingly come to be known as Disability Studies. To date, most writings that fall under this rubric have given primacy to Euro-American contexts. One of the most important early exceptions to that trend, one that is decidedly anthropological in orientation and one that was published after my mid-1990s fieldwork was underway, is the volume *Disability and Culture* (1995).

In their introductory chapter, the book's editors, Benedicte Ingstad and Susan Reynolds Whyte, emphasize that anthropological scholarship on disability must occur not only in many contexts but on many registers, including macro-historical and experiential. And in order to think about disability on numerous registers across wide spatial and sociopolitical distances, they encourage us to pay close attention to "state, legal, economic, and biomedical" institutional frameworks (1995, 10), what Mitchell Dean might call "international biopolitics" (Dean 2001, 47). For instance, Ingstad and Reynolds Whyte press us to recognize that international institutions have been highly involved in generating, disseminating, and sedimenting universalistic concepts about disability for some time, and that these processes began to heat up significantly in the 1980s as a consequence of specific organizational initiatives. Such initiatives included the U.N.'s two global development-oriented disability programs (the International Year of Disabled Persons in 1981 and the Decade for Disabled Persons, 1983–92). They also included actions by the World Health Organization, most importantly its 1980 promulgation of a gloss for disability. Reputedly universally applicable, the WHO gloss is part of a larger, tripartite definition that encompasses impairment, disability, and handicap. The tripartite definition is known as the ICIDH (International Criteria of Impairment, Disability, and Handicap). It is, not surprisingly, highly biomedical in orientation since it was created as an extension of the WHO's 1976 International Classification of Disease (see Barnes et al. 1999, 20–27).[13]

To understand the degree to which peoples and nations around the world have come to respond to the U.N.'s programs and to adopt a vision of existence along the lines of the ICIDH, Ingstad and Reynolds Whyte emphasize, one must pay a great deal of attention to institutional framing, not just at the international level but also within nation-states. They explain this in terms of two somewhat blunt heuristics, which they cast in a decidedly modernist spatial and developmental outlook:

> Disability in Europe and North America exists within—and is created by—a framework of state, legal, economic, and biomedical institutions. . . . In countries of the South, where this kind of institutional infrastructure exists only to a very limited degree, disability as a concept and an identity is not an explicit cultural construct. (1995, 10)

If Ingstad and Reynolds Whyte are correct that bureaucratic frameworks, national as well as international, are significant for the sociopolitical formation of disability as a biomedically informed identity and difference, and I strongly believe they are, then new questions are prompted. The most obvious line of questioning, which this book addresses, is how do such frameworks effect change in the ways people know and experience disability in local contexts? Yet, for anyone interested in sociopolitical formation, this line of inquiry cannot be considered in isolation. A second line of inquiry is necessary and involves a question that remains somewhat terra incognita for anthropology, a curious fact, given the discipline's interest in matters now so often referred to as globalization. The second line of inquiry is the following:

How and why, in specific national contexts, do people generate bureaucratic structures that are directly linked to an internationally sponsored portrait of existence, like the vision of disability anointed by the U.N./WHO, a portrait that is at once universal in its claim, modernist in orientation, and supposedly significant at the level of people's bodies?

This question is pivotal for this book, and I explore it specifically in terms of the China Disabled Persons' Federation. It must be emphasized, however, that this volume does not purport to provide comprehensive answers. Nor do I believe that a comprehensive chronicle of the Federation's founding is possible, as much because of the methodological hurdles facing anyone trying to conduct research on a sprawling governmental entity in contemporary China as because of the epistemological limits of sociopolitical inquiry more generally. And if this is a place for admissions, then I should hasten to add that not only are my accounts of the Federation's development in this book partial and interpretive, they are purposely so. For, as much as I strive to provide informational coverage about major facets of the Federation's formation—thereby allowing readers to make their own conclusions about the bureaucracy's development—my main intent, since well before I began fieldwork for this book, has been to explore thematic issues. As a consequence, even though there are forms of institutional action that have been consistently part of the Federation's programmatic efforts from relatively early on (like the promotion of disability arts projects), they receive far less attention here than other efforts, for example, the Federation's initial staffing policies, epidemiological initiatives, or efforts to provide mobility devices to some of its constituency.

PROFESSOR LIN

In developing the key themes of this book, as well as the arguments that animate them, I have referred to a wide variety of sources—some textual, some conversational, some produced seemingly inside China, some seemingly outside. A particularly stimulating source has been Professor Lin Mingming of Hainan University.

Lin and I first met at Hainan University in 1992 and our friendship developed while we engaged in a highly distinctive form of bodily practice: basketball. In the 1990s, whenever I was in Hainan's provincial capital of Haikou, I often ran back-and-forth with Lin and others as we participated in the university's regular late-afternoon "pickup" game. Basketball was introduced to China during the early decades of the twentieth century, a period when imperialism spawned many new things, including Chinese nationalism, and the sport has since grown in popularity among members of China's polity, especially among urban men.

One afternoon in October 1994, not long after Lin, three undergraduates, and I had been trounced by a squad of high school students, Lin and I bought refrigerated sodas at Zhu Wenping's store and then retreated to Lin's book-filled apartment to enjoy one of its greatest luxuries, an electric fan. Over the next hour, we talked formally about various subjects we had discussed previously only in passing. During our tape-recorded talk, Lin was quite clear about what he saw as the primary sources behind the Federation's emergence.

> The Federation . . . I'd guess it appeared as a consequence of the same forces that . . . that . . . have stimulated disability's visibility elsewhere. A while back, the West added disability [*canji*] to their discourses [*huayu*] about modernity and enlightened capitalism. So ideas about disability assistance and rehabilitation sciences became part of what it means to be a developed and civilized nation. Then, before long, the U.N. got in the act. That made disability an even bigger topic around the world and more important for managing a country. The power struggles within the Chinese Communist Party have been easily influenced by such discourse after Mao's death [in 1976]. Because of our history of embarrassment by Western imperialism, and because the Cultural Revolution [1966–76] allowed China to fall farther behind the West, the Party is now basing its legitimacy very much on being modern and adapting capitalist modes of production. For that to be achieved, the Party recognizes it has to do something for the most economically vulnerable, those who suffer every day because they have abnormal bodies [*shenti buzhengchang*]. To stay on top, to stay in charge, the Party has to show the most important people inside and outside the country that it is civilized and modern and that it has not completely abandoned its Maoist roots. It has to create the Federation, arrange for some of us to be called disabled, a little assistance to be given to the most visible disabled people, a lot of publicity to be produced about modern rehabilitation programs, and even for someone like you to come here and study disability. . . . That's where Foucault got it wrong. Power is not just a thing that's everywhere yet nowhere. There are places it gets concentrated. There are places it gets distinctively shaped. The state is one of them. This is especially true in China. And it is especially true when it comes to biopower in China.

Since that steamy late-afternoon in his apartment, I have stopped many times to reflect on Professor Lin's statement. His outlook, as much as any I have ever heard, seems to engage three important analytical themes. The first is one that pertains to the broad, sweeping workings of modernity, nationalism, and history. According to Lin, the expanding attention given to *canji* across parts of China is the product of long-standing, unequal relations between two sectors of the world: Euro-America and those parts of the globe that were subject to colonial authority over the last century or more. These unequal relationships are very much organized around a teleology of national development. They are relationships that order the world along gradations ranging from developed to developing countries, from advanced to backward nations. And they are relationships that both permit and necessitate norms and practices associated with modernism's supposed core, Euro-America, to expand elsewhere, serve as powerful factors in sociopolitical process, and become integral to how people understand themselves and others.

The second and third analytical themes are at once an application and a critique of certain aspects of Michel Foucault's oeuvre. Lin shows that it is helpful to draw upon Foucault's early vision of sociopolitical formation because of the authority that has been vested in several originally Euro-American and now internationally circulating discourses—most notably, discourses pertaining to disability and public health, but also those pertaining more generally to capitalism, science, and civility. Owing to historical circumstance and to the authority vested in these discourses, China's party-state identified a population of disabled persons in the 1980s and 1990s and created disability-assistance structures.

Yet, as Lin emphasized, in our post-game conversation and in subsequent discussions, he also sees disability in late-twentieth-century China as cause for scholarly innovation. Foucault's diffuse vision of power is highly limited, Lin says, because Foucault went out of his way to de-emphasize the role of the state. By contrast, and in line with much scholarly literature about the PRC, Lin believes that the State is an extremely significant loci for all kinds of power dynamics, biopower included. This brings us to the third analytical theme. Not only are state institutions and the people working within them extraordinarily influential in producing distinctive iterations of biopower, the institutions themselves are highly subject to biopower's increasingly international framework (see also Gupta 1998, 314–49). As Lin explains, when confronted with specific normalizing discourses about modernism and development that were promoted at the end of the twentieth century by many governments and international organizations, when confronted by the normalizing gazes that depict nation-states as more or less modern based on how they represent and care for the disabled, elements of China's party-state were compelled to shore up their authority by generating a new biobureaucracy, the Federation. In other words, *canji* has become an increasingly recognized subject across much of China today. The Federation was established two decades ago, and it has grown since then, Lin believes, because specific discourses, supra-local organizational frameworks, and historical contingencies spurred the party-state to embrace Euro-American styles of disability advocacy as indispensable levers of legitimacy, as tools for shoring up governmental authority while the party-state went about the risky task of recasting China's political economy along the lines of neo-liberal economics.

I assume that, by now, it does not strike anyone as remarkable that an academic like Professor Lin can be engaged with theoretical ideas that were originally laid down in texts outside of China, or that someone in his position can deftly weave together and critique such theory. But my assumption may be mistaken. Some may still presume that PRC academicians are ill informed when it comes to the social theory that has been produced in Europe and North America over the last four or five decades. The fact of the matter is that, because of post-Maoist China's unique investiture in modernism, books and journals about such theory are today available in the large cities of the PRC. For example, scores of books addressing the "post" genres (e.g., poststructuralism, postmodernity, postcolonialism) have been translated in the last two decades, and their usage by Chinese scholars has been expanding significantly. So, the fact that an academic colleague in Haikou could poignantly cite and critique Foucauldian theory in the 1990s should be as startling as news that, during my time at Hainan University, Professor Lin and his friends often informed me about recent events in North American professional sports or that they frequently gave me tips on how to improve my mediocre basketball skills.

In this book, I take Lin's commentary about the Federation and *canji* very seriously. And this volume affirms much of Lin's assessment. For instance, from chapter to chapter, I regularly chronicle that the intersection of modernism, history, and nationalism was very much at play in the founding of the Federation and in the instantiation of *canji* as a new sphere of subject-making and social action at the end of the twentieth century. I also show that, as Lin holds, ideas about discourse and normalization are invaluable for understanding the emergence of the Federation and the concomitant concretization of disability as a sphere of alterity in China. And I detail that the story of the Federation stands as a valuable illustration that biobureaucratic formation occurs in distinctive ways in distinctive settings, but also that understanding biopower's institutional expansion may require far more attention to the inner workings of the nation-state than Foucault was usually inclined to envision.

However, inasmuch as Professor Lin's arguments echo throughout this book, I also develop a set of complementary positions. These positions are as much prompted by what I saw and heard while researching the Federation and *canji* as they are inspired by insights about embodiment that have been formulated by Mauss and others. As helpful as Professor Lin's outlook on *canji* and the Disabled Persons' Federation may be, we must also ask: Was the Federation's growth and disability's rising visibility in late-twentieth-century China simply a matter of objectification driven by tectonic shifts in modernist, state, and discursive processes? Was *canji*'s concretization, the Federation's development, and their differential influence in locales like Beijing and rural Hainan simply *dictated* by the forces of biopolitical discourse, modernism, and the needs of a large-scale state, which came together to objectify Chinese bodies and to cast them as disabled? If so, we must question why, while conducting the research upon which this book is based, I met so many people throughout China who associated a single individual and his bodiliness with both the Federation's and *canji*'s expanding visibility? Why did people regularly say that Deng Pufang and his paralytic visage were both central to and utterly pivotal for the Federation's creation and for *canji*'s newly shaped notoriety as a subject position?

In other words, what role does embodiment—in the fullest Maussian sense of the term—play in the processes of emergence that make up the core of this book? The relevance of this question extends far beyond just Deng Pufang, however. For, if one exclusively utilizes Professor Lin's perspectives, it becomes easy to obviate not just Deng, but also a huge spectrum of people and the distinctive lives they have led. Included here are the tens of millions of residents who fall within the purview of what Chinese government functionaries, since the mid-1980s, have been calling the PRC's newly identified disability population. Also included, though, are the untold millions of people who have learned that they do not fit the functionaries' formal criteria for *canji*, but who nonetheless experience states of existence that they and those around them find deeply debilitating. In the late twentieth century, paralleling the uneven development of the Federation in places like Beijing and rural Hainan, there were unknown numbers of people who confronted unrelenting daily challenges; sometimes they were recognized by Federation personnel as *canji*, and sometimes they were not. Over time, some of these people have shaped the Federation's expansion in a variety of ways. Some have tried to promote the institution, going so far as becoming employees of the Foundation, while others have avoided the institution altogether. Some have tried to integrate Federation-sponsored *canji* discourses and identities into their subjectivities at specific times and in specific places, while others regularly have tried to transform or altogether spurn those discourses and identities. If we are to make sense of the emergence of the Federation and its relationship to the changing face of *canji* as a sphere of difference in late-twentieth-century China, we must cast our attention not simply on how modernist forces, biopolitical discourses, and state imperatives came to objectify such people in terms of bodies more or less disabled. We must also examine how it is that, for these people, their "bodies" have become the means and subjective springboard through which such forces, discourses, and imperatives have been concretized corporately and conceptually.

Moreover, when thinking about the Federation's and *canji*'s recent formation and the role of embodiment, we must not just interrogate Lin's perspectives vis-à-vis *canji*. Rather, we must explore, as I try to do regularly throughout this book, how was such formation, shaped by and shaping people's encounters with subject positions and categories, seemingly disconnected from *canji*? As I have indicated, it is vitally important to consider how masculinity has been involved. But beyond the categories of male and *canji*, how are the formative processes under study related to people's actively embodied engagements with other categories, such as "villager," "urbanite," "scientist," "government administrator," "foreigner," "entrepreneur," "parent," or "woman"? Likewise, how are these processes mediated by one's somatosocial encounters with overlapping normalizing discourses and practicalities (both new and old)—not just those pertaining to gender, ability, and biology, but also discourses pertaining to nationality, social standing, heritage, ethnicity, human rights, familial duty, and, more generally, modernity?

No doubt, the best way to address these questions is by delving headlong into "thick descriptions" (Geertz 1973, 6–10) of the people, places, meanings, and historical contingencies I encountered while conducting the research for this book. For it is only by enveloping ourselves in that minutia that we can begin to generate, if not comprehensive answers, then greater clarity about how matters of embodiment were influenced by and influencing Federation growth and *canji* transformations across China during the 1980s and 1990s. And, to a large degree, thick representation is what dominates most of this book.

TERMINOLOGICAL TRIMMINGS:
DISABILITY, IMPAIRMENT, AND HANDICAP

Whether produced by scientist, journalist, or novelist, every thick description is based on certain commitments, at once conceptual, political, and methodological. I have already outlined more than a few such commitments in this Introduction. But before moving forward ethnographically, I wish to elaborate one further set of definitions that undergird the representations to come. These loosely have to do with my stance toward translating *canji*.

Frequently, I do not translate *canji*, on the grounds that any English-language term which might be invoked would be too deeply imbedded in Euro-American traditions to communicate the necessary subtleties of the ethnographic moment. When I do deploy an English-language term, it is done with careful purpose, often with the desire of avoiding an undue evocation of essential difference, either cultural or national. More to the point, tapping English-language terms allows me to highlight translocal connections, new and old, actually at play on the ground, confounding the classic Orientalist perspective of "China and the Rest/West."

And when I do translate *canji*, I usually deploy a specific English-language term, although in a variety of permutations. The term I regularly tap is "disability." I draw upon this term, in part, because since the 1980s Federation functionaries and others have increasingly used it for translating *canji*. I also do so because "disability" helps flag a set of macro-level forces—the rise of a global disability-advocacy movement and the worldwide growth of rehabilitation medical disciplines—that were quite prominent during the late twentieth century and that, as I show, have been a very big part of the story behind the Federation's emergence and the recent positioning of *canji* as a sphere of alterity.

If "disability" is my term of choice, two other terms are purposefully avoided. I forgo using "handicap," a term often associated with disability, because social commentators and activists in many English-language settings increasingly have spurned that term on the grounds that its connotations are unduly negative (e.g., Shuntermann 1996). My reasoning for avoiding another term, "impairment," is more complicated and relates to how that signifier has been invested with meanings over the last three decades by the World Health Organization's definitional framework, the International Criteria of Impairment, Disability, and Handicap. I avoid the term "impairment" in large part because of the essentialism it has been saddled with by the WHO's original ICIDH wording, according to which, "impairment" is a deviation from universal norms of biomedical status, a form of acultural, apolitical, ahistorical facticity. The problem here, of course, is that such a gloss ignores the repeated findings of members of numerous branches of the academy (e.g., anthropology, culture studies, history, sociology, political science, as well as science and technology studies) that biomedicine has been very much a culturally, politically, and historically mediated set of practices and lenses—since its inception, in all its many forms and manifestations, and from place to place.

I also avoid the term "impairment" because of ongoing, worldwide criticism levied against the ICIDH. In the 1980s and 1990s many government organizations across the globe declined to formally adopt the ICIDH, often on the grounds that it is a cultural artifact of the handful of Euro-Americans who produced it, and who, when doing so, largely ignored issues of cross-cultural applicability and validity.[14] Over the last decade, in an attempt to respond to criticisms of the ICIDH, the World Health Organization underwent a seven-year process of revising the nosology, a process the WHO has lauded for involving representatives of sixty-five countries. On November 15, 2001, the WHO formally released "ICIDH-2," renaming it the ICF (International Classification of Functioning, Disability, and Health). WHO publicists extolled this new nosology, stating that it "challenges mainstream ideas on how we understand health" (WHO 2001a). The ICF's design leader, T. Bedirhan Üstün, likewise praises the nosology on the grounds that it is neutral with regard to causality (Üstün, n.d.). But when one looks at the fine print of the ICF, it is more than apparent that the nosology does not live up to its billing; this "update" of the ICIDH remains firmly grounded in a vision of "impairments of body functions and structures," overtly ordered by biomedicine (WHO 2001b).[15]

Finally, "impairment" is avoided here as a way to communicate my support for a new wave of scholarship that is on the rise within disability studies. For much of the 1980s and 1990s, even though a number of disability studies scholars criticized the ICIDH for medicalizing alterity (Oliver 1990, 4–6; Zola 1981, 242), most scholars writing about disability continued to tap, whether purposefully or not, an ICIDH-informed dyad of impairment and disability. This is a dyad based upon a Cartesian nature/culture binary wherein essential biological facts (impairment) prompt socially mediated responses (disability)—a dyad not too dissimilar from another binary medical anthropologists frequently used in the 1980s, that of "disease" and "illness" (Kleinman 1978). But, whereas many in medical anthropology have now jettisoned the disease/illness dyad, including its lead developer (Kleinman 1995), disability studies scholars have been far slower to dispense with the impairment/disability binary. This has started to change recently, however. Thanks in part to the work of scholars like Bill Hughes and Kevin Patterson (1999; 1997), not only have a growing number of disability studies scholars become openly critical of the binary's application in social analysis, recognizing that it has precluded a careful interrogation of how corporeality is at once a product of sociopolitical formation and a generative force within it, but also more and more disability studies scholars have become active in theory-building to better understand the lived body (e.g., Corker and Shakespeare 2002; Kasnitz 2003; Landsman 2001; Tremain 2002; Frank 2000).

In joining these disability scholars in moving away from an impairment/ disability binary, however, my aim is not to use ethnographic data to debunk *canji* (or any other sphere of alterity) as relative. Alterity is always a sociopolitical artifact. That is quite clear, or it should be by the time you have read this book in its entirety. Nonetheless, a single-minded relativist approach toward disability would be a great mistake. Rhetorically compelling as it might seem to some, unrestrained relativism in this area is at once analytically counterproductive and politically irresponsible.

Simply swapping one reductive metanarrative for another, exchanging biological universalism for relentless relativism, brings us nowhere closer to shedding reductivism. Nor does it bring us closer to understanding bodily experiences and their sociopolitical formation (Kleinman and Kleinman 1991). More disconcerting, though, such swapping can prompt dismissals of people's pain, thereby harming those who have the most at stake when it comes to disability. Consider rural Hainan, a venue I have already introduced. Relentless relativism could easily lead us to say that because people in rural Hainan did not regularly use the term *"canji"* in the 1990s, they did not experience the chronic conditions of suffering conveyed by the term (whether defined by the Federation or by other sources). From the little I have described so far of the woman Zeng Liping, an argument of this sort is highly misguided, if not reckless. Until her death a few years ago, Zeng's arthritic condition profoundly limited her from participating in activities of everyday life and those limitations were the source of intense suffering, both economic and psychosocial. Pursuing a purely relativist agenda would run the risk not only of belittling Zeng Liping's and her family's suffering but also of undermining arguments—built upon the ontology of pain and formulated around the lives of people like Zeng Liping and her family— for equal access to accommodation and the dampening of human vulnerability (Bourgois 1995, 14). Stated differently, just because residents in rural Hainan and other parts of China, now or in the recent past, do not regularly use the term *"canji"* or unequivocally embrace it as an identity does not mean they do not suffer. Nor does it mean that government planners and other powerful figures, like those who have backed the Federation since its inception, may be excused from equitably offering resources to and effecting social change on behalf of all the people whose lives are dramatically disrupted, marginalized or delegitimized by what they and others understand to be forms of bodily difference.

For these reasons, I try to take an alternate angle on disablement than might otherwise be expected of a relentless relativist or a WHO statistician. Following Lennard Davis, I take the position that disability is "a socially driven relation to the body" (Davis 1995, 3) and that it is, therefore, at once supralocally and locally mediated in our age of heightened bodily awareness. Yet, inasmuch as disability is something that is always culturally, historically, and politically mediated, I contend, it is never a mere construct, one that is dissociable from people's tangible, sentient, and fragile lives. Whether in China or elsewhere, it is a sphere of difference that is deeply grounded in what is most at stake for us all: the most quotidian and most intimate aspect of existence.

Chapter 1

A Biomythography in the Making

One day in early 1971 officials of Beijing University (Beida) arrived at the 301 Brigade Military Hospital. They entered and approached the bedside of the former Beida graduate student, who had lost the ability to walk two years earlier. The officials told Deng Pufang they wished to transfer him elsewhere to convalesce. Still the dutiful student, Deng consented, and in the afternoon he was packed into a jeep and moved to the Qing He Shelter (Qing He Jiuji Yuan) forty-five kilometers northwest of Tiananmen Square.

Originally a nursing home for women, Qing He had become a place of last refuge for a variety of people following the Korean War. Wounded veterans without family were brought there, and gradually all sorts of what Chinese then often called *fei ren* (social outcasts, literally, "garbage people") ended up at Qing He. These outcasts included orphans, the mentally impeded, the deaf and mute, the chronically ill, and persons with other forms of bodily difference that were viewed locally as highly delegitimizing. According to published reports, conditions at the shelter were dire at the time that Deng Pufang arrived. Most residents slept six or seven to a bed. Medical care was unavailable. Meals were usually nothing more than rice, bread, and small amounts of vegetables.

According to one of his biographers, before his arrival at Qing He, Deng was already quite melancholy. For, by then, the people plotting against him had already succeeded in stripping him of his cherished possessions: "his party membership, his university diploma and credentials, his fully healthy body, [and] his family" (Qin 1992, 205). But once deposited at the shelter, Deng's mood quickly devolved from melancholy to despair, feeling as he did that his tormentors had gone out of their way "to throw him into the nadir of Chinese society," "to turn him into living refuse" (205, 206). This mood shift is not difficult to understand, given Deng Pufang's situation in the winter and spring of 1971. During those first few months at Qing He, he was placed alone in a small room without plumbing and left to handle his own incontinence with nothing more than a rag.

FOREGROUNDING DENG PUFANG

Members of China's party-state began forming the organizational structures for the China Disabled Person's Federation in the mid-1980s and founded the institution in 1988. During that period and over the subsequent decade, we might ask, how did these government functionaries succeed in expanding the institution into a vice-ministry with offices across the country? As many have explained to me, their success was based in part on their capacity to convince people inside and outside China's sprawling governmental apparatuses that internationally recognized disability-assistance discourse and practice could contribute in special ways to agendas of great import to the nation and the party.

The positioning of the Federation in serving such agendas has not been lost on China's citizenry, certainly not on the many people with whom I have spoken since beginning the research for this book. In discussions with me about the Federation, quite a number of people, particularly urbanites, have emphasized that the ability of Federation staff to situate disability assistance as useful to the nation and the CCP was indispensable for the emergent institution in receiving the sizable resources necessary to develop it into a vice-ministry. Those resources included, but were not limited to, durable material (e.g., financial outlays, office buildings), symbolic capital (e.g., access to mainstream media outlets, publishing houses, and research institutes), and professional personnel (e.g., administrators, educators, clinicians).

But, in general, over the last decade, people who have talked to me about the Federation have tended to downplay or pass over these matters. Rather, they have emphasized a different social force as having fueled the Federation's formation. As previously highlighted, this force is Deng Pufang. And what is particularly interesting is that, when new or old acquaintances have spoken to me about the role Deng Pufang has played in Federation formation, it has been less in terms of how he has leveraged his father's authority for the institution, although that is something few discount. Instead, what people have emphasized most is Pufang's *canji*. Time and time again, people have said to me that, if it had not been for the young Deng Pufang's unique journey in becoming a *canji ren*, the Federation would not exist today. For instance, a middle-aged Beijing man, Chen Lu, gave the following in response to a general question I posed about public attitudes toward *canji*:

Oh, so you're interested in the work of Deng Pufang. If it wasn't for him, if it wasn't for all that happened to him during the Cultural Revolution, China's *canji* situation would be quite different. Because of what he's had to live through, we have the Disabled Persons' Federation.

Why do people attribute such sociopolitical significance to Deng's paraplegia and to his embodiment of *canji* more generally? To a significant degree, it could be argued, the attribution stems from Deng and his Federation associates having carefully deployed and packaged his persona, particularly his somatic presence. This strategy is plainly visible when one examines representations of the Federation found in China's mass media during the 1980s and 1990s. Not only do those representations commonly show images of Deng—for example, greeting Chinese and foreign dignitaries or overseeing key Federation events—they usually depict Deng sitting assuredly in a wheelchair, sometimes with a plastic drainage tube visibly emanating from beneath his midsection garb and ending in a storage bag affixed under the chair's seat.

When I have queried high-ranking Federation officials about Deng's appearance in such representations, several of them have unequivocally attested that what one sees in the images is frequently not a matter of happenstance. Rather, they indicate that the Federation has worked purposefully to make Deng Pufang's body visible across China. They state that—in order to generate resources for the Federation, clear away intragovernmental hindrances to Federation growth, raise popular understanding about *canji*, and curry favor for Federation objectives—Federation leaders have found it immensely beneficial to foreground Deng Pufang as possessing a highly visible disability *(hen mingxian de canji)* and as being a genuine yet unique member of a universally recognized population: the disabled.

MISSING AFFLICTION

Yet if the depiction of Deng Pufang's disability was an important resource for the Federation, how did his embodiment become so valuable, so productive, so pivotal for the institution's formation? How was this one elite male bodiliness made not just interchangeable with the category of *canji* but endowed with a talismanlike quality such that it could spark goodwill for the Federation and its programs? How were productive forces of biobureaucratic formation embedded within Deng Pufang's corporeal being?

These are the questions that I explore in this chapter. And they are questions that point us to areas of sociopolitical formation rarely examined by academicians. While cases of biomedical institution-building spawned by elites' experiences with bodiliness have been increasingly commonplace—

the "humanitarian" efforts of Franklin Roosevelt, Queen Noor of Jordan, Christopher Reeves, the current king and queen of Thailand, or Eunice Kennedy Shriver are probably the most oft-noted—rarely have scholars examined these kinds of cases. This, despite the fact that in recent years anthropologists have shown a growing interest in studying persons with great political-economic authority.[1]

Of course, this is not to say that researchers have been uninterested in the relationship between individual actors and biobureaucracy. Indeed, over the last two decades, ethnographers of science and medicine have been keenly interested in examining the ways by which culturally embedded participants come to construct biomedical apparatuses, be they psychiatric treatments, medical school curricula, or molecular research centers.

At the risk of overgeneralization, it can be said that, to date, much of this interest has led researchers in one of two broad directions. First is the study of the ways in which biomedical providers, researchers, and teachers (what we might call "biocrats") produce, learn, reconfigure, and extend biomedical knowledge and techniques in the context of global-local change (see, e.g., Latour and Woolgar 1979; Luhrmann 2000; Rabinow 1996). The second is centered on people whom anthropologists have largely treated as distinctively different from biocrats, people whom we might call "the afflicted." In this latter approach, anthropologists explore how, as the afflicted move through everyday experiences of suffering and encounter biomedical institutions, specific somatosocial processes prompt them to support, resist, or reconfigure those institutions (see, e.g., Desjarlais 1997; Jackson 2000; Rapp 1999; Lock 1993). This second stream of research, it should be acknowledged, is often closely tied to the study of embodiment.[2]

The development of these two broad approaches—one centered around biocrats, one focused on the afflicted—has been of great importance because it has promoted a deeper understanding of the ways that people in various social contexts may be, at once, biomedicine's objects and its complicit framers. But in their attempt to discern how actors in different settings shape biomedical apparatuses, champions of these two approaches have, to date, largely overlooked what for numerous biobureaucracies appears to be a potent catalyst of growth: elite affliction.[3]

SUBJECTIFICATION

By focusing closely on the case of Deng Pufang's embodiment in this chapter, I hope to help redress this oversight. It should also be noted that, by examining Deng Pufang's story, I hope to prompt the study of biopower to incorporate more fully the ideas developed by Foucault at the end of his life. In particular, I am thinking of ideas that Foucault often discussed under the rubric of "subjectification." For him, subjectification is a set of historically and socially specific processes that allowed people, initially elite Europeans, to become heroically oriented ethical subjects: "They were a set of operations that worked on many levels of the European elite's lives: on [their] bodies, on their own souls, on their own thoughts, on their own conduct" (Foucault 1980b; also cited in Rabinow 1984, 11). And they involved, at once, externally induced discipline and self-development, that is, the "way a human being turns him- or herself into a subject" (Rabinow 1984, 11).[4] In his last writings, lectures, and interviews, Foucault began to consider how subjectification might relate to the creation of new social movements and institutions and thus to new modes of normalization and medicalization. In terms of his own research on the history of the self in Europe, he struggled to see how individual cases of subjectification could precipitate "an attempt to normalize the population" (Foucault 1984, 341). But he urged other scholars to probe this question.[5]

Since then, although academics writing about many parts of the world— China being one of them—have become more and more engaged with the issue of subjectification,[6] few have overtly examined how specific cases of subjectification may be implicated in the creation of what are some of the most commonly recognized nodes of biopower: organizations deploying biomedical modes of apprehension and practice to heal and improve health. The analysis of Deng Pufang's story presented here is designed to help situate subjectification at the center of the study of biobureaucracy. In particular, I wish to show that, in order to understand how Deng Pufang's body has been positioned in contemporary China as an engine of Federation growth, we must examine how he and others made his life knowable and meaningful, and how they did so in response to the sociopolitical forces and historical contingencies in which they were embedded.

METHODOLOGY AND NARRATIVITY

Before proceeding, I should note that in this chapter I do not provide accounts of how Deng Pufang and others "built" the Disabled Persons' Federation. That comes later. Instead of the brick-and-mortar formation of the Federation, I focus on Deng Pufang's embodiment as a young man. My analysis follows the structuring of Deng Pufang's story chronologically up to 1981, several years before the Federation's founding.

It must additionally be noted that most of the information about Deng Pufang presented here does not come from the ordinary methods medical anthropologists use to gather data about illness experience: one-on-one interviews with sick people, with their kin, and/or with their healthcare providers. Rather than relying on interview transcripts, such as those from my 1998 conversation with Deng Pufang, my sources for this chapter tend to be far more publicly accessible. Indeed, my sources are predominantly the same ones through which most people in China have been permitted to peer into Deng Pufang's life.[7] They are hagiographic texts—articles published by the Federation's media outlets, as well as *The Deng Pufang Road* (Qin 1992), a book-length biography written by one of Deng Pufang's friends and political beneficiaries, who interviewed him at length.[8]

Together, these hagiographic texts comprise something akin to what, for many in China, has become a foundational narrative for the China Disabled Persons' Federation, what we might see as a publicly circulated storyline of Deng Pufang's subjectification, a tale about how he came to be a man with a disability and an advocate for disability assistance. They comprise what I call a "biomythography of statesmanship," a celebratory story of how Deng Pufang—owing to links between his birth position, body, and the surrounding social world—came to develop a vocational intentionality: a desire, a calling, to assemble institutional assistance for China's segment of an emergent transnational category of the afflicted (i.e., persons with disabilities).[9]

How should ethnographers treat such a narrative and what can they learn from examining it? I would contend that rather than seeing it as spurious and thus as an invalid object of scholarly inquiry, we should handle it in the same way that numerous anthropologists—including those working on the anthropology of China and of medicine (e.g., Anagnost 1997; Kleinman 1995; Rofel 1999a)—have treated such narratives about life and bodily experience in recent years: as truth claims that are always framed by and constitutive of personal, political, and historical contingencies. We should explore Deng Pufang's biomythography for what it is: a complex brew of fact, elision, obfuscation, genre, discourse, and ideology.

Toward that end, I draw overtly on anthropological insights into a broad set of narrative forms known as "speaking bitterness" *(suku)*. From China's May Fourth Movement (1919) to the present, "speaking bitterness" has become ubiquitous across the PRC as a set of narrative techniques for representing suffering, often subaltern experiences of suffering. In recent years, these techniques have also been frequently employed for the production of *shanghen wenxue* (the "literature of the wounded," or "scar literature"). This genre is composed of stories in which elites, most of whom are intellectuals, describe their persecution at the hands of Maoist radicals.

By transgressing received academic boundaries between literary studies, history, and anthropology, Lisa Rofel (1999a) and Ann Anagnost (1997) have illuminated the ways in which scar literature and other speaking-bitterness genres have been pivotal for the production of key sociopolitical phenomena, specifically Chinese nationalism, CCP authority, and subjectivity.[10] Among her insights, Rofel points out that speaking bitterness has established narrative tropes for subject-making and resource allocation, in which China's citizenry regularly have been called on to claim heroic stature in the eyes of the nation-state. . . . Speaking bitterness created the conditions of visibility for a new socialist subject, one whose dilemmas in life might lead to state-sanctioned rewards. Such rewards might range from symbolic praise to concrete manifestations in terms of . . . state power itself. (1999a, 141)

How have speaking-bitterness genres carried out such sociopolitical labor? In part, Anagnost argues, they have done so by focusing on and giving meaning to the corporeal. As many readers of speaking-bitterness tracts know, the somatic is commonly invoked. Indeed, it could be said that in most speaking-bitterness expressions materially rendered bodiliness functions as a central topic of narration; it is what Anagnost calls a "privileged signifier of the 'real'" (1997, 18–19). This attention to corporeality, she says, helps speaking bitterness to produce a modernist "politics of presence" (4), in which the orator claims to have or is attributed to have the force of history. By narrating one's own or another's unfolding encounters with the sociopolitics of the twentieth century, and by narrating those encounters in terms of somatic experiences, particularly extreme affliction, "the national subject is made to embody abstract conceptions" and to become "emblematic of the nation speaking with the voice of history" (4).

In this chapter, I wish to contribute to an analysis of speaking bitterness as well as of a politics of presence. By exploring how his corporeality has been scripted into hagiographic texts, I aim to highlight the ways in which Deng Pufang's body has been made knowable and has been vested with "the power to speak with the force of history" (Anagnost 1997, 4). In doing so, though, I also strive to expand Anagnost's "history of presencing" (20) into a new domain. While sharing her interest in the effects of narrative on Chinese nation-building, class consciousness, and identity formation, my goal is to explore how these effects can converge to generate the seedbed for a further effect: the formation of a new biobureaucracy. My agenda is to show how bodily narration has worked to furnish Deng Pufang's story of subjectification with a unique governmental authority, one that has been pivotal for the creation of a new biomedical/welfare apparatus within the Chinese party-state.

THE DENG PUFANG STORY: THE EARLY YEARS

The Deng Pufang storyline, as most often presented to the public, falls into four chronologically ordered phases. In each phase, Deng's body works as a privileged signifier of the "real." In phase one, specific bodily practices allow Deng to become incorporated into a distinctive, hyperelite, male, socialist subject position. In phase two, Deng Pufang makes efforts to ameliorate the sociopolitical disruptions wrought by the Cultural Revolution, efforts that lead directly to his paraplegia. In phase three, facing a strange mix of persecution and privilege, Deng Pufang struggles to address his heathcare crises. And in phase four, as a consequence of social change and ongoing challenges with bodily suffering, Deng Pufang comes to a new consciousness about the need for institutional support for those people in China who he understands to be "persons with disabilities."

To make sense of Deng Pufang's presencing in phase one, we need to illuminate the contradictory social world he and his siblings were born into. In the PRC, the term *gaogan zinu* (literally, "children of high-ranking officials") indirectly references the special privileges *(tequan)* they command due to their parents' rank. An important aspect of their existence, particularly among the older cohorts, is a deep structural paradox. On the one hand, children like Deng Pufang and his siblings were thrown into a setting of great privilege from birth, one that swaddled them with a social status unfamiliar to nearly all other Chinese people. On the other hand, they grew up at the epicenter of an egalitarian revolution that was acutely hostile to the notions of private property, inheritance, and social domination. From the beginning, Deng Pufang and his paradoxical situation gradually began to fuse, and eventually, aspects of his body, self, and social context became inextricably entangled (cf. Bourdieu 1977, 87–88; Connerton 1989, 72).

A good example of this fusing—one of the earliest—regards Pufang's naming. Biographical accounts suggest that, through naming, Deng Pufang was positioned not only within the normative expectations of daily life, such as a gendered division of labor, but also within the CCP's imaginary of China's past and future. Deng Pufang's mother, Zhuo Lin,[11] had trouble breastfeeding her newborn son, so she enlisted the services of a pro-Communist farming family (Deng 1995). That family's wet nurse, who nourished the child with her peasant, and thus, revolutionary, body, gave him the "milk name" of Pangzi, or Chubby. When the time came for Pangzi to attend school, his parents honored Deng Xiaoping's closest military colleague, Commander Liu Bocheng, by giving Liu the cherished task of choosing a formal name for their son. Liu fulfilled this task by splitting the sound of *pang* into two sounds, *pu* and *fang*; he then chose the two ideograms for these sounds that translate as "simple" and "righteous."[12] The Deng family apparently was thrilled with Liu's selection. Qin Yan, author of *The Deng Pufang Road,* relates, "Not only did the name *embody* [the family's] deep love and wishes for New China's future, but it also *embodied* memories of the many who sacrificed themselves for military victory" (1992, 100, emphasis added).

As Deng Pufang and his siblings entered early childhood, their parents pressed them to help the Maoist project. The main way Deng Xiaoping and Zhuo Lin pursued this course was by pointing their children down an "edu-

Figure 1. Deng Pufang as an adolescent watching CCP lumi-
naries Zhu De and Peng Dehui play Chinese chess. Behind
Deng Pufang and standing to his left is Deng Xiaoping.

cational road" so that they would have the skills to be China's future leaders
(Qin 1992, 107). For Deng Pufang, this involved testing into and attending
the finest schools China had to offer, many of which were all-male (or mostly
male) institutions filled with the progeny of both revolutionary martyrs
and top military figures. Deng Pufang's educational road, however, entailed
more than just attending classes with other boys from elite Communist
backgrounds and taking exams. For the developing Deng Pufang, school
life involved learning a number of somatic disciplines.

This is exemplified by a story Pufang reputedly related to Deng Xiaoping
and Zhuo Lin in 1952, just after the Deng family moved to Beijing and
Pufang was enrolled in the most elite primary school in China, Bayi.
Specially created for the "flowers of the fatherland," Bayi educated the offspring of military martyrs, mid-level Communist functionaries, and high
party and army figures such as Mao Zedong, Zhou Enlai, Zhu De, and Ye

Jianying. After attending his first day of third grade, Deng Pufang recounted to his parents:

> My teacher chided me for not sitting straight in my chair. Afterward, the teacher questioned me as to whether I avoid sitting up straight because at home I have lots of sofas to lounge around on. I said to the teacher, no, and explained that the reason [I slouch in my chair] is because I am too fat. When the class heard that, they all broke out into huge laughter. (Qin 1992, 111)

This excerpt articulates not simply that Deng Pufang's childhood involved somatic molding or that at times this caused him to suffer humiliation. So, too, it articulates that the molding was intensely guided by Maoist ideals. Although an emphasis on vertical posture is not unique to the China of Deng Pufang's youth, the concept of the upright *(zheng)* resonates strongly with the young Maoist state's project for erecting a strong national body politic—a project that Chairman Mao crystallized on October 1, 1949, when he proclaimed the country's founding from Tiananmen Square: "The People's Republic of China now stands up" *(xianzai zhongguo renmin gongheguo zhanqilai).*[13]

In addition to postural molding, accounts of Deng's childhood also emphasize various activities centered around movement *(dong)*. These activities, or "symbolic gymnastics," as Bourdieu (1977, 2) might call them, convey messages about Deng's paradoxical engagement with Maoist ideals and his somatic embrace of the social standing afforded him as the male scion of Deng Xiaoping. As Deng Pufang matured, one activity to which he and his siblings were often exposed, and which played a significant role in their rearing, was manual labor *(laodong)*. Deng Xiaoping often organized his family into a manual-labor brigade *(laodong dui)* to toil outside the home. The more difficult tasks were assigned to the Deng males rather than to the females (Qin 1992, 122).[14] Another group of activities pertaining to movement that was central to Deng Pufang's childhood was sports *(yundong)*. Some of Deng's fondest childhood memories involve attending athletic events at large stadiums with Deng Xiaoping, or joining his father for swims at the club reserved for high officials *(gaoji ganbu julebu)* and at the special resort provided for them at the Beidaihe seashore (Qin 1992, 117). Deng Pufang also frequently played ping-pong and badminton throughout his secondary and university schooling. In the summer months, he and his elite male classmates organized swimming outings to lakes in central Beijing and to the Summer Palace. And together with his largely male academic cohort,[15] Deng also played organized basketball, until the onset of the Cultural Revolution.

As with all representations of Deng Pufang's childhood, there is no single way of interpreting his sporting life. Biographical accounts of Deng's sporting activities seem to confirm his patrician pedigree, for in the early years of the People's Republic sports largely took place in relatively formal public settings (e.g., schools, military bases, government compounds). Yet many Chinese urbanites have told me that representations of Deng Pufang's athleticism may also be understood as articulating a broad-sweeping allegiance to both Maoist and Euro-American principles of modernity, nation-building, and subjectivity. Possibly because of his early exposure to the wide variety of biosocial discourses that accompanied Marxism's introduction to China and fueled the rise of nationalism there in the late nineteenth and early twentieth centuries—discourses such as biomedicine, eugenics, and Social Darwinism (see Dikotter 1992)—Mao fervently championed sports and lashed out at China's erstwhile idealization of the sedentary scholar-official (Brownell 1995, 57; Spence 1990, 308). Mao articulated this view as early as 1917, when he published an essay entitled "Study of Body Training," (Tiyu zhi yanjiu) in which he described athleticism as a source of Western domination and thus a necessity for China's own salvation, economic development, and nation-building.[16]

Before the book shifts to the events leading up to Deng's paralysis, one of the last episodes chronicled in *The Deng Pufang Road* is Deng's admittance to university. In 1962 Deng Pufang completed his secondary studies, took the nationwide university entrance exam, and was admitted to Beida. This account of Deng's college entrance conveys complex social information about his absorption into the paradoxical world of the children of high-ranking officials. Almost since Beida's creation, many in China have considered it the finest university in the country. To win admission during the Maoist epoch, students were required to fulfill several demanding criteria. They needed not only to have graduated from top secondary schools and to have achieved the highest entrance-exam scores, but they also needed to possess impeccable socialist credentials (both ascribed and achieved). Yet there was at least one additional criterion for admission, namely, good health. Even today, all Chinese universities require prospective students to take and pass a physical exam *(shenti jiancha)*.[17] For the eighteen-year-old Deng Pufang, the exam was never a concern. In the words of a Number 13 Middle School employee, Teacher Li, "[Pufang's] body was perfect. He loved to play ball. He loved to do manual labor. And he was tall" (Qin 1992, 135).

PHASE TWO: CADRE CONFLICTS

Phase two of Deng Pufang's biography describes the events leading up to the crippling of this "perfect" body. Here, the narrative follows the lines of classic speaking-bitterness literature. Not only does it tell the tale of an upstanding citizen who is wounded as a consequence of an unbearable sociopolitical predicament, it tells it in terms of a cast of known agents acting within specific contexts. As such, it uses what Anagnost describes as "telescoping vision," a technique that lies at the "very heart of" speaking bitterness: a mode of representation that collapses "abstract forces into adversaries who can be identified in local sites of struggle." Owing to these metonymic reductions, we are able to see the wounded subject as the "material embodiment" of history in the making (Anagnost 1997, 27).

The fact that Deng Pufang's hagiography has furnished him with special bodily authority stems in part from the "known personalities" (e.g., Deng Xiaoping, Mao Zedong, Jiang Qing, Liu Shaoqi) that this and subsequent phases of his story invoke and in part from the "local sites" where Deng Pufang is situated. Because biographers (Wang, n.d.; Ruan 1992; Qin 1992; Deng 1995) offer the viewing public insight into a cast of characters who are already well known (and who are known to possess the power to speak with the authority of history), Deng Pufang's wounding takes on a heightened sociopolitical presence, one that far exceeds that of most Cultural Revolution "victims." By allowing us to peer into the adversarial relationships of China's elite and to see Deng's paralysis as a product of his "virtuous" attempts to respond to those adversarial relationships within contexts such as Beijing University, his biographers help to inscribe Deng Pufang's body with a historical force few in China today possess.

To understand how this works, it is necessary to highlight some additional features of Deng's subjectification. In particular, it is necessary to relate one of the key objectives of his childhood to what is now understood by many in China to have been the political landscape of his adolescence and early adulthood. Without question, one objective underlying Deng Pufang's rearing as a "flower of the fatherland" was social reproduction, that is, he was raised to join the PRC's largely male officialdom, to become a Chinese Communist Party *ganbu* (cadre).[18]

Though seemingly innocuous to non-Chinese speakers, most well-educated PRC residents today are aware that during the 1950s, 1960s, and 1970s the term *ganbu* was a topic of fierce contention among the nation's most well known and powerful leaders, particularly Chairman Mao, Deng Xiaoping, and Mao's heir apparent in the 1950s and early 1960s, Liu Shaoqi. Owing to the recent traffic in and out of China of what we might call post-1949 "court chronicles"—some written by academic historians, others by journalists and eyewitnesses—a large percentage of well-read Chinese citizens know that Mao, Deng, and Liu all felt that cadres should be quick, efficient, and disciplined; but beyond that, these leaders had deep disagreements on the subject. Whereas Deng, Liu, and others within the party leadership increasingly believed that cadre competence needed to be defined more in terms of technical skill, the Chairman tended to equate competence with political purity. In the idiom of the period, Deng and Liu and their allies felt it was more important for cadres to be "experts," while

Mao and his closest colleagues primarily emphasized that they should be "Red."[19]

This disagreement became particularly significant after the Great Leap Forward proved to be a catastrophe.[20] In the early 1960s, with the devastation still unfolding, Deng, Liu, and others took steps to change government policy and sideline Mao. Instead of pursuing economic growth by having cadres push communist theory, the Deng and Liu group demanded that cadres should champion more pragmatic scientific, economic, and managerial techniques. Along these lines, they directed the cadres to revive the rural economy by allowing farmers to produce for themselves rather than for the collective. And, at the universities, they ousted those officials who they viewed as ideologically minded and replaced them with more scientifically oriented scholars (Schneider 1989).

What was Deng Pufang's position during this period? His biographers suggest that, to a large degree, it was one of filial allegiance to his father and his father's approach to Communist governance and competence. Deng Pufang had joined the Communist Youth League in his sophomore year of high school, and a short time afterward had become a member of the Chinese Communist Party. Two years later, he was accepted into the technophysics department at Beida. The department, then nearly an all male program, had just been created as part of Deng and Liu's mandate for building a national infrastructure based on rational planning and "high" technology.[21] In 1966, as Deng Pufang was completing his bachelor of science degree and preparing to start a master's degree in nuclear physics, he and thousands of other students throughout China went off to the countryside to help with the Four Cleanups, a campaign launched by Deng Xiaoping and Liu Shaoqi to educate rural cadres in the ways of "scientific management."

Despite this seemingly salutary merging of life and politics, texts like *The Deng Pufang Road* emphasize that as Deng progressed through college, his filial devotion increasingly put him at risk. This, Qin attributes directly to the Cultural Revolution (1966–76) and to Deng Pufang's response to it.[22] As much as he could, Deng Pufang tried to dampen the Cultural Revolution almost from the moment he learned of its launch, in June 1966, when he and his classmates were returning to Beijing after months in the countryside promoting the Deng and Liu agenda. The site of most of these dampening efforts—Beida—is quite significant. Possibly more than any other venue in China, Beida is generally recognized across the PRC today as having served as a key spawning ground for the Cultural Revolution. Indeed, it is viewed as having been something of a laboratory for the radical policies that would eventually engulf the country.

After they heard about the Cultural Revolution over the loudspeaker when their train was pulling into Beijing, Deng Pufang and his classmates went directly back to campus, foregoing stops at any of their family homes along the way. What did the group find upon their arrival at Beida? The campus was in a state of political fervor. Plastered on walls everywhere were large posters denouncing—sometimes metaphorically, sometimes directly—the policies promoted by Liu and Deng. Students of reputedly good (non-bourgeois) family backgrounds had formed paramilitary groups, named Red Guards, to insure that the Cultural Revolution would be carried out, and the Red Guards were starting to clash openly with resisters (Qin 1992, 174–75). Deng Pufang's early response to this fervor was to intervene on behalf of students who were being attacked because of their "bad" family backgrounds and to communicate what was happening at Beida to his parents. At one juncture, we are told, he even went so far as to tear down a large-character poster *(dazibao)* filled with pronouncements attributed to Jiang Qing, the wife of Mao, which he then delivered by bicycle to Deng Xiaoping (1992, 179).

It should be noted that here, as in the other phases of Deng's story, his biographers never reveal either his or their own views about Mao. A good case in point is Ruan Cishan's 1992 essay which appears in a China Disabled Persons' Federation publication. While chronicling how Deng was increasingly harmed by the Cultural Revolution and its leaders, Ruan never expresses any judgments about Mao. More to the point, as is the case with Qin's book-length biography, nowhere in Ruan's essay is Mao specifically blamed for Deng's difficulties or for the Cultural Revolution more generally. Instead, as is the case with Qin, Ruan casts blame on "leftists" or named figures from the Maoist camp, people such as Nie Yuanzi, the Gang of Four, and Kang Sheng, all of whom Ruan and Qin characterize as "fascists," "feudalists," "dictators," or "murderers." In this regard, Ruan and Qin seem to walk a fine line: they use the idiom of speaking bitterness to criticize known personalities, while at the same time they—and by extension Deng Pufang—remain in compliance with long-standing party rules, which limit open criticism of Mao's political life.

Qin and Ruan continue to walk this fine line as they explain Deng Pufang's growing predicament from 1966 to 1968. This was an intensely tumultuous period during which the Cultural Revolution spread from Beijing to nearly every community in the PRC, inflicting shock and suffering on millions. It was also a period during which Maoists continued to chip away at Deng Xiaoping and Liu Shaoqi's authority. They labeled them China's number one and two "capitalist roaders," promoted diatribes against them in the press, directed Red Guards to demonstrate incessantly outside the two leaders' homes, and then imprisoned Liu and sent Deng and his wife to live under house arrest in Jiangxi Province.

Deng Pufang's existence during this period is described not only by way of a telescoping vision but also through the technique frequently deployed in phase one of the story, that is, by using Deng's body as a privileged signifier. For instance, Qin Yan tells us that, as this period progressed, at a Deng family meeting, Deng Pufang receives a severe somatosocial blow when Deng Xiaoping announces to his children that soon their father might be of dubious value to them. Somewhat cryptically, he advises that rather than follow their parents' path, his children should take a "detour." After the meeting, Deng Pufang returned to Beida and fell into a state of deep depression. He ignored his personal hygiene, ate little, and rarely got out of bed. His classmates' pleas for him to cheer up and join them in some basketball (and their accusations that he is acting like a girl for not doing so) were of little use in unseating his malaise (Qin 1992, 183–85).

Yet in this phase of the story, by far the most important representations—for Deng Pufang's contemporary presencing, for the creation of his bio-mythography, and for the positioning of his subjectification as discursive effect—are those surrounding how he became disabled. Here, narrative attention to telescoping and bodily signifiers is thorough. According to Ruan, in the spring of 1968, as leftist-induced chaos raged throughout much of the country, one of the most notorious Maoist activists at Beida, Nie Yuanzi, directed the Red Guards to detain Deng Pufang and his sister Deng Nan (a Beida sophomore). The two were imprisoned in separate rooms of the campus physics building. Deng Nan was released relatively quickly, but Deng Pufang was held for four months. During the detention, the Red Guards subjected him to repeated interrogation, lengthy periods of food and sleep deprivation, and other kinds of abuse. As the months passed, Deng's captors became increasingly agitated by his unwillingness to give a full self-criticism. Eventually, they proclaimed that if he did not comply with their wishes—if he did not state everything he knew regarding the party, admit anti-Maoist sentiments, and expose his mother and father as traitors—his party membership would be revoked and his academic credentials invalidated (Ruan 1992, 2). Deng's subsequent moves are robustly described in *The Deng Pufang Road* as antifascist, sacrificial, and protective of family, party, and nation. Deng declared, once again, that he would not provide the denunciation his captors demanded. He then surreptitiously penned the following note:

> I am infinitely devoted to the party and to Chairman Mao. But owing to the Cultural Revolution, which I don't understand, and particularly owing to questions about my father, which I don't understand, things are being said that should not be said. This talk directly relates to secrets within the nucleus of the proletarian leadership that cannot be disseminated. The rebels demand that I talk. But I cannot talk.
>
> Under this situation there is really no road left for me to travel. (Qin 1992, 190)

Having received permission to use the bathroom, Deng then performed an arresting act of embodiment: he attempted suicide by throwing himself out of a third-story window.

PHASE THREE: THE BODY IN PAIN

On the way down from the window, Deng's body bounced off a steel guidewire and flipped before thudding to the ground (Qin 1992, 198).

After relating these vivid details, Qin repeatedly returns to a theme that Deng's other biographers regularly use to depict his post-fall existence, the body in pain. This representational emphasis, it should be noted, is central to the main question being explored here: how speaking-bitterness techniques have enabled Deng Pufang's subjectification to be fashioned into a significant force for a new institution of biomedical intervention.

Since their inception, speaking-bitterness genres have repeatedly invoked the body, particularly the body in pain. This theme has been not only a defining feature of speaking bitterness but also a central mechanism by which this genre has promoted national subjects (Anagnost 1997, 18). By "giving voice" to experiences of corporeal and psychic suffering fueled by historically framed injustices (such as Japanese colonialism or the Cultural Revolution), speaking bitterness has helped the CCP to foster moral, knowable citizens, deserving and recognizable subjects who are ready to revivify and rectify the polity.

Unlike most book-length speaking-bitterness stories set during the Cultural Revolution, in which once-upstanding citizens (say, intellectuals or government officials) find their lofty official status comprehensively inverted and themselves facing related afflictions, Deng's story has an important distinction: his first few years of post-fall suffering are frequently marked by substantial privilege. In phases three and four of his story, like most literature of the wounded, Deng is visited by attack and calamitous misfortune, and he struggles with intense pain. But his situation is not that of constant dispossession. Rather, he is frequently described as convalescing in situations of relative luxury.

This representational jumble of pain, persecution, and privilege, I would suggest, has been vital in forging Deng Pufang's subjectification as a discursive force and for presencing Deng Pufang as embodying great political power and moral authority. In recent years, when I have asked people in Beijing or in other PRC cities to explain Deng's current governmental influence, they regularly tell me that in addition to its emanating from his disablement, his authority emanates from his father, and particularly from his father's *guanxi* (sociopolitical network). And when I have pressed them further, saying, "Well, Deng Xiaoping has been dead for several years now. Why does his *guanxi* still give Deng Pufang so much power?" they often answer it is because Deng has benefited from his father's network nearly all his life, and that owing to his unique status as Deng Xiaoping's son he was forced to suffer great trauma during the Cultural Revolution and thereafter to live with enduring discomfort.[23] In other words, these explanations indicate that for many people, there is a degree to which, on the one hand, Deng's current hyperelite status seems preordained, and on the other, it is understood to be restitution for his persecution and intractable struggles with bodily damage.

In phases three and four of this story, by depicting Deng as being treated sometimes with malice but more often with privilege (and always in a state of pain), his biographers have fueled these two aspects of his presencing. They have helped promote the view that Deng belongs in the hyperelite sphere of the party-state and that he is particularly deserving of such a position. To see this, one needs only to consider the stories which follow, which involve encounters with malevolence and privilege. And when considering them, one should likewise pay close attention to how the telescoping vision of the narrator situates Deng's body in pain amidst knowable settings, people, and historical events.

As recounted at this book's outset, moments after his fall from the third story of the Beida physics building, as he is regaining consciousness on the pavement, Deng cries out for medical assistance. But because of his, the Deng family's, and the nation's political situation, help is not easily found. For many moments, people just stand watching Deng writhe in pain. Eventually, a few people intervene and carry him to the university clinic. Medical personnel block their entry, however. The people then decide to transport Deng off campus to the emergency ward of the nearby Beijing Medical College (BMC) hospital. When nobody is looking, they run away. Doctors again refuse treatment. Deng remains in a BMC hallway, lying unattended until nightfall, at which time hospital officials order an ambulance to return him to the Beijing University clinic. On reaching campus, the ambulance crew leaves him on the ground alongside the clinic's front door and then speeds off (Qin 1992, 190, 198–99).

After spending the night lying alone, Deng is brought inside by university clinic workers and left on a bed in an empty corridor. After several days, a worker assigned to watch over Deng's class, Wang Fengwu, wins approval from Mao and Zhou Enlai to have Deng admitted to one of Beijing's best orthopedic centers, Jinshuitan Hospital. There, doctors discover through X-rays that Deng has shattered his first lumbar and twelfth thoracic vertebrae. They also learn that, owing to an infection of unknown origin, he is running a high fever. When they cannot break his fever or diminish his paralysis despite months of inpatient care, the Jinshuitan staff move Deng to Beijing's 301 Brigade Military Hospital, which was, until recently, an exclusive medical facility providing the finest clinical services in China to the nation's highest government officials (Qin 1992, 200–4).

Deng resides at the 301 Hospital for over two years, until the day in early 1971 which was described at the beginning of this chapter. On that day, Beida radicals remove him from the 301 and deposit him at the Qing He shelter. As the weather begins to warm in the late spring, one of Deng's younger sisters finds her way to the shelter. She breaks into uncontrollable fits of crying upon finding her brother in the most abject of conditions.

> Several times each day and night, the bony thin Deng Pufang would lift a rag and pull his hands down toward his mucousy corpselike legs. Pulling back the long-unwashed black blanket, he would use the rag to wipe and scrape the accumulated shit and piss from his limbs and the folds of his blanket. Then, using his hands, he would drag himself across the rank floor, and at the doorway of his room shake off the rag, flinging its contents into the icy northwest wind. Performing this demeaning ritual day after day, Deng Pufang's room and the area outside it were, only a short time after he arrived, splattered thick with excrement. (Qin 1992, 206)

After making sure he is bathed, Deng's sister gives money to the Qing He staff in the hope they will provide her brother with better care; she then leaves the shelter to return to central Beijing and sends her parents a letter in which she vaguely states that Deng is sick and in a shelter. Still unaware of their son's paralysis, Deng Xiaoping and Zhuo Lin respond by penning a letter to Mao. They state that although they are elderly and have no work, they retain the capacity to feed and shelter their son and hope he can thus be sent to them. As a consequence, in the summer of 1971 Deng Pufang is delivered from the capital to his parents' residence in exile in central China (Qin 1992, 215, 219).

Deng and Zhuo soon find a way to have their son readmitted to hospital and to change his and their family's plight. In September 1971 they hear of the failed coup d'état led by Lin Biao, Mao's heir-apparent, and of Lin's subsequent death. Deng and Zhuo draft another letter to Mao. This time they request that their son be permitted to receive medical treatment in Beijing. In response, Zhou Enlai issues a central-government document directing that Deng Pufang be returned to the 301 Hospital. And shortly thereafter Deng Xiaoping's guards place Deng Pufang and his sister Deng Rong aboard a train heading north (Qin 1992, 219).

In the aftermath of Lin Biao's failed coup, pressure grows within the party to thwart expanding hostilities from the Soviet Union and to curtail the excesses of the Cultural Revolution. The pressure leads, in part, to Nixon's 1972 Beijing visit and to the political rehabilitation *(huifu)* of many cadres who had been purged in the late 1960s. During that wave of change, Deng Xiaoping and the rest of his family are brought back to Beijing, in February 1973; later that year, Deng is reinstated as vice-premier (Qin 1992, 223).

After the Deng family's return to Beijing, Zhuo Lin immediately visits her son at the 301. There she learns that because of Jiang Qing's interference and because of the displacement of urban medical personnel to the countryside during the Cultural Revolution, doctors have been unavailable to provide her son with significant attention. Zhuo reportedly becomes furious and—mirroring her husband's attempts to establish a desired state of normalcy in Chinese political life—she takes additional steps to normalize her son's health status. Using the family's reclaimed political authority, Zhuo personally arranges for top Beijing physicians who are scattered across China to travel back to the capital and care for her son and the rest of the hospital's patients (Qin 1992, 223).

Curiously, however, the main outcome of these efforts is not curative but informational: the creation of new knowledge for Deng Pufang about rehabilitation medicine and his body. In the early 1970s Deng learns that, in the past, members of his new medical team had unsuccessfully applied to government departments for the creation of a rehabilitation medical hospital of international caliber (Wang, n.d., 4). He also learns about what is going on inside his spine. In 1974 members of his medical team operate on Deng in an attempt to learn why, during the previous six years, the extent of his paralysis has expanded from the top of his legs to his chest. Because the surgeons' findings are reported in such detail by Qin, because the findings mark a bio-epistemological amplification of Deng Pufang's body as a privileged signifier of the real, and because they express strong messages about his historically contingent sufferings and thus his claim to a special moral and national authority, they are worth reporting here:

> The shattering of the 12th thoracic and first lumbar vertebrae burst surrounding blood vessels. The released blood slowly spread up the cavity of the spinal column like a hematoma and compressed the nerves between the 12th and the sixth thoracic vertebrae. . . . Since the hematoma was not eliminated, the spinal tissue died under six years of pressure. This caused Deng Pufang's paralysis to spread from the level of his upper legs all the way up to his chest. (Qin 1992, 224)

The surgeons are surprised that the blood released into Deng Pufang's spinal cavity did not spread further, something that would probably have killed him, they say. They also are disturbed by the realization that if Deng Pufang had had access to better treatment six years earlier (and if the blood between his 12th and 6th thoracic vertebrae had been removed), his paralysis would have been far less severe (Qin 1992, 225).

PHASE FOUR: NEW SUBJECT-MAKING

In phase four Deng Pufang's journey from undeserving victim to hero (Rofel 1999a, 142) moves toward its climax. In chronicling this period, his biographers portray Deng as acquiring a new reality, new authority, and new political intentions. They do this partly by using the narrative techniques discussed above and partly by tapping more intensively into a set of categories: humanitarianism *(rendao zhuyi)*, disability *(canji)*, and biomedicine (*xiyi*, literally, "Western medicine"). These categories have increasingly been invoked throughout China in recent decades, and they have been pivotal in establishing Deng Pufang's political stature and indispensable for the formation of the China Disabled Persons' Federation.

By deploying these categories, Deng's biographers are again turning to long-established speaking-bitterness practices. Anagnost posits that by drawing so heavily on universalizing Euro-American categories—history, society, class, progress, the individual—producers of speaking bitterness during the early to mid-twentieth century helped create the existential foundation necessary both for the proliferation of nationalism and Marxism and for CCP domination (1997, 8). She contends that, by regularly invoking such universalizing categories, speaking-bitterness producers nurtured a new metaphysics and subjectivities that were vital to the communist nation-state. The metaphysics—largely that of modernist teleology—portrayed Chinese existence as lacking and backward and Western existence as worthy and developed. The oft-promoted subjectivities were generally those of exploiter/exploited (e.g., landlords/landless peasants, capitalists/proletarians); yet they also included a new modernizing elite stratum: a communist leadership whose legitimacy hung on its intent to build a modern nation and to empower the very subaltern subjects that the state's own discourse, enabled by speaking-bitterness tropes, helped instantiate (1997, 20).

If it is true that speaking bitterness facilitated the dissemination of Western-generated universalizing categories, the production of a modernist teleology, and the formation of Marxist subjectivities, and that these were important in vesting the CCP with the authority to govern the nation, it would seem that such techniques are similarly at play in the last phase of Deng's story. However, as in the first three phases, there are also differences in how speaking-bitterness techniques work to fashion Deng's elite embodiment into a discursive force. The first of these differences is that, as mentioned, rather than just promoting universal signifiers such as history, progress, and the individual, Deng's biographers have deployed the globalizing categories of humanitarianism, disability, and biomedicine in this phase. Second, instead of just working broadly to legitimize the CCP, the deployment of these new categories works to support the Deng Xiaoping political agenda and, even more specifically, to imbue Deng Pufang with a contemporary, elite, internationalist agency.

In early 1977 Deng Pufang finally leaves the hospital and moves home. This return to a situation of family normalcy is closely tied to a number of monumental "achievements," which include the arrest of the "fascist dictators" known as the Gang of Four, Deng Xiaoping's ascent to the position of China's "paramount leader," and the promulgation of his sweeping political platform of making China a more normal/modern nation by opening its doors to Western investment and science (Qin 1992, 234–37).[24]

For Deng Pufang himself, his departure from the hospital is most meaningful because it allows him to reclaim the erstwhile trappings of his patrician and, as I have emphasized, androcentric childhood. Rather than just staying at home, he feels compelled to venture out into public, to play badminton and ping-pong from his wheelchair, to tinker with advanced telecommunication equipment at a television station near the Deng house, and to make chauffeur-driven visits to old chums around Beijing. As he tries to regain some of what he once had, he begins to identify himself not just as a member of an elite but also as a member of, and possible advocate for, a different group of people. After he moves home, he continues to interact with acquaintances from Qing He and the 301. These include mostly men of a similar age who, like him, struggle with problems of immobility. Their social backgrounds vary widely, from uneducated polio survivors to injured soldiers of high Communist Party pedigree. Deng's connection with and sense of nascent responsibly for this cross-section of Chinese men is strongly foregrounded in a statement he makes on his first return visit to Qing He in early 1977. In what comes across as part remembrance, part promise, Deng Pufang reportedly tells his Qing He friends: "I will never forget all of us disability brothers [canji gemer]" (Qin 1992, 231).

During the ensuing four years, this vaguely worded statement crystallizes, becoming a conviction for Deng Pufang. By the early 1980s Deng has decided to act programmatically on behalf of his "disability brothers" and others. Once again, the interaction of bodily trauma, China's quickly changing political landscape, and known social actors is of overriding importance in Deng Pufang's transformation. One morning in 1979, as Deng Pufang rises from bed, a family attendant notices a large protrusion on his back. Doctors at the 301 discover that a thoracic vertebra, made fragile years earlier, has sustained new damage and that bone fragments are moving around freely in Deng's spinal column. The doctors immediately readmit Deng and restrict his movement. Their greatest fear is that the fragments might cause a major blood vessel to rupture, which could kill him. That fear is compounded by the fact that orthopedic specialists are at a loss over how to resolve the crisis (Qin 1992, 238).

According to Ruan, the way the crisis is resolved relates directly to the very policies Deng Xiaoping is then implementing to transform the national polity. With Deng's promotion of national development through the integration of Western scientific techniques, groups of North American scientists begin to visit China in the late 1970s. One of the first groups is a team of elite U.S. physicians. Shortly after this group arrives in Beijing in the spring of 1980, doctors at the 301 approach one of its members—Dean MacEwen, a former president of the American Orthopedic Association— and ask him his views about a case. MacEwen studies the case file and tells the 301 staff that their Soviet-trained doctors have made errors in treating the patient and that the only way he can survive is through a set of complex procedures requiring surgical equipment then available in only a few Western medical centers. At this point, the 301 staff discloses the identity of the patient and asks MacEwen to see whether he can surreptitiously find a hospital in North America that would be willing to provide care for Deng Pufang (Ruan 1992, 4).

On his return to the United States, MacEwen contacts a long-time ortho-pedic colleague, Gordon Armstrong, of Ottawa Civic Hospital, and asks if, "in the spirit of humanitarianism," special accommodations can be arranged.[25] Armstrong, whose parents were missionaries in pre-Communist China, offers to operate on Deng free of charge and to convince his hospi-tal to cover all inpatient costs. And so, at the end of September 1980, Deng Pufang flies to Ottawa with a nurse, a personal physician, and a translator. Nine days later, the surgeries begin (Ruan 1992, 4).

Although they describe many of these procedures, Deng Pufang's biog-raphers seem to place far greater importance on another aspect of his time in Ottawa: the decisions he makes during his postoperative period. Armstrong's plan is for Deng to spend nearly a year in Ottawa recuperating and undergoing physical therapy at the Civic Hospital. But Deng demurs. The calculus behind his resistance is heard in his own retrospective account, in both *The Deng Pufang Road* and in a widely circulated pamphlet published by a Federation agency. In the pamphlet, Deng Pufang states, "When think-ing of the thousands upon thousands of disabled people in my country who were desperately crying for appropriate rehabilitation services, I decided to go back home immediately to help establish our own rehabilitation centers" (Wang, n.d., 4). So, shortly after his surgeries, Deng has himself moved from the hospital to the closest outpost of the PRC, its Ottawa embassy. Like Armstrong, Canada's prime minister visits the embassy and presses Deng Pufang to return to the Civic Hospital to undergo the year's worth of ther-apy. But Deng will not be deterred:

> Being a Chinese person, [Pufang] placed his motherland and its people first and foremost in his heart and as a disabled person, he placed all . . . who are disabled . . . before all else. . . . Deng Pufang could not avoid inheriting this burden; he could not avoid inheriting the hardships of his motherland, of his Chinese compatriots, and of his fellow Chinese disabled people. (Qin 1992, 244)

In February 1981, five months after leaving Beijing, Deng flies back home, prone and wrapped in a suit of plastic. He is happy and excited, Qin tells us. For, even though his health is far from certain, he is secure in his intent to become an agent for a new form of government-sponsored, science-based intervention for disabled people in China. He is "eager to introduce to China the spirit of modern global humanitarianism: the concepts of rehabilitation medicine, and the systematic science of rehabilitation technology" (Qin 1992, 244).

PUBLIC SECRETS

More than two decades have now passed since Deng Pufang's trip to Ottawa. According to Gordon Armstrong, whom I interviewed in October 1996, the Deng family, for specific reasons, demanded that the trip be kept secret. Because in the early 1980s Deng Xiaoping's position atop the party-state was still not completely secure, the Dengs feared the political fallout that would ensue if China's citizenry learned via an indiscrete international press that the family had leveraged its position so as to provide Deng Pufang special medical care in North America. Yet, why, then, over the last ten years, when I have spoken to people inside and outside of China about the Disabled Persons' Federation, have they so often provided me detailed information about Deng Pufang's body, his personal experiences with paralysis, and his time in Canada. For instance, quite regularly people have communicated details to me like the following:

· I once read an article that said Deng Pufang's Canadian doctors had to place a lot of steel in his torso to support his spine. So, now he can't get by a metal detector without alarms ringing.
· Oh, I know a great deal about Deng Pufang. I read somewhere that he can only sweat on half his body.
· I learned in a newspaper that, since his crippling, Pufang's hearing isn't very good in one ear.

Recently, while dining with my family in a restaurant near our home, another such anecdote was conveyed to me by a waiter who had immigrated to California three years earlier from his native Beijing. When I mentioned to him I was working on a book having to do with Deng Pufang, the waiter regaled me with information about the efforts Zhuo Lin had made during the early 1970s to arrange for Shanghai doctors to treat her son. He also talked to me about Deng's trip to Canada and his "years of suffering" (*duonian de xingku*).

That so many people inside and outside of China know something about Deng Pufang's life and bodily travails, and that they view the two as being pivotal for the development of the China Disabled Persons' Federation, is not coincidental. As senior Federation staff explained to me, when they were initially engaged in the realpolitik of creating for themselves and the disabled a new bureaucracy from within the party-state, they had quite deliberately disseminated the heroic account of Deng Pufang's painful journey into disablement. To enable specific activities—for example, the leveraging of Pufang's filial prerogatives as the male scion of Deng Xiaoping, soliciting large sums of state and foreign resources, and overseeing the Federation's expansion—the Federation leadership had carefully deployed a melodramatic tale about Deng Pufang.

Initially, they had circulated aspects of this tale, which I have come to call a biomythography of statesmanship, quite discretely, only communicating it to CCP power brokers and other potential Federation benefactors. But in the late 1980s their discretion gave way to an approach that was far more forthright and publicly oriented: Pufang's confidants and beneficiaries arranged for his biomythography to be disseminated widely by way of China's electronic media and through the publication of texts such as *The Deng Pufang Road*. A main reason for this change, my closest acquaintances within the Federation's upper echelons have said, was the need to improve Deng's and the Federation's stature in the wake of the 1989 political upheavals. In the spring of 1989 many of China's pro-democracy demonstrators had criticized both Deng Pufang and the Federation for their involvement in the corrupt Kanghua Corporation (see Chapter 3). The criticism not only tarnished Deng Pufang's public image, it also undermined the Federation's expansionary agenda for a time.[26]

What lasting insights might the Deng Pufang story provide to scholars who are interested in studying the intersection of subjectification, suffering, and biomedical formation? For anyone interested in political economy, the history of science, cultural studies of the body, or medical anthropology, it might seem straightforward that government officials would use the suffering of a political luminary to help them build a powerful institution. Still, we must ask how does this actually occur? What processes allow it to happen?

In the case of the China Disabled Persons' Federation, as I have shown, Pufang and his biographers deployed a number of speaking-bitterness elements in order to create for Pufang's bodiliness what Anagnost calls a "politics of presence." Aided by the speaking-bitterness techniques, Pufang and his biographers convey a tale that positions Pufang's bodiliness as a morally, historically, and nationally imbued force for an emergent institution of healthcare provision, social assistance, and governance.

Yet, in addition to demonstrating how embodiment can be made meaningful in such a way that it serves biobureaucratic formation, there is something more the Deng Pufang story can teach us. This point is highlighted by the life, not of Deng, but of Qin Yan, his most well-known biographer.

In early 1995, three years after the publication of *The Deng Pufang Road* and shortly after Qin's husband had successfully spring-boarded from a high Federation post to become the party secretary for an important city in China's interior, I had the opportunity to talk with her briefly in Beijing about the factors that had influenced her book. Qin summed up her reasons for writing the biography as follows:

> My motives were quite personal. Because I attended the same elementary school as Pufang, because I had to live through Cultural Revolution chaos, and because my husband and I have struggled to deal with our own child's disability, we've come to feel very passionate about Pufang's disability work. . . . Moreover, when we realized how the demonstrators' attacks [in 1989] had injured Pufang's integrity and, therefore, the Federation's chances for significant growth, a number of us close Pufang friends felt it our responsibility, our duty, to chronicle his troubled life. And it was plain to us that we had a very good story, one that would sway many people. . . . We knew we had all the right pieces, everything necessary to make Pufang our nation's most famous and respected disabled person.

Qin's comments are certainly intriguing for their candor in acknowledging the narrative components ("all the right pieces") that were used to depict Deng Pufang as "China's most famous and respected disabled person" and to make his corporeal presence particularly meaningful and thereby potent. But there are other comments that I found equally intriguing and instructive for the study of subjectification: Qin portrays her decision to write about Deng as personal and moral; she couches her explanation in terms of the painful events of her own life; and she frames these events by tapping into some of the same narrative components I have analyzed above. Just as she employed telescoping vision, body-in-pain tropes, and universalistic categories such as history, nation, and disability to tell the Deng Pufang story, she also draws upon these very components to situate her writing of *The Deng Pufang Road* within a personal and moral narrative. This narrative, particularly as it pertains to her raising of a "disabled child," is not something she has avoided airing in public. On the contrary, she has broadcast it extensively through the semi-autobiographical film *Mama* (Qin 1990), for which she wrote the script and in which she played the leading role of a mother struggling with a thirteen-year-old "mentally disabled" *(zhili canji)* son. Like *The Deng Pufang Road,* the film draws heavily on speaking-bitterness techniques.

The degree to which someone like Qin has gone out of her way over the last decade to presence both Deng Pufang's and her own life, the degree to which she has used speaking-bitterness techniques to do so, and the degree to which she has been politically positioned to disseminate these narratives, sheds light on an important issue that Foucault and subsequent scholars of subjectification have rarely, if ever, explored. When studying elite self-development and how such development can work as a potent personification of governmental agency, one needs, no doubt, to be attentive to discourse production. But one should also attempt to go further and study how such discourse production is intersubjectively incited by many people's most intimate engagements with symbolism, power, and, indeed, pathos. Widely circulated biographical accounts of patricians who spawn new biobureaucracies are always more than the products and extensions of symbolism. Such accounts are not only about historically situated persons who may have lives significantly marked by unexpected affliction. They are also always generated by other historically situated persons—friends, publicists, professional biographers. And the self-development of these latter persons may be informed by fusions of discourse and intimate bodily experiences that, in fact, parallel the same types of experiences that inform the accounts they generate.

Chapter 2

Why Ma Zhun Doesn't Count

As Ma Zhun pushed open the doors that chilly morning, and shuffled her way into Beijing's Xuan Wu district's Federation office, her goal was simple: to get a disabled person's ID card so she could keep her job. Ma Zhun made this very clear, first in a gentle conversational tone and finally in a loud declaration. Like many people I observed during the spring of 1995 while I was conducting research at the Xuan Wu office, Ma Zhun had been sent to the Federation by her employer. The state-owned enterprise for which she worked, a small money-losing engine factory, told Ma Zhun that her only chance of keeping her job, of not being laid off like the other 35 percent of the factory's employees, was if she could get a disability ID. That spring, the Beijing government had sent out directives instructing all work units in the capital to document that at least 1.7 percent of their full-time staff were officially recognized disabled persons (*canji ren*); if not, the factories would face stiff fines. So, like many others in the capital city at that time, Ma Zhun's bosses informed her that she either needed to get a disability ID or they would dismiss her and hire someone who had one.

The same message was delivered to Wang Zhun, who I had observed the previous afternoon stopping by the Xuan Wu Federation office. Wang showed up around 5 P.M., just as two of the office's five staff were packing up to head home. Wang gestured to Cadre Chen, one of the staff members, and then placed on Chen's desk a group of papers, which included a medical report from a nearby hospital and a set of wallet-sized photos. Cadre Chen looked over everything, asked Wang a few questions about his background, had Wang give a fingerprint on a form, and then instructed him to come back two days later to pick up his ID.

Ma Zhun's visit to the Xuan Wu office went far less smoothly. Over a thirty-minute period she struggled in vain to convince Cadre Chen that she was entitled to receive an ID. Ma stated over and over that, in an industrial accident a decade earlier she had lost the toes on her right foot, and that, thereafter, she had had difficulty walking. On the second telling of the story, Ma unlaced her shoe and showed Cadre Chen her foot, as well as the wooden block she kept in the front of her shoe to help her walk. But Cadre Chen was unmoved. Holding a Federation manual in hand, he told Ma over and over again that whether or not she could walk easily did not matter. If she was only missing toes on one foot, she did not meet the state's standards for *canji* and so she could not have an ID. Just before she left the office, Ma made this terse statement:

> Where did your *canji* standard come from? It doesn't make any sense. If that damn industrial machine that fell on my toes ten years ago had cut off more of my foot and I had trouble walking, just as I do now, I'd be able to get an ID. But because my foot isn't mangled more, I have to lose my job. That's stupid. If someone can barely walk, why doesn't that count as *canji*?

In this chapter, I will explore the questions posed by Ma Zhun. I do so to understand the processes that produced the disability criteria that I observed Ma struggling with. I also do so because her questions direct us to examine how the early development of the China Disabled Person's Federation involved the formulation of a set of truth claims about what comprises *canji* as a distinct sphere of alterity and about what constitutes China as a distinct national locality.

If a key way people come to distinguish and imagine their "locality" is through a shared understanding of who belongs and who is desirable, so, too, it is through overlapping notions of who is different and who is subject to Othering (Anderson 1991; Douglas 1966; Stoler 1991). And for those people who occupy what they view as a common locality, there are always numerous alterities that they recognize, and there is never complete unanimity on what constitutes any single sphere of otherness. Many perspectives exist for each. Moreover, since there is so much at stake for people when it comes to definitions of alterity—for example, potential assistance and empathy, but also possible stigmatization, economic ruin, and exclusion—the degree to which persons and relevant institutions vest any perspective with interpretive authority is always intensely political.

By what means do definitional perspectives or truth claims about otherness arise? How are such truth claims reaffirmed, reconfigured, or eclipsed over time? And at one juncture or another, how does a truth claim about otherness come to possess particularly significant interpretive authority for a nation-state? In order to plumb these depths vis-à-vis *canji* and modern China, there is one set of practices that demand special attention, practices that many readers might assume to be at great remove from anthropological inquiry. That set of practices is statistics.

As uncommon an anthropological topic as it might seem, statistics merits careful attention for several reasons.[1] The most important reason has to do with the criteria that Ma Zhun confronted in the spring of 1995, which Cadre Chen invoked to preclude Ma from receiving a disability ID. Those criteria are the direct product of statistical action. They were created in the mid-1980s for a large-scale statistical investigation. Entitled The China 1987 National Sample Survey of Disabled Persons *(zhongguo yijiubaqinian quanguo canjiren qiuyang diaocha)*, the study coordinated the work of thousands of data collectors and surveyed over a million and a half people. By the time it was conducted, after several years of preparation, the 1987 Survey had developed into a decidedly biostatistical study, one informed by several internationally anointed "health sciences" standards for distinguishing degrees of normalcy and pathology.

Examining statistical action is likewise compelling because it allows us to offer valuable commentary on the relationship between sociopolitics, embodiment, and enumeration. One aspect of embodiment—objectification—has been long associated with statistical enumeration. But what of other spheres of embodiment? How have they contributed to statistical inquiry? As detailed in the pages of this chapter, the statisticians who oversaw the quantification of *canji* in the 1980s were frequently preoccupied with and motivated by their own subject-making. Indeed, while the statisticians were seemingly involved in quite impersonal acts of codifying and enumerating alterity, they were also working out their own political status and identity *through* these acts. Thus, by examining *canji* quantification, this chapter offers a different reading of enumeration. It shows that, in the case of *canji*'s quantification, not only has objectification been important but so, too, a far more robust set of processes associated with the sociopolitics of embodiment (cf. Stigler 1999; Terry and Urla 1995).

Another reason to discuss *canji* quantification has to do with the historical depth this medium affords. The enumeration of *canji* and allied categories is not a twentieth-century phenomenon. For some six hundred years, *canji* and its linguistic cognates have been subjected to large-scale quantification across wide swaths of what is today referred to as the People's Republic of China. Why has *canji* been enumerated for so many centuries? Why have statistics been used to apprehend, define, and count otherness under the rubric of *canji* and its allied terms?

State formation, it would seem, has been a persistent force. Since the early Ming dynasty (1368–1644), *canji* and its cognates have been repeatedly quantified *for* the state and *by* the state. Whether in late-imperial times or more recently during different moments of the twentieth century, *canji* has been placed under a statistical lens by those aiming to build a stronger centralized government. This lens has not remained the same, though. For most of this six-hundred-year history, enumerators have been relatively vague about what they have meant by *canji*. But starting in the early 1900s, they began to define *canji* more carefully, by harnessing a variety of bio-medically informed perspectives. Thus, by examining these shifts in statistical production we are able to gather insight, however partial, on not just state involvement with the category of *canji* over time, but also on how state-making has contributed to the medicalization of *canji*.

To understand such a genealogy, to make sense of the lengthy and shifting interaction between state-building and *canji* quantification, I have found it helpful to tap the writings of Ian Hacking. In several essays and a full-length monograph (1990), Hacking provides a history of the expansion in Europe of a "fetishism for numbers" (1981, 24). He focuses on a period, the early 1800s, that was a time of tremendous development for what we have come to understand as the nation-state, as well as a time of great sociopolitical enthusiasm for the statistical objectification of humanity, particularly statistical efforts to differentiate and count ever more detailed forms of bodily "deviance."

As Hacking documents, these two trends were deeply related and they significantly contributed to the unfolding of biopower across Europe. Statistical inquiry into deviance supported the development of the nation-state; the nation-state promoted such statistical actions; and each promoted ever more specific and ever more biologically driven discourses about what constitutes a healthy, well-disciplined, and normal individual and populace. Statistical study allowed nation-states (and their colonial territories) to be understood as being populations and sub-populations residing within geographic boundaries, as being spatially fixed biological aggregates comprised of distinct numbers of individuals who were more or less normal.[2]

But, in addition to such synergy, Hacking emphasizes that the confluence of statistics, the nation-state, and biopolitics was very much an issue of basic pragmatics. In the Europe of the early 1800s statistics was a tool that allowed government employees to expand their moral and material authority over the citizenry. The quantification of deviance was "an overt political response" of state employees to quell popular discontent with government and to justify state expansion (1982, 281). State officials in Europe promoted the numeric inquiry of bodily deviance because such inquiry could help substantiate that the state was needed to perform important palliative and curative functions, that the state must be expanded so that those functions could be carried out more effectively, and that state authority was unquestionably legitimate.

In this chapter's discussion of three eras of *canji* enumeration, I develop an argument vis-à-vis Hacking's ideas. Hacking's historical accounts no doubt deepen our understanding of how the numeric objectification of otherness, particularly epidemiology, can relate to biopolitics. His accounts also situate an analysis of biopower very much within the workings of the state, something, again, that Foucault was usually hesitant to do. But, I would suggest, when examining the enumeration of alterity, one must push further, specifi-cially into the micro-workings of the state vis-à-vis embodiment. In addition to examining how the grab for greater state authority can promote objectifica-tion and a statistical rendering of bodiliness, one must be attentive to another specific set of phenomena, about which Hacking makes little mention. One must also consider the subject-making of government statisticians.[3]

As I will show, what has often fueled the quantification of *canji* in China, including its biomedical enumeration, has been government agents' own identity work. Complicit with the statecraft of concretizing disability as a dis-tinct object of intervention (one that may act as bulwark against dissent and as a lever for government expansion), what has influenced statistical inquire of *canji* and allied terms, particularly during the twentieth century, has been how state officials themselves have been "incited to subjectivity." Just as important, if not more so, than expansionary impulses of the state in the story of *canji*'s long statistical apprehension has been how government agents have negotiated their own elite and embodied subject positions.

By developing this argument through an exploration of *canji*'s statistical genealogy, I hope to answer more fully Ma Zhun's questions. I also have two additional aims. And, given that this chapter is about statistics, allow me to enumerate them. First, I hope to promote a greater dialogue between, on the one hand, disability scholars, many of whom till now have overlooked the role of quantification in sociopolitical formation (cf. Davis 1995), and that small group of anthropologists, on the other hand, who have largely ignored disability but who in recent years have been exploring the linkages between statistics and the transnational forces of state formation (Anderson 1991; Appadurai 1996; Gupta 2001; Horn 1994). Second, I hope to help fill a lacuna in China Studies. A number of observers have noted that in the PRC, as in possibly all cultural contexts, statistics represent as much the product of rigorous inquiry as they do political exigencies (AFP 1998; Huang 1996; Merli 1998; Tien 1991). Likewise, several anthropologists have shown that the PRC's party-state has used enumeration to concretize new social cate-gories and policies, such as those pertaining to China's national minorities (Gladney 1991; Greenhalgh 2001b; Schein 2000). Yet, until now, little inquiry has occurred in the PRC that focuses on the relationship between sta-tistics and the subject-making of statisticians (cf. Lee 1998).

TERMS OF ENGAGEMENT

Before considering the genealogy of *canji*, statistical or otherwise, there are two additional Chinese terms that need to be foregrounded. These are *can-fei* and *feiji*. Like *canji*, these terms date back to Chinese antiquity. *Canji*—a word which many Chinese today often mistakenly believe was a creation of the Disabled Persons' Federation—is used in documents dating from as early as the Tang dynasty (618–906 A.D.). *Feiji* appears in the *Li Ji* (Book of Rites), a text assembled during the Han dynasty (202 B.C.–220 A.D.). *Canfei* is used in documents dating as far back as the Wei (220–265 A.D.).

Mathews Chinese-English Dictionary (1931) states that the English-language equivalents for *canji* and *canfei* are the words "maimed," "crippled," or "deformed." The *Large Chinese Dictionary* (Luo 1989) offers a similar definition but adds that *canji* may also denote "an ailment or disease." For *feiji*, these dictionaries offer definitions ranging from "useless" to "diseased" to "maimed." And the lexicons define the ideograms that make up the three couplets *canji, canfei, and feiji* in this way:

- *can*: a verb, meaning to injure, to spoil, to destroy, to oppress; a noun, denoting remnant or residue.
- *fei*: a verb, meaning to do away with, to abrogate, to waste, to destroy; an adjective denoting useless, wasted, or abandoned.
- *ji*: a noun, meaning sickness, disease, or pain.

There is much to explore in these definitions. But given that my interests here lie in examining the sociopolitical formation of these terms, at this moment I will restrict my comments to just two. First, according to twentieth-century lexicons, the term *canji* and its cognates tend to revolve around that which is most visible, around the most perceivable or objectifiable of differences, around the sort of things that the American sociologist Irving Goffman called "abominations of the body" (1963, 4). Second, as their sub-ideograms convey, *canji, canfei,* and *feiji* carry strong and very negative moral meanings.

That such an emphasis has been placed on visible difference and moral negativity can no doubt be linked to the emphasis that China's classical canon gives to the preservation of the human form. Possibly the most oft-invoked example, in this regard, one which has served as a moral axiom for centuries, is found in the *Book of Filial Piety*. There, Confucius is described as teaching that all children have the filial duty to preserve the body given them by their ancestors and to not allow even their hair or skin to be injured (see Hansson 1988, 20).[4]

But rather than utilizing a simplistic vision of "Chinese tradition" or "Chinese culture," as equivalent to statements attributed to a famous sage, I prefer to examine how *canji* and its cognate terms have been framed, reframed, and made known over time. For that, I now turn to three enumerative epochs. These are the Late Imperial period, the Sino-Japanese War of the mid-twentieth century, and the decade of the 1980s. These periods, it needs to be noted, do not each receive the same degree of attention below. Because of the limited space afforded in a book chapter and because my primary interest is to respond to Ma Zhun's questions, showing how they help to illuminate important points about the Federation's formation, the most recent of these periods receives more coverage.

EARLIER ERAS OF ENUMERATION

In the Late Imperial period, the enumeration of *canji* developed as an outgrowth of a broad-based census system. This census system was called the Yellow Books (Huang Ce).[5] As Ho (1959) has explained, the Yellow Books were very much about state-building. They were produced in large part to allow dynastic regimes to calculate how much wealth each of their administrative localities regularly had to proffer in military conscripts, taxes, and service on public works projects (also see Chen 1946, 1). Unlike most contemporary censuses, though, the Yellow Books were quite parsimonious in who they counted. The Yellow Books mainly counted men, who were usually recorded under the heading of *ding*. To be male, however, did not necessarily mean that one's local enumerator would consider you a *ding*. In 1391 imperial notice was given to local magistrates that, thereafter, the Yellow Books must differentiate the *canji* from *ding* (Zhao, n.d., 4.2a–4.2b).[6] Thereafter, *canji* were to be counted under the heading *jiling* (i.e., "odd lot, fractional, or refuse").[7]

It is unclear to what degree the 1391 edict was promulgated or subsequently followed for the purpose of social assistance. Unmarked by the *ding* label, a man and his family presumably could be released from service to the polity (Ho 1959, 26). What seems clear, however, is that the edict was both a move of marginalization and part of a broader structuring of male authority and identity-making already well under way by 1391. The best way of appreciating this is to look at what, for much of China's long imperial period, was probably the most important conveyance for male social mobility—the government's civil service exam—the rigorous state screening system used to confer scholar-official status (Skinner 1976, 336–43).

Gender was a basic factor in who could sit for such exams at the end of the fourteenth century. Only men were eligible. But, then again, not all men. Some years earlier, during the Yuan dynasty (1271–1368), the imperial government had barred two groups of people from participating in the civil service exams.[8] One of the barred groups was the *feiji*. The second was a group known as the "mean people" (*jianmin*), a highly stigmatized class of people that had long been treated by the imperial regime as quasi-criminals and a source of social pollution (Hansson 1988, 19–20).[9] Benjamin Elman suggests that, whatever its catalyst, the 1391 edict was probably often used to enforce the earlier, Yuan dynasty fiat. The requirement that the Yellow

Books designate people as *canji* likely worked as a gatekeeping mechanism, allowing local magistrates to block those who were enumerated as *canji* from taking the civil service exam.[10]

Nowadays, thanks in part to colonial, postcolonial, and feminist scholarship, it is well recognized that acts of othering and exclusion are frequently linked to a striving by dominant social segments to distinguish their own identity, social status, and subject position. This insight seems apt when we consider dynastic China's statistical fascination with *canji*. More to the point, it allows us to highlight certain aspects of state-building, hitherto overlooked by scholars, at play in the production of the Yellow Books. Inasmuch as the Yellow Books bolstered the state by enabling resource appropriation, one may also see that such quantification served to define and elevate the state by demarcating the parameters of elite masculinity. By separately tracking the *canji/feiji* through the Yellow Books, and by excluding them from sitting for the civil service exams, male scholar-officials were as involved in defining their own identity as they were in defining an anomalous "Other." By positioning the *canji/feiji* as constituting a different realm of existence, male government officeholders cast the *canji/feiji* as a distinct yet separate part of a larger delegitimized and polluting range of humanity that also included the "mean people" and women (Ahern 1975). What is more, the government officeholders were arrogating not only the authority to define who they were themselves, and who they were not, but more importantly, they were deciding who could succeed them, and who could not.

Firsthand accounts of this self-making surface in such Late Imperial chronicles of the civil service exams as the *Qin Ding Ke Chang Tiao Li* (Li Bu [1887] 1989). Written by male scholar-officials, one frequently sees in these chronicles laments about how, despite the moratorium begun during the Yuan period, the *canji/canfei/feiji* were sometimes making it through and taking the exam, thereby besmirching the integrity of all justly accredited scholar-officials.

Equally important for our broader discussion, these same laments shed light on what government officials in the Late Imperial period may have meant by the term *canji*. By reading the laments carefully, one comes to understand that definitions attributed to *canji* by scholar-officials were relatively inchoate. One also comes to understand that these diverged significantly from the far more rigid institutional definitions generated in the late twentieth century, as promulgated in the World Health Organization's ICIDH and ICF. In those modern documents, the definitions of "disability" rest on the biological bedrock of impairment and they are understood to be the outgrowths of fundamental biological differences or breakdowns (WHO 1980, 2001b).

The Late Imperial laments suggest that *canji* (like *canfei* and *feiji*) was as often understood to denote an experience (e.g., a fall, injury, or illness that caused an absence or loss of ability) as it was understood to denote bodily difference or breakdown (e.g., a damaged eye or a missing finger), and that there was no epistemological priority given to one definition over another. Moreover, the administrators' laments are less concerned with chronicity than are more recent government disability criteria, such as those established by the Chinese state in the late 1980s. Unlike those criteria, which treat disabilities as largely permanent facts, the Late Imperial perspective seems to be far more open. In their laments, Late Imperial chroniclers describe people as having such potentially permanent problems as "nearsightedness" *(jin jian yan)* (Li Bu [1987] 1989, 2:659–60) or "crippling that makes it difficult to walk" *(can fei bu lu shen jian)* (2:663), but they also speak of such seemingly transitory conditions as "a painful hand" *(shou ji)* (2:664), "an injury caused by a fall" *(die shang)* (1:225), and "illness" *(bing)* (1:226).

When did this Late Imperial governmental vision of *canji* begin to be transformed by biomedical perspectives and become a topic of epidemiological inquiry? No doubt, a key transformation began, however incrementally, during the late nineteenth century with the introduction into China of biological discourses (e.g., biomedicine, biology, botany, public health, evolution), which was made possible after the Opium Wars (1839–42) by the ebb and flow of waves of European, American, and Japanese colonists. Large-scale epidemiological scrutiny did not start immediately after the Opium Wars, however. It would be several decades before epidemiology found its footing in China and possibly even longer before disability came under scrutiny.

An important milestone was the 1942 Census of the Kunming Lake Region. While certainly not the first enumerative exercise ever conducted in China to draw upon biomedical principles, the Kunming Lake Region study is notable for its handling of *canji/canfei/feiji*. Biomedical practitioners were employed to count and describe more than 600,000 residents in the vicinity of China's southwest city of Kunming, and they were required to catalogue each person in terms of several variables, including *canfei*.[11]

In large part, the census of the Kunming Lake Region was inspired by an emergent movement based on concepts and terms that were relatively novel to inhabitants of Kunming. The movement aimed to foster a new kind of political entity throughout China's former dynastic territories: a nation-state, headed by a centralized government apparatus and aimed at modernizing society based on international norms of development. The Kunming study was also heavily driven by a set of subtle processes that, as several China scholars have previously shown, were pivotal for the Chinese project of nation-state making during the first half of the twentieth century. It was fueled by the identity-making of a newly imagined Chinese citizenry and a newly forming post-imperial intelligentsia (Bergère and Lloyd 1998; Chang 1987; Saari 1990; Weston 2004; Yeh 1990).

The Kunming Lake census was organized and directed by a well-known figure from this new intelligentsia, Chen Da, one of China's first self-described social scientists. According to biographical accounts, Chen Da was an extraordinarily cosmopolitan figure for his day (Yuan and Quan 1981). As a young man, he had been trained in English-language schools in China. Until his mid-forties he was avidly involved in athletics, a set of bodily practices common in Euro-American education then but wholly incommensurate with the sedentary habitus carefully cultivated by China's earlier generations of scholar-officials (Brownell 1995; Yuan and Quan 1981). After completing his M.A. and Ph.D. at Columbia University of New York, with a grant from the Boxer Rebellion Indemnity Funds, Chen worked for a short time at the U.S. Bureau of Labor Statistics (Yuan and Quan 1981, 60; Chen 1946, viii). On his return to China, he became professor of sociology at Tsinghua University and director of the university's Institute of Census Research, and he subsequently went on to become a member of the International Statistical Association and vice-president of the International Population Association.[12]

Despite this pedigree, we would be mistaken to depict Chen's life as involving either an outright embrace of an a priori West or a complete rejection of an equally imagined China. Rather, his cosmopolitanism was to a large degree animated by the mission of building a new China, using what he understood to be the tools of modernist internationalism. As was the case with Sun Yatsen, Liang Qiqiao, Lu Xun, and Fei Xiaotong (as well as many lesser-known intellectuals, including Tao Menghe, Sun Benwen, Pan Guangdan, Wu Jingzao, Wu Zelin, Lei Jieqiong, Chen Xujin, Li Jinghan, and Li Jianhua), Chen Da strongly structured his life in terms of broad modernist standards, which he saw as common to the West but not exclusive to it. And, like these scholars, Chen also fiercely identified himself as being Chinese and as a champion of a strong Chinese nation-state. He was part of a coterie of new intellectuals fixated on harnessing modernism's most heralded techniques—most notably, "science"—for political-economic ascendance, in order to throw out the imperialists and create China as a sovereign national entity.

In their embrace of science these early-twentieth-century scholars reframed the Chinese polity in terms of a national organic. Steeped in the social evolutionary rhetoric that undergirded nationalist and modernist discourses worldwide during the period, this emerging intellectual elite sought out scientific education at home and abroad (and especially in the medical and social sciences) for the purpose of "healing China," "saving from decay" a newly conceived Chinese "race," jettisoning the humiliating "sick man of Asia" label, and building the Chinese polity into a healthy body politic (Dikotter 1992; Fei 1992, 5).[13]

This emergent intellectual vanguard saw statistics as an indispensable tool in its efforts. In order to create a strong and fit nation, social scientists like Chen Da argued, it was necessary first to appreciate the full spectrum of the Chinese citizenry—not just select male residents. A sizeable portion of this intellectual initiative, not surprisingly, was driven by the tenets of eugenics and its social-engineering techniques of promoting fertility among the "strong" and discouraging or prohibiting reproduction among the "weak." This propensity is evident at the end of Chen Da's survey report on the Kunming Lake census, where he included a policy paper that fervently urges government authorities to mold a stronger Chinese race and nation by systematically manipulating fertility based on *canfei* status (Chen 1946). Unlike the United States in the early twentieth century, or Germany during World War II, this type of policy report in China never precipitated eugenic intervention. Largely because of the escalation of the Sino-Japanese War, such eugenics initiatives thankfully found no sound administrative foundation upon which to grow into actual practice in pre-Mao China (Dikotter 1992, 185).

For our discussion here, however, what is most important about a statistical exercise like the Kunming Lake census has more to do with how the census contributed to and reveals the social processes that were acting upon the categories of *canji/canfei/feiji*. First, the census illustrates that well before Ma Zhun hobbled into a Federation office in 1995 to request a disability ID, modernist processes were biologizing *canji/canfei/feiji* and the use of statistics was a key piece in that biologization. Second, the census shows how both the individual and the national body was becoming visible in early-twentieth-century China. Unlike the Yellow Books, the Kunming Lake census's more "scientific" orientation dictated the cataloguing of every inhabitant of the survey region—after all, each inhabitant was a member of the nascent Chinese nation—and it further dictated the differentiation of each person in terms of *canfei*.[14] Third, the census underscores Hacking's argument that modernist state-formation may be an important calculus promoting the proliferation of statistics. The Kunming study (and other statistical projects Chen Da conducted during his career) was clearly aimed at transforming Chen's research object, "Chinese society," into a powerful organic mass, guided by a strong and health-inducing state. Fourth, the Kunming Lake census also had much to do with modernist discourse concerning intellectual identity. Indeed, inasmuch as the Kunming Lake census appears to have been spurred by strategies for building a more strongly governed society, it also seems to have been fueled by the modernist desires of its creator and like-minded colleagues to have China's intelligentsia conform with and be seen as respectable members of a new international community of policymakers and social scientists.

And in this regard, it seems far from incidental that Chen Da arranged for an English-language version of his Kunming census report to be published by the University of Chicago Press, or that he included in both the English and Chinese-language versions of the report a foreword by the famed U.S. sociologist and statistician William Ogburn, extolling the Kunming study as "the beginning of modern census-taking in China" (Ogburn 1946, viii).[15]

THE MAOIST ERA IN BRIEF

The transition from the pre-Maoist to the post-Maoist era was relatively uneventful for the enumeration of *canji*. During the early Maoist years, even though Communist officials saw themselves as the vanguard of Chinese modernity and were highly driven to reframe China as a "developed" nation, they invested little energy in epidemiology, paying scant attention to *canji / canfei / feiji*. There are several explanations for this. Mao had a strong distaste for one of the earlier engines of epidemiological development in China—the optic of eugenics, which he saw as being part and parcel of "Malthusian trickery," as a bourgeois ideology designed to limit population growth in poorer countries, and as a Western tactic to keep nations like China small and weak (Tien 1973; 1991). Everyone in China with either an inclination or a professional mandate to quantify was therefore under immense pressure, after 1949, to provide nothing more than the statistical proof that Mao's call for unfettered growth was being realized. Also, when the emergent party-state did focus on bodily difference, such as in the terrain of health care, its approach often paralleled that being championed during the time by international organizations like the WHO, that is, it was one of finding, quantifying, and eradicating communicable diseases. It must also be noted that, in terms of alterity, during much of Mao's reign the CCP was often far more interested in rooting out and labeling antirevolutionary forms of deviance than any kind of bodily difference (Greenblatt 1977). Thus, until Mao's death in 1976, it was generally understood that those who were locally thought of as *canfei* (which, rather than *canji*, was the term in far greater usage at that time) were not to be medically diagnosed or healed by the state. Instead, they were to be defined in terms of socioeconomic inequity, a product of the nefariousness of the antirevolutionary element. Instead of being clinically cured, the *canfei* were to be aided either through the struggle against antirevolutionaries or through the socialist techniques of resource allocation—that is, "from each based on their ability, to each based on their need" (Huang 1989, 67–68).

Nonetheless, there were spheres in Maoist China where statistics and the categories of *canji* or *canfei* did cross paths. This probably occurred in the most systematic way in the military (cf. Skocpol 1992). In the 1930s the Red Army had begun providing benefits to injured soldiers.[16] And in 1950 the People's Liberation Army (PLA) expanded that entitlement infrastructure and created unified criteria for identifying and compensating "revolutionary *canfei* soldiers."[17] The 1950 criteria, updated in 1980, were divided into four levels *(deng)* consisting of six grades *(ji)*. While the levels were largely functional—ranked along a continuum based on the "ability to work" *(lao dong neng li)* and "ability for daily life" *(sheng hua neng li)*—they were regulated by biomedicine.[18]

Because of the highly secretive orientation of the People's Liberation Army, typical of most armies, it is hard to know how much statistical inquiry the PLA has done on *canfei* soldiers over the years (although we can certainly assume some such inquiry has occurred). Also, owing to its secrecy, it is difficult to know why the PLA came to use biomedicine to define *canfei* and how the identity-formation of military personnel may or may not have played a part in the creation of the PLA's criteria. Nonetheless, what we can say with a fair degree of certainty is that, although *canji/canfei/feiji* had come under the lens of epidemiology in the early part of the century, by the early 1980s, such objectification was relatively infrequent and it was mainly confined to a limited, notably masculinist, sphere of the country.

POST-MAO ENUMERATION: THE 1987 NATIONAL SAMPLE SURVEY

Why, then, it remains to be answered, did branches of the PRC central government mount a nationwide survey of disability in the late 1980s? And why did those branches create a biomedically informed disability criteria potentially applicable to any PRC citizen? Was not the primary engine of all this simply the needs of the nascent Federation?

In the mid-1990s, not long after I began researching the Federation's early formation, several members of the Federation's leadership talked to me about the ways in which their programmatic aims had helped prompt disability enumeration in 1980s China. They emphasized that when Deng Pufang and his staff had become involved in the business of disability assistance in the mid-1980s, when they had begun placing themselves in the role of disability advocates, they had quickly come to some realizations. One was that they needed to create a broad-scale institutional infrastructure within the party-state. Another was that, to create and adequately develop such an infrastructure, they recognized that they required specific kinds of knowledge. Most importantly, they needed to produce criteria to delineate what their target population was—that is, who China's disabled were—and they needed to produce irrefutable statistical information about that population's special conditions. With such information in hand, the Federation leadership could more easily justify to people both inside and outside of government why the People's Republic required a high-profile, national *canji*-assistance organization. Such information would allow them to demonstrate that it was reasonable and indeed beneficial for national resources to be directed to the creation of a new institution, and it would ease the way for the Federation to draw upon whatever advantages it had, including Deng Pufang's family status, to speed resource acquisition.

Thus, it would seem that Hacking's arguments—about the relationship between statistical enumeration, biopower, and the formation of bureaucracy—are quite incisive for understanding this third era of *canji* enumeration. Clearly, the push to produce statistical information about disability in 1980s China was tied to the production of state bureaucracy. The push, as Hacking would prompt us to consider, was also integrally tied to the preservation of state authority. As I explain further in subsequent chapters, since the mid-1980s government proponents of the Federation have shrewdly framed the existence of a newly enumerated disability population as not just justification for the Federation's existence but also in terms of the continuance of the Chinese Communist Party's preeminence during the first decades of the tumultuous post-Mao period. Whether in the mass media or in internal government documents, these functionaries have portrayed the state's willingness to acknowledge China's disabled—as well as the Federation's programmatic agenda to aid the disabled—as proof of the Communist leadership's ongoing moral commitment "to serve the people." And while no doubt useful for the Federation's expansionary agenda, this kind of representation has clearly been aimed at helping the CCP dissuade dissent. Most importantly, it has been designed to dampen popular disgruntlement toward the party for what many across China now see as the dark side of the post-Mao reforms, for example, escalating social stratification, the dissolution of former Maoist social guarantees, expanding waves of unemployment, rising crime levels, and surging healthcare costs.

Yet, inasmuch as Hacking's ideas help guide us, there are clearly many questions that remain unaddressed. For instance: Why did Chinese government agencies that had no prior commitment to disability advocacy become interested in enumerating China's disabled in the 1980s? Why did the nascent Federation's functionaries and other party-state officials place such a special premium on statistical knowledge about disability rather than on other kinds of knowledge? And why did these cadres come to believe that they needed to produce disability criteria that were distinctively biomedical in orientation?

When addressing these questions, we must be highly attentive to the fact that the 1987 survey was undertaken at a unique moment for the category of disability, just after the conclusion of the U.N.'s International Year of Disabled Persons in 1981 and in the midst of the U.N.'s subsequent Decade for Disabled Persons (1983–92). This was a moment when the power and authority vested in the social signifier "disability" were reaching new heights, owing not just to the U.N. campaigns but also to an intensifying fusion within Euro-America of disability-related discourse, research techniques, modes of provision, medical developments, and emergent rights movements.

We must likewise pay close attention to the fact that the survey was developed during a unique chapter in China's political history. When planning for the survey began, Mao had been dead for only a few years and the Cultural Revolution was still fresh in people's memories. In this period, many within the CCP were intensely deliberating the question of China's national identity, and specifically the question of how China and its people measured up to other nations in terms of economic and civilizational "development" (fazhan). Many worried that the "ten lost years" of Maoist radicalism had caused China to lag even farther behind other nations in the race for modernity, that the Cultural Revolution had left China shamefully "backward." It was against this backdrop that Deng Xiaoping established not only market reforms but also the Open Door policy, a primary goal of which was to strengthen China by giving its citizenry greater access to Western science, something that Chinese intellectuals since the early 1900s had viewed as the outside world's main means to modernity.

Yet to understand why and how the 1987 survey came about and how its disability criteria were created demands that we consider more than just the wider international environment of the era and the sociopolitical setting within China itself. We must also examine the ways in which the survey's designers responded to these cross-cutting sociopolitical spheres. The formulation of the 1987 survey was far from a simple case of Chinese government agencies being disciplined by either their local environment or translocal forces. The survey's development was instead very much a matter of Chinese officials struggling to negotiate multiple and frequently contradictory agendas, at once personal and public. Moreover, although in my discussions with them, survey officials have often explained that their agendas were more or less framed by "foreign" and "Chinese" imperatives, in fact, many aspects of the survey defy such simple binary distinctions, owing in large part to China's lengthy and complex historical engagement with modernism.

How then—against the backdrop of Deng Xiaoping's Open Door policy and in the midst of a U.N.-facilitated global disability-advocacy movement—did Chinese government officials come to count canji in the 1980s? One of the first ways the post-Mao regime signaled its commitment to its newly enshrined Open Door policy was by welcoming back United Nations agencies. Two decades earlier, just before the PRC had entered the Korean War, China's freshly established party-state had "suspended" ties with U.N. agencies (Hanson 1984, 81). On their return in the 1980s, U.N. representatives found that the Chinese government officers with whom they interacted were extremely eager for engagement. Specifically, the government agents wanted U.N. assistance in assessing China's socioeconomic situation. This was particularly the case for UNICEF. Joe Judd, UNICEF's representative in Beijing from 1984 to 1985, told me that Chinese government officials "seemed hungry to have us serve as their eyes, to assess where they stood internationally. Given we had just returned, it was amazing the access we were given."

Faced with such enthusiasm, a Beijing-based UNICEF representative invited the former director of UNICEF's U.S. Committee, Norman Acton, to come to China for two weeks in 1981 in order to assess China's disability infrastructure. This consultancy was the beginning of what has become a multifaceted relationship between Chinese government agencies and Rehabilitation International (R.I.), the New York City–based organization which employed Norman Acton as its Director General. R.I. is an organization which for many decades has remained at the heart of the globalization of a biomedically centered portrait of disability.[19]

While I do not attempt to review the history of R.I. here, several pieces of information are in order. Rehabilitation International has been known by different names over the years—the International Society for Crippled Children, the Council of World Organizations Interested in the Handicapped are two—that in many ways reflect the development of much disability-advocacy discourse and practice over the course of the twentieth century. R.I.'s first iteration was launched in Elyria, Ohio, at the start of the 1920s. Members of Elyria's Rotary Club established the National Society for Crippled Children soon after a train accident left a group of local children seriously injured and their families struggling to find appropriate hospital treatment for them. The society benefited from the internationalist fervor over how to respond to the legions of wounded and maimed soldiers that came home in the wake of World War I, and then again after World War II. One result was that, after World War II, Rehabilitation International (then called the Council of World Organizations Interested in the Handicapped) began a protracted lobbying effort to convince the U.N. to promote rehabilitation programs for the handicapped.[20] In the late 1970s, because of a confluence of factors—including the growing successes of transnational disease-prevention programs and the gradual globalization of Euro-American concepts of rehabilitation care and disability rights—the U.N. General Assembly bowed to pressure from Rehabilitation International and other organizations, passing a resolution to launch the 1981 International Year of Disabled Persons.

Thus, when Norman Acton visited China in March 1981, his Chinese counterparts were interacting with an organization and a man which, whether they knew it or not, had been central to international policy-making in the area of disability for over fifty years. Following his fortnight in China, Acton submitted a report in which he made several recommendations. The first recommendation was for the Chinese government to conduct a detailed "household survey" in order "to obtain more complete information about the prevalence of disability among children" (Acton 1981, 11).[21] Soon thereafter Acton's recommendation was inadvertently bolstered by the United Nations; in support of the world body's Year and Decade programs, the General Assembly passed a resolution on December 3, 1982, by which "developing countries" were encouraged to create methods of "data collection" on various disabilities, "to be used as essential tools and frames of reference for launching action programs to ameliorate the condition of disabled persons" (United Nations 1990, iii).

Not long after, China's National Statistical Bureau, in conjunction with several other government offices, carried out a survey among children ages one to fourteen, living in 137,000 households across China. Among other things, the survey found that 1.4 percent of the children were "obviously and seriously unhealthy."[22]

According to my interviews with those who oversaw the survey, they had been motivated not by the idea of building an organization like the currrent Disabled Persons' Federation. Rather, the key stimuli for the survey, they explained, were the PRC's new Open Door policy, the U.N.'s disability initiatives, and how these dovetailed with the politics of identity-creation that were then circulating through and structuring the Chinese polity. As previously mentioned, identify politics at that time were greatly informed by modernist perspectives that framed China as, at best, a "developing country," and, at worst, "backward."

In the early 1980s, with the growing strength of the Open Door policy, many high-ranking Chinese officials increasingly interacted with visiting foreign dignitaries. Prompted by the U.N.'s Year and Decade programs (and the encompassing global fervor around disability), the foreign dignitaries asked many epidemiological questions about China's disability situation. Because the Chinese government had never made disability an object of wide-ranging study, its officials had no way to answer. This caused a number of the Chinese officials to feel not just personal frustration but also a sense of national embarrassment. On more than one occasion, my informants described the situation in terms of the highly embodied idiom of "face." As one of the officials responsible for the survey of disabled children told me, "To stem this problem, to stop China from losing face, we felt our only choice was doing a big study based on the most scientific of international techniques."

Not long after the survey of children got under way, officials within China's Ministry of Civil Affairs notified UNICEF's Beijing-based officials that the Chinese government planned to do an even more ambitious study of disability. That study became known as the China 1987 National Sample Survey of Disabled Persons.

Why did officials make this decision to do a much larger survey so soon after undertaking the survey of children? As I have come to learn, it was at that juncture that Deng Pufang's unfolding interest in providing disability assistance had started to play a role in the decision making having to do with the quantification of *canji*. A second impetus for the decision to conduct a large national survey was the fact that, for many Chinese officials, the 1983 survey of children had not allowed them to "save face," but instead caused them to "lose face." This "loss of face" relates again to Norman Acton, more specifically something Acton wrote two years earlier. When the U.N. was preparing to launch its 1981 International Year of Disabled Persons campaign, it asked Acton to help draft U.N. Secretary General Kurt Waldheim's opening speech for the campaign. In his contribution to the speech, Acton inserted a statistical figure that he hoped would have a marked effect on the global development of disability. As Acton explained to me, he wrote that 10 percent of the world's population was disabled. The 10 percent figure was not altogether new; Acton and others at Rehabilitation International had been citing it for more than a decade. But, as Acton further explained, "This 10 percent figure was not a rigorously derived rate. It was something we at R.I. largely invented. Based on limited evidence, we created the figure. We wanted to have a weapon to make people respond to our issue. People don't tend to think an issue is big unless you have big numbers." One official in the U.N.'s Statistical Division, to whom Acton has also made this admission, commented to me that "Norman thought 10 percent would both stimulate disability activism around the world and give it lots of clout. . . . His 10 percent figure was prompted by nothing other than political expediency."

Because it was included in Waldheim's 1981 speech, Acton's 10 percent figure was disseminated widely thereafter.[23] And in the ensuing years, given modernism's fetish for numbers and the fact that Acton's statistic carried the U.N.'s imprimatur, the 10 percent figure took on tremendous normative authority.[24] The 10 percent figure, together with the survey of children, strongly influenced many Beijing officials, as is evidenced by my conversations with New York–based U.N. staffers. As one of these staffers explained to me:

> The 1983 survey of children made many [Chinese officials] terribly embarrassed and frustrated, so much so they tried to hide their results from us. The U.N. and Rehabilitation International hoopla had sent the message to the Chinese that their 1983 result would be around 10 percent. And they didn't get 10 percent. They didn't get anywhere near to 10 percent. They got 1.4 percent.

In light of such embarrassment, it is not surprising, then, that the Ministry of Civil Affairs asked the State Council to approve and finance a far more ambitious national sample survey, or that the Council quickly agreed.

PREPARING AND LAUNCHING THE SURVEY

With approval granted, the new survey's leadership group had a "tough job ahead," as its director obliquely quipped in an April 1985 *China Daily* news item (Chen 1985). Not only did it have to organize and conduct a survey large enough and complex enough to satisfy what it and its potential critics understood as international norms of scientific validity, but it also had to guarantee a final prevalence rate that would offer China the maximum benefit. And, according to a number of people involved in the survey, conflicting pressures made it very difficult to discern what final figure would be best for the nation.

On the one hand, the 10 percent rhetoric created pressure for a certain kind of number. If the survey's rate did not fall at or above 10 percent, some within China and in international circles might view the leadership group (and by extension the CCP and China) as unequipped to handle basic scientific methodologies and thus as backward and incompetent. On the other hand, there were powerful forces within China militating against a 10 percent or higher figure. For example, some government agencies that the leadership group consulted thought a figure of 10 percent or higher might be damaging to the CCP's authority. Because of how many people across the PRC historically viewed *canji* (and its more idiomatic cognates *canfei* and *feiji*)[25] as shameful and to be hidden, and because of the colonial legacy inherent in the "sick man of Asia" concept,[26] the worry was that a 10 percent or higher prevalence rate could potentially call into question the very ground upon which the CCP rested its legitimacy in the early 1980s: the purported successes of Mao's revolution. Li Zheng, the leadership group's director, may have been implying this when he said in 1985 that PRC citizens tended to see the disabled as "dirty linen which they would not like to wash in public" (Chen 1985). What is more, during survey planning meetings, several officials from the Ministry of Finance expressed strong concern that a 10 percent or higher prevalence rate could create a huge drain on the nation. Specifically, they worried that such a figure might unduly erode Deng Xiaoping's modernization program, by exacerbating China's welfare burden and by sanctioning a large portion of the population to withdraw from the work-based economy.

These pressures—some pressing for 10 percent or higher, some pressing for less—had several effects on how the leadership group decided to handle the survey. Before noting some of these, I should point out an important facet about my research on the 1987 survey. Although my interviews with survey leaders occurred in the informal setting of their or my private Beijing residence, during which we talked warmly about family and friends, leadership group members were nevertheless often wary about describing the process by which they had designed their survey. Unless I introduced a fact that I had learned about the survey elsewhere, many interviewees were extremely parsimonious in what they would relate, and they tended to take pains to describe everything they did as having been structured by unanimity and the most rational of scientific techniques.

As time has passed since those meetings, which took place in the intensely politicized setting of Beijing, I have become even more convinced that all this parsimony of expression and obfuscation of events was closely related to the thorny matter of identity-making which my own presence in the meetings amplified. In our talks, my wary interlocutors each labored to craft a specific subject-position—that of the highly competent, cosmopolitan scientist and caretaker of the PRC's image—while at the same time, they were also being forced to deal with the troublesome intersection of two locally and translocally acknowledged realms of Otherness, two realms of alterity that were viewed as suspect and potentially dangerous in China and in many sociopolitical settings. My leadership group interviewees were not only being confronted with a "foreign investigator," but one who was asking questions having to do with the "abnormal body."

Owing to the challenges of conversing with leadership group members, some of what I ultimately learned about their design work only occurred because of chance encounters with others who had also contributed to the design of the survey, but in more ancillary ways. One example of how such serendipity deepened my understanding of events has to do with the means by which the leadership group chose to parse and define *canji*.[27] In the end, they divided *canji* into five separate categories:

- *tingli yuyan canji* (hearing and speech disability);
- *zhili canji* (intellectual disability);
- *shili canji* (visual disability);
- *zhiti canji* (physical disability);
- *jingshenbing canji* (psychiatric disability).[28]

Initially, leadership group members indicated to me, these categories had been chosen early in the design process, after the group had consulted a variety of "foreign standards" *(waiguo bioazhun)*. Yet, because of a chance conversation in Beijing during the spring of 1995 with a psychiatrist, one Dr. Liu, I learned that reaching a final decision on this five-part categorization had been far more complex and far more political than group members had led me to believe, and that it had occurred at a very late stage in the survey design. Dr. Liu, and subsequently others, explained that the leadership group, after having consulted national disability criteria for a number of countries, had settled on the first four categories above quite quickly, but they included the fifth category, "psychiatric disability," only after being intensely lobbied by elite Chinese psychiatrists.

It seems the main reason the psychiatrists pressed to have mental ill-ness included was their wish to expand psychiatry's institutional strength. According to Dr. Liu, the psychiatrists had concluded that the soon-to-be established Disabled Persons' Federation, under the tutelage of Deng Pufang, would probably grow into a powerful institution, and that the medical discipline of psychiatry would enjoy far more national support if it were to ally itself with the Federation than if it were to simply remain affiliated with the Ministry of Public Health's Association of Neurology and Psychiatry.

The psychiatrists finally succeeded in having mental illness included in the survey by getting Deng Pufang to take up their cause. Their approach, when meeting with Deng Pufang, was to argue their case along three main themes: the optics of modernity, national identity, and the foreign assess-ment of China. As Dr. Liu explained, he and colleagues convinced Deng by asserting that if mental illness were excluded from the survey, others would think that China was out of step with modernity, since Western governments considered the quality of care offered to the mentally ill to be one mea-surement of "civilizational development."[29]

According to one high-ranking Ministry of Civil Affairs official, who spoke to me somewhat grudgingly about this matter, the survey's leadership group initially did not want to include mental illness because the soon-to-be-launched Federation did not want to be responsible for or associated with a social group—the mentally ill—that many in China and the Chinese state had long viewed as unpredictable and thus as a threat to social order. Another reason for excluding mental illness from the definition of *canji*, the same Civil Affairs official implied, was that leadership group members saw the mutability of mental illness as challenging to their subject-positions as scientists and government officials, charged not only with conducting rig-orous research but also saddled with the vexing need to be sure that their research reflected well on the State.

> Back then, the survey group just thought that the concept of mental illness was too broad and mutable. Not only is mental illness hard to diagnose, but one day a person may be mentally ill and then tomorrow they might be okay. You know, if this [finger] is cut off, then it's gone—its not going to come back and everybody can plainly see that. . . . The leadership group felt that disabil-ity had to be things, physiological things, that were not only permanent but easy to grasp and control (*zhang wo*). Only that way could they ensure that their disability research came out right and was good for the nation.

Beyond categorizing disability, the leadership group's desire to carefully manage the production of data also had a strong influence on how each cat-egory was ultimately defined. During one of my research trips to New York City, I learned from a U.N. official that initially the survey's leadership group had not planned to organize its study around a biomedical vision of the body. It had not planned to draw upon empirical concepts like those that inform the WHO's ICIDH/ICF standards. Instead, to determine whether or not people were *canji*, the leadership group had at first planned to outfit its local data gatherers with a relatively idiomatically worded and social function–oriented questionnaire, which would have employed loosely worded queries about social adaptation and self-sufficiency (e.g.: Is that person able to see well enough to differentiate ideograms on a newspaper? Are you able to cook a meal for yourself?). I inquired about these plans on my next visit to Beijing and leadership group members told me that they had initially designed the questionnaire in this way so as to protect their less capable provincial data gatherers from the complexities of biomedical criteria.

Such self-flattering paternalism was jettisoned, however, not long after the group piloted its initial questionnaire. The leadership group was startled by the disability prevalence rate that the pilot produced: a rate of 13 percent. According to one U.N. official:

> When they got 13 percent [in their pilot], my New York office started getting constant phone calls from them, in which they said "We got 13 percent. It's too high." They were very uncomfortable. They thought, "Oh, my lord, now everybody is going to think we have too many disabled."

As a result, the leadership group, acting on advice from a number of international consultants and Ministry of Health officials, decided that a more internationally recognized and biomechanically based questionnaire should be employed, and they changed their methods accordingly. This new emphasis not only influenced how each category of disability came to be defined but also who would ultimately designate a research subject's disability status. In their revised methodology, the leadership group required that local, government-employed biomedical practitioners should be enlisted for the survey. These clinicians would examine each person that non-medical surveyors deemed as being potentially disabled and would then make a designation (Di 1987).[30]

These definitional and methodological revisions bring us back to one of the questions raised by Ma Zhun at the start of this chapter. Why would a Chinese person who is unable to walk well not merit a disability ID?

In late 1987, after the national survey had at long last been launched, China's State Council publicly certified that the survey's criteria would henceforth become the nationwide standard for civilian disability. Thereafter, *canji* would be a state-recognized and officially codified modality of existence potentially applicable to any PRC citizen, a modality around which government provisions could be offered and other actions taken. Within a few years, the State began extending some provisions, such as tax reduction, disability hiring quotas, residency permit exemptions, educational opportunities, and access to state-subsidized forms of health care. These provisions, to be sure, have helped many. They have also, however, created painful predicaments for numerous others, possibly numbering in the tens of millions. These are people, like Ma Zhun, who feel both undermined by what they view as their bodily condition and bereft of important abilities *(nengli)*. These are people who may want or are being compelled to seek out *canji* accreditation, but who are ineligible because they are mismatched with the state's new criteria.

In Ma Zhun's case, she is ineligible because the methodological revisions that occurred shortly before the survey was conducted involved a remapping of *zhiti canji* (physical disability) as being narrowly defined in terms of physiological integrity and physiological mechanics. What is more, she is ineligible because the shift to a more bio-material approach allowed the leadership group to insert several provisions at the end of the new *zhiti* criteria, one of which states that "loss of forefoot with the heel intact" will not be recognized as a physical disability (Di 1989, 1478).

Why were these provisions added? As explained to me by a key leadership group member, the provisions were born of the same reasoning that guided much of the survey's design: "Being that we were scientists and government officials, our duty was ensuring that the survey struck the best balance between good science and China's social and political needs. That provision, the one about the forefoot, we felt accorded with both of those goals."

This statement, like much of what has been presented in this chapter, shows once again that it would be an error to simply attribute Ma's plight to vague notions of objectification. As I have tried to convey, Ma's situation is not so much a result of biostatistical modes of apprehension, or any other form of objectification, for that matter. Biostatistics no more "created" disability in 1980s China than it did in 1940s China. Rather, biostatistics is a medium through which members of the Chinese state in the 1980s formally made disability knowable. And that knowledge-production process was highly mediated by thorny political-economic, ethical, and self-referential negotiations that state employees struggled over within a biopolitical environment increasingly obsessed with quantification. The modes of viewing human existence that ultimately informed the 1987 survey were just that, modes of viewing human existence. While they certainly influenced the survey's development in the 1980s, how in the end these modes of viewing were deployed in the survey—as well as what thresholds they enabled for dividing up who is and who is not *canji*—was significantly shaped by the multifaceted decisions the leadership group had to make about what reflected best upon China, the CCP, and the Federation, not to mention themselves.

A few other facts about the 1987 survey need to be mentioned. Not only were the group's revised criteria nearly never adopted by the State Council, but the group almost kept the 1987 survey's results from being released. To understand the reason for this, one must know more about the final stages of the leadership group's work.

Once its revised, two-step methodology had been created and its earlier functional criteria jettisoned, the leadership group was finally ready to implement the survey. And so, in early 1987, the group's locally based research teams descended upon neighborhoods across China. With great specificity, the leadership group then published the *Survey Report,* which describes how the research teams canvassed 424 communities and determined that 77,345 of their research subjects possessed one or more kinds of disability. But something that cannot be known by reading the report's twenty-nine capacious volumes is that this final tally of 77,345 disabled people initially made many members of the leadership group very upset. Why? Given that the total number of research subjects was 1,579,000, the figure of 77,345 disabled people meant that the carefully planned survey had produced a national disability prevalence rate of only 4.9 percent. And as a senior public health scholar/official in Beijing explained to me, that rate caused the leadership group members to worry they would be viewed as "backward, unscientific, and out-of-step with reputedly universal standards of disability quantification."

Not surprisingly, the leadership group considered shelving its results. That it finally did release the survey data in December 1987, and that the State Council certified the criteria, had much to do, once again, with the interplay of the local, the translocal, and identify formation. After the results had been tabulated and the 4.9 percent figure was known, the group's director, Li Zheng, began seeking out foreign-trained statisticians, a number of whom were either foreign nationals or Chinese citizens recently returned from overseas. The ostensible goal of Li's visits was to learn what the experts thought about the group's data. But, according to at least one of these sought-out PRC experts, "It was also quite clear the goal was to see how, in the eyes of international experts, the data reflected on the professionalism and competence of the leadership group."

One of Li Zheng's statistical consultations in this period involved travel to the U.N. headquarters in Manhattan. There, he and other group members talked at length with quantitative specialists in disability research. One of these specialists described what transpired:

> Li and his entourage came to tell us they were considering quashing the survey because they wanted 10 percent and they didn't get it. We carefully looked over everything they brought. We then told them that, as far as we were concerned, the survey was just fine and that they had proven themselves highly

effective researchers, that they had experimented with various methods and, with each, come up with different scientifically verifiable results. We told them that everything they had done was good and reputable science and that they shouldn't worry about not getting a rate closer to 10 percent.

In addition to the role played by such processes, it should be mentioned that the survey's results were released, in all likelihood, also because Deng Pufang and his staff needed them to legitimize their institution-building efforts. On December 7, 1987, China's State Council and the National Statistics Bureau formally released the 1987 survey results. Then, two days later, on December 9, the State Council drew upon these results when it announced to the Chinese people that it was creating the Disabled Persons' Federation. From that moment forward, Federation officials have invoked and celebrated the "scientific validity" of the survey. And as they have gone about building broader bureaucratic and financial support for their organization and China's disabled, they have frequently cited aspects of the leadership group's findings.

STATE SUBJECTS

Of course, it is unlikely that someone like Ma Zhun knows much about the inner workings of the 1987 survey. What is more, given the institutional and identity politics undergirding so much of the 1987 survey, it is unlikely that Ma Zhun will ever know much about the efforts to standardize, medicalize, and normalize disability that have been described in this chapter. To be sure, over the last decade, because of the Federation's purposeful circulation of disability statistics in China's mass media, more and more people in China have become familiar with the survey's results. But because, like most government agencies, the Federation requires the local and translocal legitimacy afforded by statistics' supposed remove from social processes, few people in China are likely to know anytime soon why it is that someone like Ma, someone deemed disabled by her employer and told to get Federation accreditation or lose her job, someone who walks with difficulty, cannot receive a disabled person's ID. Few people will understand why it is that at the same time that disability is becoming a more and more recognized form of being, it has been defined by China's party-state largely in terms of a range of biomedically informed standards and not in a discourse more amenable to everyday human experiences, such as social functionality or occupational need.

I would like to emphasize that the point of my discussion of the statistical genealogy of *canji* has not been to criticize specific research efforts. Rather, my goal has been to highlight processes by which such research is made manifest. I have wanted to show how research projects like the 1942

Kunming Lake census or the 1987 survey are generated as much as a consequence of the intersecting movements of elite subject-making as by the political-economic needs of a nation-state. Giorgio Agamben, in his volume *Homo Sacer: Sovereign Power and Bare Life* (1998), has encouraged us to move beyond Foucault's portrait of biopower to examine how biopower proliferates within state structures. Yet, to do so, as I have tried to show here, we need to focus not just on institutional structures within nation-states, on their internal administrative logics, or on the internationalist structures that may animate them (such as NGOs, globalizing discourses of development, worldwide campaigns of social justice, colonial histories, and flows of scientific knowledge). We must also examine more fully the actors that animate the institutions of the nation-state, those for whom the idea of the nation-state is not just a vague political notion but a workplace, a set of professional duties, a set of turf battles, and a locus of identity-making (also see Litzinger 2000, 24–31).

I believe there are vitally important issues at stake in pursing this type of scholarship. In a sociopolitical setting like that of post-Mao China, and no doubt in many other states, the people who formally codify disability and create government-assistance programs for the disabled usually live at great experiential remove from bodily alterity and other forms of Otherness. In the case of the 1987 survey, nearly all the people who orchestrated that study achieved their political authority well in advance of the 1980s through processes—education, professionalization, and political training—that demanded that their lives should be largely free from any question of deviance, difference, and Otherness. And as I have tried to highlight, for a number of those people, the ongoing need to demonstrate a high level of ability, to conform to perceived international normalizing benchmarks of scientific competence and national respectability, were important factors in how they framed disablement.

Chapter 3

Building a ~~Corporeal~~ Corporate Body

A CLUB'S RISE AND DEMISE

In the early 1980s a group of people had to prevaricate their way past a guard at Beihai, Beijing's sprawling metropolitan park. The guard had stopped the men and women as they were attempting to pass through the park's front gate, asking the several dozen people in the group why they wanted to enter the former imperial gardens located across the street from the Forbidden City. An answer had been prepared in advance, one designed to win the group's entry into the park and to avoid political repercussions. "We're all friends," members of the group said, "and we've come here to have a picnic and enjoy the trees and flowers."

According to some members of the Beihai group, with whom I have become acquainted over the last decade, it is still unclear what precisely raised the guard's suspicion that day, thereby prompting them to lie. Quite possibly it was the size of their group. More likely, they say, it was the fact that so many among them were polio survivors who had arrived at the park either on crutches or using a sort of hand-crank Chinese tricycle that is fashioned for people who have trouble walking.

There is little uncertainly, however, about why the group had assembled at the park that day. Friendship notwithstanding, what drew them to Beihai was their desire to participate in a meeting of the newly formed Bingcan Qingnian Julebu, or "Disabled Youths Club," which is the translation the new club's leaders affixed to its publications. The club, founded in 1982 by a few Beijing residents, would grow quickly over the next few years. Hundreds of people in cities all across China would join—that is, until the late 1980s, when the club abruptly fell apart.

Quite possibly the first non-governmental disability-advocacy association to exist in the People's Republic of China, the Disabled Youths Club was launched with the objective of transforming personal and collective political economics: to enhance the well-being of its members and of other "disabled" people by stimulating changes not only within Chinese society but also within the party-state.

A confluence of factors, many at the intersection of the bodily and the governmental, seems to have spurred the club's creation. On one level, there were accrued sentiments of stagnation and marginalization. In the early 1980s the men and women who would form the club were in their twenties and thirties. Unlike most Beijing residents their age, who had experienced the previous two decades as a mix of schooling and Maoist activism, for most soon-to-be club members the 1960s and 1970s had been marked largely by inactivity, parental cloister, and social exclusion. So, as they entered adulthood in the early 1980s, these youth were hungry to step outside of their homes, create meaningful relationships, and become productive members of social and national life.

Also triggering their decision to form the club was exposure to what the youth viewed as an array of foreign and distinctively Western discourses, practices, and initiatives centered around the term "disability." Of particular importance here was the U.N.'s 1981 International Year of Disabled Persons. The founding figures of the Disabled Youths Club had come together initially as a direct consequence of the U.N.'s year-long global program, when the Chinese party-state had sponsored programs in Beijing to mark the start of the U.N.'s initiative. To lend credibility to these ceremonies, as club members have explained, the party-state had enlisted the participation of youth with easily recognizable *canji* bodies.

Following the ceremonies, several of the *canji* invitees began to meet informally in homes around the capital. During the meetings, participants talked about a wide variety of subjects, but their focus consistently returned to one theme: the party-state's continuing inattention to societal discriminated against *canji*. By late 1981, the group decided to take action collectively by enjoining the party-state to build an assistance agency for people like themselves. They drafted a proposal in which they asked the government, in the spirit of the U.N. Year program, to form a state-directed association to enhance the well-being of China's "physically disabled" *(zhiti canji ren)*, so that *canji* could live more complete lives and thus contribute more fully to the party's goals of national modernization.[1] One of the proposal's key arguments was a lack of equity—both between the disabled and the able-bodied *(jianquan ren)* and among different *canji* people. Not only were the *canji* treated unfairly in China, some enjoyed more state support than others, group members insisted. In particular, in the 1950s the Chinese government had created an organization to assist the blind and the deaf, but it had never established any such organization for the "disabled," in general, or for the "physically disabled," specifically.[2]

Ministry officials to whom the group submitted its proposal cordially received it and, following bureaucratic convention, promised it would be given due consideration by the proper authorities. But after they had waited several months for government offices to take action, the proposal writers were informed that, because the nation was turning toward a market economy and away from a collectivist social state, there existed insufficient interest among officialdom.

At that juncture, the men and women determined that they would have to demonstrate the value of their proposal themselves. So, in July 1982, seven or eight of them created the Disabled Youths Club. This was a bold move, given the encompassing political climate. In the early 1980s the political environment in Beijing was acutely inimical to grassroots organizing, perhaps more than at any other time in the history of the People's Republic. After the turmoil of the Cultural Revolution, most Beijingers were exhausted by collective action, and the metropolitan and national government administrations were intolerant of any sort of independent organizing.

Despite this climate, the club flourished. In its initial two years, its accomplishments were numerous. By dint of its highly committed members, the organization published magazines, staged sporting events, held various kinds of study sessions, established "consultancy" relationships with famous "revolutionary *canfei* soldiers," solicited donations from individuals and organizations such as the Chinese Red Cross, coordinated medical treatment for members, and contributed to state-directed civic campaigns.[3]

At its apex, the club had more than 750 members, most of them polio survivors. Outbreaks of polio in China during the late 1950s and early 1960s had been frequent. Beijing alone had reported more than 1,600 new cases of polio-induced paralysis in 1959, most involving children ranging from a few months to five years old (China's Academy of Preventative Medicine, personal communication, March 11, 1995). By the early 1980s most of those who had been paralyzed by China's mid-century polio epidemics were now young adults in their twenties.[4]

This large cohort of 20–30-year-old polio survivors played a key role in the expansion of the Disabled Youths Club beyond the confines of the capital. Whereas the Beijing residents who created and ran the club were not all polio survivors, the club found it relatively easy to enlist polio survivors living in other urban contexts because most of them felt ignored by the state and discriminated against by society. Moreover, polio survivors had no special communication barriers (as did, say, the deaf and blind). Thus, by January 1984, when the club's various urban chapters held their first national meeting in the northeastern city of Shenyang, more than 90 percent of its members were polio survivors (Han 1984).

It was at this point in the club's development that the organization took a decisive turn: its leadership started to splinter and the club began to fall apart. The main reason this occurred was the emergence of Deng Pufang as a force in disability advocacy. Deng did not shut down the club. Rather, his organizational efforts led to the club's co-optation. Several former club leaders described this to me in detail during taped interviews. Among them, Ms. Jiang provided one of the clearest explanations:

> Deng Pufang's staff contacted us in late 1983, early 1984, around when he began publicly working for the disabled. Before then, many of us didn't even know his name. When we met Pufang, we couldn't believe our luck. We were thrilled to have somebody like him sharing our agenda. It was like a dream. We were just a group of folks cranking tricycles around Beijing and other cities, trying to get people to support our movement [*yundong*]. By contrast, Pufang had so much power, and he was in a hurry to use it for both disabled people and national development. . . . He was the emperor's son and his body's crippling was closely connected to the national tragedies of the Cultural Revolution. With that power he could help people do almost anything, and so people were ready to do anything for him, including us. Most of us had desperate work and living situations, and we were happy to join his effort in order to improve our lots and achieve our goal of having the government help disabled people in China. Pufang had a few disabled people with elite backgrounds working at the top of his new organizations, but he needed people like us so his efforts could be better connected to the general public, and so his programs could develop across the country more quickly.
>
> But a downside of joining Pufang was how it hurt our movement and caused our club to bust apart. In the mid-1980s, a bunch of us were invited to work for the Beijing Association [what would eventually become the Beijing chapter of the Disabled Persons' Federation]. Two or three men among us— people the Association bosses viewed as particularly competent—got real government positions within the Association. Most everyone else, though, was offered posts that were largely symbolic. That created huge tension among us club leaders. More than a few members were irritated. Some were angry for being deemed not able enough to receive real jobs in the Association. Some were angry that the symbolic work offered didn't directly help disabled people and that it involved spending lots of precious state money on public events rather than on disability assistance.

Because of this discontent, and because many of the previously active club members now eagerly involved themselves with Deng Pufang's efforts, the youth association that Ms. Jiang and her friends had worked so hard to build soon collapsed.

Like many of her former club colleagues who had also thrown their lots in with Deng Pufang's organization, Ms. Jiang made it clear that by the mid-

1990s she had come to harbor a strong sense of displeasure at what her club's rise and fall had wrought.

> In building the club, many of us came to understand what it meant to have our own organization and our own movement. But now that's all gone. It's all gone. What exists, this Federation, is like most state institutions: it's a big highly centralized bureaucracy run by a bunch of able-bodied men, who fight for resources with other state bureaucracies and who are motivated mostly by their self-interests. Sure, many people running the Federation, including Deng Pufang, are sincerely interested in helping the disabled. But, you know, lots of them are very focused on personal interests. And since most Federation employees are career cadres and since most Federation employees are able-bodied, it's hard for them to understand the disabled, which means it's very hard for them to make either their self-interests or the interests of the state fit the interests of the disabled.

USEFUL GOALS

Ms. Jiang's description of how the Disabled Youths Club was co-opted and her characterization of the Disabled Persons' Federation structure, sets the stage for the material in this chapter. My ethnographic aim here is to describe the form and effect of administrative tactics that promoted the Federation's first decade or so of development (from the early 1980s to the mid-1990s). More specifically, I hope to chronicle some of the strategies of institution-building put in place by Deng Pufang and his staff and how these strategies helped create an organization that, while it strove to provide benefits for those persons who fit the state's 1987 disability criteria, also tended to be highly centralized, male dominated, and paternalistic in its actions. In the 1980s and 1990s, these actions often reinforced not only party-state authority but also, ironically, many of the very power relations that had been marginalizing people who, by one means or another, were understood to be *canji*.[5]

Yet, if this chapter examines how the Federation was assembled and how it developed some distinct characteristics, it does so from a specific angle.[6] What I explore here are some of the ways that Deng Pufang and those around him utilized bodies—variously defined and imagined—as the medium through which to develop the Federation. As I have demonstrated in the first two chapters, processes of embodiment like those commonly associated with objectification and subject-making undergirded the Federation's genesis. What, though, of another form of embodiment: the way that bodiliness may work as a medium of social action? If our heightened biopolitical moment demands that we become increasingly aware of how existence is frequently objectified in terms of bodies, as well as attentive to how bodiliness involves subject-making, then we must also be ever more cognizant of how we and others *use* the corporeal as a medium for practical action and of how this serves to instantiate new and old structures of domination. In the case of the Federation's early development, how was corporeality a modus operandi not just for institutional production but also for social domination?

This chapter's account of ways Deng Pufang and his staff, in their institution-building efforts, drew upon forms of bodiliness is presented as a chronological and thematic history of the Federation, starting around the time that Deng Pufang returned from Ottawa and ending in mid-1995. The bodies addressed include those of Deng Pufang, his father, the nation-state, and Federation employees. These bodies, as I will show, have not functioned as isolates, but instead have been highly interdependent mediums of sociopolitical formation—which allows for an interesting commentary on some key literature in the study of bureaucracy.

WEBER

Max Weber was one of the first theorists to create an analytical framework for understanding the development of new bureaucracies, especially those relating to the state. A centerpiece of Weber's theorizing is that bureaucratic formation is ineluctably linked both to patterns of domination—of which Weber offers three typologies (charismatic, traditional, and rational/legal domination)—and to formulaic aspects of the leaders who oversee these patterns ([1914] 1978). Charismatic leaders, Weber contends, are most important for the formation of new bureaucracies. Bureaucracies are frequently born as a consequence of the imperative placed upon charismatic leaders to sustain in perpetuity the authority vested in and delimited by their unique existence. This process involves the transmutation of power, from the leader to institutional authority, and usually results in the formation of either traditional organizations or legal/rational organizations, the latter type having become particularly prevalent with the rise of modernist forms of accumulation.[7] All such transmutation can be referred to as the "routinization of charisma" (Weber [1921] 1946, 196–244; 1978, 246–54).

According to Weber, charisma is a "quality of an individual personality" which makes that person "extraordinary and treated as endowed with . . . exceptional powers" (1978, 241). Whether a leader "really" possesses such charisma is not at issue; what matters most is that people view the leader as extraordinary (Giddens 1971, 160–62). And, as Weber emphasizes, one source of extraordinariness, and thus charisma, is frequently the body. Charismatic leaders are usually "holders of specific gifts of the body and spirit" (Weber 1946, 245), such as "epileptoid seizures" and "spells of manic passion" (1978, 242).[8]

To what degree is it helpful to examine the China Disabled Persons' Federation in Weberian terms? It could certainly be argued that the Federation is an institution that closely resembles the paradoxical features of the rationalizing bureaucracy that Weber wrote about throughout much of his career. During its first two decades of existence, the Federation was an institution that claimed it bettered the human condition by creating managerial responses to specific problems, yet it simultaneously bound people to a growing web of rationalizing administrative and categorical constraints. Moreover, as I show below, bodily authority and processes of corporeal transmutation can certainly be seen as vital for the Federation's initial formation.

That noted, one can critique Weber's routinization thesis as being saddled with at least four interrelated problems for understanding bureaucratic genesis. Of these four critiques, the first three are not particularly novel; they are largely restatements of standard scholarly commentaries on Weber (see Hall 1980; Maneker 1991).[9]

First, Weber depicts bureaucracy builders as too hermetic and formulaic—as self-contained, acultural individuals with predictable if not predetermined agendas. Second, Weber's approach leaves unexamined how emerging organizations and their advocates might be shaped by changing local and supralocal fields of power and knowledge. Third, Weber's dependence on typology can easily cause one to miss the most important specificities of any bureaucracy's genesis. For instance, allegiance to a Weberian approach would likely prompt us to puzzle over whether the Federation is the product of a charismatic leader (Deng Pufang) or simply an extension of a preexisting modernist bureaucracy (the Chinese party-state). But is that the most important question for understanding the Federation's formation? Fourth, the Weberian approach, although certainly more suggestive about corporeality than most frameworks that academics have thus far proffered for making sense of institutional formation, remains quite myopic with respect to embodiment. In particular, it does not consider the possibility that numerous people and their bodies can be implicated in a bureaucracy's development, that these bodies are never pre-given but always known through language and social processes, and that such overlapping bodies may not only enable institutional formation but also limit it (Herzfeld 1992).

This chapter should be read as a response to these four critiques, particularly the last. And toward that end, let us again return to Deng Pufang's embodiment.

PROBLEM SOLVING: TRANSMUTING DENG XIAOPING'S
SOMATOSOCIAL CAPITAL

As noted earlier, Deng Pufang's hagiographers state that he began to develop a programmatic aim in the late 1970s, and that this aim was crystallized while he was in Ottawa. Initially, that aim was aiding people like those Deng had befriended at Beijing's Qing He hospice and the 301 military hospital. How this initial aim was pragmatically transformed into the Federation after Deng Pufang's return from Canada was the result of a unique fusion of somatosocial entities and strategies.

One of the most important of these entities was the authority vested in Deng Pufang's body-self, authority vested through processes like those described in Chapter 1. Another was Deng Pufang's somatosocial ties to an aging Deng Xiaoping. Even before the mass circulation of Deng Pufang's biomythography, many in China during the 1980s viewed Deng Pufang as enjoying an utterly unique and indissoluble relationship to Deng Xiaoping. This relationship was at once corporeal and existential and predicated upon various tenets and cosmologies (e.g., filial piety, biology, and Confucian ideas regarding patrilineal essence). What is more, as time passed, the somatosocial relationship between father and son was understood to have become ever more powerful. This is because, as he entered his final years, Deng Xiaoping became increasingly dependent on his five offspring to serve as his spokespersons. During his last years, Deng Xiaoping was rarely seen in public without one of his children by his side, serving as interpreter.

A further entity of great importance was obviously Deng Xiaoping himself. During the decade and a half after Deng Pufang's 1981 return from Ottawa, Deng Xiaoping was at the apex of the party-state. Although he retired from most of his formal posts in the late 1980s and early 1990s, Deng remained China's "paramount leader."[10] As such, he wielded tremendous influence over nearly all aspects of sociopolitical organization: from the party, the state, and the military, to the economy, mass media, popular culture, transportation, and health and welfare provision.

The sovereignty enjoyed by Deng Xiaoping during this period was a direct extension of the bureaucratic supremacy of China's nation-state. What may be less obvious is the degree to which that supremacy, for Deng, was structured by bodies. Deng Xiaoping's power was not just mediated and built upon bodiliness, it was delimited by it. To a large degree, Deng Xiaoping's authority in the post-Mao epoch was predicated on memories and media representations of mass bodily suffering and the promise of palliation. Using its control over symbolic mediums, Deng's post-Mao regime sold itself from the very outset as a recuperative balm for the nation (narrated as a body politic in pain). Drawing upon ideas of the national-organic introduced into China during earlier decades, Deng's regime framed much of its claim to legitimacy as one of rescuing the Chinese population from the cycles of misery, privation, and violence that had been engendered by leftist radicals. Another equally important way by which Deng Xiaoping's authority was deeply embedded in bodiliness was the notion of death. By the time Deng Pufang returned from Ottawa, his father was quite advanced in age. And many in China generally understood that Deng Xiaoping—like Mao before him—would remain the final arbiter on key matters of party and state until the finest medical services in the country could no longer keep his body functioning and the central government announced his death.[11]

In light of these somatopolitical circumstances, when Deng Pufang returned from Ottawa, he found himself in a particularly opportune and challenged position to provide for China's *canji*. On the surface, Deng Pufang had all the power needed to alter aspects of Chinese society for the enhancement of the country's unknown millions of disabled. But at the same time, Deng Pufang was fighting the clock. Once Deng Xiaoping's physicians could no longer keep him alive, the power vested in Deng Pufang and his siblings, one consequence of their somatosocial ties to their father, would invariably wane—possibly gradually, possibly precipitously—and thus the political-economic window for the fulfillment of Deng Pufang's aspirations would begin to close.

Deng Pufang faced another constraint as well. One might assume that, throughout the 1980s and 1990s, not only was Deng Pufang quite influential, but that he could wield his influence wherever, whenever, and however he wanted. In fact, his situation was far more complicated. For many of the very reasons Deng Pufang was powerful—his proximity to Deng Xiaoping, their patrilineal ties in a highly patriarchal society, and the desire of others to curry favor with the father through the son—Deng Pufang could not wield that power frivolously. This largely has to do with the way Chinese Communist political organization has structured the somatopolitical relationship between government officeholders and the nation's patrimony. Because the Communist nation-state was built upon claims of being more egalitarian, more progressive, and more rational than China's earlier, "feudal" (as party historiographers still refer to them) dynasties , the children of PRC officials have had to modulate deftly how they utilize parental authority. That is not to say, of course, that they have not taken advantage of this authority. One of the most common commentaries one hears about PRC politics is that princelings *(gaogan zinu)* have been regularly exploiting formal and informal modes of parental authority to advance their own political-economic condition. What is more, in the English-language literature for China Studies as well as in "foreign" journalistic reports there is ample anecdotal evidence to support the existence of such princeling opportunism at many levels of government. What is usually overlooked in these accounts, however, is the manner by which these princelings (as well as the children of lower-level officials) have used their parents' authority. Rather than being directly invoked, parental power has usually been applied through subterfuge—through the informal trading of favors and through what we might view as "authority laundering." The use of subterfuge has been particularly important for the children of China's most powerful politicians, and especially during the first decade after the Cultural

Revolution, when many in the highest levels of government, like Deng Xiaoping, had only recently been "politically rehabilitated" from the turmoil and accusations of the previous period.

Such subterfuge is evident in Deng Xiaoping's relative silence about his son from the early 1980s forward. Indeed, before his death in 1997, Deng Xiaoping never made a single publicly reported declaration of support for his eldest son's disability-advocacy work.[12] At first, I found this silence somewhat confusing and asked myself: With so many other high-ranking PRC officials making public pronouncements in support of disability assistance in the 1980s and 1990s, why did Deng Xiaoping remain silent? Then, shortly before Deng Xiaoping's death, one Federation official commented to me:

> The Dengs have been very aware that, to successfully use their family power to help Pufang, it has made sense for Deng Xiaoping to stay quiet, to not make public statements [on behalf of Pufang]. Leaders have had to be careful not to be seen supporting their children; otherwise they and their children may come under criticism for misusing state authority.

How did Deng Pufang and his staff respond to this situation? One way, I would suggest, was by devising strategies that allowed them to convert Deng Xiaoping's tremendous, although fleeting, authority (as well as Deng Pufang's patrilineal tie to that authority) into capital far more durable and more directly under Deng Pufang's control (cf. Marcus and Hall 1992). By patching together a number of techniques, they were quickly able to convert the Dengs' *corporeally* structured capital into *corporately* structured capital.[13] They fashioned a set of strategies that enabled them to transmute the power delimited by and contingent upon Deng Xiaoping's aging body, and the power infused in the living tie between the father and his "disabled" son, into their own bureaucratic entity within the Chinese party-state. Over the years, this new bureaucratic entity would grow to consist of a large rehabilitation hospital, a foundation, a trading company, media outlets, welfare factories, and a national advocacy organization.

A number of the strategies that seem to have been most pivotal for the transmutation of Deng family authority and the formation of the Federation are described in the following section. It should be noted first, however, that Deng Pufang, as far as I know, has never spoken publicly about how he has personally benefited from building the Federation. In line with his taciturn father, he has made only cryptic statements, such as in 1984 when, following a disability fundraising event, he told journalists, "My engagement in this work is itself a kind of rehabilitation" (Bradley 1984). With only this kind of veiled data, it is difficult if not impossible to separate the "cause" and "effect" of Deng Pufang's broad actions during the 1980s and early 1990s. At best, we can only assume that, as far as Deng Pufang was concerned, creating significant support for the "disabled" and shoring up his own status were each necessary.

Figure 2. Main office of metropolitan Beijing Disabled Persons' Federation.

THE EARLY PROJECTS: THE CRRC, THE FUND, AND KANGHUA

After returning to China from Canada, one of the first programmatic ways Deng Pufang applied himself was by assembling a state-of-the-art medical facility along the lines of the Ottawa Civic Hospital. His declared aim in building this facility was to create a Chinese flagship institution for the development of rehabilitation medicine techniques like the ones he had encountered in Canada. Deng Pufang oversaw the design and approval of the facility, as well as its construction in southwestern Beijing, during the mid-1980s. Today, the China Rehabilitation Research Center (CRRC) covers more than 100,000 square meters and consists of a large hospital and a series of administrative and residential buildings.[14]

Beyond the interpersonal capital of Deng family contacts, the construction of the CRRC was buoyed by an array of factors. These included the bureaucratic support of Deng Xiaoping's network of party stalwarts; China's post-Mao appetite for acquiring "modern" techniques of all kinds; the modern image granted to rehabilitation medicine in the late twentieth century by such events as the U.N.'s 1980s disability programs; Deng Xiaoping's newly launched reform and Open Door policies; and the desire of foreign governments and corporations to show goodwill toward both Deng and his political initiatives.

According to CRRC staff, these were the factors that led the State Council to declare the CRRC's construction a "key" project of China's Seventh Five-Year Plan. These factors also prompted the governments of Canada, Japan, and Germany to fund the vast majority of the building costs and stimulated Western companies to donate a large proportion of the CRRC's medical equipment. And after the first wave of CRRC building was finished, many of these same factors stimulated the construction of additional large rehabilitation facilities in other major Chinese cities during the late 1980s and early 1990s.[15]

In this period, internal debates sometimes erupted among Chinese health planners about whether the party-state should be spending money on rehabilitation centers, which were deemed capital-intensive and centralized rather than low-cost and community-based, but rarely were these debates aired publicly. Moreover, little discussion occurred in public or private about the ableist underpinnings inherent to rehabilitation medicine. Possibly because of the long-standing negative coding of *canji*, possibly because of China's embrace of modernism's teleological vision of the biosciences, possibly because twentieth-century China could not spawn a more radical domestic disability community like other countries, and possibly because starting in the early 1980s a growing bevy of small Euro-American NGOs had barraged Chinese government planners with offers to help develop rehabilitation medicine facilities across the country (see Mindes 1991), few in China questioned the prevailing English- and Chinese-language discourse that framed rehabilitation medicine around ableist precepts. These precepts, again, are that bodily "differences" resulting in a perceived lowering of one's functional level are "problems" (biomedical pathologies) which need to be ameliorated as quickly as possible.

THE DISABLED PERSONS' WELFARE FUND AND THE KANGHUA CORPORATION

To help finance the CRRC and subsequent projects, Deng Pufang and his inner staff created two other elite organizations. These were the China Disabled Persons' Welfare Fund and its subsidiary, the Kanghua Development Corporation.

During the Maoist era, of which the early 1980s were residually still a part, most Chinese elites remained publicly hostile to the formation of philanthropic or commercial institutions because, according to the received Maoist wisdom, such structures were capitalist and/or "bourgeois liberalist" (*zichan jieji ziyou hua*) and thus politically unacceptable and dangerous. But since Deng Xiaoping was sending out signals in the 1980s that he was leading China in a less socialist direction, "since it was the emperor's crippled son who was backing the Fund and corporation, and since that son was trying to help people harmed during the Cultural Revolution," as a former Kanghua employee once quipped to me, Deng Pufang's philanthropic organization and trading company were initially immune from public rebuke.

The fundamental tactic of the Disabled Persons' Welfare Fund—to have a powerful and well-connected individual, that is, Deng Pufang, raise cash and other resources for the weak—has worked quite well over the years. The success of this paternalistic strategy stems from the fact that organizations and individuals, both inside and outside of China, have been eager to donate to a charitable institution controlled by the Deng family. In the 1980s and 1990s offerings to the fund were provided sometimes as a consequence of solicitation, but frequently, individuals and agencies approached the fund on their own. Donors included Chinese government agencies, top figures in China's rapidly expanding private-business sector, as well as foreign nationals, companies, organizations, and governments. Donors also included the People's Liberation Army (PLA). For instance, when Deng Pufang needed office space shortly after returning from Ottawa, he received a PLA building in central Beijing. Similarly, when he needed a prestigiously sited plot upon which to build his administrative headquarters, he was given a large military tract located at 44 Beichizi, a tree-lined street abutting the eastern perimeter of the Forbidden City. And when he needed technical assistance to carry out one of his first large-scale good-deeds-oriented programs, the Three Targets Rehabilitation *(san xiang kang fu)* initiative, Deng Pufang received it from the armed forces.[16]

It is unclear to what degree the Deng regime exchanged favors for such donations.[17] What is clear, however, is that many government agencies, companies, nations, and wealthy individuals assumed that exchange was possible, and so they directly gave to the Fund, the CRRC or, later, the Federation. As suggested by Li Rubo, an official formerly with the central Federation office, this assumption was predicated at least in part on notions of the well-integrated familial body:

> Of course, everyone would like to have good ties with Deng Xiaoping. So, if they have a chance, people will do things to make his children happy. . . . Everyone has been fully aware that the Deng family has been very close knit, that Deng Xiaoping and his children have lived together in a big house since the Cultural Revolution. They know that, in that household, the head, hands, and feet know what each other are doing.

The Fund's success also stemmed, at least initially, from the special freedoms enjoyed by its subsidiary, Kanghua. From the very beginning, the Kanghua staff conducted its business with unique permits that allowed the company to function almost completely untethered from the government institutions that controlled the Chinese economy so tightly during the 1980s. Because it enjoyed self-fashioned "welfare enterprise" permits, because it had almost no competition in what, then, was a nascent domestic market economy, and because people throughout the country were fearful of interfering with anything associated with Deng Xiaoping, the Kanghua corporation quickly mushroomed into a huge money-making machine with branch offices in most major Chinese cities.

This corporation, it should be said, was in many regards a forerunner of the market system that would soon transform China, a system that would come to place greater and greater emphasis on certain kinds of productive ability. And, more than almost any other institution of the period, Kanghua embodied and affirmed China's nascent market system and its ableist structures of dominance. As Quan Yanchi (1994) has shown, the staff of Kanghua's many branches were to a significant degree comprised of the highly educated male offspring of China's political elites, many of whom were eager to exploit the protective aura of the Deng family enveloping Kanghua in order to enrich themselves and the welfare fund.[18]

DISSEMINATING PROPAGANDA

Deng Pufang and his staff also deployed the even more visible strategy of top-down symbolic production. This strategy requires considerable attention, and I will begin with the matter of lawmaking. In the early 1980s, to expedite the development of rehabilitation medicine in particular and Deng Pufang's disability-advocacy goals more generally, Deng Pufang's staff along with staff of the Ministry of Public Health decided that a disability law should be created. A year or so later, in consultation with the State Council's Judiciary Department *(sifa bu)*, they began circulating successive drafts of a bill throughout the top stratum of the government. In 1989 Deng Pufang agreed to take charge of the bill's final version and to use his influence to win ratification. The process then moved very quickly. The bill was approved by the State Council on October 17, 1990, and ratified by the National People's Congress (NPC) on December 28, 1990.[19]

Thereafter, Deng Pufang and his aides regularly invoked the new legal code—the Law on the Protection of Disabled Persons—to extract more and more capital from the party-state. They found the law of particular value for elite-level lobbying. High-ranking members of the Chinese polity were understandably disinclined to deny resource disbursement to a Deng scion who was assembling structures of state assistance for a "legally protected" population.

But despite the utility of the protection law for elite lobbying, this piece of legislation was something that individual citizens rarely invoked for personal "protection" during the late twentieth century. Why? There were likely several reasons. To begin, of those who learned about the protection law in the 1990s, many were chary to request its invocation because they felt that the ignominy of formal association with the term *canji* would eclipse benefits possibly won through litigation or arbitration. Second, the protection law, like most NPC legislation of the period, was vaguely written and highly paternalistic; it was not a regulation aimed at guaranteeing entitlements or personal rights but a loose declaration of ethics, one that called for society and government to take such actions as treating the disabled fairly and providing them with access to rehabilitation medicine, education, and employment. Third, not until the late 1980s did the party-state begin affording people limited opportunities to use laws and courts for adjudicatory action. A fourth reason, one that also speaks to the significant unintended consequence of the legislation, has to do with an aspect of legal process in China. During the late twentieth century, it was generally only those most lavished with a sense of social status—for example, educated men with strong political networks—who had either the temerity to file a legal case or the political leverage to use judiciary structures successfully.

And so, however well intentioned some of its framers might have been, and however useful the law might be for a modest segment of society, over its initial decades of existence, the protection law had a number of less salubrious consequences. Among these was the affirmation of paternalistic, androcentric, and ableist attitudes.

MEDIA PRODUCTION

In addition to lawmaking, a more far-reaching symbolic tool that Deng Pufang's group drew upon extensively in order to garner resources was the media. Not only did Deng Pufang's group regularly utilize the state-controlled news services throughout the 1980s and 1990s, but his staff created three state-sanctioned media outlets between 1984 and 1989. These were two magazines and a publishing house.

The main goal of these three outlets was to produce what within the Chinese government and among Federation staff has been commonly called "propaganda" *(xuanchuan)*. During their first decade, the three outlets disseminated a wide variety of propaganda that dealt with many topics, from Federation policies and assistance programs, the institution's success at destigmatizing disability and rehabilitation medicine, the positive application of the disability projection law on behalf of individual constituents, to current events, economics, philosophy, history, and the arts.

As with Deng Pufang's earlier projects, there are strong reasons to assume that his father's status played a vital role in his media efforts. Without the highest level of party-state consent, it is hard to imagine that China's mainstream news services would have begun giving significant and regular coverage to *canji*, raising its official profile to that of an important "social problem" *(shehui wenti)*. What is more, since the PRC's infancy, high-ranking leaders have tightly controlled the licensing of new media outlets. Yet, it was just those kinds of officials who rallied around Deng Pufang's media ventures. His initial publishing enterprise was the magazine *Spring Breezes*, launched on September 9, 1984, at a ceremony overseen by Deng Xiaoping's then hand-picked General Secretary of the CCP, Hu Yaobang. On September 17, 1986, Deng Pufang and his aides created the Hua Xia publishing house. Nearly every top Chinese leader (e.g., Wang Li, Peng Zhen, and Li Peng) affixed their imprimatur on an early Hua Xia publication, usually by penning the publication's opening inscription or foreword. Next, on January 1, 1989, the official voice of the Disabled Persons' Federation, the magazine *Disability in China*, was established.[20] With blunt symbolism, publicists adorned the first page of the inaugural issue with a color photo of a smiling Deng Xiaoping shaking hands with a soldier seated in a wheelchair; and on successive pages, they published signed calligraphy especially produced for the issue by such political elites as Yang Shangkun and Li Xiannian.

USING CONTRADICTIONS

As expected, Deng Pufang's propaganda cast his agenda in the most flattering light. But beyond that, the propaganda was formulated in careful ways to help him use the vast capital of the party-state managed by Deng Xiaoping. To understand how this worked, one must review key aspects of China's transition from Maoism to Dengism.

In the late 1970s Deng Xiaoping and other top party-state leaders had begun ousting Cultural Revolution "extremists" and arrogating to themselves control over the Chinese nation. One way they regularly justified their actions to the Chinese people, as already mentioned, was by invoking notions of a national body politic. These were notions infused with a mix of classical Chinese precepts and strong modernist and ableist overtones. Deng and his supporters publicly excoriated Cultural Revolution leaders for (either through incompetence or guile) having visited suffering on China and for having fostered chaos *(luan)*, weakness *(ruo)*, and backwardness *(luohou)* among the Chinese masses. The Dengists promised that, in contrast to the leftist extremists, they would offer the Chinese people a more competent and ethical leadership, one which would foster stability, heal the wounds of the Cultural Revolution, and more rationally achieve the modernist goals of national enhancement and self-strengthening as set out by the 1949 Revolution.

Broadly speaking, Deng Xiaoping sought to fulfill this mandate by marrying Leninist notions of party-state dominance to neoliberal models of development, political-economic competence, and managerial proficiency. The latter part of the marriage, as is well known, was centered around utilizing foreign investment, science, technology, and medicine; breaking up collectivist forms of labor in favor of neoliberal notions of efficiency; and steering Chinese society away from a social contract based on the idea of "each according to his need" and toward the idea of "each according to his ability."

As innumerable China scholars have noted, this sociopolitical marriage, from the very start, was plagued by severe contradictions, of which, two were especially significant. First, Deng Xiaoping was attempting to create personal/party/state/national strength and stability by embracing modernist techniques of development while at the same time spurning concepts (like democracy, individualism, and human rights) that nurtured those techniques' initial formation in the "west." Second, Deng Xiaoping's policies— by increasingly emphasizing competition and profitability over social provision and guaranteed employment—contradicted communism as the Chinese people understood it and thrust vast segments of the Chinese population into positions of greater susceptibility to basic human suffering.

From the 1980s forward, Deng Pufang and his staff shrewdly promoted responses to these structural problems—responses intended to serve and feed off of Deng family authority and ideas of the national body politic. On the symbolic level, the responses came packaged in sometimes subtle, sometimes boldfaced rhetoric. In reports designed for circulation within government agencies, Deng Pufang and his staff argued that disability assistance was a vital tool for shoring up support for the CCP and dampening political dissent.[21] In media releases, Deng and his staff criticized the Cultural Revolution as a fascist-directed epoch of chaos and mass human suffering; presented cases of persons disabled by leftist radicals as illustrative of the broader harm wrought by the previous regime; championed "Deng Xiaoping thought" as a recuperative, stabilizing, and modernizing force; depicted disability assistance as exemplary of the party-state's commitment to heal and protect China's citizenry; and asserted that building structures to aid those who were most likely to be "left behind" by the reforms (the *canji*) was vital to party, state, and national construction.

DIRECTIVES

Armed with such rhetoric, the soon-to-be-ratified Disability Protection Law, and international mandates like the U.N.'s calls for disability intervention, Deng Pufang and his staff found it relatively easy to deploy another symbolic technique for transmuting his and his father's immense capital into institutional structures for disability advocacy. This was the administrative directive. Starting in the early 1980s, a growing number of central-government decrees were issued pertaining to *canji*. These dealt with numerous issues— everything from the creation of the Welfare Fund, resourcing local fund offices, micro-management of the Three Rehabilitations Program, and the distribution of disability ID cards, to the organization of intra-Fund/ Federation party members, the launching of disability sporting events, and the dissemination of *canji* propaganda.

Deng Pufang's staff issued many such decrees independently. But when it came to projects involving the use of resources they did not yet possess, Deng's staff co-issued directives with numerous agencies (e.g., the Ministries of Finance, Public Health, and Civil Affairs, and sometimes the State Council and the State Planning Commission). How were these multi-endorsed directives generated? "Pufang's crippled body [*canfei shenti*] was a helpful tool [*gongju*]," one high-ranking Federation official noted to me. Quite often, multi-endorsed directives were issued after Deng Pufang made face-to-face (or was it body-to-body?) appeals to the ministers and directors of the co-signing institutions. "When those leaders were put in the same room with Deng Xiaoping's disabled son, with Pufang sitting there in a wheel-chair," the same Federation official asserted, "few were willing to deny us their chop on a document."

CREATING THE FEDERATION

In the mid- to late 1980s, buoyed by their growing victories in garnering resources, Deng Pufang and his aides began pressing top party-state officials to support an expansion of the Welfare Fund. The plan was to have the Welfare Fund grow into a broader network of government-funded offices that would have a wider state-sanctioned mandate to initiate disability-assistance projects. As outlined in its founding documents, this network was to develop as a top-down government and Communist Party institution that would be part administrative apparatus, part advocacy organization, and part medical provider. On December 9, 1987, China's State Council formally endorsed this plan in a nationally distributed directive. And then, in March 1988, the party-state's top officials (sans Deng Xiaoping) christened the founding of the China Disabled Persons' Federation at a three-day event held in Tiananmen's Great Hall of the People. Not surprisingly, these events were enthusiastically reported throughout the mainstream media.

ENABLING THE ORGANIZATION

During the next decade, sundry strategies were pursued for promoting the Federation's institutional development. Some of these strategies were quite overt, while others were more cloaked or latent. Some were carefully designed, while others appear, in hindsight, to have been patched together. A key organizational orientation that appears to have guided a number of these strategies was what Federation staff sometimes referred to as *jianquan*

TABLE 1

Year	Number of Federation Chapters
1989	30
1990	403
1991	2,700
1993	45,117

Chu et al. 1996, 616–18.

zuzhi (Liu 1995, 38). To understanding the irony of this term, to grasp how it reflects ableist underpinnings of the Federation's early development, and to flesh out how it has related to the somatosocial structuration of Deng family authority, one must begin by unpacking the term's literal meaning. The second of the term's two couplets, *zuzhi*, in this context acts as a noun and means "organization." The first couplet, *jianquan*, may function as either an adjective ("able-bodied" or "fully healthy") or a verb ("to enable" or "to make fully healthy"). Since its founding, the Federation consistently has used the adjective *jianquan* to represent the opposite of disabled (e.g., *jianquan ren*, meaning a person who is "able-bodied" or "fully healthy"). In the case of the idiom *jianquan zuzhi*, though, *jianquan* usually acts as a verb. And, as such, the full phrase *jianquan zuzhi* can be translated as either "to make the organization fully healthy" or "to enable the organization."

What did *jianquan zuzhi* mean for Federation leaders on the administrative level, and how did they direct subordinates to fulfill *jianquan zuzhi* during the 1980s and 1990s? In part, the term can be viewed as a policy prescription to create as many Federation chapters as possible, spanning the full breadth of the Chinese administrative system. The Federation statistics above seem to indicate that this objective was easily met.

GROWING PAINS

Impressive as these figures may be, they should be interpreted with more than a bit of caution, for according to the Federation's own estimates, by 1993, 96 percent of the Federation's 45,000 offices were what we might call "virtual chapters" (Chu et al. 1996, 616–18). Such chapters usually constituted a plaque outside a regional Ministry of Civil Affairs office, a few overburdened local officials who were required to fold their Federation duties into their MCA portfolios, and little else.

How did the Federation create these "virtual chapters"? And what did it have to gain by them?

The Federation had to do little to create these offices. When the State

Council certified the Federation in December 1987, it made the disability-advocacy organization subordinate to and a part of the Ministry of Civil Affairs. Thus, wherever an MCA office existed, in theory, so, too, a Federation chapter should surface. On the one hand, this arrangement was very beneficial to the Federation. At a time when Deng Pufang was struggling to emerge from the cloud of the 1989 democracy demonstrators' accusations, his staff was able to gain a significant foothold on institutional formation. It also meant that, throughout much of the country, at least a modicum of disability advocacy could be done relatively efficiently by experienced local MCA cadres at almost no cost to the Federation.

On the other hand, as far as the Federation leadership was concerned, being attached to the MCA was problematic because laboring from within the MCA meant that the central Federation and its many chapters lacked the key markings and prerogatives of a full-fledged government ministry, namely, a semi-autonomous, nested hierarchy of salaried staff with the authority to create local work plans, issue documents across local government sectors, and manage internal budgets relatively independently. In other words, the Federation network had very little formal administrative clout of its own, which was necessary if it was to wrestle more capital from an increasingly decentralized state and come to constitute a durable and efficacious bureaucracy. This brings us to another meaning Deng Pufang and his staff had for the term "enabling the organization." For them, this term meant not only establishing local Federation chapters, but also elevating the Federation to a full-fledged Ministry, thus making local chapters independent from the MCA.[22]

LOCAL GOVERNMENT RESISTANCE

One of the initial ways they sought to accomplish such institutional independence was through a spate of top-down directives.[23] These directives, as it turned out, were relatively ineffectual, particularly when it came to separating local chapters from the MCA. What greatly contributed to that inefficacy, it could be said, were aspects of Deng family authority: its strengths and weaknesses, how it was already being applied, and its somatosocial structuration. There is a timeworn phrase in Chinese politics: "The mountain is high and the emperor is far away" *(shangao huangdi yuan)*. This phrase has been invoked over the centuries to describe the limits of centralized government authority, and I often heard it when discussing with Chinese acquaintances the inability of the Federation to get local government administrations to implement disability policies. In this phrase, the emperor serves as a personification of state authority; what orients state power within and over the polity is space and the idea that space is defined as the distance between the administrative center and the locality. But the emperor is always more than a personification of state power. He is also a living, breathing, performing embodiment of state power. As such, what can be important for state sovereignty is the immediacy of the emperor's bodiliness and how that bodiliness is imagined. To create a sense of greater immediacy, top PRC leaders over the decades have increasingly performed at public events, and those events have been covered extensively by the mass media. Likewise, taking advantage of ever-faster transport conveyances, leaders have regularly made highly publicized "inspection tours" of the country. Underwritten by modernist bodily ideals of strength and mobility and older Chinese ideals of energy and vitality, public performances and tours help leaders present themselves to the citizenry as fit, healthy, and potent (both politically and somatically).[24] But by the early 1990s Deng Xiaoping could participate in few such performances or trips. Because of his advancing age and growing frailty, he had to stay increasingly out of the public eye.[25]

Also greatly adding to the inefficacy of Federation directives was the Deng regime's ongoing fiscal restructuring of China's body politic. This requires some explanation. In the 1980s, as part of its post-Mao "reforms," the party-state's new leadership under Deng Xiaoping began pressing for all levels of the Chinese state to adopt a new funding system. This was a move away from the 1950s and early 1960s model of intragovernmental financing and toward one of fiscal decentralization. In the language of government as consumptive bodies, this has been known as "eating in separate kitchens" (*fenzao chifan*) (Shirk 1993). A key feature of the shift to "eating in separate kitchens" was that regional government agencies—whether they were branches of the MCA, the Ministry of Public Health, the Ministry of Culture, or some other agency—were increasingly funded by money raised locally, by regional People's Governments, rather than by money allocated from supralocal government coffers.[26] This prompted many in the regional People's Governments to resist all the more intensely any new fiscal obligations foisted upon them from above, especially obligations that might require the regional People's Governments to either expand their annual budgets or to divert money from preexisting obligations. And, according to my central and local Federation acquaintances, top-down directives that called for the building of able-bodied Federation chapters often ran up against this type of resistance. Throughout the early 1990s, People's Government officers across China frequently eschewed supplying the funds that local Federation chapters needed to become independent of the MCA—funds for everything from staff salaries, to office space, to general administrative materials (e.g., desks, electricity, vehicles, etc.). Shortly after I arrived in East Hainan, this problem was explained to me by an MCA official, Cadre Gao, who worked for the Wenchang County's Federation chapter.

Yeah, most counties in Hainan haven't had much success establishing independent Federation chapters. The main reason is that county-level People's
Governments haven't wanted to give us the money. We show them all the
directives we've received from Beijing and they say, "We know about those
directives, we want to help you, but it is very hard."

To be sure, resistance to the Federation's institution-enabling directives
was not limited to provincial government officials. It also came from people
like Cadre Gao—that is, from county-level MCA functionaries who worked
on Federation issues. Some cadres in Gao's position were opposed to
Federation autonomy because, given the longtime negative coding of *canji*,
they did not wish to be seen as working exclusively on such matters. Many
were also reluctant because they calculated that institutional autonomy
would erode their and their families' socioeconomic status. This latter issue
also emanated, in part, from shifts in government financing. To compensate
for the proportional decline in top-down allocations that accompanied
"eating in separate kitchens," and to promote economic growth across
China, central government planners began in the early 1980s to expect
local governments to create entrepreneurial ventures. Regional MCA
offices, like other local governmental branches, often responded with great
alacrity to this expectation, and their entrepreneurial fervor frequently created a strong disincentive for local Federation independence. The
Federation and the MCA leadership had an agreement during the 1980s
and 1990s that, when local Federation chapters became autonomous, MCA
officials who were handling Federation duties would be officially transferred out of the MCA and would become the first employees of some of
these free-standing chapters. A large proportion of MCA cadres, like Gao,
were opposed to Federation independence because they recognized that if
MCA–Federation division occurred, they would stand to lose the perquisites
of MCA enterprises (e.g., bigger end-of-the-year bonuses, more robust
administrative budgets, and lucrative employment opportunities for their
children within the enterprises).[27]

Not surprisingly, one strategy that the Federation leadership developed
in response to these various forms of resistance was to deploy Deng Pufang
to the provinces. During the 1990s, Deng Pufang frequently flew from
Beijing to provincial centers to meet with local governors, MCA directors,
and Federation staff. These promotional trips on behalf of the Federation
were widely publicized in local media, often with accompanying hagiographic accounts of Deng and frequently with pictures of soldiers carrying
Deng down airplane stairs or of local officials conferring with him in their
offices. The trips proved effective in breaking down resistance to Federation
independence, to a degree. As one Federation functionary in Hainan's
provincial capital explained, "Although it had little influence on the situa-

tion out in the counties, all kinds of doors started flying open for us in Haikou when Deng Pufang visited in the early 1990s and was wheeled around the meeting rooms of the provincial government compound." The inefficacy of Deng Pufang's travels for sparking Federation building outside of provincial capitals highlights a paradox Deng and his staff have confronted that is inherent to his bodiliness.[28] As Geng Bailu, who accompanied Deng Pufang on many provincial tours during the 1990s, explained:

> We've found these trips very useful because, out in the provinces, so many people view it as quite special that Pufang—someone with such a fragile body, who suffered so much during the Cultural Revolution, and who's the son of Deng Xiaoping—takes the time to make a visit. But the trips have also been very taxing on Pufang because his body is so fragile. So, even though he wants to travel more and meet with people in the counties, we've had to limit his activities. We wouldn't want him to spike a fever out in the Anhui countryside and be without medical care. He could die. Then where would we be?

FEDERATION EMPLOYEES

Thus far, this chapter has focused on how Deng Pufang and his staff used (and were hampered by) three socially informed bodies (those of Deng Pufang, Deng Xiaoping, and the nation-state) to build the Federation. The Federation's development also involved the use of other bodies as well. A large and important group to be considered in this regard is the thousands of individuals who the Federation enlisted as employees during the 1980s and 1990s. When writing about these employees, it is difficult not to do so (as a good Weberian) in terms of typology and generalization. It is difficult because typologies are what many of my Chinese acquaintances have utilized when responding to my inquiries about the Federation's rank and file. What are the typological frameworks they have tended to invoke? Federation hiring in the 1980s and 1990s, they say, revolved around three somatosocial binaries: male/female, connected/unconnected, and *canji/jianquan.* The Federation hired mostly men, mostly those it considered able-bodied, and often those with connections.

What were the sources of such hiring practices? How did they feed off of and reinscribe normative structures of embodiment? And how do they expand our understanding of the ways in which bodily authority was used for Federation expansion in the 1980s and 1990s?

When asked in general terms, high-ranking Federation officials have usually explained the inclination to hire men by dismissing out-of-hand any role of policy and by instead offering two rationales. First, the preponderance of men in the nascent Federation, they say, was not unique but mirrored gender ratios found in most party-state agencies at the end of the twentieth century. Second, they emphasize that the preponderance of male employees was not a matter of intentional policy but rather the result of social structures that had long existed in China.

Aspects of these two rationales strike me, even now, as largely irrefutable—if not overdetermined. According to an assessment by China's own party-state, nearly 80 percent of those working for "government agencies, parties, and people's organizations" in 1990 were male, as were nearly 90 percent of "heads of governments, parties, people's organizations, enterprises and institutions" (Xiong 1995, 47–50). Such figures no doubt highlight gender inequalities long present in and dependent on Chinese state organization (Bray 1997; Stacey 1983; Watson and Ebrey 1991). That Federation hiring during the 1980s and 1990s reflected the same inequalities is strongly evidenced not only by informants' assertions but also by the fact that the sectors of the institution where one was likely to find the highest numbers of women employed were those at the lowest rungs of the system: district and subdistrict offices in large cities.[29]

The assertion that the institution's general penchant for hiring men, particularly in leadership roles, was unrelated to policy decisions I find somewhat less convincing. Although they do not communicate much information about gender equity in the area of hiring, the Federation's publicly circulated documents of the 1980s and 1990s clearly articulate that an overriding logic for staffing was established quite early in the institution's history. The documents state that the Federation's designers determined that "efficacy" *(xiaoneng)* was to be the preeminent principle in staffing decisions. Moreover, the principle of "efficacy" was not only framed in juxtaposition to the principles of "representation" *(daibiaoxing)* and "democracy" *(minzhuxing)*, it was expected to trump them (Chu et al. 1996, 468–69). The documents indicate that Deng Pufang was involved in this conceptual framing from the very beginning. Deng stated at the Federation's founding ceremonies that, when hiring employees and trying "to resolve the contradiction between democracy and efficacy," the Federation must act in accordance with the "Chinese environment" and err on the side of "efficacy" and be satisfied with "small democracy" (ibid., 19).

The policy to err on the side of efficacy and small democracy no doubt helps explain why a specific set of practices played such a large role in Federation staffing. These are practices that to some extent are common to bureaucracies everywhere. They constitute a form of sociopolitical exchange. They involve the granting of employment to those with connections *(you guanxi)*: people who are relatives, friends, or clients of powerful individuals. And during the Federation's first decade of development, my Federation acquaintances have told me, intragovernmental cronyism was particularly significant in staffing decisions. Many Federation employees throughout the system received their positions at least in part as a favor to their parents, aunts, or uncles who were powerful figures in other areas of

Figure 3. Disability symbolism was a rare sight in the 1990s. Here, the international symbol of disability marks the guarded entryway to a ramped underpass in Tiananmen Square.

the party-state. Sometimes Federation officials granted these favors out of individual avarice, hoping that an outside patron might help them with a personal matter. But there is also plenty of evidence that jobs were often issued preferentially in the hope that, by extending such favors, the Federation would become a more efficacious body politic, one that would have blood relatives throughout the party-state ready to help advance its institution-building priorities.

While such hiring techniques generated goodwill for the Federation across numerous governmental layers, it came with several downsides. Preferentially employed functionaries often had little loyalty to the Federation and frequently departed once they found a better job elsewhere. They usually had neither experience with nor interest in disability assistance, and thus regularly avoided their *canji* constituents or treated them paternalistically. Finally, their presence amplified the view that many Chinese citizens had held since the era of Kanghua—that the Federation was a corrupt organization.

How, though, did the policy of erring on the side of small democracy and efficacy shape the Federation's gender composition in the 1980s and 1990s? When I explored this question with Federation directors, their answers usually went as follows. Because of the programmatic emphasis placed on efficacy, because the upstart Federation was competing with older party-state offices for limited resources, and because the Federation's greatest window of opportunity for expansion was understood to be during the then twilight of Deng Xiaoping's life, directors of Federation chapters across the country felt they needed to enlist staff that would possess the greatest strengths in such areas as "advanced thinking," "political savvy," and "competitiveness." And as Federation directors have often added during our conversations, seemingly with a glimmer of self-satisfaction, in the 1980s and 1990s the candidates who possessed the greatest competencies *(nengli)* in such areas most frequently were men.

Stated somewhat differently, owing to a variety of sociopolitical factors (including policy directives), Federation leaders were inclined to seek out persons reputedly vested with characteristics—often couched in the idiom of ability *(nengli)*—which the encompassing patriarchal environment dictated as being more constitutive of male than female bodiliness.

LIMITING *CANJI* EMPLOYMENT

These same forces were likewise at play in how another binary—that is, *canji/jianquan*—patterned Federation hiring during the same period. Unlike gender, the *canji/jianquan* dyad and its role in staffing has been a visible part of Federation policymaking from the very beginning. And, curiously, it has taken some contradictory forms. For instance, from the moment the institution was founded, its leadership stated that it should have employees that the general population would recognize as *canji,* and a minimum employment quota for *canji* staff was implemented. Deng Pufang himself regularly emphasized the importance of *canji* staffing in speeches during the 1980s and 1990s; he frequently intoned that the disabled must always be part of the Federation's "flesh and blood" (e.g., Deng 1995, 16–17). To a large degree, this emphasis on *canji* hiring should be interpreted as a matter of somatic credibility or, in Herzfeld's terms, "mass suasion" (1992, 12). People inside and outside China would only deem the Federation legitimate if it lived up to its own calls that all sectors of Chinese society should treat the *canji* fairly. The Federation needed to be an institution *for* disabled bodies but also *of* disabled bodies.

Yet, inasmuch as the Federation needed easily recognizable disabled employees, its own documents indicate that detailed hiring guidelines were created which established barriers for the employment of the vast majority of persons fitting the institution's 1987 criteria for *canji* (see Appendix B). When I have asked senior Federation employees about these guidelines, they have usually interpreted them in terms of efficacy, claiming that from the moment the Federation was founded its leaders were compelled to limit the number of *canji* employed so that all chapters nationwide would enjoy the highest level of efficacy possible.

However, when I have raised the matter of hiring guidelines with various persons knowledgeable about the Federation who self-identify as *canji*—persons such as "disabled" Federation employees and former Disabled Youths Club members—I have often heard a more robust interpretation. They say that the design of the hiring guidelines and the paucity of *canji* staff within the Federation have stemmed from how the Chinese state has historically fostered discourses about significant/obvious bodily differences *(mingxiande shenti chubie)*. One of these discourses is that significant bodily differences are usually coterminous with incompetence, hampered opportunities, ill fate, and weakness. Another discourse is that these differences, particularly those cast as "imperfections" *(quedian)*, are tantamount to a kind of somatosocial power. This is a distinctively negative force—a corrosive, destabilizing, chaos-inducing power—that, for organized authority, is anathema and thus to be avoided, controlled, or eliminated (cf. Hansson 1988).

As former Disabled Youth Club members have told me, with the birth of the Federation this second discourse was increasingly instantiated in the *canji/jianquan* binary through the institution's hiring practices. This discourse, they say, prompted Federation officials from the outset to fear what might transpire if the institution was managed by *canji* and not just managing *canji*. As was to be expected, most of the staff at 44 Beichizi Street (the address of the Federation's national headquarters in Beijing) and employees at other Federation offices have been uneasy talking with me about this issue. Privately, however, a number of Federation officials have described how they and their other "able-bodied" colleagues in national, city, and provincial offices have worried that having a large percentage of "disabled" Federation employees, particularly in positions of authority, would make it difficult to control their rapidly developing multilevel organization. They have said that many "able-bodied" officials have feared that "disabled" colleagues would be more likely to question top-down government directives, to challenge superiors, including Deng Pufang, and to take highly activist positions which could alienate other parts of the party-state.

Determining whether the driving motive for limiting *canji* employment within the Federation at the end of the twentieth century was one of conforming to dominant views of administrative efficacy or whether it was to keep the Federation as a docile party-state institution, I must admit, exceeds my understanding of the institution. In general, my sense is that both were abiding and mutually constituting factors in the 1980s and 1990s. This seems to be illustrated by two additional recruitment strategies that under-girded the Federation expansion during that period.

DISABLED PEOPLE HIRED BY THE FEDERATION

The first of these strategies was to hire what Federation directors have characterized as "the most able of the disabled." Employing the most competent *canji* meant, once again—following the androcentric logic described above—mostly hiring men. So, too, it meant that most of the *canji* hired were those the Federation deemed "physically disabled" *(zhiti canji).*[30] Federation officials have repeatedly told me that they have preferred to fill their *canji* hiring quotas with the physically disabled because most Chinese believe that the *zhiti canji* have the highest cognitive and communication abilities from among the Federation's five *canji* categories (the physically disabled, the blind, the deaf, the mentally ill, and the mentally impaired).

But the institution's preference for the physically disabled must also be understood in terms of a second strategy. This strategy strongly influenced who—among supposed *canji* candidates—should be hired during the Federation's first two decades.

My use of the word "supposed" is prompted by the curious fact that many of the *canji* Federation staffers to whom I have been introduced do not actually meet the Federation's 1987 disability criteria. An example of this came to my attention in 1995, when for several months I conducted fieldwork at Beijing's Xuan Wu district Federation chapter. Two employees in that chapter were referred to as *canji* by their colleagues and both possessed disability ID cards inscribed with the categorizations "physically disabled" and "male." But only one of these men came close to meeting the 1987 disability criteria, and on several occasions the other man acknowledged to me that "I'm not actually *canji.*"[31]

How was this possible? These apparently non-*canji* employees were former soldiers. In the late 1980s the Federation formally extended a special accommodation to the military. This accommodation stated that any veteran meeting the military's relatively broad Disabled Revolutionary Soldier criteria is automatically recognized as *canji* by the Federation, and is therefore eligible for all local civilian disability benefits.

When needing a new staff member and feeling compelled to hire a *canji ren*, Federation office directors, like those of the Xuan Wu and Beijing city chapters, often invoked the military accommodation and hired Disabled Revolutionary Soldiers. Several Federation directors have explained this as stemming from at least one of five motivations. First, it allowed them to hire people—most notably former commissioned officers—who enjoyed educational levels and managerial experience far in excess of what would usually be found among the civilian *canji*. Second, China's central government has long required the MCA to look after and extend favors to decommissioned soldiers, and, owing to their intimate relationship with the MCA and their desire to develop goodwill among military elites, local Federation directors have felt obliged to continue the custom. Third, Federation directors claimed that recruiting retired soldiers allowed them to hire those *canji* least preoccupied by bodily difference—because soldiers cannot become *canji* until adulthood (and therefore have less time to develop what one director called a "strong *canji* attitude") and because the military's *canji* criteria include conditions far less debilitating than the Federation's criteria. Fourth, hiring decommissioned *canji* soldiers permitted the institution to leverage and enshroud itself in the authority of the hero/martyr which the party-state had for decades vested in the injured bodies of the nation's primarily male protectorate, the military. Finally, and likely most significantly, hiring decommissioned *canji ren* allowed the Federation to employ people whose discipline and allegiance to party, state, and nation were well proven.

CARING FOR CADRE ZHOU

During one of our conversations in Beijing, Ms. Jiang explained that, as the Disability Youth Club was beginning to implode in the early 1980s, she had been one of the only female club members to be offered a salaried job in the embryonic Federation system. Rather than taking the post, she had decided to pass the position on to her husband, Zhou Lili, a polio survivor who had begun courting Jiang not long after he had joined the club.

> The two of us could see how the Fed [Canlian] was starting to develop and how our club was falling apart. It irritated us. What could we do? We could throw away the Fed's job offer. But I was convinced the Fed, with Pufang behind it, was the best hope for China's *canji*, for their liberation, and I wanted to do something to help it grow for many years. So we asked if Lili could take the position. The job was more valuable for him and better suited to his life. I already had a job, one in a profession of my choosing. Lili had nothing, and that was very hard on him, making him feel increasingly incompetent. Also, I didn't really want to be known as a *canji* worker or one of those women who battle away in an aggressive branch of government. The young Fed was quite aggressive. It had to be. They were creating a new government agency. So better he take the higher-profile Federation post. He likes that scene, all that strategizing, all that sitting around smoking cigarettes and negotiating with other government agencies, all that traveling around the country trying to build up disability services. It's good for him. It's made him feel better about himself and allowed him to be a stronger model for our son. That's not to say it's been particularly easy for Lili in the Federation. Lord knows how many times he's been passed over for promotion or acceptance into the party while able-bodied staff or colleagues with military backgrounds have been upped. It's embarrassing. But he endures it, recognizing that to be a good cadre, one must make sacrifices for both the nation and those in need.

Ms. Jiang's reflections help highlight facets about the Federation's early formation, facets that might otherwise be overlooked if we were to adhere tightly to the post-Weberian analysis developed in this chapter thus far. As the preceding pages indicate, the Federation's initial development was clearly contingent on the ways bodies have been understood within China as differentially "charismatic" and on how Federation superiors selectively leveraged such bodies. Moreover, these framing and leveraging processes were not sociopolitically benign: they often involved the inscription of old and new cultural orders of dominance and subordination. But inasmuch as Federation superiors objectified and used bodiliness—and thereby often affirmed hegemonic structures pertaining to gender, somatosocial integrity, and centralized state authority—those superiors did not act alone. Numerous people participated, even, at times, the very people who were offered jobs in the institution because they fit the 1987 *canji* criteria.

Ms. Jiang's reflections seem to highlight the fact that the leveraging of bodies by the young Federation was more than simply a set of top-down activities involving a few of the institution's directors. The reflections illustrate that this leveraging was also mediated by acts of self-objectification and self-making. To be sure, the response of Ms. Jiang and her husband to the Federation's offer of employment can be understood in terms of economics. After all, Zhou's taking the position allowed both of them to be salaried employees in the inflationary environment of 1990s Beijing. But just as importantly, the decision that Zhou should occupy the Federation post was fueled by an aspect of embodiment, subjectification, that has not been emphasized in this chapter until now. As much as economics, Jiang's and Zhou's decision to place his *canji* body instead of hers in service to the Federation was incited by how such a step would allow each of them to position him/herself vis-à-vis the complex and oftentimes contradictory set of normative discourses and expectations about men and women, *canji* and *jianquan,* then circulating in urban post-Mao China. Their decision enabled Jiang to make a long-term contribution to the Federation's modernist mission of *canji* "liberation," which Jiang holds dear to her heart, though it also allowed her to make her contribution without acquiring the moniker of *canji* worker, which she feels would be corrosive to her desired identity. Their decision permitted Jiang to continue in the non-*canji* profession of her choosing while at the same time acting as committed mother and wife, one who nurtures family advancement and the development of husband and son. As for Zhou? The decision allowed him to demonstrate his competence along conventional masculinist lines, by not just gaining a job but, notably, one in a high-profile, "aggressive" state sector. It also permitted Zhou to situate himself, however retrospectively, as the exemplary socialist actor, as the "good cadre," someone willing to endure hardship for the betterment of the nation and the needy.

Chapter 4

Speeding Up Life in Beijing

In spite of their size and pageantry, I initially found the Far East and South Pacific Games for the Disabled (FESPIC) to be an ethnographic disappointment. This sporting event, held at Beijing's sprawling Asian Games Village in early fall 1994, was sparsely attended, and it was nearly impossible to speak with any Chinese athletes or the government representatives responsible for them.

I had thought that attending FESPIC '94 would provide an interesting interlude between my first and second years of fieldwork. But, well before the games were over, I was thinking of leaving Beijing and heading south again to Hainan. As it turned out, that trip to Beijing—a city where I had studied for two years in the mid-1980s but had subsequently barely visited—fundamentally changed my research agenda.

There was a rumbling din as I exited the ping-pong stadium and began my trek across the pavilion toward another of the towering athletic facilities that are part of the Asian Games Village. Before I knew it, I was enveloped by the sound of small engines, as a convoy of thirty motorcycles zoomed around the ping-pong stadium and shot across the pavilion, their riders whooping and waving as they raced by. In the twenty seconds or so it took them to pass, I realized that they were like no "bikers" I had ever seen before. Rather than black leather, these riders sported polyester pants, bright white T-shirts, and yellow-brimmed baseball caps. And their motorcycles were configured differently, too; they did not resemble the brand-name vehicles I was most familiar with—brands like Sanyang, Yamaha, Harley-Davidson, or BMW. These motorcycles had three wheels (one in front and two in back), their seats were shaped like straight-back chairs, and their chases and fenders were painted vermilion. Adding to the sight was the fact that, alongside most of the drivers, was lashed a set of crutches.

"Who are all these people?" I wondered to myself as I stood in the pavilion. "And why are they all driving these motorbikes?"

When I reached the other side of the pavilion, most of the riders had already dismounted and were making their way into the stadium with canes or crutches. I introduced myself to a few of them and learned that these sports fans, mostly men, were all from Beijing and that they had been organized months earlier into a cheering squad *(lala dui)* by the Disabled Persons' Federation. When I told these cheering-squad members that I was intrigued by their motorcycles and that they must possess the only vehicles of that kind in all of Beijing, their faces shifted from smiles, to blank looks, to unbridled laughter.

"The only ones in Beijing? You haven't been here very long, have you?" one man said between the group's collective guffaws. "Look around. These bikes are everywhere. There are thousands of them in this city."

The next day, rather than attend more FESPIC events, I decided to follow that man's advice. I borrowed a friend's bicycle and spent the day pedaling through central Beijing, visiting many of the neighborhoods for which I had developed fond feelings in the mid-1980s. On my ride, I counted more than fifty of the three-wheeled vermilion motorbikes, some parked amid a jumble of bicycles in front of stores, some being driven along Beijing's wide boulevards. Nearly all the drivers I saw were men, more than a few of whom traveled with a pair of crutches. And many of the motorbikes bore the transnational markings of disability; in particular, many brandished license plates or decals with the disabled's international icon, a stick figure seated on a wheelchair.

Thus, there in Beijing I encountered an everyday engagement with the category of *canji* that I had not expected, one which contrasted vividly with pictures of daily life that I had painted in my own mind, based on my research to that point. In rural Hainan I never saw anybody using a wheelchair, motorized or otherwise. Nearly all my village acquaintances who might benefit from such conveyances either got along by using homemade crutches, by hobbling, or, in some cases, by crawling. Just as significant was the fact that very few of my Hainanese informants ever articulated any sense of connection with a broader national—let alone international—disability movement. Moreover, most people in the village where I had been conducting research up to that point were unaware of the Federation.

My encounter with the Beijing motor tricyclists during those first days of September, and my subsequent conversations with them, significantly influenced not only my understanding of *canji* and the Federation but also how I would handle the subsequent segments of my fieldwork. Based in part on that September trip to Beijing, I decided to rethink my initial research design. Instead of continuing to concentrate my fieldwork in Eastern Hainan, complemented by only a few days in the nation's capital, I decided to pursue what Marcus (1998) has called "multi-sited" research and what Gupta and Ferguson have termed "a multistranded methodology," that is, a focus on the "interlocking of multiple social-political sites and locations" (1997, 37). From that point forward, most of my remaining research time was spent at great distance from Hainan, much of it in Beijing, some as far away as the archives and offices of the United Nations in New York City.

In this chapter I discuss important aspects of what I learned in the days, months, and years following that event outside the ping-pong stadium at the Asian Games Village. I have placed the motorized tricycles and their riders at the center of my discussion here because they were so influential in the development of my fieldwork, and also because these machines and their riders reveal a great deal about how specific processes of embodiment— once again, ones that cross-cut a Maussian tripartite framework—were implicated in the emergence of the Federation and the concurrent texturing of *canji* as a sphere of alterity.

An important assertion in the previous chapter was that the Federation's development in the 1980s and 1990s was regularly undergirded by a set of political and no less bodily forces—most notably ableism, patriarchy, and party domination—forces seemingly antithetical to the Federation's espoused goals of advancing the condition of all *canji* in China. The reader may ask, How does focusing on motorized tricycles help us understand more deeply the role those political forces played in the Federation's formation? And how can attention to motorcycles for the disabled help us to begin a discussion of issues that as yet have been little addressed in this book?

In this chapter I argue that by tracing the genealogy of these motorized tricycles we are able to gain important purchase on ways that the Federation and *canji* were influenced by a distinct set of modernist processes of embodiment. These are processes having to do with speed, political economy, and technology, which in late-twentieth-century China were deeply rooted in notions of ableism, patriarchy, and party domination. By sifting through the history of the motorized tricycles, we can glean how these processes affected what the Federation did in the 1980s and 1990s. So, too, we can grasp how the processes shaped popular understandings and experiences of *canji*. And finally, we can understand better how the Federation and *canji* mutually constructed one another.

FORDISM AND THE RISE OF THREE-WHEELER TECHNOLOGY

North American and European scholars have demonstrated that, in their countries, the long-term proliferation of wheeled mechanisms has been tied to specific modes of modernism pertaining to mass production, accumulation, and consumerism. Often, these processes have been grouped under the heading of Fordism.[1] Named for the American industrialist Henry Ford, Fordism has several features. One of the most important is the idea of time-space compression, a process whereby power—both institutional and monetary—is expanded by harnessing technology to speed up human action so that the temporal and geographic distances of productive tasks are reduced. Scholars have shown that the role of time-space compression in Fordism has involved dramatic transitions, not just in the ways people approach labor in industrial and post-industrial contexts, but also, and perhaps more significantly, in the ways in which lives are understood, evaluated, and experienced in relation to a modernist telos (Gramsci 1971; Harvey 1990; Martin 1992). All this has led to personal difference being measured in terms of one's capacity to move, think, act, and consume quickly and flexibly. It has spawned new and purportedly transposable identities relating to everything from ethnicity, athleticism, and communication, to professionalism, music, and sexuality (Hall 1996). And it has affected bodiliness in other ways. Coinciding with the growth of the biosciences and their role in economic production, an emphasis on time-space compression has contributed to the framing of bodies as mechanical entities that people experience as differentially virtuous, depending on the bodies' ease of movement and adaptability to socioeconomic change.[2]

Scholars of Fordism and its successor, post-Fordism, have most often documented the emergence, presence, and effects of regimes of time-space compression in societies with highly developed market economies, usually those characterized as "Western." Such myopia is ripe for correction, as has been suggested by several scholars. For instance, contributors to the volume *Ungrounded Empires: The Chinese Politics of Modern Chinese Transnationalism* (Ong and Nonini 1997) point out that in large tracts of East Asia over recent decades the instantiation of modernization as a set of practices, visions, and commitments has been no less contingent on the circulation of Fordist-like principles than anywhere else in the world. Of course, one must be careful to avoid analytically transposing to China, or elsewhere, specific historically situated encounters with modernism, for example, those that are distinct to automotive centers in Northern Italy or in the Great Lakes region of the United States. Nonetheless, to discount the long-standing global flows of key modernist ideas and practices such as those clumped under the heading of Fordism, or to ignore how these ideas or practices have come to be manifest in a China context, is an equally problematic proposition because to do so would reaffirm the Orientalist binary of the "West and the rest" and limit our ability to understand how sociopolitical formation in any context is shaped by tensions between the local and the global (Rofel 1999a). *Pace* such Orientalist propositions, in this chapter I try to make sense of Federation and *canji* formation in the 1980s and 1990s. I pay special attention to processes of time-space compression, and in particular to how such processes have served to differentiate and animate the national, the institutional, and the individual in China. Toward that end, I now turn to the history of motorized tricycles for *canji ren*.

POURING ASPHALT, PEDALING BICYCLES

In much of what now comprises the PRC, for centuries people have considered speed to be of great value.[3] But it was not until the twentieth century and the rise of Chinese nationalism that compressing time and space became a paramount agenda of the Chinese state. Chinese Communists have been particularly invested in speed. A perennial goal of the Communist Party, although somewhat less so during the Cultural Revolution (1966–76), has been the speeding up of human activity so as to catapult China and the Chinese people to the forefront of modernity. After 1949, one of the first ways Communist authorities symbolically and pragmatically pursued the modern was by building urban roadways. By crisscrossing cities with clean, wide, surfaced roads, the leadership not only made the landscape more conducive to speed but also symbolically pronounced to the nation and the world that a "New China" was advancing rapidly toward a socialist modernity.

Inasmuch as it was aimed at moving the entire nation toward the modern, road building also served national construction in another way by helping to configure internal frames of power and difference within a nascent People's Republic. The CCP neither expected nor allowed the Chinese people to utilize the country's freshly paved roadways equally, however much the socialist ethics of egalitarianism may have stated otherwise. It was mainly the "dictatorship of the proletariat"—the CCP's largely male elite—who were permitted to quickly and freely traverse China's newly built urban boulevards and its thousands of kilometers of unpaved roads. And the method by which this CCP elite moved about was not an inconsequential matter. Upper-rank members of the party regularly journeyed via motorized sedan. For nearly everyone else, at least during the first few decades of the People's Republic—save for truck drivers and a few others—the only motorized devices to which they had access were overcrowded buses.

One type of transportation that was increasingly visible on city roads after 1949, one that required no petroleum, was the bicycle. In what ways did bicycles serve to forge spectrums of difference and authority at the dawn of the PRC? Despite the fact they were lauded by communist leaders as an egalitarian means of transportation, bicycles helped demarcate difference and authority among "the people," as much if not more than cars or buses. They did this by marking the cyclist in two areas: residency and gender. That bicycles facilitated such differentiation likely had many sources. These include the bicycle's initial scarcity after 1949, its convenience, and the premium

CCP leaders paid to speed in their rhetoric and through their own use of the automobile. They also include patterns of resource provision emergent in the young PRC; urban-rural structures of control set in place starting in the early 1960s; long-standing linkages in China between gender, power, and space; and, no doubt, transnational flows of concepts having to do with speed, cosmopolitanism, and personhood.

After 1949 the Communist leadership took a distinctive approach to cycle technologies. On the one hand, it banned the once common hand-drawn rickshaw, on the grounds that the device was an imperialist vestige. On the other hand, it created a huge demand for bicycles by celebrating this Euro-American creation as an essential component of Chinese self-sufficiency. Yet, during that era, like many objects, bicycles were not easy to obtain in China. Until supply caught up with demand in the late 1970s, access to bicycles and most other durable goods was strictly limited by the coupon system called *gongyequan*.[4] These coupons were issued by work units *(danwei)*, and because most work units were located in cities, the coupons quickly became key benefits and markers of what in the Maoist era was an increasingly restricted right to urban residency.

As a consequence, in a relatively short amount of time, pedaling a bicycle became an important demonstration of the celebrated modern body-self; those who did so were seen as individuated urban citizens who possessed the ability and the privilege to use technology to traverse space quickly and thereby speed up society.[5] This is somewhat reflected in the Mandarin term for bicycle: *zi-xing-che*. *Zi* means "self"; *xing* means "movement, performance, or competence"; and *che* means "vehicle or machine." These separate words reflect a cultural logic—one imbricated by notions of individuality and ability—that accompanied and fueled the proliferation of bicycle usage in Chinese cities.

But bicycles were more than just about distinguishing urbanity, modernity, and competence. Many older people have explained to me that during the 1950s and 1960s bicycles were also important tools for the articulation of family formation and its relationship to masculinity and male authority. According to these older acquaintances, when bicycles were initially hard to come by, the devices had mostly been used by *jiazhang*, heads of households (a term which idiomatically and administratively has almost always been coded in the PRC as male), and, to a lesser degree, sons. The reasons seniors give for this usage pattern is that in the 1950s and 1960s a metropolitan family usually could accumulate only enough coupons to acquire one bicycle at most, and that husbands, concerned about perceptions of their male vitality, their patriarchal household position, and their commitment to national agendas, were disinclined to let their wives or daughters use the family's only transportation device

Much of the cachet associated with possessing and riding a bicycle in urban China, particularly a bicycle with a good brand name, remained strong through the 1980s and early 1990s.[6] It was during this period that production finally caught up with demand and bicycles became a ubiquitous aspect of urban citizenship for both men and women.[7]

THE HAND-CRANK TRICYCLE

The post-Mao economic reforms greatly expanded the production, consumption, and use of non-motorized cycle technologies. In the early 1980s profit-seeking manufacturers increased the supply and variety of pedal-powered devices, which now included female bicycles, child bicycles, and, eventually, mountain bikes.[8] There was at least one additional type of non-motorized cycle that began to appear in cities during the early 1980s, one that served a highly specialized domestic market. This was the "hand-crank tricycle" *(shouyao sanlun che)*, the first widely used "disability" conveyance in China.[9] Initially, most hand-crank tricycles were built in homes from old bicycle parts. But before long, factories began producing them.

Who used hand-crank bikes, what prompted them to cobble together or buy this technology, and how did such a decision relate to meanings and attitudes about bodily difference? Anecdotal observations, informal interviews, and discussions with local residents indicate that the vast majority of people in Beijing who used hand-crank tricycles were men whose lower bodies could not provide the balance and propulsion needed to operate a bicycle. Many of these men, although not all, were polio survivors.

DELEGITIMIZING *QUEZI*

Earlier, I described the importance of polio survivors in the formation of the Disabled Youths Club. What still must be explained is how a specific term, *quezi*,[10] significantly framed people's conceptions and experiences of polio at the end of the twentieth century.

After the Federation's launch, *zhiti canji ren* (physically disabled persons) was the term that government officials increasingly used to describe polio survivors and others with weak or damaged legs. But during the period of my fieldwork, I found that local citizens usually used a different term: *quezi*. A close English-language equivalent for *quezi* might be "the lame." Such a translation is wanting, however, because it underemphasizes two crucial characteristics of the word.

The first characteristic is that in late imperial China *quezi* was generally used to signify those with either a "sick hand or foot" *(shou jiao bing)*. In the wake of the Qing dynasty's demise (1911), however, the term increasingly came to designate those who had trouble "moving" *(dong)* (Lu and Dao 1996, 10–12). And, second, Chinese people have long considered *quezi* to be a pejorative term, far more so than English speakers have usually considered the term "lame" to be.

The disapprobation encoded in the term *quezi* reflects the fact that, for some time, those in China understood to have certain bodily differences have persistently undergone what Kleinman et al., in their study of Chinese epileptics, call "intersubjective delegitimation" (1995, 1328). Through complex processes, Chinese citizens have often and relentlessly objectified polio survivors, epileptics, and others with supposed defects, transmuting their so-called spoiled bodies *(shen)* into objects of flawed social and moral status *(shenfen)*. As a consequence, polio survivors and others have for years been denied educational opportunities, made the butt of jokes, shunned as potential marriage partners or employers, and treated with paternalism or bureaucratic indifference.

As I discussed in Chapter 2, such delegitimation and discrimination occurred in the 1990s partially because of the importance Chinese "tradition" (as inscribed in, reified by, and passed on through the recitation of classic texts) has long placed on bodily perfection as an indicator of moral and spiritual standing. But, to be sure, beyond visible bodily perfection (however defined), people in the late twentieth century also considered the lives of *quezi* as "spoiled" because they were lacking in the ability to traverse space.

SPEED, CYCLE TECHNOLOGY, AND THE TRANSFORMATION OF *QUEZI*

Two assertions I make in this chapter are that modernist concepts of space, speed, and mechanization have played significant roles in strengthening the delegitimation of both the *quezi* and *canji* categories and that this has caused the two terms to undergo similar transformations in meaning.

If, as Lu and Dao tell us (1996, 10–12), the term *quezi* morphed during the last century from referring to someone with a "sick hand or foot" to denoting a person who has trouble "moving," should we be surprised that a parallel transformation occurred with the word *canji*? During the late imperial period, *canji* often signified an inchoate array of conditions loosely associated with injury and disease (see Chapter 2). Yet, by the time I was conducting fieldwork in Beijing's Xuanwu district and Hainan's Wenchang County, people were affixing a far more circumscribed array of meanings to *canji*. For instance, whenever I asked residents in those two locales to tell me about someone in their neighborhood who they considered *canji*, I consistently received responses that closely matched that given by Mr. Zhang Li, a twenty-five-year-old Wenchang shrimp farmer.

> *Canji, canji* . . . uh . . . Yes, there is one of those guys who lives nearby. His name is Ah Wen. He lives over there near the tea house. . . . He can't walk. He

has to use a pole to hop around. He hasn't been able to move around [*dong*] for years. He's such a *quezi*.

The conceptual link *canji*–immobility–*quezi* present in Zhang's reply also surfaced regularly when I asked Beijing and Hainanese residents: "Who's *canji*?" Of the innumerable replies I was offered to that question, the vast majority closely matched the following one by Ms. Lin Lichen, a forty-five-year-old Wenchang resident: "Who's *canji*? Oh, they're people who can't get around [*dong buliaode*], people who can't walk [*zou buliaode*]. You know, *quezi*."

To be sure, in Beijing the responses I received to the question "Who's *canji*?" were frequently more broadly worded than the one provided by Ms. Lin. One might conjecture that capital city residents' more expansive understanding of the term may have stemmed from their relatively greater exposure to global disability discourse and to the rhetoric of the Federation and its antecedent, the Blind, Deaf and Mute Association. This was regularly suggested to me when I questioned Xuanwu residents, such as Chen Meilin, a fifty-two-year-old factory worker, about *canji*:

> MK: Could you tell me who's *canji*?
>
> Ms. Chen: The *canji* . . . they're simply people who can't walk, *quezi*, people who have a crippled foot.
>
> MK: Could anyone else be *canji*?
>
> Ms. Chen: Other than *quezi*? Well, I think you could also say the blind and the deaf are *canji*. Yeah, they probably could be included, too. After all, we used to have that Association, the Deaf, Mute and Blind Association. Isn't that what it was called?
>
> MK: Does anyone else qualify as *canji*?
>
> Ms. Chen: You might say that dwarfs are also *canji*. And I think other countries say that the *sha* [the mentally retarded] are, too.
>
> MK: Anyone else?
>
> Ms. Chen: No. That's it. I think that's it.

What this exchange and many others like it helped me to grasp during my research was that, although Chinese citizens' understanding of *canji* is elastic and responsive to various forms of discursive intervention (global, national, and local), in the 1990s, at the core of their understanding of *canji* was often the term *quezi* and the concept of immobility.

BICYCLES AND CATEGORIES OF DIFFERENCE

To understand how technologies of time-space compression helped intertwine the notions of immobility and the terms *canji* and *quezi*, it is helpful to turn again to the bicycle. As many Beijingers have explained to me, the rise in bicycle usage from the 1950s through the 1990s greatly amplified the perception that certain people were slow and unable to move through space easily and, thus, that they were undesirable. Initially, because they were engineered to be powered by bodies of a specific sort, bicycles often had little to no positive application for people, such as polio survivors, who could not produce the necessary coordinated leg movements. More importantly, bicycles were devices that—rather than salubriously expressing social rank, personhood, and belonging—accentuated an aura of moral, political, and economic decline among polio survivors. As a Beijing survivor named Meng told me, "The sudden growth of bicycles in China didn't help us a bit. They just made people like me slower, more incompetent [*geng bu nenggan*], and more *que*."

Ironically, it was because the proliferation of bicycles delegitimized persons like Mr. Meng that he and many others chose to cobble together a form of cycle technology that was amenable to their needs. "To *keep up* with everyone else, to participate in the quickening pace of social development," remarked an older man named Zheng, "we had to devise something to help us move around, and to help us move around independently." By transforming bicycles into hand-crank tricycles, and later by buying the mass-produced replicas of these cycles, many urbanites like Messrs. Zheng and Meng found a way to keep up.

No doubt, hand-crank tricycles afforded some of the most visible expressions of "bodily difference" in Chinese cities during the 1980s. And, although these machines allowed many people to travel by themselves at speeds faster than ever before possible, thereby allowing them to demonstrate an ability to use time-space compression, the overall speed of the vehicles was slower than that of bicycles. Owing to such visibility and relative slowness, hand-crank tricycles further contributed to the common view in the 1990s that *canji/quezi* were those people who had difficulty traversing space, that, in the words of Celeste Langan, they were at once "hostages to speed and to a failure to maintain speed" (2001, 462).

GENDER, SPACE, AND CYCLE USAGE

To sort out further how understandings of the *canji* and *quezi* categories were changing in the late twentieth century and how cycle technology may have been implicated in those changes, one must also consider more fully the relationship between time-space compression and gender, because during that period, male/female differentiation greatly informed how the categories of *canji* and *quezi* were used and how tricycle technology was distributed.

First, however, I should clarify how I use the term "gender," by which I do not mean a strict and fixed binary, that is, one demarcated along the lines of all men sharing an essential set of traits and all women sharing another, equally essential, set of traits. Nor do I mean the all too simplistic and epistemologically untenable dimorphism of "sex is biology/gender is culture." Rather, following the insights of third-wave feminist scholars, I see both male/female and sex/gender as socially constructed, historically mediated, and relational frameworks that are always in flux (Butler 1990; Nicholson 1990). That is not to say that those two binaries have no saliency in the People's Republic of China today or that they have not been dominant logics for identity-making there in the past. That would be foolish. But instead of treating the binaries a priori, as pre-given, I take it as the intellectual's task to understand the sociopolitical processes that reinforce and amplify gender distinctions and inequalities. What is more, in the spirit of Nietzsche, who argued there is no "being" behind doing, effecting, and becoming (1967, 45), I see it as the goal of all anthropologists to investigate the means (e.g., administrative, technological, performative, discursive) by which people define and fashion themselves, whether in terms of gender or any other method of identification.[11]

A number of authors, writing about people of non-Chinese ancestry, have discussed gender and technologies of time-space compression. They have argued that such technologies have frequently been props for the performance of gender, serving to define the masculine in relation to the feminine and disproportionately benefiting men (Bourque and Warren 1987; Bolton 1979; Connell 1995; Mosse 1985; Oldenziel 1999; Scharff 1991).[12]

In the 1980s and 1990s technologies of time-space compression were no less pivotal for demarcating and celebrating the *nanzihan,* the "real Chinese man" (or, more literally, the "the Han male"). After Mao's death and the subsequent loosening of residency regulations, more and more men and women of working age in China became willing, if not eager, to venture away from home to earn a better living, thereby ostensibly challenging the synchronicity of the public/private and male/female binaries that scholars have noted as long being a character of life in China.[13] But while many Chinese were keen to work, live, and travel away from home, and they regularly used machines of time-space compression to do so, the control and operation of those machines in China (particularly the fastest ones) was generally normatively prescribed as a performative aspect of masculinity. Whether it was tractors or trucks, motorcycles or cars, ships or trains, buses or airplanes, it was male subjectivity that was generally expected to be driving those machines and it was male more than female subjectivity that was wont for affirmation through such actions.[14]

My acquaintances, from all walks of life in Beijing and Hainan during the 1990s, were more than willing to discuss with me connections between gender, space, and speed. Some of the most poignant comments came from female taxi drivers, then a relative rarity in many parts of China. When I asked them about challenges they had faced in their profession, the female drivers consistently said that they felt that operating a taxi was "less suitable" for women because it contradicted expectations that they should be "watching over the house," because venturing alone away from the hearth was "more dangerous for women than men," and because "it [was] more important for men to use vehicles to move around quickly than it [was] for women."

Statements like these, I would suggest, go a long way in explaining why over the years tricycle technology (be it hand-crank or motorized) has been so highly associated with male *quezi*, why at one of the county's largest retailers of three-wheeled conveyances for the disabled, the staff in 1995 were unable to remember ever selling a vehicle either to or for a woman.

Less transparent, however, is another gender-specific phenomenon that strongly influenced who adopted hand-crank or motorized tricycles technology. This phenomenon is intersubjective delegitimation. During interviews and informal conversations with people in Beijing, I repeatedly confronted the fact that being a polio survivor or having any kind of easily perceived difficulty with mobility has often been excruciating. But what I came to understand more slowly is that how such pain manifests itself has been notably differentiated in terms of a male/female gender binary. This juxtaposition is strongly evidenced in the comments of Beijingers regarding tricycles. Many women who have trouble walking have told me they would never drive a hand-crank or motorized tricycle because it would only draw attention to their appearance *(waimao)*. As a Ms. Cai once said, "Women who have trouble walking are less able to endure people's looks and comments about our appearance when we go out in public. We're much happier staying at home. In some ways, staying at home just makes us feel like good traditional women." Many men in the same situation, by contrast, have articulated sentiments similar to that of a Mr. Lin:

> Sure, the stares hurt. But, in the past, when I was young, what hurt even more was being closed up in the house. I'm never going back to that kind of life. . . . I'm not going to be a hermit because people look at me. I'm going to get outside any way I can. You know, move around, find work, show people I can participate in all this rapid economic development going on around me.

In other words, it would seem that in the 1990s the most challenging and corrosive aspect of not being able to walk easily for the performance of masculinity was immobility, whereas the most worrisome aspect for femininity was visible imperfection.[15] And whereas these sociopolitical crosswinds were likely to compel those wanting to present themselves as decidedly masculine to venture out into public, the same winds were more likely to drive indoors those wishing to be seen as adequately feminine.

GENDER DIFFERENTIATION AND THE CATEGORIES OF *CANJI* AND *QUEZI*

In light of the en/gendering of space, pathos, and subjectivity described thus far, how did most people I met apply the terms *canji* and *quezi*? Lao Wen usually set up her cart outside the courtyard home where I lived during one of my longer field stays in Beijing. Although I often stopped to chat with her, I never bought any of her glistening product. Wen sold unpackaged, brick-sized blocks of coagulated pigs' blood, a favorite item among some of the retirees in the neighborhood. One evening, not long after Wen and I had chatted briefly about some of my research, she knocked on my door. "Why, Lao Wen, what a surprise to see you," I said. "Xiao Gao, I was thinking there is someone you'd like to meet," she responded. "Why, thank you. Please, please come in and sit down, have some tea." "Oh no, that's not necessary. You said you're interested in learning more about the lives of *canji ren*. I thought I'd take you around and introduce you to *canji ren* who live nearby. There's a couple of *quezi* who've lived here for years. Maybe you've seen them. Either way, you should meet them. I can help you with that. They're the grandsons of some of my regular customers."

My exchange with Wen that evening was far from exceptional. When I would ask Beijing and Hainan residents to describe a *canji* neighbor, not only did they tell me about residents who had trouble walking, but nearly every time they described the neighbor, it was in the language of so-and-so's grandson, brother, son, nephew, or husband.[16] When I first noticed this trend early in my Hainan research and then again in Beijing, one reaction was to reexamine the 1987 National Sample Survey of Disabled Persons, particularly its data about interactions between the binaries of *canji/jianquan* and male/female. After all, the survey had collected information from both Beijing's Xuanwu district and Hainan's Wenchang County. What I found was that the survey's findings for these two locations conflicted with the highly male vision of *canji* that residents in each community had been providing me. According to the government's survey, in both Xuanwu and Wenchang, female inhabitants had slightly higher rates of disability than males.[17]

I found similarly conflicting portraits of *canji*—one portrait appeared to be more government-driven and female in orientation, and the other appeared more community-driven and male—when I scrutinized disability registration records. These are documents that, over the years, central Federation leaders have expected individual Federation chapters to create in order to catalogue who in the given region is eligible for disability benefits. In the 1980s and the early 1990s, the central Federation had issued no unifying methodology for how registration should occur. Local offices had the criteria from the 1987 survey to lean on, but little else. As a consequence, registration techniques varied widely from place to place. This variability is illustrated by the registration records of Xuanwu district and Min Song village (my Wenchang field site). In the case of Min Song, one of that community's four cadres had created the registration records in October 1992, at the request of the county's Federation office, and he had based his records on the 1987 criteria. But he also did this without the consent of village residents. In Xuanwu, by contrast, Federation officials had been adding the names of residents to registration records since 1987. This occurred usually only on request from individual residents or their family member (who sometimes were compelled to make such requests under duress, as was the case for Ma Zhun in Chapter 2).

Particularly interesting is how the different recruitment methodologies undergirding these two sets of registration records—one methodology more government-driven, one less so—appear to have generated somewhat contrasting gender portraits of who was *canji*. For the more government-driven case of Min Song, the gender ratio of registrants was 0.7 males for every female. But for the Xuanwu case, the ratio in December 1994 was nearly the inverse: 1.4 males for every female.

What data like these helped me understand as my study progressed was that for most people I met—whether they were Beijing merchants or Wenchang farmers—the archetypal image of the *canji ren* (the disabled person) was not simply someone who had trouble walking. More specifically, it was often someone who had trouble walking and who was male. In other words, the paradigmatic popular portrait of a disabled person was the very sort of person who most frequently adopted hand-crank tricycles.[18]

ENTER THE MOTORIZED TRICYCLE AND THE FEDERATION

In the late 1980s a new transportation device became available to such paradigmatic disabled people. This was the machine I had first observed outside the Asian Games Village. Chinese citizens usually refer to these gasoline-powered conveyances as three-wheelers, disability bikes, or motorized tricycles. For the informed PRC observer, the machines appear to be spin-offs of at least two preexisting and originally quite hypermasculine devices of time-space compression: the hand-held tractor and the police motorcycle with side-car.

From whence did China's motorized tricycles emanate? On the most specific level, they are the product of one of the Federation's earliest subsidiaries, having been designed and brought to market by the China Rehabilitation Research Center. But on a more general level, these machines—their genesis, their proliferation, and their subsequent bureaucratization—are the product of social forces that include the institution-building agenda of the Federation and ongoing Fordist-oriented processes.

As noted, from the 1980s forward, Deng Pufang and his staff employed several strategies to garner support for the emergent Federation. One of these pertains to the disability-assistance programs the Federation launched in the first decade of its existence. At that time, when Federation leaders designed and coordinated modes of disability assistance, they did so with an important agenda in mind: that their assistance programs might easily and effectively be represented to the general public as concrete proof that the Federation was doing tangible good (i.e., that it was allaying the suffering and improving the livelihood of the disabled).

From the very instant that Deng Pufang left Ottawa and began his advocacy work, one sphere of technological assistance took center stage in this emergent institution-building strategy and that was the vaguely conceived realm of rehabilitation medicine *(kangfu yiliao)*. In order to understand how modernist notions about power and mobility were implicated in the Federation's deployment of rehabilitation medicine, several Federation projects might be considered. The one central to this chapter is the Federation's three-wheeled motorcycle initiative. But before moving on to discuss that initiative, it is useful to analyze another Federation program briefly.

THE THREE REHABILITATIONS PROJECT

The Three Rehabilitations Project (TRP) was the Federation's largest assistance program from the mid-1980s to the mid-1990s. It consisted of three modes of intervention: (1) cataract surgery, (2) polio-correction surgery, and (3) oral-language training for deaf children. When the TRP began in the mid-1980s, Federation leaders in Beijing, with the support of central party and government agencies, set up national quota figures for the three interventions, and they directed local Federation representatives to ensure that the quotas were fulfilled with the cooperation of local government officials and healthcare providers.

By the mid-1990s the TRP had provided treatment to hundreds of thousands of disabled people across the country. The program had also spawned, it must be mentioned, a steady stream of local and national media reports about individuals who had been transformed by the humanitarian rehabilitation efforts of the Federation.

Throughout the TRP's first decade, as its quotas were met and its attendant media reports were generated, Deng Pufang often spoke in public forums about the importance of the Three Rehabilitations Project. During his presentations, Deng regularly invoked an argument to justify the TRP that went as follows: the key mission of the TRP (and the Federation's emphasis on rehabilitation medicine more generally) is to use the most modern scientific techniques to help those people who would otherwise fall behind to *speed up* and actively contribute to the rapid economic developments that have been stimulated by Deng Xiaoping's reforms (Deng 1988).

To appreciate how the logic of time-space compression informed the TRP, though, one must look beyond this kind of rhetoric (of the speeding up of the *canji*) to the project's very design. During a visit to Beijing in 1996, high-ranking Federation officials explained this to me. They said that the decision to conduct the tightly defined TRP and the choice of what forms of rehabilitation technology would be used had had as much to do with the Federation leaders' desires to speed up people's lives as their desires to speed up the institution's own development. More to the point, I heard that the specific TRP treatments had been chosen because (1) the Federation leadership saw these treatments as quick and effective procedures for mollifying specific areas of disability, (2) they could easily be used to expedite the flow of positive publicity for the Federation, and (3) as previously mentioned, the Federation recognized that Deng Pufang's power to persuade military medical personnel to do a sizable amount of the initial TRP work, and thereby move the Federation's rehabilitation agenda along faster, was fleeting.

CATEGORICAL INEQUALITY

Before proceeding further, several characteristics of the TRP need to be fleshed out—some of which, I would suggest, reflect tendencies inherent to a vast majority of Federation activities from the mid-1980s to the mid-1990s and which were clearly present in the Federation's motorcycle initiatives.

First, the TRP did not include provisions for two of the five categories of disability recognized by the Federation, "psychiatric disability" and "mental disability." A high-ranking Federation official responsible for the design and implementation of the TRP, who I will call Mr. Zhao, explained this oversight to me one evening while we were eating at a Beijing restaurant. I wrote the following dialogue in my notebook a few minutes after it occurred:

> *Mr. Zhao:* When we designed the TRP campaign, we at the Federation wanted to produce propaganda that would help the Federation grow quickly. So, at that time it was decided that focusing rehabilitation resources on the mentally ill and mentally disabled would not be a priority.
>
> *MK:* Why couldn't rehabilitating the mentally ill and the mentally disabled help you?
>
> *Mr. Zhao:* At that time people didn't associate the mentally ill [*jingshen bing*] or retarded [*sha*] with disability, so propaganda about their rehabilitation wouldn't have been seen as relevant to the Federation. But more important than that, as was our understanding at the time, rehabilitating the mentally ill and retarded was just too difficult, too slow, and too costly.

These statements illustrate two significant Federation features. First, the organization did not assist its constituents equally in the 1980s and 1990s.

And, second, the unequal way the organization meted out care during this period was both a reflection of the vision of disability then circulating throughout the Chinese polity and of the Federation's developmental experience (its institution-building imperatives and the constraints confronted by those imperatives).

The most slighted of the Federation's five categories of disabled constituents were certainly the mentally ill and the mentally disabled. Some Federation chapters in some circumscribed geographic locales, to be sure, did coordinate a limited number of programs for the mentally ill and mentally disabled during the 1980s and 1990s. Yet, no matter what area of Federation outreach one examines—rehabilitation care, educational services, vocational training, job placement, arts and sports programming, entrepreneurial development, or intradisability socializing—a general pattern persisted: the Federation provided far fewer resources to the mentally ill and mentally disabled than it did to people in the institution's three other categories of disablement. Moreover, it would not be an overstatement to say that, during this period, the Federation system generally either left the survival of the mentally ill and the mentally disabled up to individual families or expected responsibility for them to be picked up by the three government branches already charged with "managing" such people, that is, by China's acutely understaffed psychiatric community, the State Education Commission's small network of special education providers, and the Public Security Ministry (which historically has been the disciplinary arm for mental health provision in the PRC).

In terms of Federation attention and resources, two other officially recognized categories of disability—the deaf and the blind—did not fare much better. On the surface, this is somewhat difficult to discern, since the existence of the TRP, as well as the numerous blind and deaf schools across the country, seems to indicate that the Federation was committed to aiding its visually and hearing-disabled constituents. But aside from the two pertinent branches of the TRP and a limited number of other small initiatives, the Federation provided few sizeable benefits for the blind and the deaf. What about the special schools? While some of them were built with administrative assistance from the Federation, a large percentage of them were created earlier under the auspices of the now defunct Blind, Deaf, and Mute Association. Moreover, during the 1980s and 1990s, the Federation played only an ancillary role in either building or running the schools and instead left responsibility for them in the hands of the State Education Commission.

MOVING ONTO MOTORCYCLES

Thus, as I have been illuminating, a convergence existed in the 1980s and 1990s between the popular portrait of the *canji ren* and those people the

Federation aided most fully. To better appreciate this convergence—how it was influenced not only by modernist principles about speed but also by the Federation's developmental patterns during the era of the Deng Xiaoping reforms—let us now more fully consider the three-wheeled motorcycle.

As noted, these vehicles were originally designed by the China Rehabilitation Research Center (CRRC). More specifically, they were created by an arm of the center, the Rehabilitation Engineering Institute. One of the institute's engineers in charge of the three-wheeled motorcycle project from its inception explained to me how he and his cohort of largely male colleagues conceived of the device. Two particular features of his explanation that have struck me as especially significant are that the creativity and resources the engineers marshaled were directed by male-to-male empathy, and that this empathy was contingent on a Fordist-like reverence for speed and productivity.

> Shortly after our institute was formed, a group of us engineers were trying to think of items we could create that'd be highly beneficial to disabled people and that'd help the Federation. At that time, here in Beijing, there were all these people struggling to use hand-crank tricycles. We at the institute knew some of these people. It was really pitiful to watch them! The tricycles they used were so slow and they took so much effort to propel. So, one day, somebody at the institute suggested that our first product be a motorized tricycle. Looking back, it turned out to be a very easy thing to accomplish. We came up with a few designs, took them to a Beijing factory, and had some prototypes made. Since then, the Federation has licensed a number of factories around the country to make the machines. . . . Overall, it's been a great success, probably the most successful product our institute has ever created. Now all the people who once struggled to crank a few kilometers an hour are able to race around. They're able to be productive. They're able to find work, to get jobs, or to start their own business.

THE PROLIFERATION OF THREE-WHEELERS

By the early 1990s, motorized tricycles could be found in greatest concentration in China's highly structured metropolitan transportation landscape. To anyone visiting China for the first time during that period, urban traffic probably seemed anything but structured. Yet, despite the growing malady of vehicular gridlock, branches of the state remained committed to keeping urban roadways under tight control.[19] This meant that getting around urban China by any method besides foot, human-powered cycle, or mass transportation remained very much a privilege and a mark of high status.

The fact that three-wheelers enjoyed such a privileged position stemmed, in large part, from their institutional and symbolic link to Deng Pufang. In the beginning, the Federation, vehicle manufacturers, and users barely had to emphasize the Deng connection in order to keep traffic authorities in major cities from stepping in and restricting three-wheelers. But this changed in the early 1990s when the numbers of motorized tricycles started to surge—to such a degree that, by 1995, Shanghai had at least twelve thousand of them and Beijing more than thirty thousand (Li 1995; Zhang 1995).

One force behind the exponential growth in motorized tricycles was their unregulated status and speed, both of which made them extremely useful tools for entrepreneurs, disabled or otherwise.[20] Another force was how tricycle-enabled entrepreneurship melded so well with the neoliberal tenets being promoted by the CCP's post-Mao leadership and how early Federation development became increasingly contingent on those tenets. The clout of Deng Pufang notwithstanding, the young Federation neither had the resources nor the backing from the party-state to provide cash outlays for *canji ren*. Instead, taking its cues from the prevailing political winds blowing out of Beijing, the Federation opted to promote small-scale private entrepreneurship as a means to *canji ren* and Federation well-being. During our interviews, senior Federation staff regularly conveyed two points to me with great pride: that growing numbers of *canji ren* across the country had registered for tax exemptions under a special provision created for independent *canji* businesses, and that the Federation's motorized tricycle project was indispensable in promoting this kind of activity.

Something the Federation staff never pointed out, however, was that the Federation's emphasis on independent entrepreneurship tended to serve male constituents disproportionately and to exalt masculinist formations that were deleterious to women. Small-scale entrepreneurship, as it gradually reemerged in the years following Mao's death, was a significant domain of gender differentiation. According to a national survey conducted by China's Social Science Academy, possibly as many as 90 percent of China's private business people in 1992 were male (Institute of Sociology 1994).[21] What's more, as Everett Zhang (2001) has demonstrated, this burgeoning socioeconomic sector was contingent on the Othering of women and tended to fuel misogynistic undercurrents in China's gender regimes. Most notably, business activity in the 1990s was dependent on and fostered patterns of manliness, what Zhang calls "entrepreneurial masculinity," which were predicated upon, at once, male-to-male exclusivity and the commodification of women's bodies and sexuality. Perhaps these trends explain why, despite my best efforts, I encountered relatively few women over the course of my research who had established independent businesses with *canji* entrepreneurial status.

Something else that Federation staff members were not inclined to mention was that motorized tricycles had become cash cows for the institution since the primary purveyors of the devices at the retail level were Federation chapters. By the mid-1990s, selling motorized tricycles had become a big business for many chapters and a primary source of funds.²² Initially, when supplies were limited, chapter staff created waiting lists and restricted sales to only those people who they viewed as demonstrably disabled. But, as supplies grew, many chapters began selling three-wheelers to anyone who wanted them.²³

POLICING THREE-WHEELERS

In 1994 a number of city governments—alarmed by the growth of three-wheelers and their unbridled use of public space—banned them. One outcome of the moratorium was that groups of people in several cities joined together to resist the bans. Many of these people represented themselves by a social category that, in China's long history, quite possibly had never before been invoked as a unifying signifier for popular resistance. Who were these protesters and what category did they invoke? Nearly all of them were men who called themselves *canji*. Initially, they protested locally, descending en masse upon city government buildings and demanding that the ban be lifted. When that failed, many brought their grievances to the eastern edge of the Forbidden City, to 44 Beichizi Road, the headquarters of the Central Disabled Persons' Federation. A senior Federation official, who recounted these events to me under condition of anonymity, said the most ardent of the regional protesters was a group of men from the northeastern industrial city of Shenyang. They traveled to Beijing twice in 1994, requesting that Deng Pufang intervene. Deng responded by inviting Shenyang's mayor and Liaoning Province's governor to 44 Beichizi for extensive meetings. But before the meetings had gotten very far, the Federation's main office in Shanghai began reporting that similar protests were breaking out there.

Realizing he had a national problem on his hand, Deng Pufang again exercised his prerogative as Deng Xiaoping's son. He contacted the government functionary who had possibly the greatest administrative authority over public space in China, the Minister of Public Security. Deng and the minister met several times during the spring and summer of 1995. Their meetings were paralleled by lengthy discussions between high officials from both the Ministry and the Federation. Ministry staff initially reasserted the stance that three-wheelers were dangerous and disruptive to public order and thus should be banned. The Federation cadres countered with arguments for an alternative intervention, one that would involve licensing regulations and would permit three-wheeler sales to continue.²⁴

After only modest resistance, the Ministry of Public Security accepted this alternative and in early 1995 signed a detailed set of regulations. The staff at 44 Beichizi were jubilant. It is easy to understand why. Besides being an important revenue stream for local chapters, the vermilion tricycles were

Figure 4. A snowy day in Beijing.

quickly becoming the most visible icons of the Federation and its constituency—disabled people—to be found on a daily basis in urban China.
Local government attempts to banish three-wheelers were a direct challenge to both the Federation and its constituents' attempt to "speed up," to
amass more power.

THE CONCEPTUAL REIFICATION OF DISABILITY

By the end of the 1990s, it was not clear if or how Federation–Public
Security intervention had affected popular definitions of disability across
the country. But based on my time in Beijing, where such an intervention
had gone into affect some years earlier, it seemed the agreement was probably going to help promote *canji*'s visibility as an emergent form of state-
sanctioned alterity and that it would intensify the linkage between the term
canji and the concept of immobility. The national-level intervention had
entailed a major and very public bureaucratization of three-wheelers. To
avoid fines, users of the devices thereafter had to register as legal owner-
operators, and to do this they had to cross a series of administrative barriers
and subject themselves to intensive institutional scrutiny.[25] Also, from that
point forward, police increasingly monitored motorized tricycle drivers vis-
à-vis disability; that is to say, police increasingly stopped tricyclists and evaluated their credentials and bodily status.[26]

This was strongly evident in March 1995 when I witnessed Beijing's Fourteenth Automatic Tricycle Rectification Campaign and followed its coverage in the mass media. One hundred police teams spread out across the city, stopping three-wheelers that either lacked a license plate or that were operated by anyone the police suspected might not be legally certified as a *canji* driver. According to a *Beijing Evening News* article of February 21, 1995, the previous citywide rectification project had occurred a year earlier and had resulted in 16,330 drivers being fined and the impoundment of nearly 6,000 trikes. All this surveillance, one can only assume, prompted people on the streets to scrutinize drivers all the more and to wonder, "Is that person really disabled?" Indeed, Beijing friends have said that, during both campaigns, daily conversation often turned to two questions—Who should be driving these vehicles? And who really counts as disabled?—with the seeming supposition that the answer to one was the answer to the other.

Of course, it is impossible to discern how these campaigns may have been a reflection of what was happening in urban settings elsewhere across China during subsequent years. Yet, if "rectification" projects occurred with similar frequency and intensity in other Chinese cities, which anecdotal evidence indicates they did, it is reasonable to assume that more and more persons countrywide came to occupy their time thinking about *canji* and to think about it the way ever larger numbers of people did during my field stays in the capital. As one of many Beijingers answered when I asked her "What constitutes *canji*?": "Oh, *canji*. They're the ones the police permit to drive motorized tricycles. You know, *quezi*. People who can't walk."

MEN AND FEDERATION ASSISTANCE

Before moving on to the final portion of this chapter—in which I address the ways that use of motorized tricycles shaped the lives of some owner-operators—a few more words must be said about how the Federation developed during the 1980s and early 1990s.

Over that period, as already noted, Federation-directed assistance tended to have at least two effects on the production of *canji* as a sphere of alterity. First, the ways by which Federation assistance attracted and benefited people seemed to be refracted through binaries, most notably those of male/female and physically disabled/other-kinds-of-disabled. Second, "men," and, more specifically, "physically disabled men" tended to receive the greatest amount of Federation support.

As indicated above, these patterns no doubt stemmed from how various forces—like the cultural logics of space, movement, and entrepreneurship, as well as bodily integrity—made the public presentation of a *canji* persona more problematic for the management of a female as opposed to a male subject position. Other factors also contributed, though, including the gen-

Figure 5. A now former employee of the Xuan Wu District Disabled Persons' Federation repairing his mototrike outside the entryway to his office in the mid-1990s.

eral circumstance that, despite collective exposure to decades of Maoist rhetoric on gender neutrality, Chinese citizens during the 1980s and 1990s continued to organize their lives around a male/female binary so intensely that men and women often occupied highly differentiated social spaces, behaved in contrasting ways, and used different linguistic techniques for goal achievement. No less important, I should add, was the degree to which that very same binary was then structuring Federation hiring.

How did these various factors militate against the Federation being a social-assistance agency equally welcoming to male and female subjectivity? As Ms. Lin, who had been laid off from a factory in the Xuanwu district, said about Federation staff:

> Since there are so few women running the Federation, I usually stay clear of that place altogether. It's just too much trouble trying to figure out how to talk with the male officials. They're so often gruff and worried about face. I get confused trying to say the right thing to them. Whenever I've tried, I've always seemed to do it wrong and end up feeling more miserable.

Another explanation came from Mai Dilie, a Beijing Federation official. He provided this comment a few weeks after I told him that a program he was developing—the "affirmative action" hiring initiative that required cap-

ital city work units to employ a certain number of disabled people—seemed
to be enlisting few local *canji* women. The affirmative action initiative had
been launched, in part, to deal with the exceedingly high rate of unemployment among those urbanites fitting the Federation's *canji* criteria.[27]

> You know, I've thought a lot about what you said earlier. I can see now that
> there is a discrepancy in the numbers of *canji* men and *canji* women . . . being
> enlisted in this program. I think a big reason is that people like me, men work-
> ing at local Federation offices, find interacting with women a lot more incon-
> venient. We're just not used to talking with women. So, you could say, we're
> less likely to take note of their needs.

This statement, I would suggest, also helps shed light on why the CRRC's
Rehabilitation Engineering Institute responded the way it did back in the
mid-1980s: why its cohort of mostly male scientists were inclined to take
notice of, to show sympathy toward, and to engineer their first device for a
relatively small population of men who were operating hand-crank tricycles
around Beijing.

Yet, complicit with this sexism both inside and outside the Federation,
there was a further reason why, during the 1980s and 1990s, the Federation
generally underserviced women, and that was the strong desire on the part
of the Federation's leadership to "enable" its many chapters quickly.
Federation officials in Beijing and Hainan told me on a number of occasions that, because of the Federation's need to develop rapidly, they had felt
considerable pressure to succeed whenever they organized assistance programs. Such pressure, many conceded, had strongly influenced their selection criteria when the time came to decide which disabled people should
participate in programs. More to the point, officials said they tended to
favor those *canji* constituents who were the most able, the most well educated, and the most comfortable being in public. Because many in the country continue to undervalue female educational achievement, and because of
the view running through much of contemporary China that men are (and
should be) more able than women, especially in domains involving the
state,[28] women were perforce placed at a competitive disadvantage in terms
of selection for Federation programs.

THE EXPERIENCE OF AUTOMATIC TRICYCLE USE

Now that I have described several processes that influenced the Federation's
three-wheelers initiative, it is time to switch gears and consider, however
briefly, some of the ways these processes and devices shaped the lives of *canji*
motorcyclists. Too often, I would suggest, anthropologists and historians
provide effective analyses of how new mechanisms come into being without
giving attention to how these technologies relate to the coming-into-being

of local people. In other words, scholars must do more than simply chronicle the "social life of things," to borrow a phrase from Appadurai (1986). Indeed, it is incumbent upon us to detail the lived experiences of the people who use the things.

Given the circumstances described above, what was it like for people, like the men I met outside the ping-pong stadium, to buy and use three-wheeled devices to facilitate their time-space compression? My taped interviews conducted with Beijing tricyclists are helpful in this regard. Peng Dushan, who in 1995 ran a convenience store not far from Lao Wen's home, told me the following:

> Those old hand-crank tricycles were remarkable devices. They let disabled people like me have concrete contact with society, often for the first time. I got my first hand-crank tricycle in 1985, when I was 22. I started working at a factory a little less than a year afterwards. It was utterly transformative getting a tricycle. With it I was able to leave home and go out and see the multi-colored world. Before then, I rarely had contact with anyone. I was closed out.
>
> I purchased my first disability motorcycle three years later. I was still at the factory then, so I was able to pay for most of the three-wheeler myself. The initial feeling of driving a hand-crank bike and driving a motorcycle was very different. My initial impression of my first motorcycle was how much quicker it was than bicycles. The second impression was that, without any force, I could go incredibly fast. At first, I was spooked by it being so much faster than bicycles. I was scared to take it out on the big boulevards and drive rapidly with all the cars. Coping with this fear took a long time. I didn't dare drive more than 20 kilometers an hour back then. Not like now. Now I'll go 50.
>
> Getting a three-wheeler, at first, gave me a deep sense of satisfaction. I couldn't drive a car, but I had the ability [*nengli*] to drive this sort of motorcycle. That gave me a real sense of power and vanity [*xurongxing*]. I think all men have this sort of vanity. That I could drive this kind of vehicle really boosted mine. That heightened feeling of vanity has pretty much disappeared, however. Now, after six years on the road, I just look at my motorized tricycle as a transportation tool. It's something I can't survive without. If I go out the door, I must use it. I couldn't live or run my business without it.
>
> Still, as I see it, there are clear pros and cons to motorized tricycles. My scope of activity is much greater. That's one pro. I've driven as far as 150 kilometers to a tourist spot in Hebei with a bunch of disabled friends. Another [pro] is that the motorcycle has given me the ability to open my own business and start supporting my parents.
>
> One of the cons is, physically, I'm nowhere as strong as when I used a hand-crank bike. Before, I was strong enough to crank myself 10 kilometers in less than twenty-five minutes, almost as fast as some bicycle riders. Now, I probably couldn't crank 10 kilometers an hour. Another con is the danger of accident. That's why I wear a helmet. If I crash and become more disabled, I'm done for. As an independent businessman, I have no national health insurance, no nothing. If I have a serious accident, I'm dead.

The next excerpt is from a thirty-nine-year-old man, Liu Guoze. Like Peng Dushan, Liu contracted polio before he was old enough for grade school. This left his lower limbs so weakened he could not walk without leg braces and crutches. Liu rarely left his house until 1988, when, with the help of his parents and siblings, with whom he lived, he purchased his first disability motorcycle. A few years later, Liu opened a tobacco store by taking advantage of the Federation-sponsored regulation that allowed certain officially registered disabled persons to receive tax-exempt status for their own businesses. By 1995, Mr. Liu was making a good living from his store, and he contributed more to the family's finances than his retired parents combined.

MK: Can you tell me about getting your first three-wheeled motorcycle?

Liu: Before I got it, my life was pretty miserable. I had my hand-crank tricycle. But it was so slow. I couldn't accomplish much with it, and I certainly couldn't use it to make a living. And because it was only *quezi* who used them, I think my hand-crank tricycle made people see me as that much stranger.

 I purchased [my first motorcycle] from the factory, very near the Rehabilitation Research Center. The quality was dreadful. It's funny. The first thing I did after buying that motorcycle wasn't learn how to drive it, but go out and purchase a manual and study automotive repair (laughs). Everyday I had to fix something, the carburetor, the wheel bearings, the brakes. It was fun learning how to fix a motorcycle, but it was also a real pain in the ass. The big advantage was that, when I'd go out on the road and the bike broke down, I didn't need others' help. After so many years depending on people—my parents, my siblings—I just wanted to take care of myself. That motorcycle, as horrible as it was, allowed me to become much more self-sufficient.

 My second motorcycle, the one I'm still using, I got at the Disabled Persons' Service Center [run by the city Federation]. It's a Jia Ling. Jia Ling has become the most popular brand of motorcycle among disabled people because it has a Japanese-designed engine. I got my Jia Ling by pulling a nice little trick. It's quite an interesting story. At first, the only place to get a Jia Ling was the Service Center and the boss there was a real bastard. He'd take your money for a new motorcycle, but he wouldn't hand over the bike for months. So, when I'd saved up enough money, I spoke to one of the boss's men. I told him, "Sir, I don't have a motorcycle and I need one right away because the government has just moved the factory where I work to the suburbs." The guy was very skeptical. He thought I was going to resell the vehicle for a big markup. So he had me write and sign a guarantee saying I wouldn't do that. Afterwards, he said, "OK, you're a disabled guy, you deserve to have a motorcycle." Later that day I drove my Jia Ling home [laughs].

 But, the truth is, I really didn't like lying to that guy. In general, I never lie. Well, almost never. Sometimes, if I'm giving a person a ride and the police stop me, I'll fool the cop by saying I'm on my way to do some business and my passenger is coming along to carry me up the stairs to the office I must reach. I think lying to a cop in that way is okay.

MK: Have you always been this bold?

Liu: [laugh] No. I was pretty childish before. I was just like an infant, always at home, always needing others to do things for me. Once I started to get out of the house, once I set up my own store, I became much more pushy. My parents frequently urge me to be more cautious, particularly when I drive. Going out on the Beijing streets on a three-wheeler is very, very dangerous. But what choice do I have? To make a living, to help the family, I need to drive one of these bikes. Still, its hard not to think about the fact that an accident might leave me even more crippled [*canfei*].

Several points stand out from these excerpts. Purchasing time-space compression devices altered Mr. Peng's and Mr. Liu's lives enormously, and these transformations were framed by a paradoxical mix of sensations. Traveling alone at increasingly higher speeds was, to a large degree, a joy for Peng and Liu. It gave them the power—or ability [*nengli*]—to expand their experiential and economic reach, and it bolstered their sense of self-worth, both as men and as modern consumers/producers. This joy, however, was dampened by deep feelings of fear and dependence. Peng and Liu clearly state that their lives and businesses were, at once, contingent on and threatened by their access to motorized tricycles. To sustain their current situations, they needed the speed of the devices. Yet they and their families worried—and for good reason—that such speed might either kill them or cause an injury that would worsen their disablement.[29]

LIVING A PARADOX

There were several ways in which men like Peng Dushan and Liu Guoze responded to the paradoxical mixture of feelings (pleasure, fear, dependence) that entered their lives as a consequence of their use of the motorized tricycle. Here, I will delineate three. As is the case with all of the accounts of people's lives appearing here, it should be emphasized that these sketches are not presented as "essential" truth claims—as either foundational features of *canji* existence or even as traits characteristic of, say, all urban, male mototrikers in the PRC at that time. Any attempt to posit such claims would be infelicitous, not just because it would overstate a sense of coherency but also because it would aid the agenda of nation-building common to what Stoler has termed the "taxonomic state" (2002, 206), something that this book, like Stoler's work, is designed to decipher and disrupt. So, rather, my sketches should be treated as propositions (filtered as they are through my and my informants' polyvalent subject positions) about how some men in Beijing responded to mototrike use in the mid-1990s.

One response among these men was to foster a relationship with the Federation—a patron/client connection—that situated the men as quasi-appendages to the Federation's body politic. Walder (1986) describes patron–client relations as a key feature of rulership in Communist China. As he explains, they are built around government agencies, like the Federation, exchanging privileges for client loyalty. The primary way mototrikers articulated such cliental loyalty in the 1990s was by becoming public-relations figures for the Federation. As previously noted, even before its formal founding, the Federation understood the necessity for easily recognized and highly functional "disabled people" to perform at the public events it regularly sponsored. The mostly male, mostly polio survivors enlisted by the Beijing Federation to work as cheerleaders during the FESPIC Games exemplified this pattern. For the cheerleaders, performing for Federation offices and being public relations icons were ways to guarantee that the joy entering their lives as a result of motorized tricycles would not be eroded but instead enhanced. In the 1990s many mototrikers gave time and deference to the Federation in exchange, they hoped, for informal assistance with a host of issues like the dismissal of traffic fines, career advancement, housing assignments, residence permit transfers, the enrollment of children in choice schools, and tax reduction.

A second response of Beijing mototrikers to the paradoxical feelings associated with three-wheeler usage was the development of social networks among themselves. In some instances, these networks were facilitated by overlapping patron/client relationships with the Federation. But, more generally, they stemmed from less formal interaction among mototrikers. Through regular interaction with one another, which was facilitated by tricycle ownership, the operators of the devices developed tightly knit circles of what in the 1990s some called "disability brothers" *(canji gemer)*. At the heart of these brotherhood circles was the shared experience of being, simultaneously, privileged to live in the nation's capital and radically delegitimized for being *quezi*.[30] Also at the heart of the circles were the principles of mutual assistance and male-to-male conviviality. Disability brothers pooled finances when one fell on hard times. They shared instrumental contacts. They swapped professional services, consumer advice, and business insights. They drank together and treated one another to meals at restaurants, often battling in received masculine fashion over who should pick up the check. Disability brothers went on group trips. They acted as matchmakers. And disability brothers provided emotional support when trouble struck. The intensity and importance of these circles was strongly reflected in a statement uttered by a man, Wu Guoqiang, while he, several of his "brothers," and I shared a home-cooked meal. Also at the meal was the host brother's wife, as well as Wu's longtime love interest, Ms. Pei. Near the end of the meal, after Wu had had his fill of food and beer, he intoned across the table: "The only people I really trust, the only people with whom I'm willing to express my honest feelings, are my disability brothers. When I'm away from them, when I'm with others, say my parents, people at work, I'm a fake, I'm a liar."

A third and related way in which mototrikers responded to the use of three-wheelers in the 1990s was by carrying out acts of collective justice, acts that for at least some were imbricated in the received ideal of masculine assertiveness. Examples are the protests that popped up across the country when city governments tried to ban motorized tricycles. Beijing mototrikers who have discussed the protests with me extol the participants for alerting society that *canji ren* can be *xiong* (male, strong, and/or gallant). As Liu Guoze said, "Those protests were great. I thought those brothers really showed everyone that they were *xiong,* that *canji ren* can be heroes [*ying-xiong*]." At times, collective justice by mototrikers also involved direct criticism of the Federation. For instance, in late 1994 a group of mototrikers in Beijing sent a letter to the mayor in which they accused the city Federation's main tricycle dealership, the Service Center, of financial impropriety. One of the organizers of the petition told me that, to help garner signatures, "I went around and told my brothers that, by signing the petition, they would show that we brothers are not Federation lackeys, that we're not its court eunuchs, that when it does something wrong we're going to make it act properly." At times, collective justice was targeted at non-governmental sectors of society, as occurred in early 1995. That year, on a cold and gray day in Beijing, a group of male mototrikers blockaded a company office for several hours until they received accident compensation. The day before the blockade, a driver of one of the company's sedans had sideswiped a mototriker as he was heading home with his wife. Both the husband and wife had been injured in the collision and their tricycle badly damaged. One of the men who took part in the blockade was Peng Dushan. "In the end, those company bastards learned their lesson," Peng told me. "We showed those bastards that we can't be bullied, that we'll fight back. We showed them that, as all brothers are supposed to, we *canji* will defend another brother and his woman whenever necessary."

VARIEGATED ALTERITY

In this chapter I have explored the ways in which social processes and everyday practices shaped Federation programs and popular understanding of *canji* during the 1980s and 1990s. Because of these processes and practices, which were to a large degree informed by Fordist-like precepts, there existed a strong convergence, if not a mutually enforcing relationship, between Federation programs and changing local definitions of disability. In the case of one Federation program, in particular—the three-wheeled motorcycle initiative—the convergence fueled palpable transformations in the lives of certain urbanites.

How should these transformations be assessed? On first look, they might be characterized as a form of legitimization. By facilitating access to modes of time-space compression, the Federation enabled people to project themselves out of their homes and to create financial and community structures. In doing so, the Federation helped these people to make enunciations to themselves and those around them about their own value, social status, and subjectivity. The Federation helped these people declare that they were not just highly competent disabled people who were adroitly responsive to China's market transformation, but that they were also manly and moral men.

But, on closer examination, I would suggest, these victories were quite ambiguous. For inasmuch as disability motorcycles allowed some people, like Peng Dushan and Liu Guoze, to transform aspects of their lives, the men continued to feel unrelenting discrimination. Whether it was in the area of business, government work, education, housing, or marriage, Beijing residents regularly considered people like Peng and Liu to be "damaged" or "useless" and thus undesirable as potential colleagues, students, spouses, or neighbors. To a degree, this discrimination was dampened by the Federation's propaganda, the vaguely worded Disability Protection Law, and by the assertiveness of people like Peng and Liu. But, without more systemic efforts—that is, without changing people's outlook that mobility and ability are coterminous, or without making the built world in China more accessible for all people who have difficulty walking—discrimination continued unchecked.

We must recognize also that men like Peng and Liu represented only a small fraction of the millions of people in China who fell within the Federation's criteria for "disability" during the 1980s and 1990s. The lives of most *canji ren* were not subject to legitimization anywhere to the degree of most disability brothers in Beijing. Evolving cultural proscriptions, like those that blocked women from using motorcycles, compounded by the Federation's institution-driven emphasis on quick-fix rehabilitation and by socioeconomic distinctions between urban/rural residency, caused significant disparities in how people under the Federation's aegis were served.

To that extent, it could be argued that the Federation during this period framed disability not just as a space of identity-making and state intervention, but also of biopolitical stratification, what Ong has termed "variegated citizenship" (Ong 1999, 217). For men lucky enough to reside in Beijing or in China's other major metropolitan centers, for men whose bodies fell within certain parameters (i.e., within the Federation's criteria for *canji* and within the even more narrowly understood notions about lower-body disablement), there existed the opportunity for distinct, although still quite limited, social, political, and economic advancement via motorcycle assistance and other means. For those whose bodies did not fall within those parameters, unfortunately, such advancement was far more illusory.

Chapter 5

Troubled Sociality

*The Federation-*Canji *Relationship
in Wenchang County*

Before Chen Lu gave up his government post for a more lucrative job in Haikou, his colleagues regularly asked him to handle the paperwork. Whether it was income reports, census updates, or marriage applications, the task of filling out the village's government forms nearly always fell to him. Neighbors and friends humored Chen that this was because he was the most educated cadre in Min Song village, but Chen knew, somewhat bitterly, that his pencil-pushing duties stemmed from his junior status within the community's government bureaucracy, the "village committee."

So Chen was hardly surprised when one day in 1992 his supervisor—Min Song village's party secretary—told him to visit the township government building to retrieve some forms. The next day, Chen rode his 80cc motorcycle to see Lao Zhen, the frosty-haired official responsible for the township's accounting and Civil Affairs duties. As he entered Wenjiao government's office building and walked toward Old Zhen's doorway, Chen assumed he would be receiving another stack of dreary accounting forms. But on that day Old Zhen had something else for Chen, a bundle of forms from a newly created government office. Chen recounted to me Old Zhen's explanation:

> As you may know, during the last few years, the Ministry of Civil Affairs has been creating a new administrative system to deal with crippled folks [*canfei ren*]. That system is now building up steam in Hainan and its bosses have chosen our township and several others on Hainan to pilot a handful of programs. One program will provide rehabilitation medicine and another program will offer interest-free loans. But before these projects can begin, we must first conduct a local survey to learn about who's *canfei* around here. Take this criteria list and use it to fill out these forms. For each person in your village who meets the criteria, fill out one form, and then bring the documents to me in a couple of days.

Figure 6. Keeping track of the community: Chen Lu filling out some annual statistical forms about Min Song village.

That evening after he and his wife finished making dinner and putting their two children to bed, Chen sat at his desk beneath the bare electric bulb illuminating the only habitable room in his family's dilapidated house. Wedged between his son's crib and the wall, Chen began reviewing the criteria—which as he quickly learned included more than just what he would call *canfei*. He then replenished the ink in his fountain pen, pulled out his copy of the village's household registry, and set to work. The task of filling out the forms, while tedious, was relatively simple. After all, Chen had grown up in Min Song. So of course he knew the names and backgrounds of everyone there who generally resembled the government's criteria for "physically disabled," "blind," "deaf," "mentally ill," and "mentally disabled." Entering the particulars—birth date, family size, and educational level— was also quite simple to accomplish, since all Chen needed to do was refer to the household registry and transfer the information.

To keep things even simpler, as he explained to me later, Chen opted not to divulge his work to villagers.

Of course, I decided to let very few people around here know about the reg- istration work. Letting them know would have just created a big mess. If folks learned they were being registered, some would get embarrassed and curse

me. Others would figure out that registration was being done, in part, to pick
people to receive those loans, and then so many would badger me to help
them be nominated. I didn't have time for that. No way! That was right in the
middle of my first watermelon-growing venture and I had to deal with a
mountain of things to get my melon patch harvested and shipped to North
China on schedule. As it turned out, I lost a lot of money on that first patch.

Several months after Chen finished his registration work, Ming Luli felt
a tingle in his right foot. He noticed the sensation while making his usual
afternoon trek from his peanut field to his residence, a 6 foot by 15 foot hut.
By the next morning, the tingle had turned into palpable ache. So, instead
of tending to his crops, Ming stayed indoors, lying upon his typical South
China farming bed of elevated planks. For two days Ming barely moved save
for boiling drinking water and using a chamber pot. By day three, he was in
agony. His lower leg had swollen to twice its usual size and was oozing puss.
But an equal cause of Ming's suffering was the fear that he had contracted
polio again. At age six, polio had left his now swollen leg paralyzed. And,
thereafter, the leg, together with his family's penury, had prompted innumerable setbacks for Ming, like being forced to give up his studies at age
seven, never finding a woman to marry, and being subjected to a stream of
village ridicule.

Knowing he could not endure another sleepless night and fearful that he
had contracted polio again, Ming took a hold of his crutch and hobbled out
to the road to ask a neighbor for a tractor ride to the village center. On arriv-
ing there, he went to see the village doctor, Ren Xiaodong. Dr. Ren made a
quick examination and then exclaimed that Ming's problem was not polio
but a staph infection that had been caused by an unclean cut. Once Ming
promised he would borrow money to pay for treatment, Dr. Ren injected a
large cocktail of antibiotics and painkillers into Ming's buttocks.

While leaving Ren's clinic, Ming spotted one of Min Song's community
officials, Peng Luzheng. Ming hobbled over to Peng and they had the following exchange, which Ming later recounted to me:

> *Ming:* Oh Peng, look how things have fallen apart. My foot is all swollen up
> like a melon. I don't have the ten yuan to pay Dr. Ren for the injection
> he just gave me and I have no money to buy any more medicine. I've
> asked you before, isn't there something the government could do for
> me? Last year, the village committee generously gave me a blanket and
> sixty yuan as poverty relief, but isn't there anything more that could be
> done to help somebody like me?
>
> *Peng:* I'm sorry about your foot. I hope it doesn't hurt too much. With luck,
> that injection should help. But, unfortunately, there's really nothing we
> on the village committee can do for you. You should ask your brother's
> family.

Ming: But you know my sister-in-law hates me because I use a crutch to walk and for all the struggles I've had in life. It was because of that my brother and I split apart two years ago and I had to move into that hut. Since then he's closed up the house and run off to the city. Now I'm sixty-three and living all alone. There's no one here for me. No one to look after me. No one to even boil water for me. Isn't there anything more the committee could do?

Peng: I'm sorry. It really is your brother's family who should be helping you.

According to Ming, Cadre Peng then excused himself, got on his bicycle, and pedaled away.

THE FEDERATION, THE DISABLED, AND RURAL TRANSFORMATION

In the previous chapter I highlighted how the Federation's early formation was characterized by and contingent on the significant disjuncture between the institution's formal claim that all *canji ren* in China merited special government and social support, on the one hand, and patent disparities among Beijingers who fit the institution's criteria, on the other. I also showed that this disjuncture was not simply an outcome of Federation intentionality; it often stemmed from a complex set of social, political-economic, historical, and phenomenological processes of embodiment, which both drew upon and fused a Maussian tripartite somacentric epistemology of subject, object, and means.

How, we must ask now, did the Federation–*canji ren* relationship manifest itself elsewhere during the same period? More particularly, what was this relationship like in those communities of the PRC far removed from Beijing or other major urban centers? This begs attention if for no other reason than so many of the Federation's statistically conceived constituents—*canji ren*— reside in China's countryside.[1] It also merits consideration because so little is still known about the interaction in the early post-Mao years between the state's framing of health and welfare outside of large cities and the ways people in communities across China were at once experiencing and making identities, like *canji ren.*[2]

To be sure, over the last decade, China scholars have been informing us more and more about daily life in villages and small towns across China. Relatively few of these researchers, however, have examined the state's involvement in health-related issues from a sociopolitical perspective. Fewer still have paid significant attention to the effects of health and health care on the intersubjective processes that enable or undermine identity-formation.[3]

If an abiding aim of this chapter is recursive, that is, to help fill in the gaps in our knowledge, it does so with a specific eye toward biopower. Here, I examine the ways in which the party-state's involvement in the definition and management of "populations," particularly in terms of health, textured the interpersonal environment through which identities emerged. And by discussing these issues vis-à-vis one community—the village of Min Song— I hope to enhance what is known more broadly about how the intersection of state and sociopolitical transformations situated bodies, however disabled, however able-bodied, as sites wherein the relational messiness of identity-formation took place.

In other contexts far from Min Song, far from China, an approach to biopower and identity that has drawn a good deal of attention in recent years has been Rabinow's thesis on biosociality (1996). This is the idea that the social, political, and technological framing of discrete bodily differences in terms of health—defined biologically—can spawn a "network of identity" around those differences (1996, 99). For instance, drawing on Rabinow's ideas, Rapp (1999) has described how major biotechnological transformations in genetic screening in the United States have cast social attention on specific biologically defined disabilities (e.g., Down's syndrome) and how, in turn, that has facilitated people (either those understood to have such disabilities or their family members) to form identity-based community structures (the "support group" being an exemplary form).[4]

Rapp's account of biosociality has some resonance with the "brotherhoods" formed by the men in Beijing who bought mototrikes from the Federation during the 1990s. It also has some commonality with the short-lived Disabled Youths Club, described at the start of Chapter 3. That noted, several characteristics of biopolitical categorization need to be remembered, particularly when working in a place like China. First, the nation-state often shapes significantly the emergence of new categorizations within community contexts. Second, these contexts, while possibly supportive of new categorization regimes as well as novel forms of intersubjectivity, may not necessarily nurture forms of sociality that are salubrious to identities centered around the new categories. Third, identity-formation around new, biomedically defined categories can occur without that identity-formation triggering the weaving of webs of mutual support (e.g., village-based webs of disability brotherhoods/sisterhoods).[5] More to the point, modes of biomedically informed categorization (like *canji*, as promoted by the Federation) may incite people to embed themselves within an imagined nationwide matrix of identity (like China's "disabled population") while simultaneously undermining the production of sociality, biological or otherwise, for those people in their community settings.[6]

Of course, one does not have to leave the Chinese metropole and head into towns and villages in order to consider these admonitions. Yet, at least for this book, there is a compelling reason to do so. If the party-state and those who have trouble walking are the centerpieces to this narrative, if the Federation and men with mobility difficulties were pivotal to the category *canji* becoming a site of expanding sociopolitical formation in late-twentieth-century China, it is intrinsically interesting to ask what kinds of intersubjective forces framed disability for such men in a rural location like eastern Hainan, a place where distinctive party-state modalities, allied with those in Beijing yet vastly different from them, existed during the 1990s.

It is not my intention, however, to proffer a meta-narrative for the workings of biopower in "village China" at the end of the twentieth century. Rather, the accounts provided here should be understood as highly delimited in terms of place (Wenjiao township) and emergent subject position *(canji ren)*. This is particularly important to emphasize, lest this chapter reinscribe a specific kind of academic ableism: the expectation that "China hands" will establish their professional authority, that they will affirm their disciplinary title, by asserting a specific kind of representational competency, an ability to generate explanations that are reputedly generalizable across and encompassing of an entire sector of the Chinese nation-state—for instance "the countryside." Thanks to the research of numerous scholars over the last decade, the pitfalls of trying to make nationwide generalizations about the PRC or to conceptualize that polity neatly in terms of rural and urban spheres have become ever clearer. Indeed, the immense complexity and variability of life in this vast country makes meta-narratives—such as gleeful economic growth in cities or a post-Mao state retreating from the countryside—more than a little problematic.

In light of all this, I have organized this chapter as follows. First, I sketch a historical landscape. I briefly describe the political, social, and biomedical shifts that occurred in and around the tropical venue of Min Song in the post-1949 epoch: that those shifts helped spawn distinct intersubjective processes when I was living in the community; and that those processes facilitated a form of sociality centered around kinship. I then consider how some Min Song residents who the Federation system recognized as *canji* experienced that sociality. From there, I outline the ways that party-state efforts pertaining to health and welfare—most notably, efforts associated with the Federation—developed in the region during the 1990s. Finally, I explore the degree to which such efforts intermingled with everyday practice to not only make *canji* known in Min Song, but also to make it appear there as a category patently risky to one's well being and thus as a category often acutely unkind to any distinctive and separate disability sociality built upon face-to-face relationships.

MIN SONG: A BRIEF PORTRAIT

How to describe Min Song's biopolitical transformation up to and through the latter part of the twentieth century. I start with the themes of geography, migration, demography, kinship, and political economics because during my time in Hainan, Min Song acquaintances and Hainanese scholars seemed to invoke those themes with as much regularity as they did the theme of changing healthcare provision.

Min Song is part of Hainan Island, the PRC's youngest and most southern province. Hainan is similar in geographic size to Taiwan, and it sits off the Vietnam coast adjacent to China's Guangdong and Guangxi Provinces. Min Song is located in Hainan's northeastern county, Wenchang. During the period of my fieldwork, the easiest way to reach Min Song from the city of Wencheng (which is the Wenchang county seat) was to travel east 20 kilometers down a dirt road past fields of rice and sweet potato—the region's main staples—to the town of Wenjiao, and from there continue several kilometers more down another dirt road skirting the Wenjiao River's mangrove and palm-dotted levy.

Wenchang County has long possessed some of the finest farmland on Hainan. As a consequence, from the late nineteenth through the early twentieth century, the county had a high rate of population growth, probably the highest anywhere on the island. Most of that growth came from mainland Han Chinese in-migration. But then, from the 1930s through the 1990s, Wenchang's population grew only modestly, in part because the land could not sustain more people and in part because the shortage of land prompted an extremely high level of out-migration. By the early 1990s, nearly all preexisting "minority groups"—those citizens that contemporary Chinese officials categorized as having ethnicities other than "Han"—had left the county, and possibly as many as 60 percent of Wenchang's 500,000 residents had family members who either were living or had lived beyond the territorial boundaries of the PRC (Si 1992, 98–108).

Both because of and despite these migration patterns, the lives of the Wenchang villagers were quite similar to those of people living in many of the Han regions of rural South China during the pre-Communist era. Life was largely built around the soil and family relationships. Nearly all land was privately held and was farmed by "joint" or "stem" family units. The rules and practices of filial piety and ancestor worship were strictly followed. All males were expected to extend their father's line by marrying and producing heirs. Women were expected to live with their husband's family, to bear offspring (preferably males), and to contribute to their husband's family's labor pool. The rules of filial piety and ancestor worship required that children respectfully care for their parents until the parents died and then to propitiate them in the afterlife.

Following the founding of the People's Republic in 1949, Min Song, like nearly all villages in Wenchang County, underwent decades of sweeping transformation as a consequence of the blunt and sometimes destructive penetration of the newly forming Maoist state. Before Communist "liberation," the active hand of government *(zhengfu)* was rarely felt anywhere on

Hainan, save for the island's county seats and its main city, Haikou. But from the early 1950s forward, the state visibly entered Min Song and nearly every other community on Hainan and began socially engineering local life based on edicts that came from atop the government hierarchy. At the local level, the most visible and important force for implementing these top-down edicts were village cadres. These were people, like Chen Lu, who had been born in Min Song of "good class" backgrounds and who had proven themselves to be committed socialist revolutionaries.

Rather than trying to discuss all the top-down restructuring that the Min Song cadres performed during the Maoist epoch, let me mention just three broad areas—economics, ancestor worship, and health care. According to Min Song cadres and villagers, these areas were important in influencing the well-being of the community, and, more specifically, what they often referred to as the health of the population *(renkou de jiankang)*. Initially, some of the most important edicts that Min Song's cadres implemented related to collectivization. By the late 1960s, in the name of the state, cadres had appropriated nearly all property and had organized the village into a "brigade" *(dadui)*, and its five hamlets into "production teams" *(shengchandui)*. Thereafter, in military style, villagers reported to team leaders, who reported to brigade leaders, who reported to commune leaders (whose offices were in the market town of Wenjiao). Under this new system, material differences between Min Song residents were significantly eradicated, as income levels were determined by brigade and team officials. Cadres distributed goods and money to villagers based on various factors, most importantly, the villagers' needs, "work points," Maoist attitudes, and class standing.

During the collective era, cadres used their new paramilitary chain of command to propagate a wide variety of Maoist ideals. One subject about which they regularly disseminated information was ancestor worship. According to the Maoist world view, ancestor worship was both outdated and dangerous. It was outdated, in part, since care for the elderly and others in Mao's "New China" *(xinhua)* was to be handled by the society's new collective structures of production and redistribution. It was dangerous, in part, because it placed the health of kin over the health of the collective and the nation-state. For these and other reasons, party leaders determined that ancestor worship must be stamped out. And by the mid-1970s, Min Song's cadres had so fully transmitted this "party line" that nearly all signs of ancestor worship at the village level were obliterated, including lineage halls, gravestones, and ancestor tablets.

Another hallmark of Maoism's penetration of Min Song—one which was pivotal to building local confidence in the party and its commitment to "serve the people"—was the widespread provision of efficacious medicine. Prior to the 1950s, death by communicable disease was common in the villages of Wenchang. Smallpox, cholera, measles, leprosy, and a host of other illnesses were endemic. As Min Song residents regularly explained to me, they were largely defenseless against such diseases because they had almost no access to biomedicine *(xiyi)*. "Pre-liberation" Wenchang had just a handful of private doctors trained in *xiyi*, nearly all of whom were located in the county seat and a few market towns. Beyond them, the only caregivers that Min Song villagers could engage when misfortune struck were various for-profit spirit mediums, herbalists, and healers (the latter two offering treatments loosely associated with contemporary notions of traditional Chinese medicine).

As the Maoist era progressed, a multilayered public health infrastructure was created in Wenchang, one which was based on biomedicine and which proved highly successful at fighting communicable diseases (Feng 1990). A critical layer of this infrastructure was built in the late 1950s when Wenchang County's twenty-two communes established "central hospitals" in their host towns. These hospitals—which usually had a dozen or so beds and twenty or more staff members—were responsible for and had jurisdiction over all medical and public health matters within each commune.

Yet, as far as Min Song residents were concerned, the most crucial transformation in medicine occurred from the mid-1960s to the mid-1970s, when the state created a collective healthcare system that covered nearly all Wenchang inhabitants.[7] The point of entry to the system for Min Song villagers was the "health station" *(weisheng zhan)*, a one-room clinic established in 1966 next to the brigade's government offices. This station was one of 320 such clinics established across rural Wenchang. Like the rest of them, it was run by a *chijiao yisheng* (barefoot doctor), a local resident educated outside the community for short periods in a variety of basic biomedical techniques. In theory, Min Song villagers had unlimited access to the barefoot doctor, and whenever they presented a medical problem that was beyond his expertise, he referred them up the system to the Wenjiao commune hospital. Villages had to pay only a few pennies for the barefoot doctor's treatments, the medicines he distributed, and any services provided as a consequence of referrals.[8] Nearly all costs were covered by the collective earnings of the Min Song brigade.

SIZING UP THE POST-1949 EPOCHS

What were some of the ways the transition from the Maoist era to the Deng period textured life in Min Song at the level of what Arthur Kleinman (1995, 97) has called the intersubjective "felt flow" of experience? When I lived in Min Song during the 1990s, most adults looked back on the changes I've outlined here—the intrusion of the Maoist state and its transformation of fundamental aspects of daily life—with varying degrees of nostalgia and displeasure. And how they blended that mixture had a great deal to do with both a pre-concern with "health" *(jiankang)* and with the way that they understood the emergent Dengist state to be supporting or undermining the local population's health in relation to an imagined past. While most villagers expressed distaste for aspects of the Maoist era (such as the tumultuous political campaigns, food shortages, and infringements on various personal freedoms), those who denounced Maoism to the greatest degree often did so by talking up how, in the 1980s and early 1990s, the local population *(difang renkou)* had enjoyed increasingly better means to bolster their health, with nutritious food, pharmaceuticals, and advanced clinical care. Similarly, while most I spoke to waxed romantic for what they remembered as the simpler, less competitive, and kinder aspects of the collective period, those in Min Song who tended to be the most sentimental about Maoism were also the ones who tended to say that their and the local population's health was increasingly threatened by the Deng transition. The point I am trying to make is that, by the 1990s, a requisite of biopower—the language of health (both that of the individual and that of the population)—was a well-established feature by which experience (past, present, and future) was represented and measured in Min Song.

And yet, if both condemnation of and nostalgia for Maoism echoed across the sandy landscape of Min Song via a language of health, nostalgia certainly echoed the loudest. The only sound that might have exceeded nostalgia was likely the din of foreboding, which was also often articulated by community members in terms of health.

What prompted this foreboding? People in Min Song often ascribed it to several shifts in state-formation. The first was economic deregulation. In 1979 the Wenjiao commune had been decollectivized and family farming had returned. Thereafter, incomes in Min Song grew, but only modestly for most. By 1993, average per capita income for the village's nearly two thousand residents had reached only 350 yuan (US $42).[9] At the same time, a huge divide had opened up between the rich and the poor. Community cadres reported that in 1993 a twentyfold difference in yearly income existed between Min Song's wealthiest and poorest residents, and at least 5 percent of community members survived on less than 200 yuan per annum.[10] Something that paralleled these shifting incomes, something that made economic disparity all the more significant, was the sharp inflation attendant to the deregulatory policies of the post-Mao era. This inflation was usually talked about in terms of food prices and nutrition. For instance, villagers repeatedly told me that from the early 1980s to the early 1990s, rice prices in Wenchang had nearly doubled and the cost for such things as pork and green beans had jumped tenfold. This meant that, as was often explained to me, only the newly gilded could consistently afford to eat highly nutritious foods.

Another notable and not unrelated topic of popular unease was the speed with which resources circulated in and out of the village. During Mao's long reign, the state had strictly limited not just where people could live and travel, but also the kinds of information and goods they could attain and from whom they could send or receive funds. By comparison, after a decade of the Deng reforms, Min Song's was a far looser, far more permeable environment, one simultaneously marginal to yet loosely incorporated in a growing array of social, symbolic, and economic circuits. Residents now had comparatively many more items at varying prices to choose from, whether print media, music, and videos, or toiletries, foods, building materials, and pharmaceuticals. Adults regularly parted ways with younger and older relatives in order to work in cities across South China. Those who remained in the community often received visits, mail, and remittances from newly departed relatives or from those who had left Hainan before 1949.[11] Certainly, many in Min Song, particularly the better off, spoke positively about this new and more fluid environment. For instance, my landlord—who had children working successfully outside the community, who regularly traveled to Hainan's cities for high-priced health care, and who often watched pornographic rental videos late at night—had many panegyric things to say about the end of Maoism. Yet, almost everyone in the community with whom I conversed also expressed deep distress about the disruptions they associated with this new fluidity. Theft, youth violence, transportation accidents, prostitution, desertion, the decline of mutual assistance, as well as an overall loss of social order *(shehui zhian)* were just some of the many phenomena through which Min Song villagers gave voice to this distress.

Medical care was another major contributor to and possibly the most common means by which many Min Song residents expressed the unease that they and their neighbors increasingly felt as the Maoist era faded into the distance. As a consequence of the late-1970s dissolution of the brigade and production team structures, Min Song and most other villages across China were no longer able to maintain health stations. A large percentage of the stations had folded or gone bankrupt. What happened to the barefoot doctors? In Wenchang County, from 1976 to 1987, four out of every five had stopped practicing medicine, and those that remained worked on a fee-for-service basis (Feng 1990, 53–55).

But to grasp how Min Song residents in the 1990s understood these transformations in medical care as being, at once, threatening to and a medium through which to make sense of their world, one must also consider health indices and hospital services. An archetypal trope for biopolitics, health indices were often harped on by my Min Song acquaintances. The most commonly fretted over index was quite likely that of infant mortality. This was not without reason, it should be noted. According to county epidemiologists and village cadres, infant mortality in and around Min

Song took sharply negative turns during certain periods in the 1980s and 1990s.[12]

Yet, whatever clamor existed about such indices, it paled in comparison to what I heard about hospitals. With the demise of the country's village-based healthcare network, most Chinese farmers, and certainly nearly all Min Song residents, had been thrown into a situation where they had to pay for hospital treatment on a fee-for-service basis. Even though most Min Song residents were quick to suggest that the general quality of care in Hainan's hospitals had improved over the course of the 1980s and 1990s, they nearly all found the switch to a pay-as-you-go system deeply disturbing. And for the majority of community members, whose incomes did not keep up with inflation, their reasons for distress only grew as time passed. Because government subsidies issued to Hainan's hospitals declined relative to the growing costs of running such facilities during the 1980s and 1990s, patient prices at the province's hospitals skyrocketed. By the early 1990s, prices had became so high relative to average per capita income that many hospitals across Hainan were demanding patient deposits before administering treatment, even when patients presented with obviously life-threatening conditions. Min Song villagers, in their efforts to emphasize how harrowing this situation was, repeatedly told me stories of Wenjiao residents who had been turned away from hospitals and who had subsequently died while lying in the entranceways to these facilities.[13]

FAMILY, TRADITIONALISM, AND SOCIALITY

With such sociopolitical and, indeed, biopolitical winds swirling across Min Song, it is neither surprising that villagers experienced foreboding or that such foreboding helped trigger activity at the level of sociality. Nor is it surprising that residents often conceived of this sociality as a revivification of tradition. Although Maoism was missed by many, nearly all viewed it as being untenable as a model for community organization. And while everyone I met in the community seemed to wish for greater modernity, nearly all made it clear that they saw Wenchang as unalterably mired in backwardness in comparison to the economic vibrancy that characterized city life or that of the villages in nearby Guangdong Province. As a consequence, community members increasingly promoted a selective traditionalism, one organized to a significant degree around kinship.

Much of this found expression in family formation. During my stay in Min Song, most residents ardently extolled the idea of a "traditional household" *(chuantong hu)*, one marked, as they explained, by multiple generations living under one roof, members remitting money from elsewhere, strong male leadership, and kin giving great attention to intrafamily welfare. An important aspect of this traditional family orientation was a renewed concern with the androcentric cult of ancestor worship. As the 1980s gave way to the 1990s, lineage halls in the region were rebuilt; gravestones were reset; ancestor tablets were reinstalled; and many rituals for propitiating dead patriarchs were being practiced with growing vigor. Through all these activities, people in Min Song and elsewhere hoped to rekindle a sense of stability, to foster feelings of native place, and to create local and supralocal kin-based ties with the aspiration of generating a steady supply of mutual assistance (cf. Jing 1996).

COMMUNITY CHANGE AND THE EXPERIENCE OF DISABLEMENT

As the post-Mao period unfolded, who in the village had the greatest cause to feel unease (and thus was in most urgent need of kin-based support)? Answers I often heard while hanging out in community teahouses and homes were these: the chronically sick (*laoyoubing*), the crippled (*canfei*), or those whose bodies were otherwise different (*shenti bu yiyang*) or abnormal (*shenti bu zhengchang*).

The name of Ming Luli, whose story appears at the outset of this chapter, surfaced regularly during these discussions. That his name was invoked so often no doubt stemmed from how precarious his life was when I lived in Min Song. Ming Luli regularly emphasized this during our chats. And, like his neighbors, he attributed his vulnerability in large part to his polio-addled body and post-Maoist economics.

> Things were pretty secure for me when Mao was around. Like everyone else in this hamlet, I worked for the production team and I was given enough to eat and get by. But then, oh . . . [sigh] . . . Mao died and my polio-damaged body and I were left behind. Sure, after Mao's death, I was given a contract for a piece of land like everyone else around here. I've been farming that land, mostly growing peanuts and a few vegetables. But I don't have enough strength to survive on farming. Now I earn about 190 yuan a year. Without help, I don't know how I'll make it. I'm all alone here. My brother deserted me. Mao deserted me. What am I to do?

That Ming was "deserted" by Mao and his brother and that he was destined for permanent bachelorhood (an issue I address further in the next chapter) reveal the degree to which the emphasis on kin-based sociality that was increasingly at play in Min Song had become not just deleterious to but also constitutive of life with bodily difference/abnormality. As Ming explained:

> Back during the time of Mao, everyone here treated me as part of the brigade. People used to stop by and say hello. They'd chat. They'd ask how things were. They'd offer to serve as my matchmaker. Sometimes neighbors would ask me if they could help me when they saw me trying to carry a heavy

load. Government officials would stop in and ask if I had enough to eat. Now, everybody is racing around trying to make money, to get ahead, government officials included. So naturally they have less and less time to do things like stop by and talk.

Around here, before, lots of things were done collectively, so everyone had chances to know what was going on in each others' lives. But now collective action is almost all gone and everything is about the individual and the family. Now everybody lives very separate lives. Because of that, neighbors know little of what's going on in each other's homes. And the people that everyone wants to know the least about are those like me. That's what it's like being crippled [*canfei*] here: being ignored and watching neighbors building family.

Ming also understood his vulnerability, his inability to partake in a kin-based sociality, and his unwanted *canfei* subject position in terms of what, on more than one occasion, he termed people's growing "love for the competent and beautiful" *(ai nengren, ai meiren)*:

The big thing now is having ability and looking good. Many people have become absolutely obsessed with it. All they want, all they're after, is demonstrating that they're more competent than everyone else and that they're as good-looking as what they see on TV. And, of course, that affects how certain folks around here interact with me. During the time of Mao, some people avoided me. But now it's so much worse. Now, not only do some people avoid me, they also tell their family members to stay away from me. They say, "How will we raise our status if you interact with him? What does that incompetent [*ganbuliao*] *quezi* have to offer? He's a cripple. He's abnormal [*bu zhengchang*]. The last thing you should do is associate with him." That's been my brother and sister-in-law's response. They took off for Haikou to make money, to get away from me, and to show others that they're competent.

On more than one occasion, Ming approached me and said he had been hungry for several days and asked me for assistance. These and other encounters prompted me to buy bags of bulk rice and other foodstuffs for Ming, and to inquire of village and township cadres whether there was not more they could do for him. I mention this not so much to reveal how at times I responded to the ethical immediacies that so frequently characterized my fieldwork, and that color all ethnographic inquiry in settings where scholars are interacting with people who are suffering outright privation or less overt kinds of inequality. Rather, I mention it in order to contextualize some of the last reflections I ever heard from Ming. In 1996 he died of unknown causes, according to a village friend. Shortly before I left the village at the end of 1994, this is what he had to say:

Old Mao . . . who'd have thought his assent to heaven would make me into such a miserable cripple. Before, when Mao was still around, I couldn't walk well. Did that affect me much? Not really. But now, I'm hungry. I've got no family to help me. And there's no one in the village willing to interact with me. I appreciate you giving me this rice, this meat. Who knows how I'd get by without it. But, damn, how it makes me seem so much more miserable, so much more crippled.

THE STORY OF RU LIN

No matter how poignant his words might be, no matter how much Ming's reflections seemed to reveal about aspects of the symbolic, political, and historical mapping of bodily difference in Min Song in terms of the perceived rise and decline of government care, learning only about Ming's life in this chapter would be a mistake. Attention to Ming's situation and that situation alone might imply that I interacted little with others in the village. Just as erroneously, it might imply that only men like Ming were struggling with post-Maoist political economic transformations, the community's increasing family focus, or the ways those two factors seemed to foster negative views about inability and bodily difference/abnormality. Even though aspects of Ming's life dovetail with the portrait of *canfei/canji* that I most often heard espoused by Min Song and Beijing residents (i.e., an adult male who had trouble walking), it would be wrong and certainly irresponsible to suggest that the type of difficulties highlighted thus far by Ming's case were altogether unique to men.

Ru Lin was thirty-five years old when we met. She was married to Xing Fujia, a man of approximately the same age. According to Federation criteria, both Ru and Xing could be called *canji*, although I heard few ever use that term to speak of them—or, for that matter, anyone else in Min Song. Instead, the operative terms that were applied to both were either "incompetent" or "abnormal." And during the period I lived in Min Song, villagers were inclined to say Ru was far more incompetent or abnormal than Xing. This discrepancy, Ru and Xing said, had to do with the contrasting visibility of their "differences." Xing had begun experiencing intermittent schizophrenic episodes at age twenty. He openly and often acknowledged his diagnosis to me, and he indicated that his episodes had become far more infrequent, thanks to the drugs he took daily, which had been prescribed during one of his visits to a Haikou psychiatric hospital. By contrast, Ru had developed her hunchback as a young girl. By the time she had reached her late teens, her spine had become distinctively bowed and her height barely reached four feet.

Beyond visible difference, a significant reason that villagers were far more likely to refer to Ru as incompetent or incapable, she believed, was because of her precarious family situation. In the early 1980s, after each had attempted to find a spouse for years, Ru and Xing were introduced to each other and got married. But whereas marriage had expanded Xing's family network, it had meant a diminution for Ru. In part, this was because traditional custom required brides to move from their birth home to their husband's home, thereby breaking her ties to her own family. In part, it was also because Ru and Xing did not have children, a fact that nearly everyone blamed on Ru's "abnormal" body. Without children, Ru was deprived of the social standing afforded motherhood and the long-term protective intimacy of offspring, both of which, as Wolf has shown, have been pivotal for women's well-being in Chinese cultural contexts marked by patrilocality (Wolf 1972).

To be sure though, Ru's tenuous family situation had become even worse after Xing's uncle returned to live in Wenjiao from a thirty-year hiatus in Taiwan. As she explained to me, in the wake of the uncle's unannounced arrival, Xing and his father had become more and more hostile toward her. They increasingly told Ru that, if the uncle had returned sooner, they never would have agreed to the marriage because, with the cachet of the uncle's presence, they could have found a "better" wife than Ru, one who was not so "abnormal."

These poor and deteriorating affinal ties had direct consequences for Ru's survival. About eight months before I arrived in Min Song, Ru fell ill. She visited the village doctor, who made a preliminary diagnosis of tuberculosis and instructed her to report immediately to the Wenchang County hospital. Ru did not follow the doctor's directions. She had no personal savings to pay for hospital treatment, and her natal kin lived many miles away in another township. Of course, Ru's husband's family had money enough to pay for treatment. But they did not volunteer, and, feeling very proud, Ru did not ask. Fortunately, one of Ru's friends sent a note to her natal family describing her plight. This prompted Ru's aunt to travel to Min Song to deliver Ru to the Wenchang County hospital. The aunt paid a large deposit and then stayed on at the hospital to help Ru as she was treated over a period of several days.

This story of illness and rescue was something Ru told me several times during the year I lived in Min Song. She recounted the details, usually, whenever our conversation turned to her future, something that she obviously approached with great unease. More than anything else, the story symbolized for Ru the tremendous precariousness of her situation. For as she conveyed to me on several tear-filled occasions, she had come to understand that if she ever confronted serious illness again she would likely perish in the cold and uncaring house of her husband.

STRUCTURES OF ASSISTANCE

In light of the worrisome state of people like Ming and Ru, in light of the more general foreboding that people in Min Song felt as a consequence of the post-Maoist sociopolitical turn, and in light of the party-state's continued monopoly over large-scale organization, it makes sense that most people I met in Min Song longed for governmental structures that would protect them. While state employees in and around the community, or at least the employees I spoke with, knew of these longings, little government response seemed forthcoming during the 1990s. But what of the Federation? And what of the broader *fuli* (welfare) system that Dengism had promised would address the greatest hardships created by the demise of Maoism?

Other than the Federation's projects (to be outlined shortly) and military stipends issued to a negligible number of "revolutionary" veterans, there were only three state "welfare" programs functioning in Wenjiao township during the early 1990s. All three were started in the Deng era. All were modest in scope. And all were designed to provide aid for the needy. One program was called the "Five Guarantees Households," which was targeted at those elderly who lacked family or independent economic support. Another was "Relief for the Severely Poor," which as the name indicates was targeted at the most destitute. These countrywide programs provided cash and food subsidies. But because they were funded almost entirely with small national and provincial allocations, their effect was skeletal. When I lived in Min Song, fewer than half of one percent of the villagers were enrolled.[14]

The third government "welfare" structure was Wenjiao township's nursing home. The home was established in 1990 with seed money from Wenchang County's finance bureau. Thereafter, nearly all of its expenses were covered by the township government, a fact that greatly limited its size.[15] When I visited the home in 1994, it was at half occupancy, with five residents.[16]

FEDERATION DEVELOPMENT: A SNAPSHOT

Rather than trying to detail the full sweep of the Federation's structural development across Hainan during the late 1980s and early 1990, let me begin with a snapshot description of how far that development had come by 1993. However grainy, this snapshot outlines what one would likely perceive if s/he were to "move down" *(xia qu)* through Hainan's state hierarchy from Haikou to Min Song. In the island's capital there were two full-fledged Federation chapters: the Hainan provincial office and the Haikou city office. Housed under a single roof, these chapters collectively employed about twenty staff members whose portfolios were solely devoted to the Federation. In the county seat of Wencheng, the Federation had a virtual chapter, one that was set within the Wenchang Civil Affairs (CA) Bureau. It was staffed by three local CA officials, all of whom were former soldiers and none of whom claimed to be *canji*. These three officials carried out Federation-directed assignments, but they also handled a spate of CA-related tasks. In the town of Wenjiao, the Federation had neither a chapter nor staff members. Its de facto proxy was the frosty-haired official Lao Zhen, who, since leaving the military, jointly handled CA and accounting responsibilities for the township. Min Song had neither a Federation chapter nor any formal Federation employees. Instead, as noted above, Cadre Chen served as the Federation's ad hoc agent in the village—that is, until the summer of 1994 when he decided to forgo government service for a private-sector job in Haikou.

Given this thin structural edifice, it is probably of little surprise to readers that, from the perspective of most Min Song residents, and perhaps most others in Wenjiao township, the Federation was nearly invisible as the 1990s unfolded. Yet, for me, this remains somewhat ironic. In the early 1990s, as I was initially conjuring up the idea of conducting village research on *canji*, Federation officials in Haikou and Wenchang's county seat regularly encouraged me to work in Wenjiao because they considered the institution's footprint there to be relatively large for rural Hainan, a fact I later came to understand as stemming from the preferential treatment, real or imagined, that the township enjoyed because the Federation's provincial director had been born and raised in a Wenjiao village.

REHABILITATION MEDICINE IN WENCHANG

The Federation's near invisibility for Wenjiao residents during the 1990s was no doubt fostered by how the institution administered aid in eastern Hainan. During the Federation's first five-year plan (1988–92), it had only one nationwide program that was even nominally directed at Chinese villages. This was the previously mentioned Three Rehabilitations program. In Hainan, that program initially was staged almost entirely at the supralocal level of the county seats, and most of the labor it necessitated was performed not by Federation staff but rather by personnel attached to China's county-level public healthcare system. The total number of people who benefited from this program across Wenchang County in 1992 was miniscule. Of the county's 24,383 officially recognized *canji*, less than 3 percent had received any of the program's three modes of treatment.[17]

In part because Wenjiao township's hospital was one of the better-administered medical facilities in east Hainan, Wenchang County's Federation and public health leaders began using it as a staging area for the Three Rehabilitations program at the end of the Federation's first five-year plan. It was also, in part, because of Wenjiao Hospital's quality that supralocal Federation officials during this period selected Wenjiao as one of three townships across Hainan to serve as a pilot site for two additional programs.

These programs were designed to provide locally registered disabled people with "Community-Based Rehabilitation" *(shequ kangfu)* and interest-free "Rehabilitation Poverty Loans" *(kangfu fupin daikuan)*. In the case of the first program, the locus of provision was supposed to be the township hospital itself. And to mark that fact, county Federation officials hung a sign outside the hospital's side entrance that read "Wenjiao Township Community-Based Rehabilitation Station" *(wenjiao zhen shequ kangfu zhan)*. Yet, during the period of my stay in Min Song, little ever happened in Wenjiao under the auspices of Community-Based Rehabilitation (CBR). One of the hospital doctors who was formally affiliated with the Wenjiao CBR station explained its dearth of activity to me (cf. Ingstad 1997, 267):

> Community-based rehabilitation, ha! What's that? From what I've heard, it's just some term cooked up by a bunch of foreigners and officials in Beijing. As far as I can tell, it means local communities are supposed to pay for special kinds of treatment. But I'll tell you, there's none of that going on around here. [If and when] money and directions come down from the provincial Federation to the county Federation, and then from there to our [CBR] station, some rehabilitation medicine happens—say, somebody gets sent out for some polio surgery, a few deaf kids get some language training, or a few old people get brought in for cataract surgery. Otherwise, nothing occurs in Wenjiao under [the heading of] community-based rehabilitation. During the Maoist era, I think community-based rehabilitation could have worked fine. But not now. Why? Because everything is so expensive. Because, unlike before, there's no way to raise money from local people. And because nobody around here has the desire to make anything happen.

A LOST OPPORTUNITY: THE POLIO ERADICATION CAMPAIGN

Even if no Federation employees lived in or near Min Song, even if Federation activities were staged at supralocal levels, and even if those activities were often hollow ventures, were there not other means by which villagers might learn about the Federation in the early 1990s?

One avenue might have been the PRC's practice of mounting national medical campaigns. Medical campaigns became a common occurrence across China during the Maoist era. At the village level, the key people behind the implementation of these campaigns from the mid-1960s onward were barefoot doctors and local cadres. These government functionaries made sure that community members not only participated in the campaigns, but that they learned various kinds of related information as well.

When I lived in Min Song, there was only one national health care campaign I witnessed: a polio vaccination effort. At first blush, this campaign struck me as the perfect mechanism for transmitting knowledge about the Federation and its social-assistance agenda. After all, if the Federation was not about polio-related issues, what was it about? But for most people with whom I discussed it, the overall message conveyed by the campaign was far more about state struggles to enforce biopolitical control than about delivering either assistance or knowledge regarding assistance.

Part of an ongoing WHO initiative to eradicate polio worldwide, the mid-1990s inoculation effort was orchestrated by several branches of China's vast governmental apparatus and was billed in the press as intended to reach every community of the PRC. All Chinese children four years old and younger were to be administered oral polio vaccine during two forty-eight-hour periods, the first in late 1993 and the second in early 1994.

Given its scope, one would have expected that quite a number of people would have been involved in the campaign in Min Song. In fact, Dr. Ma, an employee of the Wenjiao Hospital, was the only person who actively worked to fulfill the basic goal of the campaign (i.e., distributing vaccines), and he was not a Min Song native but an outsider. What about the sorts of village personnel who previously had worked on the Maoist medical campaigns? Because he was functioning as a private physician, Dr. Ren, who was Min Song's primary healthcare provider, was neither expected to participate nor did he desire to help with the anti-polio campaign. Likewise, since they were more interested in their own economic ventures and were under little fear of reprisals from supralocal authorities, Min Song's cadres also largely flouted their explicit duties to assist with the campaign—a fact that greatly angered the township physician, Dr. Ma.[18]

What angered Dr. Ma even more was that, despite notices delivered to them in advance through the mail system, relatively few Min Song households brought their children to the village center to receive the vaccine. This meant that Dr. Ma had to spend four days going from house to house to track down children of the appointed age, receive parent or guardian permission, and then administer vaccine.[19]

Facing such difficulties, Dr. Ma had little interest in communicating public health messages, let alone information about disability-related services or the existence of the Disabled Persons' Federation.

OTHER MEDIUMS FOR LEARNING ABOUT THE FEDERATION

Even though institutions like the Disabled Persons' Federation could no longer expect medical campaigns to deliver information directly to their target audience, were there not other mediums in eastern Hainan that might have filled that void? In particular, what about the newspapers, radio stations, and televisions broadcasts that increasingly penetrated Min Song during the 1980s and 1990s? Intermittently, these media did offer some knowledge about the Federation and its projects. But since a large number of Min Song residents who might fit the official disability criteria were impoverished and barely educated, they were some of the least likely in the community to access or react to the mass media. Moreover, as several of Min Song's more well-off and better-educated *canji* registrants told me, they generally had little incentive to pay attention to news about Federation programs. As Lu Yi, a polio survivor who was one of the community's more avid newspaper readers, explained:

> Yeah, I've seen some stories about how that institution—What's it called? The Disabled . . . The Disabled Persons' Union?—has helped people in one place or another. But until anyone in this place sees that the government is willing to give the disabled around here some tangible aid, why should anyone pay attention to all that propaganda? If I have little chance of getting something for my trouble, why should I embarrass my family and friends by making noise that I'm *canji*? Why should I holler "I'm *canji* and I want this or that from the government"?

DELIBERATIONS: WHETHER TO INTERACT WITH THE FEDERATION?

Lu's remarks bring two things to light that require further attention. First, some Min Song residents did gradually learn about the Federation in the early 1990s. Second, among this small group, some deliberated whether or not to reach out to the Federation in the hope of gaining assistance. During my interviews, I found that a specific equation was often at the center of such deliberations: whether the potential benefit of Federation assistance outweighed the cost that assistance might exact in the way of community disapprobation on the individual and family. Before commenting on a Federation area of programmatic outreach that often prompted this sort of calculation—the rehabilitation poverty loans—a few words must be said about the cost side of the equation.

Min Song residents expressed different levels of shame, embarrassment, and discomfort whenever they discussed with me the possibility of seeking out any form of government welfare, and these differences seemed to have as much to do with people's backgrounds as they did with whether the assistance discussed was poverty relief, Five Guarantees subsidies, or something else. Irrespective of that, though, people often made clear that they and their neighbors felt that nearly all forms of government welfare were somewhat damaging to their personal and/or family status. Receipt of welfare, they said, was a mark of failure, something which could undermine the recipient's face as well as his/her family's social standing.

While this might not seem particularly unique to Min Song or even China, one can observe greater specificity if we examine the shame of welfare over the course of the Deng reforms. For, as most of my informants explained, that shame *(chiru gan)* became increasingly more pronounced during the 1980s and early 1990s as Min Song shifted away from Maoist forms of social organization. As one acquaintance succinctly explained:

> Before Mao's death, it didn't matter so much around here if somebody got a little extra help, a little extra subsidy from the state. Everyone was contribut-

ing to the state, everyone was living off the state. And the expectation was that we'd all live relatively equally. But now, because ability is such a big deal, because family is so much more important, it's pretty embarrassing if you get state aid.

This quote highlights a critical point being argued in this chapter, namely, that Deng Xiaoping's market reforms created a paradox in the area of welfare delivery. The paradox was that, on the one hand, the reforms stimulated the need and desire for welfare assistance, and, on the other, they created or fueled intersubjective processes—concerns with ability, family status, and economic prowess—that made such assistance embarrassing.

THE FEDERATION LOANS

To understand how such embarrassment textured state-sponsored disability advocacy in Min Song, consider the second of the two programs the Federation piloted in Wenjiao township during the early 1990s. Depending on how much they knew of them, Min Song residents viewed the Federation's rehabilitation loans with a varying mix of desire and antipathy. The antipathy was partially a result of the loans being a form of government assistance, but it also stemmed from the fact they were administered by an institution—the Disabled Persons' Federation—whose name most residents quickly associated with bodily "defect" *(quedian)*. The loan program's positive image, on the other hand, emanated from the idea of receiving a large lump-sum of cash rather than a protracted and modest stipend. It was further rooted in language. For most community members, the term "rehabilitation" *(kangfu)* was relatively unfamiliar, and they generally associated it with the concept of health *(jiankang)*—not with sickness, disability, or deviance, as some readers might expect. And among my acquaintances in Min Song and elsewhere, "loan" was a fairly attractive term, falling somewhere between the highly positive notion of "profit" and the more negative idea of "handout."

But simply because people found the title and notion of "rehabilitation loan" to be somewhat innocuous, if at times attractive, did not mean that everyone in Min Song eligible for a loan had a chance to apply or even desired to do so. The person in Min Song responsible for accepting loan applications—Cadre Chen—tried to limit people's knowledge about the program. His efforts proved to be relatively effective. When I lived there, not only were the vast majority of Min Song residents unaware of the loan program, but they also did not know a related fact: that Cadre Chen had formally registered community members as disabled. Over the course of my fieldwork, I found that among the 125 Min Song villagers Cadre Chen had registered—those I have been referring to as *canji* registrants—only a small fraction knew they had been officially categorized as *canji*, and most of them only knew because Chen had contacted them to say he wanted to nominate them for a loan.

Mentioned at the beginning of this chapter, Chen's decision to hide the loan program was motivated in part by his desire to avoid having people come and "bother" him for an opportunity to submit an application. But, as he also explained to me during a number of conversations, he felt that he was morally obliged to "protect" families from the discomfort of learning that one among them had been registered as *canji*. Thus, he only let families know about registration if their *canji* member was going to have the opportunity of possibly receiving a loan. In other words, Chen seemed to see the opportunity to apply for a loan as a kind of "compensation" for the pain attendant upon a family learning that one member among them had been officially labeled *canji*.

The concern that *canji* labeling might cause people pain was not misguided. People in Min Song who learned, by happenstance, that Chen had formally registered them or someone in their family as *canji* were generally quite upset by that news. And in terms of my own research, that reality, compounded by the fact that residents rarely knew of their own registration, meant that I had to be extremely careful not to inadvertently divulge registration information, lest my research become a source of informant suffering.

UNEQUAL ACCESS TO ASSISTANCE

This brings us to a further aspect of how the emphasis on a family-based sociality framed, and at times undermined, disability advocacy in Min Song. Most of the individuals Chen nominated for a loan in Min Song were men between the ages of twenty and fifty, and nearly all of them were friends or relatives of one or more of the village cadres. While it was never politic (or, for that matter, really necessary) for me to ask why friends and relatives were nominated, I did ask Cadre Chen on a number of occasions to explain why he had selected men. His answers consistently echoed the social forces discussed in Chapter 4. Here is how he accounted for his gender bias in a conversation we had shortly after I arrived in Min Song:

> Well . . . I guess I chose men because the village committee was under pressure from superiors to make sure that the loan program was successful, that local loan recipients established money-making ventures and paid back the principal on time. So, of course, I felt I had to choose those *canji ren* who were most competent, who were most likely to succeed in business. Here in Wenchang, men do business. Women farm.

That Chen felt obliged to reinforce such local gender expectations—men do business, women farm—did not necessarily mean, however, that his job of selecting promising entrepreneurs was that much simpler.

After the introduction of Deng Xiaoping's reforms, men around here became much more concerned with face. As a consequence, many men I've offered a loan to aren't willing to try their hand at launching a *canji* business. They see it as just too much of a public display of their failings. They'd rather just remain poor.

This concern with face-saving, it would seem, was also amplified by clumsiness on the part of the loan program's designers. By the time I left Min Song in the fall of 1994, Wenchang County's Federation office had allocated no loan money to anyone in Wenjiao township, and there seemed to be little evidence that it would do so in the future. Why? The main reason, as township cadres explained, was that the county bank administering the loans would not release funds until applicants submitted cash collateral, and few or no Wenjiao applicants had access to large sums of cash.[20]

As a consequence, by the time I left Min Song, the trade-off that Cadre Chen had assumed would occur—villagers receiving loan money in exchange for knowledge of their disability registration—had not transpired. One upshot was that many loan applicants felt a growing mix of shame and frustration at having been categorized *canji* and having nothing positive to show for it. Many of these men and their family members told me that when they had been originally approached by Cadre Chen they had been happy to apply for a loan because they assumed they would get something for their trouble. But, by mid-1994, a majority felt they had been not only cheated by the loan program but they had also been afflicted by it. Villagers sometimes teased loan applicants and their families for failing to win succor and, as applicants further explained, that teasing often involved such epithets as "hoodwinked *canji*" or "stupid *quezi*."

GUO LI'S COCONUT GROVE:
FROM LATE-NIGHT DEATH THREAT TO A COMMUNITY PARABLE

In this final section of this chapter, I wish to explore the fact that Federation assistance in the 1990s often had the broader effect of making *canji* a category that was not only more known in Min Song but also more disdained.

I got to know Guo Li halfway through my research in Min Song. His name, however, was already familiar to me, since villagers had often mentioned him during the previous six months. Cadres had frequently invoked his name when I asked about local loan applicants, and community members had often mentioned him when I queried, "Who around here is *canji*?"

During my initial chat with Guo Li, which took place as he sat husking coconuts beside the tiny structure he occupied, I quickly learned several reasons why people had so often invoked his name. In the early 1990s, the Wenjiao government had installed Guo Li on the Wenchang Federation's *canji* representative committee (a largely symbolic body comprised of Guo Li and eight other *canji* Wenchang men). Guo Li matched perfectly the Federation's unofficial model of the disabled person: he was male, in his late thirties, smart (despite having no formal education), and a polio survivor. An even more important reason why villagers so often invoked Guo Li's name was because, by the mid-1990s, he had became known locally as the village's (and possibly even the township's) most assertive disabled person (*jiji canji ren*).

This was not a positive moniker. And on more than one occasion people who knew of their *canji* registration in Min Song mentioned Guo Li's assertiveness as reason why they would not consider banding together into any kind of *canji* friendship circle along the lines of what I described to them as existing in places like Beijing. How was Guo Li so negatively coded? To understand this, I must describe the genesis of Guo Li's coconut grove.

The story starts in the 1980s. As the decade progressed, as Guo Li experienced the death of his parents and the departure of his sisters to marriages outside Min Song, he realized he needed to find a successful means of livelihood so that he could not only feed himself but also make himself a viable marriage candidate and thereby partake in the family-based sociality that was becoming increasingly central to local survival. For a number of years Guo Li had tried to find a wife, but not one of the women he had set his sights on would have him because they were repelled by his paralyzed legs, his penury, and his apparent inability to achieve financial success.

In the early 1990s Wenchang's Federation officials approached Guo Li and asked him to serve on the county's *canji* representative committee. He agreed, and shortly thereafter he decided to follow a strategy that he had seen other Min Song residents pursue in the previous decade: planting palm trees and eventually living off the sale of coconuts. The problem with his strategy was that Guo Li only had a small parcel of land in his name and no broader family land claims to tap. His response was simple: he began planting coconut saplings on the land adjacent to his own.

Many in Min Song were not pleased. Before long, people complained to the village cadres, cursed Guo Li, and threatened to tear up his saplings. Guo Li countered these acts in a unique way. He argued with his detractors that he possessed "special rights" guaranteed by China's Disabled Persons' Protection Law, and that those rights allowed him as a *canji ren* to grow his coconut palms without fear of discrimination.

Village and township officials disagreed with Guo Li, and before long neighbors began ripping up some of his trees. Late one night, Guo Li awoke to an angry villager holding a knife to his throat and demanding that the trees be moved. These actions prompted Guo to seek supralocal intervention and to associate himself even more with a protected demographic entity: China's *canji* population. Emboldened by the various Federation magazines he had subscribed to and had been studying over the previous few months, Guo sent a petition to the central Federation office in Beijing. Within a short time, central Federation officials had redirected the petition to the Wenchang County government with a cover letter requesting that appropriate intervention be taken. This spurred county officials, including members of the Wenchang Federation office, to make investigative trips to Min Song.

When Wenjiao township and Min Song officials learned of these trips and of how Guo Li had petitioned Beijing authorities, they became enraged and verbally abused Guo. In the end, however, the township and village officials had little choice. They had to swallow their anger (if only for the time being) and allow the county-level functionaries to investigate the situation in Min Song. In late spring 1993, under the protective eye of the county government, Guo Li and the village committee signed a contract that dictated he could continue to use the land upon which his saplings were growing for a period of twenty years.

While the contract legally blocked local cadres and villagers from pushing Guo off the disputed land, it did little to diminish the overall community hostility toward him. A key source of this hostility was the claim put forward by the Fengs. A well-respected local family, the Fengs had lived in the Min Song area for generations, and in the early 1990s one of their kinsman was on the village committee. A few weeks after Guo Li had begun planting saplings, Feng family members had accused him of colonizing their pasture—a field which they said not only had been their property long before Communist collectivization, but which generations of Fengs had sanctified as an ancestral burial ground. Much to their dismay, the Fengs' case against Guo Li had a serious legal flaw. They lacked the requisite documentation to prove their land claim.[21] Because, in the 1960s, the Fengs had burned their deeds and destroyed the family grave stones—like many other devout Maoists during the Cultural Revolution—they had no evidence to use against Guo Li. Of course, most community elders in Min Song knew that the disputed land had belonged to the Fengs. But in the eyes of the county officials who had intervened on Guo Li's behalf, that did not matter.

Interestingly, on a certain level, it can be said that the conflict between Guo Li and the Fengs was one of competing moves to foster family-based sociality: Guo wished to establish his own family so he could survive and prosper, and the Fengs wished to protect the sanctity of their patriline. In pursuing these aims, each was drawing upon distinct discourses having to do with the privileged body. Guo was invoking the modern, international concept of the legally protected disabled body. The Fengs were invoking a re/emergent concept of the sacrosanct ancestral body.

On the surface, it would seem that Guo Li came out ahead. But appearances are deceptive. A result of his actions—that is, the *fury* of the Fengs, of large segments of the Min Song community, and of local cadres—was deeply troubling for Guo. The rationale for Guo's concerns might not be immediately apparent, so allow me to elaborate.

From 1949 forward, survival in rural China had depended on the goodwill of not just one's co-villagers but of one's village cadres. This was particularly true for those, like Guo Li, who lived with negatively marked kinds of bodily difference. Yet, owing to Guo Li's land grab, to the Federation's legalistic defense of his behavior, and to the reemergence of ancestor worship in the post-Mao period, Guo's chances for goodwill had been almost completely shattered. Instead, if and when disaster struck, he could only expect aloofness if not outright hostility from nearly everyone in the community. As Guo Li indicated:

> Looking back, I have real doubts that I did the right thing. The downside of my coconut farming enterprise has been huge. Now, everyone around here really hates me. People are always threatening me, cursing me, and calling me demeaning names. People even accuse me of abusing women. They'll say anything to get at me. And what have I won? I've been able to find a wife, yes, that's very important. But how about my economic future. I have only a twenty-year contract on the land. What good does that do when I'm old? I can't depend on some local network of disability brothers, like those in Beijing you told me about. I can't depend on the Federation. They're all the way in Wencheng. Sure, the Federation helped me get a twenty-year window [to use land]. But they can't stop people from cursing me. They can't stop someone from slipping into my house and cutting my throat. They can't give me a pension so I'll be able to live securely later in life. They can't make people around here help me if I get sick or if a big typhoon hits and knocks down my house. What would I do if something like that happened? I only have one good leg.

If he had done nothing—if he had not shrewdly used the Disabled Persons' Federation and its loosely worded Protection Law as a legal buttress to create a livelihood for himself—would Guo Li be facing any less precarious a situation? If he had done nothing, he would have had little chance of finding a wife and having children who could potentially provide him at least some support in his old age. Indeed, if he had done nothing, he would have become increasingly like Ming Luli, an impoverished elderly man dependent on the haphazard and often illusory sympathies of distant kin, co-villagers, or the state.

Ultimately, it is impossible to know whether Guo Li would have been better off on his pre- or post-coconut-planting trajectory. And, I would argue, the fact that he was seemingly destined to be thrust into some sort of precarious situation no matter what he did vividly demonstrates the presence of overt hostilities toward bodily differences associated with the category of *canji*. It also reveals forces inherent to post-Mao social organization, forces that, alas, during the period of my fieldwork, too often amplified such hostilities and, even more troublingly, inhibited constructive responses to them.

Chapter 6

Dis/ablement and Marriage

Ridiculed Bachelors, Ambivalent Grooms

When Lin Gemei got off the bus in front of Wenjiao's meat and vegetable market, it did not take her long to find a jitney driver heading to Min Song. The driver already had a number of passengers on board, so before long he started the engine and set off. During the bumpy fifteen-minute ride to the village, Gemei struggled to understand what her co-passengers were saying, since they were all chatting in Wenchangese. Fortunately, the driver knew Mandarin and he kindly served as the young woman's interpreter. Shortly before they arrived in Min Song, on Gemei's request, the driver asked some of the passengers for directions to the home of Zhang Pinxin. His query, the driver later told me, had been met with a mix of knowing responses and snide remarks. But he didn't tell that to Gemei when they pulled into the center of Min Song.

Pointing her toward a sandy path, the driver told her which turns to make and where. Within a few minutes, Gemei had successfully navigated her way to the courtyard house that Zhang Pinxin shared with his parents and his brothers' families. At the gate, Pinxin's father and several children warmly welcomed her and invited her in. Struggling in Mandarin, the father told her that Pinxin was off fishing but that he was expected home within the hour. As she waited, the father provided Gemei with tea, a towel for some long overdue washing, and a bit of polite conversation.

After an hour or so had passed, Pinxin arrived and introductions were made. It was only a moment before Gemei's eyes welled up with tears. She continued to cry most of the way through lunch and into the early evening. The next day, after family members had spent hours trying to convince her to stay, Gemei left the Zhangs' house and began the long journey back north to her mainland village. According to a neighbor, on her way out of the house Gemei had screamed at the Zhangs:

You bastards. You're all cheats. We wrote all those letters back and forth and you never told me the truth. Why would I want to marry a cripple? My family's poor. Big deal. I don't need to marry someone like him. Even if I was a cripple [*quezi*], I could do a lot better. I wouldn't have to marry a *quezi*. You should know that. Everyone knows that. I could marry a good man, not some eunuch.

Pinxin barely ate or slept in the days following this calamity, his father explained to me. "We all felt so terrible."

CHINA, DISABILITY, AND MARRIAGE EXCLUSION

For more than a few people in post-Mao China, marrying has been an acutely difficult and conflict-ridden proposition when certain bodily differences are perceived as being in the mix. Invectives, tears, and accusations of wrongdoing regularly spill forth, leaving in their wake feelings of frustration and disappointment.

In this chapter, I explore this troublesome terrain. And I explore it from the perspective of men like Zhang Pinxin—men who, like so many others discussed in this study, are frequently viewed by those around them as "crippled" or "disabled."

Why orient this penultimate chapter around such a topic? Why focus on the courtship travails of men like Zhang? Because they are so commonplace and so distressing, these travails afford a poignant and quotidian way to take up once more a central thesis of this book: that embodiment significantly mediates two interrelated and unfolding processes of sociopolitical formation—the development of biobureaucracy (in the guise of the Federation) and the production of Otherness (in relation to the category *canji*). As much as any other place, today or in the past, finding a spouse in China involves not just quotidian but so too embodied practices. Finding a spouse involves assessments of the somatosocial and somatopolitical vis-à-vis complex notions of normativity. It entails or heralds the production of intimacies, sentiments, and interactions that are deeply contingent on corporeality. And usually it is sexually saturated and presages procreation.

Another reason to consider courtship and its calamitous contours among men like Zhang Pinxin is that such a focus can help clarify further not just the significance of the nation-state but that of the masculinist nation-state for the interrelated production of *canji* as a realm of Otherness and for the Federation as an institution. Why was the nation-state, even before the Federation was formally accredited, concerned with whether the *canji* married? And why, after it came into existence, did the Federation make it a fundamental part of its mission to help disabled men find a life partner to partake in a heteronormative system of marriage?

A further rationale for discussing marriage, beyond prompting us to explore such questions, is that it affords a unique vantage point from which to return to a sphere of embodiment, subjectification, and to analyze in particular an aspect of subject-making that, as of yet, has not been considered in sufficient detail here. In previous sections of this book, I have noted that many, if not most, people in China who fit the Federation's *canji* criteria were quite reluctant to embrace *canji* as a signifier of self and personhood. Likewise, I have also shown that among those people potentially eligible for Federation intervention (symbolic and/or practical), those most likely to have that eligibility refashioned into a demonstrable *canji* persona often tended to be men who had difficulty with walking.

What remains inadequately discussed is that, while I wended my way through my fieldwork, there were many people I encountered—with lives profoundly affected by what the Federation would call *canji* and what English-language observers might characterize as "disability"—who had quite ambivalent sentiments toward *canji*. These were people who would, at one moment, characterize themselves to me and fellow community members as *canji,* and who would display affinity toward others that they called *canji ren,* but who would, at another moment, either spurn any association with *canji ren,* disparage them, or speak of themselves highly gratuitously as being able-bodied *(jianquan).* These were people for whom a commitment to *canji* was far from fixed; how much they affiliated themselves with *canji,* how much they reviled *canji,* was mutable. What's more, these were people who, as they explained it to me, did not always find such mutability particularly gratifying. In fact, they made clear that traversing this dyadic borderland of difference, of *"canji,* yet not *canji,"* was often quite painful.

In recent years, I have come to think about such people as occupying a deeply indeterminate zone, an ambiguous space, of theirs and others' making. One might call this space dis/ablement. And in splitting the word "dis-ablement," there is a temptation to explain this space by drawing on disability scholarship that is centered around ideas having to do with liminality.[1] I resist that temptation. Informed by his own confrontation with a degenerative spinal disease, which ultimately took his life, and based on research among persons suffering from mobility impediments, Robert Murphy posited in the 1980s that the disabled in the United States "dwell in twilight zones of social indefinition" (1988, 237). This existence is analogous, he and his co-authors have argued, to the liminal condition that Van Gennep ([1909] 1960) and Turner (1969) characterize as a central structural phase in rites of passage. Disability is a "juncture," Murphy and his co-authors wrote (1988, 237). It is "an in-between state, for the disabled person is neither sick nor well, neither fully alive nor quite dead" (238). It is "an arrestment in life history that is dramatized in a rite of passage frozen in its liminal state" (241).

While quite helpful, particularly for avoiding viewing disability as something that is biologically given, I find Murphy and his collaborators' approach unsatisfying for making sense of *canji* as a sphere of subjectification. First, since they see disability as always characterized by incompletion, their approach seems to render implausible sentiments of fulfillment that are felt or desired by people, such as some of the motorcyclists I came to know in Beijing, people who strongly identify with both the category *canji* and social networks of *canji ren*. Second, although a liminality model can potentially help highlight the degree to which *canji ren* was a socioculturally mediated subject-position in late-twentieth-century China, it is less promising for helping us understand that *canji ren* was a subject-position that was not fully embraced by the people who were thus categorized, and that, more often than not, they tried to dodge that label and only came to inhabit it at the level of identity with sizable ambivalence and through significant negotiation. Last, but not least, a liminality approach seems to obviate the possibility of either active agency or process—whether personal, interpersonal, discursive, or institutional—in the formation of a "*canji*, yet not *canji*" persona.

To better appreciate the issues of agency and process, it is helpful to think about time. For, if there exists a temptation to draw on a liminality model, so too there is a temptation to think about dis/ablement as nothing new for China. Did not the hybridity of being "*canji*, yet not *canji*" pre-date the Federation's formation, although within an alternative symbolic network? Were there not, for example, people in pre-Dengist China who at one moment called themselves *canfei* and at another moment called themselves normal *(zhengchang)*? My stance is that such a continuity outlook—such a "there's-nothing-really-new-here view"—is misguided. I insist that, while we are dealing with something that has deep roots, there were factors quite unique or certainly far more intensely at play in the late twentieth century when it came to the category of *canji* (as compared to *canfei*) and which helped to promote the presence of a distinct yet indeterminate space of "*canji*, yet not *canji*."

At play, for instance, were a set of translocal discursive forces. These forces, as I have already chronicled, rained down on the term *canji* after Mao's death in ways and degrees that they never did with *canfei* or any other antecedent term of bodily alterity (like *canfei, bozi, shazi, mengren,* or *xiazi*). These forces have had much to do with modernization, nationalism, and science. After the Maoist epoch ended, *canji* began to be increasingly attached to a set of contradictory precepts and bureaucratic imperatives animated as much by local as by transnational notions of modernity, empiricism, and the nation-state. *Canji* began to be discursively imbued as a social category holding special promise for the Chinese nation and its people. That promise, even if only realizable in a distant future, was one of affording personal and national progress. Such progress was to be achieved in two, quite paradoxical ways: by dint of advancements in governance and/or science, *canji* was either to be developed as a special and well-endowed form of citizenship or it was to be medically mitigated, if not removed.

No less pivotal for promoting dis/ablement as an ambivalent terrain of subjectification during the late twentieth century and for differentiating it from anything that came before in China, was the bureaucratic body-politic, which was then working so hard to create a newfound symbolic prominence for *canji*. More to the point, dis/ablement's distinctiveness and frequency was fueled by features of Federation development. At the broadest level, it was fueled by the institution's symbolically substantial yet politically and economically limited power during the 1980s and 1990s. That the Federation disseminated sizable amounts of information regarding the hitherto rarely used term *"canji"* and about the lives of supposed *canji ren*, that the Federation demanded that Chinese people help the disabled by actualizing what in the 1980s it increasingly called socialist humanitarianism *(rendao shehui zhuiyi)*, caused many a person across the country to be subject to *canji* categorization. But, because the Federation's and the party-state's investments in the realm of disability advocacy during this period were quite unevenly applied and generally modest in scope, and because extant sociopolitical disapprobation toward bodily difference remained fierce, and no less because the privileging of individual competency was on the rise countrywide, sparked by the promotion of neoliberal economics, people I met up and down eastern China in the 1990s rarely felt enticed to fashion a strong *canji* identity or to do so unequivocally. Rather, in Hainan as in Beijing, people I got to know were far more inclined either to discount *canji* as a fixture of their personhood or to think of themselves as *canji* quite selectively and strategically.

That such strategy has been a key part of dis/ablement is important for thinking about *canji* as a space of subjectification. It means that people experiencing *canji* as a life form and as a target of objectification have not been simply disciplinary objects in an early Foucauldian sense. Nor have they been inert initiates encapsulated in some unchanging rite of passage, frozen in a liminal volitionless state of betwixt and between without a life history (see also Frank 2000). In the 1990s, whether it was informants of mine who ran *canji* businesses, or whether it was acquaintances who less publicly attached themselves to *canji* as a moniker or persona, nearly all seemed to emphasize that they had an engaged role, however circumscribed, however profoundly textured by discrimination, in fashioning their day-to-day existence and their unfolding trajectories.

What can discussing spouse-seeking offer in an effort to understand dis/ablement? What can it reveal about how multiple layers of agency and process—including those tied to Federation development—were involved in shaping people into being "*canji,* yet not *canji*"? And what can the struggle to find a spouse tell us about how masculinity related to dis/ablement at the end of the twentieth century? To consider all this further, it is useful to peer through the lens of state statistics, if only briefly. In Chapter 2 I went out of my way to deconstruct state statistical inquiry. Be that as it may, such enumerative inquiry remains rich ground for this and other forms of anthropological study. Beyond demarcating key sites of governance, beyond illuminating what state officials want to know and manage, state-sponsored statistics afford powerful insights, even for critical medical anthropologists, about aspects of everyday sociopolitical formation (as they unfold within those realms of management and governance).

A case in point is a 1988 study on marriage which had a nationwide sample of nine hundred thousand PRC residents. One could certainly suggest that the government's mere decision to conduct such a large national marriage survey highlights, as others have commented (Diamant 2001; Erwin 2000; Stacey 1983; A. Wolf 1986), that the party-state has long treated the marital bond as foundational for the Chinese Communist nation. But there is more to be gleaned about marriage from this survey than just that. For instance, the survey found that by age forty-four, only 3 percent of those studied had never married (National Statistical Bureau 1990, 530–35).[2] A possible surprise to readers unfamiliar with China, this low rate fits with, and amplifies, the predominant image of heteronormativity among many people in Chinese cultural contexts: that nearly all men and women should and do marry (Rofel 1999b; Stockard 1989; Tien 1991). The 3 percent figure also corresponds closely with how marriage in Chinese society settings has been understood as a bulwark for economic survival, an organizational centerpiece of Chinese ideals about personhood, and a normative feature for the development of a proper life (see also Brownell 1995, 244–48; Cohen 1976; McGough 1981; Mann 1991; R. Watson 1986; J. Watson 1989; Wolf and Huang 1980).

Still, it must be remembered, not all people in China have been able to marry or to do so easily. Finding a spouse has often been a vexing endeavor for many people. Of great importance here has been *difference.* As much as any other practice in China—today and in the past—finding a mate is something profoundly entangled with received visions of differentiation: everything from class, ethnicity, professional occupation, and regional background, to education level, legal status, and political history. But not only have distinctions of these kinds been implicated in whom one marries, so too they have been decisive in whether one marries at all.

What of distinctions like those understood along the lines of bodily alterity if not abnormality? How might they be implicated in who marries and who does not? While few scholars have addressed these questions in detail, the same cannot be said about government functionaries.[3] Branches of the

TABLE 2

Population	Percent Never-Married (ages 30–44)
General population	4%
Canji population	25%

Di Ya 1989, 134–37, 1002–43

party-state carefully considered marriage when they co-sponsored the 1987 National Sample Survey of Disability. And one of their key findings was that persons who fit the survey's *canji* criteria were six times more likely to have never married by midlife than those not fitting the criteria.

Owing perhaps to a sense of fixity often imparted by numerical abstraction, the above table could easily be viewed as indicating that many people deemed to be *canji* by the government were suffering from arrested lives, that they were locked in an inescapable state of liminal unmarriedness. After all, if marriage is a long-established normative feature of life development in China, is not the statistically demonstrable fact that a quarter of all *canji ren* were out of step with the broad social expectation of conjugality in the late 1980s duly indicative of a suspension of their life histories? As already indicated, this chapter is designed to argue the contrary. And I support my stance in two overlapping and nonsequential ways. First, I outline that the Federation and its constituents did not handle being single as a forgone conclusion for *canji ren*, but rather as a mutable state, one that effective management could eliminate. Second, I show that actions taken to promote marriage—both institutional and individual—worked to foment a distinct existence, one wherein people were not locked in a twilight zone of liminality but instead one in which they actively participated in constructing an open-ended, often painful and marginalized hybrid sphere of becoming.

INSTITUTIONAL MATCHMAKING

Ever since its 1987 national survey and its 1988 founding, the Federation has viewed the fact that many of its constituents are unmarried as a programmatic problem. And since its founding, the Federation has taken steps to promote marriage and to let others know about that work. This initially came to my attention in 1992, a day after my closest acquaintance in Hainan province's Federation headquarters, Ma Zoufu, introduced me to Gao Xiaoqi, one of the cadres in the Wenchang County Civil Affairs department responsible for Federation activity. The next day, Cadre Gao gave me what I came to learn later was his standard tour of Wenchang County's Federation activities. After a breakfast of dumplings enjoyed at the Civil Affairs Restaurant on the ground floor of Gao's office building, the tour's second stop was the dusty main street of a nearby town, where Gao joyfully and proudly introduced me to a man who owned and ran a medicinal herb shop. The third stop was a nearby village home, where Gao similarly introduced me to a forty-three-year-old man who ran a small but bountiful papaya and jackfruit plantation. In both instances, the men were polio survivors and had established their tax-exempt "*canji* enterprises" with Gao's assistance. What Gao emphasized most of all on our jeep ride back to his office for lunch, however, was not that he had helped coordinate the creation of these men's entrepreneurial ventures, but rather that these ventures had afforded the men enough status and wherewithal that they each could marry.

Whereas Gao's marriage-promotion efforts were relatively indirect—in fact, I probably would never have understand them as such if he had not pinpointed their conjugal effect—his was not the modus operandi adopted by all Federation officials. On the contrary, numerous Federation officials were far more overt in agitating for marriage. Some regularly sponsored "singles events" in their offices. Some ran karaoke parties at nightclubs for unwed constituents. Others set up *canji* dating services in cities like Beijing and Shanghai. More than a few orchestrated public weddings wherein *canji* registrants married en masse. And many worked tirelessly to publicize instances whereby, owing to some Federation intervention or another, a long-unwed *canji* protagonist had met someone (possibly also *canji*), courted, and married:

> Four disabled couples from Guiyang city in Southwest China's Guizhou Province were recently joined together in a group wedding ceremony. The ceremony attracted people from all walks of life in Guiyang city. Vice-Mayor Situ Guimei and more than 100 guests attended the ceremony to wish the happy couples the best for their new lives. Dai Jinping, one of the bridegrooms, sang the popular song "If Everybody Shows His Love for Others . . ." and his rendition of "The Mating of the Goddess" from the famous Anhui Province opera was the high point in the ceremony. (Xinhua News Agency, October 12, 1990, republished in the *China Daily*, October 12, 1990)

> A group wedding ceremony for ten disabled couples was held today in the Gloria Plaza Hotel in downtown Beijing amid flowers and laughter filling the wedding hall. Officials of the China Disabled Persons' Federation, the China Association for the Physically Disabled, the Beijing Disabled Persons' Federation, and the Beijing Municipal Civil Affairs Bureau attended the ceremony and wished the ten couples well. (Xinhua News Agency, January 30, 1999)

Why were Federation officials so keen to both help *canji* constituents find spouses and to extol their success in finding marriage partners for *canji* in

the mass media? What were the effects of these efforts? There are many answers to these questions, some which have been conveyed to me directly, by
either Federation officials or observers of the institution in Beijing and
Hainan.

Several answers have to do with perceptions of well-being and institutional legitimacy during the Deng era. My acquaintances emphasized
that by a certain stage of life—the early twenties in village Hainan, later in
Beijing—being single was a likely source of significant dissatisfaction for
Federation constituents. Such unhappiness could have multiple sources:
disapprobation that one is flouting an expected organizational practice
while others in one's age cohort are complying; unmet desires for sex and
adult intimacy (even though conjugality was rapidly becoming less of an
absolute prerequisite for fulfilling those desires as the millennium drew to
a close); and anxiety that one was abrogating the overarching duty of
extending descent. But beyond such sources, being single was a common
fount of displeasure, since it placed a person in an extremely precarious situation. Because China's Maoist welfare net was growing increasingly thread-
bare in the 1990s, and because a spouse and progeny were expected more
than ever to be one's primary social security backstops, being single had
become anathema for many, especially those who were infirm and/or otherwise marginalized. So, by helping constituents marry, it could be said that
the Federation was simply striving to fulfill its preordained administrative
mission of bringing happiness to *canji ren*. But is that all the institution was
striving to achieve through its efforts? It could just as confidently be argued,
I would suggest, that by laboring to help constituents marry, and by publi-
cizing its successes in this area whenever possible, a further effect was being
sought and consciously generated, one vital for Federation development:
proof of the institution's efficacy. As Cadre Gao once quipped to me: "Helping *canji ren* marry makes them look good and it makes the Federation look
good. The Federation is a new department *(bumen).* To survive, it has to be
constantly showing everyone it cares for these kinds of people."

A related explanation for why and to what effect the Federation promoted marriage has to do with moral and political liability. By helping *canji
ren* create their own conjugal unit, the Federation was shielding itself—as
well as its main benefactor, the party-state—from something of potentially
tremendous significance: a population decrying that it was not being properly looked after. It must be remembered that by publicly recognizing over
fifty million people as constituting a "special population" of *canji ren* at the
end of the 1980s, Deng Pufang and his leadership group had created a massive new sector of potential claimants on the party-state. To delimit demands
by such claimants and to curtail their disgruntlement over perceived unmet
commitments of basic well-being—in other words, in the language of the
party-state, to delimit *canji ren* as a potential source of "instability" within the

TABLE 3

| | Percentage of "never-married," ages 30–44 | |
Population	Female	Male
General population	0.5%	7.0%
Canji population	4.0%	45.0%

Di Ya 1989, 134–37, 1002–43

country—marriage was an apt and credible arrangement for the Federation to promote. After all, it was far cheaper for the party-state to facilitate social assistance and political equanimity by promoting conjugal-unit creation and heteronormativity than it would have been by providing cash outlays or costly government services.[4]

A further explanation for why and to what effect the Federation promoted marriage, I would suggest, has to do with the gender politics of those patrons and clients who had the most to gain from these efforts. And to begin grasping this, one needs to not just recall that most Federation employees in the 1980s and 1990s, particularly among the institution's upper echelons, were male, but also consider the data from the 1987 National Sample Survey of Disability. These data differentiated along male/female and able-bodied/disabled binaries and painted a very distinct portrait of the Federation's spouse-seeking clientele (see Table 3).

According to Brown (1995), in highly patriarchal state-centric environments, the sociopolitical embodiment that is masculinity is built upon men's "power of access to women" (for sex, sentiment, and progeny, as well as for care and labor), and the credibility of government in such an environment always depends on the state's ability to ensure men such access (Brown 1995, 167). Are these insights about the workings of masculinity any less valid for China? On more than one occasion, Federation employees made it quite plain to me that they understood their institution's credibility to be highly contingent on its ability to provide male constituents with spouses, thereby affirming their place in the gender order. So, too, it was plain that one effect of this phenomenon, beyond affording male constituents access to women and the affirmation of their masculinity, was that it often fostered feelings of male self-worth, potency, and occupational legitimacy for the institution's employees.

This was visible in 1992 during my tour of Wenchang County with Gao Xiaoqi. Not only did Cadre Gao feel it important to demonstrate the Federation's potency by introducing me to Wenchang men for whom he had helped find spouses, but he also made it quite clear that he and his *canji* clients drew much personal pride from those conjugal outcomes. As he and I motored back to his office, he quipped:

> Something that's great about working for the Federation is that I'm able to help one of these *canji ren* put his life together well enough that he can convince a girl *(guniang)* to marry him. It's good for everyone. It makes the *canji ren* feel wonderful. It allows him to become his own family head *(jiazhang)*. And it really makes one feel like Lei Feng.

Lei Feng is a mythic soldier in the People's Liberation Army, a creation of Maoism, who is often depicted in socialist realist imagery as upright and strong, a do-gooder extraordinaire. The legend goes that Lei Feng persistently and without want of credit helped those in need, until his untimely death in 1962 in an accident while driving his army truck to repair a rural electrical outage. Up to the present, the party-state regularly launches "Study Lei Feng" campaigns. And from its outset, the Federation has depicted itself as the institutional embodiment of this masculine paragon of Maoism; it has represented itself as the bureaucratic exemplar of "Lei Feng spirit" *(leifeng jingshen)*.

Several years after my jeep ride with Cadre Gao I heard another Federation official who was involved in marriage promotion invoke Lei Feng. This occurred in Beijing at a karaoke party. Organized by the Xuanwu district's Federation office, this party was like most such functions I attended in the capital, illuminated by disco lights and overshadowed by a preponderance of unmarried male, "physically disabled" registrants. Near the end of the evening, the male Federation official who had orchestrated the function turned to me with a smile and began reflecting on his job:

> My wife and I regularly laugh at the fact that my work demands that I find these *canji ren* partners. She likes to call me Matchmaker Lei Feng. Plenty of disabled people exist who want a mate. There's a lot of them out there in the woods, particularly men, who wander in for these kind of parties. My main job, and a key Federation goal, is finding women who are attracted to these kinds of men and who have the same needs. Women like that are quite rare. Still, when I'm successful, when people hook up and marry, it's always great.

GROOMING *QUEZI*

When considering comments like these, comments like Cadre Gao's and Matchmaker Lei Feng's, two issues must be reemphasized. First, the Federation's actual programmatic reach remained relatively modest in the 1980s and 1990s, and so the institution's practical role in helping constituents marry was quite limited, even though its propaganda made it seem otherwise. Second, whereas Federation officials matter-of-factly referred to their married and unmarried constituents as being *canji ren*, those constituents often experienced that appellation as an alien/alienating self-descriptor and, only after a significant series of life events, did they begin to appropriate it, however ambivalently, however strategically, as a mode of self-identification.

In light of the Federation's developmental pattern of symbolic outreach outstripping programmatic profundity, how did people in local community settings—and more specifically, the kinds of people most often subject to local categorization as *canji, canfei*, or allied terms, that is, men with difficulty walking—seek out a mate for marriage? And how through these processes did such men at once enact and live an identity of dis/ablement, of being, yet not being, *canji*? These are questions I address in the remaining pages of this chapter.

Quite a number of scholars have noted and tried to explain why men in China have historically had a harder time finding a spouse than women.[5] Several others, writing about women, have paid attention to the generative relationship between marriage, embodiment, and identity (e.g., Bray 1997; Ebrey 1993; Hershatter 1997; Jaschok 1988; Ko 1997; Mann 1991; Watson 1991). But while these academics have produced rich historical studies, few have given focus to marriage as it may pertain to bodily markers other than gender (cf. Ebrey 1993, 63). Also, because they have mostly examined secondhand retrospective documents rather than informants in the midst of spouse searches, their studies provide scant detail on how the interplay of marriage and embodiment has shaped identity-formation at the interpersonal level.[6]

To help redress these lacunae, in a moment I will turn to two spouse-search stories. In each, the primary protagonist—one named Ah Bo and the other Chen You—is a man I came to know during my fieldwork, a man who was viewed by many in his community as different.

Before delving into these stories, though, a brief digression is required. These stories are about two men in 1990s China who matched not only the paradigmatic image of *canji*—of men who had difficulty walking—but, more particularly, these were men who had often been called *quezi*. As I was conducting fieldwork, my plan was to forego using the term *quezi* when I began my writing. Owing to the pejorative meanings attached to *quezi* and to the pain its usage regularly inflicted on many Chinese acquaintances, my initial intention was to follow the linguistic rules set by the Federation: to limit my vocabulary to *canji* and to its official English-language equivalents.[7] But I have decided that it is important to deal directly with the term *quezi* here. For one thing, despite the Federation's expurgatory efforts, most Chinese have continued using idioms like *quezi* (and its cognate, *bozi*, which can be similarly translated as "lame," "cripple," or "gimp"). Second, a defining practice of anthropology is to examine societies' culpability in the production of suffering, and this can only be done by direct observation of common terms, no matter how disparaging. Third, as I detailed earlier in this book, restricting my usage to the seemingly neutral and historically far more formalistic term *canji* is no less problematic because that term has also been long associated, like *quezi*, with deviance and marginalization. Fourth, as the American polio survivor and author Leonard Kriegel has noted, ostensibly neutral terms like "disabled" often do "little more than further society's illusions about illness and accident. . . . For to be 'disabled' or 'handicapped' is to deny . . . the rage, anger, and pride of having managed to survive as a cripple" (Kriegel 1991, 61). Lastly, I have been inclined to use and write about the category *quezi* because I have had many acquaintances who, as with *canji*, have bounced back and forth between denouncing the term and invoking it when speaking about themselves and others. So, by having the term appear here, I hope that readers will continually be alerted not only to the power and pain attendant to the word but also to how ambivalent some of my informants were toward it, and thus to how *quezi* has been inexorably linked to the experiential terrain I am calling dis/ablement.

NARRATIVITY AND MARRIAGE EXCLUSION: TWO STORIES

To analyze how seeking a spouse in 1990s China fostered subjectification for Ah Bo, Chen You, and others, we must, of course, be keenly attentive to the overarching influences of normative structures, what Foucault would include under the heading "technologies of domination" (quoted in Keenan 1995, 424). But so, too, we must be equally attentive to how, as Foucault suggested at the end of his life, these technologies bump up against "processes by which the individual acts upon himself" (ibid.).[8] And to do so, I begin by focusing analytical attention squarely on the issues of narration and expectation. For, as people like Ah Bo, Chen You, and others have explained to me, often what was most immediate in shaping their being, yet not being, *canji* were interactions between, on the one hand, how they and community members talked about aspects of their lives (often, their damaged legs, their wobbly gait, their crutches, or their wheelchairs) and, on the other hand, their hopes and expectations for the future. Mr. Li, who badly fractured his leg as a teenager, provides an example:

> After I began walking with a wobble, everybody started looking at me and talking. Looking and talking. Looking and talking . . . My leg kept me from attending school. . . . [But] the looking and talking wasn't so bad when I was young. It didn't happen so often and I barely noticed it. It became really bad, though, when I tried to marry. Growing up, I saw all these people around me finding themselves or their children a partner [*duixiang*] and marrying. This made them feel good and valuable. Naturally, my family hoped for me to marry as soon as possible. More than anything else, they thought it would

make me feel better, make me feel valuable. But it hasn't. Whenever I've tried to find someone, people start laughing and talking about how foolish my hopes are.

One way to make sense of how the interplay of talk and hope unleashed during spouse searches contributed to people like Mr. Li undergoing a transformation at the level of identity is by, once again, engaging narrative theories, particularly those attentive to issues having to do with expectation. As mentioned earlier, anthropologists of the body have turned increasingly to narrative approaches in recent years to illuminate links between meaning-making and subject-making. This interest in narrativity has been stimulated in part by some now commonplace recognitions about ethnography: that one primary avenue ethnographers have for understanding informants' experiences is the narratives they and others tell; that informants' experiences, like their narratives, are always to some degree processual or unfolding; and that the shaping of such experiences is linked to how informants can be both the source and object of narration. Just as important, however, attention to narrativity in the anthropology of the body has been piqued by sophisticated studies conducted elsewhere in the academy during the last two decades. These studies indicate that the mechanisms underlying narrativity—such as storytelling, dialogue, and audience reception—may, in fact, be closely akin to, and thus may potentially shed valuable light on, mechanisms driving various sociopolitical processes, including identity-formation (e.g., Bakhtin 1981; Bruner 1986; Habermas 1984; Ricoeur 1981).

During the search for a partner, how did the making and remaking of narratives and expectations contribute to specific men's *canji* subjectification? For men in Beijing and Hainan who potentially fit Federation *canji* criteria, and even for those who did not, finding a partner and marrying often involved intervention by a large number of people, such as parents, friends, relatives, and professional matchmakers. These people usually hoped to put men and women together who could provide enunciations of each other's vibrancy and strength (past, present, and future), who could serve as positive symbols of the other's family and personal ability *(nengli)*. In Beijing, as far as most marriage-age men and their families were concerned, for a prospective wife to project vibrancy, strength, and ability she was expected, at the very minimum, to possess the markings of a big-city upbringing and full health *(jianquan)*. In agrocentric areas like my east Hainan field site, the emphasis given to regional association was somewhat less than that which stressed full health.[9]

Whether in eastern Hainan or Beijing, people that I knew who were involved in finding a partner for a brother, nephew, or son often began their search by formulating a narrative: they created an "introductory description" about the groom-in-waiting. This description (which some called a *jieshao shu,* an "introductory script or book") was designed for verbal presentation to prospective women and their families and friends. The presenters generally strategized among themselves and with the male suitor about what elements would make a good and effective description (cf. Bourdieu 1977, 58–71). A common description at this early stage was generally assumed to be one that simply listed the positive attributes of the man and his family—what could be viewed as their collective *nengli*[10]—while downplaying or avoiding mention of any perceived problems.[11]

The expectation that they would emphasize *nengli,* though, was especially problematic for certain men, that is, for men who it was understood had difficulty moving "naturally" through space. This has much to do with historical forces shaping notions of *nengli,* forces not unrelated to my earlier discussions of bicycle proliferation. Throughout the twentieth century, *nengli* has been linked increasingly to a set of ideas about mobility, national development, and gender. Reinforced by the global burgeoning of western body discourses like biomedicine (Bullock 1980), public health (Lamson 1935), athletics (Brownell 1995), and Social Darwinism (Dikotter 1992), the Chinese image of the able body, from the beginning of the twentieth century onward, has been defined more and more as the active body: the body that can halt China's "withering" and instead promote a racially powerful nation-state (Dikotter 1992, 111), the body that can realize Mao's dream of "continuous revolution" (Brownell 1995, 57), the body that can leap, whether through collective or individual action, to the forefront of industrialized modernity (see Mao [1917] 1978).

That *nengli* has become increasingly coterminous with mobility and national development has deeply informed gender. And by the start of the post-Mao epoch, it would seem that a generally unspoken compact had emerged having to do with manhood and public space. Not only were men, more than women, expected to occupy and control public arenas for the grand mission of national development but they were also expected to be the driving force of mobility within those arenas: being a man far more than being a woman demanded demonstrating and generating status by moving around quickly outside the home and by having greater authority over where and how movement was made.

In light of these transformations, it should not be surprising that men in contemporary China who wobble when they walk are often considered either less manly than other males or more incompetent than similarly troubled women. Echoing countless comments on the subject, an elderly woman from Hainan once told me:

> The problem with *que* men around here is that they don't have the *nengli* it takes to be successful. More than women, men need to get out of the house and be fast on their feet. That's why *que* men are such a miserable lot. They

just don't have what it takes to be a man, to go out and do what's expected of them. That's why they have such a hard time marrying.[12]

Nor should it be surprising that, when seeking a spouse, many men who have trouble walking want to leave out any mention of immobility from an introductory description. Depending on a number of factors, including how much information the woman's side is able to acquire independently about the man, the presentation of an introductory description often leads to a direct meeting between the man and woman and, frequently, their families. Sadly, as illustrated at the beginning of this chapter by the story of Lin Gemei and Zhang Pinxin, such meetings often are disastrous because, when the woman and/or her family finally see the man, they feel deceived, they feel that the expectations projected by the man's introductory narrative have been shattered. Failed meetings and the invectives that frequently result are traumatizing events for the man's side as well, since their collective hopes and expectations likewise are broken.

FINDING MEI LING

Ah Bo's predicament provides a more lengthy illustration of these dynamics. Ah Bo was in his mid-thirties when I moved into the village of Min Song. He grew papayas and had a large house that he and his older brother inherited when their father died twenty years earlier. Around the time of the father's death, Ah Bo's brother married and began having children. In the mid-1980s, as Ah Bo was maturing into young adulthood, his brother, mother, and sister-in-law began pressing him to marry. But finding a local woman for Ah Bo proved nearly impossible. In part, old and new sociological forces were to blame. In addition to the ongoing pattern in Wenchang County of there being a greater numbers of males than females growing into young adulthood,[13] China's market reforms there tended to push marriage-age men and women apart. From the mid-1980s onward, many young women of eastern Hainan opted to leave home for cities like Haikou, Shenzhen, and Guangzhou in order to work in the many newly created service-sector jobs, thereby escaping the farming duties which local families had traditionally foisted upon women. Young men of the region, by contrast, generally were less inclined to move to the cities, until they had children to support, in part because the urban jobs available to them were mostly in construction, a vocation they considered dangerous and arduous.

To overcome this shortage of local unmarried women, Ah Bo's mother decided to enlist the help of several female friends who worked as matchmakers. Two of the matchmakers immediately encouraged Ah Bo to consider marrying a neighborhood woman who was deaf. But, a matchmaker

Figure 7. Gambling in conjugation: Married Wenchang County residents playing *majiang.*

told me, Ah Bo and his brother proclaimed that a union with someone deaf
or any other way "abnormal" would be unacceptable. Like their mother,
they felt that marriage to a deaf women would be incommensurate with Ah
Bo's status. In addition to rejecting the matchmakers' initial idea, the two
brothers asked the matchmakers to avoid discussing with prospective brides
anything regarding either Ah Bo's childhood polio episode or his withered
leg. Instead, they instructed their mother's friends to emphasize the realities
that they perceived as most central to Ah Bo's existence: his friendly manner, his intellectual acuity, his quickly expanding papaya grove, his family's
big house, and his brother's lucrative shrimp farm.

Using such a description, the matchmakers were able to arrange four
separate introductions over an equal number of years. Each of these meetings ended up a failure. In every case, the young woman arrived, saw Ah Bo
standing with his homemade crutch under one arm, and quickly asked the
matchmakers to bundle her home. Two of the women had burst into tears
on seeing Ah Bo. On one occasion, a father who had accompanied his
daughter became irate, blasted Ah Bo and the matchmaker with invectives,
and demanded that Ah Bo's brother compensate him for his travel expenses
and the ridicule he might receive from his co-villagers if the story followed

him home. Ah Bo's brother refused to compensate the father and was chided the next day by the village secretary for trying to cheat others and nearly causing a brawl.

For Ah Bo, the four introductions orchestrated by the matchmakers were extremely painful events that deeply affected him. As he told me:

> After each meeting, news spread. . . . For many days, people in the village and the nearby town were talking and laughing. They shouted out to me, "Ah Bo, you're such a silly *quezi* thinking you can marry a regular girl." It made me feel terrible and very depressed. I couldn't sleep. I didn't want to eat. Everything felt uncomfortable and strange. Everything I hoped for seemed out of reach. . . . After a while I got better, but not completely. I've never felt really the same since those meetings.

Men like Ah Bo and their families usually continue searching, often gradually adjusting their expectations to include women with whom a marital relationship would project less ability: women from poorer or less culturally sophisticated backgrounds, women who are in another way locally defined as abnormal, or women who live in less advantageous areas of the country. These searches sometimes extend for hundreds of miles and go on for years, sometimes with the direct involvement of the groom-in-waiting, often surreptitiously, in order to avoid his opposition. With each new stage of the search, with each reorientation of a family's expectations, the seekers commonly rethink and revise their introductory description, often transforming it from a non-linear list of positive attributes into a compelling story line about family tragedy and how this tragedy has resulted in a man who possesses both strengths and weaknesses.

This effectively describes the continuation of Ah Bo's story. After years of failure, Ah Bo's brother told me, he and his wife, together with neighbors, increasingly pressured Ah Bo to lower his expectations of the kind of bride he could have. "We kept after him to let us find him a woman befitting the reality of his personal condition." In spite of this heavy pressure, Ah Bo demurred.

His brother and sister-in-law then took matters into their own hands. More and more irritated at Ah Bo for not keeping pace with their changing expectations and for not fulfilling the overarching expectation of having a spouse to contribute to the joint family's housework, the brother and sister-in-law paid a matchmaker to bring two women from a neighboring township for Ah Bo to meet. These women, the brother explained, were different from any of the previous ones because "they had defects" *(you quedian)*. The first was mute, and the second was what the Hainanese call *gnou hui*, meaning "mentally ill" or "retarded."[14]

One afternoon, as we sat in the family courtyard cleaning a basket of peas, Ah Bo's sister-in-law quietly told me how she, her husband, and the matchmaker had remade Ah Bo's introductory narrative in preparation for its delivery to the families of the two women. The revised narrative was quite unlike the original; it described a different unfolding of Ah Bo's past, present, and future life. According to the sister-in-law, it went something like this:

> When he was born, Ah Bo was a big healthy baby. He was everybody's favorite. One very rainy winter when he was about three, Ah Bo got a bad fever. Nobody thought to take him to a doctor right away. A few days after the fever went away, Ah Bo's left leg became very painful and weak and he had a hard time walking. His mother and older brother carried Ah Bo to see many doctors. The doctors gave him massage and burn treatments. They burned him up and down his little legs. Ah Bo cried for days. But it didn't work. Nothing worked. After that, Ah Bo, spent most of his childhood crawling around his home and the area just outside it. . . . An older cousin, who felt bad that Ah Bo was a *quezi* and could not walk, taught him to read. Now he can read and write everything. He's always helping his friends write letters. He's smart, that Ah Bo. With the money his brother loaned him, he planted a bunch of papaya trees. Now he has more than a hundred trees. Most of the trees are still young, but when they get big they'll produce many, many papayas each year. . . . Even though he'll always be a *quezi*, Ah Bo will do well, just like his brother, with his big shrimp farm.

When a narrative like this works, when people like Ah Bo's family present it to potential mates and the potential mates find it at once attractive and an accurate reflection of the man's life, it is often the case that the man then rejects the woman on the grounds that she does not meet his minimal requirements.[15] Such refusals frequently cause relatives and nearby observers to lash out at the man for being arrogant, for not humbly accepting the reality portrayed in the revised narrative.

In Ah Bo's case, the introduction of the two women—one mute, one *gnou hui*—and Ah Bo's rejection of them incited a series of squabbles between Ah Bo and his brother's family that ultimately resulted in Ah Bo and his aged and infirm mother moving out of the family's sprawling white-stucco house and into a dark, small, brick hut. This hut is located on the community's outskirts, in a veritable no-man's-land that is only accessible to the other village households via a very pitted, kilometer-long sandy track. For Ah Bo, being forced out of his home was a source of enormous suffering, both because of his embarrassment as well as the daily difficulties he had to endure caring for himself and his mother. It was, indeed, a sad paradox that, in the end, Ah Bo's resistance to what he considered his brother and sister-in-law's attempt to throw him into a marginal marriage resulted in those same people physically casting Ah Bo out of his home and onto the social and geographic margins of local life.

Ah Bo's story does not end there, however. At the time I met Ah Bo and his mother in the spring of 1993, approximately four years after their exile, they were sharing their cramped hut with a third person: a twenty-two-year-old pregnant woman, Mei Ling, whom Ah Bo introduced as his new wife. Because I knew nothing of Ah Bo's life at that point, Mei Ling's presence did not seem particularly significant. That was until she and I began speaking. In response to a local greeting I expressed to her, Mei Ling spoke to me, not in Wenchangese, but in a distinctively accented Mandarin that is common to only one part of China—Guangxi—an economically underdeveloped region of the People's Republic located about 150 miles northwest of Hainan.[16]

As my fieldwork progressed and our friendship developed, Ah Bo and Mei Ling often talked about their situation with me. They told me that they initially had learned of one another in 1992 through a personal ad Ah Bo had placed in a national magazine. Mei Ling was not the first Guangxi woman to visit Ah Bo as a result of his ads. She was the fourth. The previous three women, after traveling to meet Ah Bo, had stayed with him and his mother only a short time before returning home.

Ah Bo and Mei Ling also disclosed that, even though they were about to have a child, the two of them had never officially wed. The reason they had not been able to legitimize their "marriage," Mei explained, was her father. After learning that she had chosen a man who was "a little *canji*," as Mei said, her father had barred the Communist party secretary in her natal village from issuing her a premarital certificate. On a number of occasions, Mei flatly stated she was willing to endure her father's scorn and to live out of wedlock with Ah Bo, in part, because of Hainan's economic advantages. But she also stressed that Ah Bo's honesty played a large part in her thinking. "One of the things I like about Ah Bo is he didn't try to hide things from me before I came here. He described everything in his letters."

Despite the friendship I developed with Mei Ling and Ah Bo, it was never appropriate for me to see their letters. But, on one occasion, Ah Bo did explain to me how he had represented himself in the ad that initially caught Mei Ling's eye.

MK: Did the advertisement that Mei Ling spotted vary significantly from the previous ones you wrote?

AB: I was more careful when I wrote that ad to describe myself and my physical condition very accurately.

MK: Do you remember what you wrote?

AB: I pretty much just said I was a thirty-two-year-old Hainan man, that I had a small house and a papaya grove, and that my leg was no good.

MK: You said there was something wrong with your leg?

AB: Sure. If I didn't, anybody who answered the ad would become very resistant once they found out. I had to say I was a disabled person [*canji ren*].

MK: You wrote you were a *canji ren?*

AB: No. Actually, I didn't use that word. I just said I was a polio victim [*shi xiao-er-ma-bi-zheng de*].

MK: Did you consider using an other, more idiomatic word in your ad, the word *canfei?*

AB: No. I wouldn't use *canfei.* I hate it when people call me that. *Fei* means useless and I don't consider myself useless. I'm just a little bit lame [*que*]. When people call me *canfei,* I'll often tell them the only thing worthless around here is what they see in the mirror.

MK: And the term *canji?*

AB: I don't mind that term so much anymore. I use it sometimes, although I try not to.

MK: You use it to describe yourself?

AB: Sometimes. To describe myself or parts of my life. But only when I think it's appropriate. Sometimes I feel *canji.* Sometimes I don't. You know, I'm also very competent [*nenggan*] and my health is good. Those are things that I'd like people to know about me. And when Mei Ling and I were writing each other, I emphasized them a lot, as much as being *canji.*

READER-RESPONSE THEORY

The events leading up to Ah Bo and Mei Ling's common-law marriage, it could be said, were a set of processes whereby Ah Bo's and others' expectations of who he was and what he could accomplish were repeatedly shattered and he came to occupy an unusual experiential space. Because of his spouse-seeking travails and because of confrontations with other aspects of the normative, above and beyond just marrying, Ah Bo reluctantly came to live a life distinguished by an ambivalent relationship to alterity, wherein he felt at one moment (or level) *canji* and then at another moment (or level) not.

In terms of theoretical analogies, the processes undergirding Ah Bo's marriage travails seem to echo, I would suggest, ideas explored by the reader-response theorist Wolfgang Iser (1974). Iser's main objective was to investigate how narratives are "organized and reorganized" over time through the intersubjective interactions of authors and readers (Iser 1971, 281). Iser's work is relevant to anthropology, Byron Good (1994, 143–44) has pointed out, because it allows one to think about how, through practices of everyday interaction, informants make meaning of and about their own unfolding experiences. The pieces of Iser's theory that seem particularly relevant to our discussion of marriage exclusion are his ideas about expectations and negation. In his volume *The Implied Reader* (1974), Iser details how, based on past shared events, readers tend to expect specific things from narratives. As readers progress through a story, the unfolding sentences fulfill expectations at the same time that they form new expectations for readers—expectations which are themselves modified by succeeding sentences (278). The processes of anticipation and retrospection, however, may not develop smoothly. Sometimes what readers find as they move through a narrative does not fulfill their expectations. Sometimes stories have unpredictable gaps or ruptures which cause readers' expectations to be suddenly negated (280). To overcome such negations and continue moving through the story, readers must create new expectations. They must, through processes of trial and error, use their faculties of comprehension (59) to organize and reorganize the various meanings offered them by authors and fellow readers in order to create a new horizon for themselves (281). And because readers have overlapping backgrounds yet possess personal "dispositions," negations may be handled differently (281).[17]

What utility might these ideas have for our present discussion, for understanding how Ah Bo was experiencing less an arrestment of his life history than an ongoing process of becoming? Iser's ideas suggest a way to think about how people's expectations of who they are and what befits their somatosocial situation are influenced as events unfold.[18] As such, Iser's concepts lead us toward a framework for viewing how hopes that are part and parcel of a person's sense of himself—such as those held by Ah Bo—are influenced intersubjectively over time by communication among myriad persons involved in acts like those of marriage-making.

Prompted by Iser's ideas of expectation and negation, the following analysis could be made of Ah Bo's story. As Ah Bo progressed into early adulthood, he and his family observed people around them fulfilling the perennial Chinese goal of marriage. These observations (or readings) promoted expectations among them for Ah Bo. Built upon these expectations, Ah Bo and his family created introductory descriptions that projected a certain somatosocial vision of Ah Bo for potential mates. But the potential mates and their families, on meeting Ah Bo, saw something different from what they had come to expect. And what they apprehended they communicated forcefully through invective, which caused Ah Bo to experience a sharp negation of who he felt he was and wanted to be. Under pressure to marry, Ah Bo and his family decided they had little choice but to create new introductory descriptions, ones marked by claims of both normalcy and alterity, that gradually projected a different horizon for Ah Bo. This narrative progression, which continued throughout my time in Hainan and no doubt beyond, was not easy for Ah Bo to accept. Nor was it altogether disciplining, however. Although Ah Bo was increasingly willing to narrate himself as being *canji* so that he could make marriage part of his life history, he remained ambivalent about *canji* becoming his fundamental identity.

SEARCHING FOR LIFETIME ROMANCE

As the next anecdote demonstrates, the analytical promise of Iser's ideas for discerning how practices of spouse-seeking can contribute to dis/ablement is not limited only to the reputed "backwaters" of China like Hainan Province. Indeed, many of the same processes that Iser's ideas prompt one to glean in Ah Bo's story can be found shaping people's lives elsewhere, including Beijing.

In 1994 Chen You was in his mid-thirties and lived in Beijing's working-class district of Xuan Wu, located southwest of Tiananmen Square. Chen ran a tobacco shop. Opened in 1989, the shop increasingly provided Chen with an admirable income. Two miles down the road from the shop, Chen shared a relatively spacious apartment with his parents, who were retired factory managers. To get back and forth to his shop and to conduct business, Chen at first used a hand-crank tricycle and then a three-wheeled motorcycle. Chen and I met at a karaoke party organized by the Xuan Wu branch of the Disabled Persons' Federation. At that event and during our subsequent encounters, he told me about his ongoing spouse-seeking travails.

In 1990, through a friend's introduction, Chen You had begun his first courtship experience with a woman his parents once described to me as a "lovely and fully healthy [*jianquan*] girl from a good family." The friend explained how he made the introduction between Chen and the woman, Geng La:

> Chen You asked me several times to help him meet somebody like Geng. I knew both Chen and Geng for a number of years and they seemed like a good match to me. So, sometime during 1990, I approached Geng using a pitch Chen and I had prepared. It basically went like this: "I think you might be interested in meeting my friend Chen You. You have a lot in common. You're the same age, from similar families, and both like studying English and collecting classical music. Like you, Chen is unattached and interested in meeting somebody. Everybody who knows Chen says he's extremely competent and has a strong future." . . . Of course, I told Geng about Chen's legs, how he had polio when he was young. Chen and I had decided that I should tell Geng about that up front. I did and then quickly moved on to wow her with all the good stuff.

Through this introductory description, Chen and Geng La, met, became friends, and dated for several years. Chen's legs were apparently not an overriding concern for Geng. But they were for her mother and father, who could not accommodate Chen's body to their long-term hopes for their daughter. From the very beginning, Geng's parents hounded her to stop seeing "that *quezi*." One afternoon in 1991, while Chen and Geng were at their respective workplaces, Geng's parents had come to Chen's home and, before storming off, had shouted at his parents: "This relationship has gone on long enough. We will not have our daughter marry your son. It's not right. You should have your son marry somebody of his own kind." When Chen You came home that night, his parents told him what had happened. The next day, a mutual friend delivered a letter to Chen, in which Geng La stated she could never see him again. The words of Geng La and her parents shattered Chen's expectations, leaving him painfully confused about himself and his future.

> This was one of the most hurtful and traumatic events of my life. For many months after Geng dumped me, I felt as if I had been in a terrible crash: that I had run into something while driving a motorcycle, been tossed over my handlebars, and slammed into a wall. The pain was so intense and my sense of confusion so severe, I really thought I might go insane.

The people with whom Chen found the most solace after losing Geng La were men who he described as high-functioning *(hen nenggan)*. Most of them had suffered polio paralysis as children, drove three-wheeled motorcycles, and, as was the case with Chen, increasingly were taking advantages of the privileges the state had extended to *canji ren*. As Chen explained:

> When the Federation began to make noise in the 1980s, I had no interest in it. Why the hell would I want to be connected with it. The last thing I wanted back then was for people to call me disabled. I had plenty of people calling me a useless cripple [*canfei*] when I was a kid. I hated it. [But] then the Federation started to produce these motorcycles. The advantages of having one of these bikes in Beijing, where regular motorcycles are illegal and where nobody can afford an auto, was just too great. So, I got one. Besides helping me with my own business, I figured having a motorcycle would make me seem more competent [*nenggan*] and thus eventually help me find a good wife. It would demonstrate to people how normal I am.

About six months after Chen's and Geng's breakup, some of Chen's friends introduced him to another woman, Lin Famei. The man most responsible for the introduction, Su Shande, recounted to me the basic message he conveyed to Chen You and Lin Famei. Something important to note is how this introduction, like Chen's description of his growing involvement with the Federation, frames him spanning several dyads: same/other, normal/different, able-bodied/disabled.

> Basically, what I told each [Chen and Lin] was, "I think the two of you might make a good couple. You're both Beijingers, are intelligent, have similar families, and have something making it difficult to marry an able-bodied person [*jianquan ren*]. Chen You, you're a polio survivor, and, Lin Famei, you're legally blind. If you can accept these realities, you might greatly enjoy each other's company." . . . I just told them that I thought they were a good match since both were a bit *canji*, yet both were very normal and had a lot of talent [*caineng*].

Figure 8. On the move.

Chen and Lin Famei subsequently dated, fell in love *(tan lianai)*, and con-templated marriage. Yet, once again, parental disapproval intervened. Both Chen's and Lin's parents staunchly forbade wedlock. As Chen explained to me, both sets of parents agreed with his friend's narrative. Both sets of parents agreed that the other set's child was at once a little *canji* and very tal-ented. But each set was unwilling to accept a *canji* narrative as applicable to their own child, feeling it was at odds with the expectations they had for their own progeny.

On a number of occasions, Chen You and his parents argued so intensely about his desire to marry Lin that Chen You moved out of the family apartment and stayed in guest houses and with various friends. During this extended period of intergenerational conflict, Chen You's friends encouraged Chen and Lin to steel themselves against their parents' disapproval. But family pressure eventually won out, and Chen and Lin resigned themselves to never marrying one another. Shortly before I left Beijing in the spring of 1995, Lin Famei informed me that she had con-sented to her parents introducing her to a rural man. Chen You told me that his parents also wished to introduce him to somebody from outside Beijing. Chen stated, however, that he intended to have absolutely no part of his parents' plans. Central to his refusal was how marrying a country woman, he felt, would undermine his commitment to a vision of masculine respectability:

I've told my parents over and over I will only marry somebody raised in Beijing. . . . I refuse to marry a country bumpkin. I know what many Beijingers, particularly young ones, say about polio survivors who marry hicks. They speak of them as being pitiful *quezi* who are so hungry for sex, offspring, and caregiving [*zhaogu*] that they'll take in a woman with whom they have almost no chance of ever developing real love. . . . I refuse to endure a loveless marriage or that sort of commentary. . . . I'm an urbanite. I should marry an urbanite. Why should I settle for a loveless marriage with some hick? Even when I'm old, I'd rather quietly buy sex from a prostitute before letting others pity me as a guy who has to buy a rural wife.

By the time I had returned to Beijing for a brief visit in 1998, it seemed that Chen's parents had entered a new phase, one in which, at least for the purpose of marriage, they were willing to think about and represent Chen You in a new way. Apparently, they had been swayed by Chen's need to protect his sense of masculine propriety. As his mother told me during that visit:

My husband and I were wrong to stand in Chen You's way for so long. At first we didn't like him driving a *canji* motorcycle. We didn't like him interacting so much with the Federation. We didn't like him being *canji*. And we didn't want him marrying someone who was *canji*. But his struggles to be happy have changed our views. I hate to see my son in so much pain. And he has to marry. So, my husband and I have decided, as long as Chen You doesn't marry someone who's too obviously *canji*, we're willing to support his desire to find an urban girl through the Federation.

This new willingness to support their son, as long as the woman he might marry was not "too *canji*," even found its way into the realm of formal text production. In the late 1990s Chen You's father, a retired editor, helped his son craft an ad to be circulated within the Beijing Federation's dating service system. In 1998 Chen showed me the ad, but only after he made me promise never to describe its contents and to reaffirm our earlier agreement that I would protect his anonymity. Why was Chen You so concerned about anonymity? Why did he always expect me—which I would have done anyway—to refer to him by a pseudonym and to alter the details of key aspects of his life (he does not actually run a tobacco shop)? As he explained to me in 1998, it was not because he worried about reprisal should a government agency find out that he regularly spoke to me, a North American academic. Rather, his worry was about categorical essentialism.

I don't want anyone to know that I've been one of your book's *canji* informants [*bei caifang canji ren*] because then people will always look at me as *canji*. That would be intolerable. How would I ever marry just the right person? And after I marry that person, if you've written about me in your book, then the Federation might go and publicize something about my happily married *canji* life. That would be even more intolerable.

Although comfortable enough at this point to sometimes identify himself as a *canji ren*, Chen You is loath to have *canji ren* reified as his sole appellation, whether by this book, the Federation, or by any other means. While comfortable enough to identify himself as *canji* in limited-circulation advertisements, government registry archives, and verbal communications to facilitate marriage, transportation, and employment, he bridles at the thought of *canji* becoming his sole moniker.

Much as in the Ah Bo example, Iser's ideas can be drawn upon here to help discern how Chen You's protracted marriage efforts transformed the ways he and his family understand his situation. Chen and others have repeatedly revised certain expectations for him that could be seen as constitutive components of his bodiliness. More than Ah Bo, Chen anticipated certain troubles when he began looking for a spouse. Probably because of earlier life disappointment he had experienced, he and his friends sensed the possible difficulties he might face in fulfilling conventional marriage expectations. So, they were more declarative about bodiliness when drafting Chen's introductory description. But this did not prevent significant new disappointments, or as Iser might say, negations. Geng La's parents rejected Chen because of his withered leg and because they interpreted it as meaning that Chen was an unacceptable mate for their daughter. That Geng La accepted her parents' reading and broke off the relationship deeply unsettled Chen—inflicting a trauma, as he described it, that was like that of a high-speed motorcycle accident. Indeed, losing Geng La shattered the sense of self that Chen had possessed up to that point and threw him headlong into an ill-defined realm so troubling that Chen thought he might go insane. Chen then increasingly affiliated himself with other polio survivors and increasingly made use of Federation services. Through these interactions, Chen was able to reframe his self-narrative and he allowed others to introduce him to the nearly blind Lin Famei. Chen's and Lin's parents, however, could not accept this romance. The two sets of parents, unmoved by the recent overlay of love and residency discourses (Zhang 2001), would rather have their children marry so-called *jianquan ren* ("fully healthy," or "able-bodied people") from outside Beijing than *canji* neighbors. Such a horizon was unacceptable to Chen in large part because it would visit upon him a poisonous narrative of masculine debasement. For Chen, it was better to be seen as *canji* and single then depraved and married. After some intervening years, Chen's parents became open to his self-reading, eventually affirming this by helping him write an ad aimed at finding a *canji* spouse in Beijing, with the proviso that his future wife not be "too obviously *canji*." Yet, if Chen's parents remained ambivalent about their son too closely affiliating himself with *canji*, so, too, did Chen. Whereas he and others had become increasingly willing to narrate him as *canji* in a multiplicity of contexts, he continued to be ardently opposed to being essentialized as *canji*, by me or anyone else.

CODA

In the politics of difference, ambivalence is not a symptom of the problem
but the modus operandi of the cure.
TANYA LUHRMANN, *The Good Parsi*

Although invoking a few ethnographic stories to make observations about a
culture area or set of theoretical issues is quite problematical, the stories of
the spouse-seeking travails of Ah Bo and Chen You provide insight, however
murky, on important facets about the Federation, *canji*, and subject-making.

It has been vital for the development of the Federation, ever since its
founding, to draw public attention to the plight of its constituents, to
demonstrate its success as a state institution of palliation, and to depict its
constituents as being a distinct social entity, a distinct people, worthy of
unique government intervention and community empathy.

Many persons subject to the Federation's *canji* gaze have, gradually, been
drawn to it. At the same time, however, many of those drawn to the gaze—
including those seemingly most likely to benefit from it, men with difficulty
walking—have often been quite ambivalent about how and to what degree
they want to identify as *canji*.

Far from experiencing a termination or arrestment of their life history,
people subject to *canji* are involved in complex negotiations about who they
are, how they will manage their bodiliness and marginalization, and what
their futures will look like. One terrain where this occurs, as I have explored
in this chapter, is that of family formation.

People that I have come to know whose bodiliness has been treated as different, abnormal, or deformed have been incited as they try to marry to
make that alterity a persona, a state of being, an identity. Yet, this has not
meant that these people have been docile and pliant, inertly accepting marginalization or essentialization. On the contrary, men like Ah Bo and Chen
You have not allowed themselves to be either excluded from marriage,
blithely framed as *canji* grooms, or thrust into matches they find demeaning.

Rather, they have often been involved in complex acts of enunciation or
perfomativity. As they have tried to marry, they have been involved in highly
symbolic, highly political communications with a wide array of people: family members, potential spouses, neighbors, Federation officials, and even, at
times, a North American academic. Through these complex practices, they
have created a hybrid space of identity, a space I have named "dis/able-
ment," one that is not at great variance, it would seem, from the hybrid
spaces of identity that scholars, over the last few years, have chronicled in
sociopolitical contexts outside the realm of disability.

As with other cases of individuals confronting somatosocial regimes often
associated with globalization, men like Ah Bo and Chen You have created

identities that do not neatly serve or outright challenge the "homogenizing, unifying force" which undergirds "the national tradition of the People" (Bhabha 1994, 37). Instead, they have created identities that are "continually, contingently, opening-out," wherein "difference is neither One nor the Other but something else," an "ambivalent process" (37, 219).

Should they, should we, bemoan such ambivalence? Should this state of being be perceived as either failed resistance or derailed development, whether at a personal, institutional, national, or transnational register? Not necessarily. For, if the domains of abjection, sociopolitical control, and institution-based palliation recently framing *canji* have all been highly dependent on essentialism, perhaps it is only through the techniques of ambivalence that the rising ranks of people who confront disability on a daily basis in China can best navigate those domains and thereby, we hope, fashion lives to their own liking.

Epilogue

Late on February 19, 1997, China's top government offices sent a statement to the Chinese Communist Party and its media outlets. Within hours, the statement had been transmitted around the world. It announced that Deng Xiaoping had died at 9:08 that evening. In distinctively clinical terms, it explained that Deng "had suffered advanced stages of Parkinson's disease with complications of lung infections," and he had "passed away because of failure of respiration-circulation" (*China Daily*, February 20, 1997). While the news was worrisome to many, few were surprised. Deng's failing health had long been a topic of public discussion among Chinese citizens and "China watchers."

In the days following the announcement, Deng's death was marked in the manner many expected. The Chinese government quickly proclaimed the formation of a nearly all-male funeral committee, comprised of almost five hundred of the party-state's elite, with President Jiang Zemin as the committee's chair.[1] Solemn and restrained ceremonies were held across the country. Chinese and foreign media ran obituaries that had been prepared long in advance. World leaders made respectful statements of condolence.

Inasmuch as these steps projected what seemed like a stable and carefully choreographed transition, they did not quell many foreign observers and Chinese residents from posing myriad questions about the broad course of China's party-state. Would Deng's handpicked successor, Jiang Zemin, cement his authority as supreme ruler of China? Might the power vacuum left by Deng's death cause disgruntled government factions to launch an anti-Deng backlash? If not, would the macro-social frameworks put in place by Deng Xiaoping continue? Could Jiang Zemin and others sustain Deng's precarious balancing act of party supremacy and market liberalization?

Beyond broad-ranging questions such as these, there were also many that related directly to the Deng family. Would the party-state subject the Deng children—Deng Lin, Deng Pufang, Deng Nan, Deng Rong, and Deng Zhifang—to investigation and prosecution for corruption? Would the Dengs be allowed to continue enjoying their many perquisites, including retaining their state-subsidized Beijing villa? Would the Deng children continue to hold formal and informal positions of influence within China's party-state apparatus?

As I have explained at a number of junctures during this book, the death of Deng Xiaoping was something that many people involved with the Disabled Persons' Federation had worried about for years. And, as one might expect, such worries were thrown into even sharper relief once Deng had finally died. When I revisited China not long after Deng's death, more than a few people who had sizable investments in the Federation's success peppered our conversations with anxious questions: In the years to come, would the Federation be closed down or absorbed by another branch of government? Would Deng Pufang remain influential enough that the Federation could continue developing?

My anxious acquaintances emphasized that these questions would probably remain open for some time. To understand their angst better, I tried anew in late 1997 to arrange an interview with Deng Pufang, one that had long eluded me. Starting in the spring of 1994, I had been working with staff in the central Federation's foreign affairs office to try to arrange for such a meeting to take place. But for one reason or another (no doubt including my lackluster moniker of social scientist and my thorny status as a U.S. citizen), an interview had not been possible.[2] That my request for an interview was granted at long last, and that it occurred in early July 1998, likely stemmed from several factors, at least two of which highlight how much the Federation's functioning has been contingent on matters of embodiment, biomedicine, and international and national politics. First, in the spring of 1998, on my request, Gordon Armstrong, the Ottawa surgeon who had treated Deng Pufang in 1980 and therefore a key person in Deng's embodiment, sent him a letter proposing that he meet with me. Second, President Bill Clinton was scheduled to make a long-awaited trip to the PRC in early July of 1998. This trip was being heavily promoted in China's media as a mark of improving U.S.–China relations (which had foundered since the Tiananmen massacre) and as an affirmation of the party-state's and Jiang Zemin's ongoing success at guiding China to the forefront of global modernity (Zhong 1999).

On July 1, Deng Pufang and I met in the central Federation's office on Beichizi, a road that runs along the eastern edge of the Forbidden City. We talked for almost ninety minutes in a second-floor conference room.[3] We chatted about a number of subjects. Deng inquired about my past research, encouraged me to offer suggestions on how the Federation could better serve the disabled, and asked about my background, particularly any encounters I had had with *canji* in my own life. When I asked Deng questions, his impulse was generally to answer with a blend of cheerfulness and calculus. This was certainly the case when my questions dealt with the linkages between him, his father, and the Federation's development. For instance, Deng did not hesitate to smile when acknowledging his personal role in the Federation's formation, but he was also quick to situate that role within an earlier, broader context:

> I got involved in the disability cause because of my personal needs (laughs). But the disability cause was already underway in China and elsewhere before I got started (laughs). When I founded the Disabled Persons Welfare Fund, the U.N. International Year of Disabled Persons had recently ended and the U.N. Decade for Disabled Persons was getting going. In response to those programs, disabled people all over China created clubs. So, already, there were waves of activity. This was social progress in action. It had nothing to do with me. All I did was stimulate the waves to grow even larger. Those waves would have continued even if I had never gotten involved. They just would've gone in different directions.

Deng did not refrain from saying that his unique status as the son of China's paramount patriarch had been of pivotal importance for the Federation's formation. Yet his general inclination through most of our conversation was to depict Deng Xiaoping's role in the Federation's development as being far less than it could have been:

> My work has certainly been made more convenient as a consequence of my father. One of the most important ways has been that, whenever I've asked to meet with high-ranking officials, they've met with me. Whereas an average disabled person would not get an audience, I've been able to. That had to do with my father (laughs). I've used this. I've met with many leaders and explained to them about disability issues.
>
> [But] the Federation has never been dependent on my father's direct support or pronouncements [about the institution]. From the perspective of building a disabled persons' advocacy organization, I should have asked him to speak or write a few words on behalf of the disabled. But I did not.

And what of the Federation's future? Deng Pufang repeatedly went out of his way to paint a decidedly confident portrait of how the Federation would fare in the post–Deng Xiaoping era, a portrait that he framed in terms of deft bureaucratic planning and the irrefutable size and needs of the nation's recently recognized disabled population:

> My father is dead. . . . This is something I have thought about well in advance, and from the very beginning I've prepared for it. . . . The Federation has

become very large. It has offices in every province and at nearly every level of Chinese society. . . . So I have quite a secure foundation. This foundation has been created on rational bases. . . . It's been created based on a societal necessity: that China's 60 million disabled people suffer and need assistance.[4] . . . The foundation is based on this, not whether my father is alive or not.

Further framing Deng's portrait of the Federation's future, I should add, were distinctively gendered forms of expression: oaths of filial veneration for China's fallen patriarch and proclamations of fraternal esprit de corps among party-state elite:

When my father died, I really felt his greatness. Everyone expressed respect and thoughts about him. And, since then, I haven't seen any changes in how people express their respect and thoughts. Many ministers have come up to me and said: "Pufang, whether the old man is around or not, I'll be the same. There is absolutely no problem. Regarding my support for you, there is no problem." Last year the central Federation organized an award ceremony. Chairman Jiang [Zemin] came, met with the disabled awardees, talked with them, and he penned a celebratory passage. I asked him to come and do these things. And he agreed to do them all. I invited the rest of the leaders and they all responded. Whenever I host an event and invite leaders, they all respond. And what does that mean? It means that our Chinese leaders are not those kinds of people who only help you when you're "up" and spurn you when you're "down."

So, this concern that one hears, that the Federation might be dissolved after my father's death, is not warranted.

To date, such assertions of Deng's—that the Federation's trajectory in the aftermath of his father's death will remain unchanged—seem to be bearing out. Several years have now passed since Deng Xiaoping's death. The Federation has not disappeared and its momentum has not been quashed outright. Nor, for that matter, have its publicly discernable strategies for helping the disabled shifted significantly. For example, in August 2002 Deng Pufang made a widely publicized pronouncement at a Federation event. He announced that China's government had set a goal to provide all disabled persons in China with at least some free rehabilitation medicine by 2015. Although open to critique (say, as a further move to clinically normalize the body rather than alter societal expectations of it, or as another move to delay disability provision), one could also applaud this announcement as a nod toward equitable assistance for all Federation constituents, a move away from the Federation's penchant to direct its energies to programs that most benefit the urban, the male, and the immobile. That noted, only a few months later, in December 2002, Deng's next major pronouncement seemed to reaffirm earlier patterns. At ceremonies marking China's eleventh Annual Day of Disabled Persons, Deng announced that, on the urging of the Federation, the country's State Council and Ministries of Construction and Civil Affairs had issued unprecedented regulations to help "the disabled." These regulations require that wheelchair access be part of all new and renovated city civic architecture.

Besides continuity in the deployment of palliative resources, such pronouncements reflect the fact that Deng Pufang's personal involvement in Federation development has been unflagging in the years since his father's death. What is more, they show that Deng's involvement continues to be directed to national and international platforms. For instance, Deng was a common figure in the English- and Chinese-language media between late 2002 and early 2003. There, one can glimpse him meeting with members of the International Olympic Committee for discussions about the 2008 Paralympic Games in Beijing, traveling to Hong Kong for the annual sessions of China's National People's Congress and People's Political Consultative Conference, and delivering a speech in Sapporo, Japan, at Disabled Peoples' International's Sixth World Assembly.

Despite these activities, or maybe because of them, several people I have encountered recently continue to wonder out loud about the Federation's future. Not long before this book entered the publication process, I spoke with a person I had met initially in the mid-1990s, someone who has been a long-time client/activist of both the Xuan Wu district and the Beijing city Federation offices:

> These days it's really hard to know what will happen to the Federation. On the surface everything seems okay. Yes, there's been a little gossip about Pufang being snubbed by this leader or that leader. But his political position seems stable for now. He was even given the title of Alternate to the [CCP's] Central Committee after his father died. . . . So, at this stage, it seems to me that, as long as there is no major instability within the nation that leads to an attack on the Deng family (which it looks like there won't be right now), the biggest issue is Pufang's *shenti* (body/health). Think about it. What happens if his doctors miss something and he gets sick? So much of his motivation to build this institution and so much of his ability to do it has sprung from his own experience [*jingyan*], his own disability. But, you need to remember that his disability also makes him very susceptible to illness. People paralyzed like him usually don't live long. He could easily get sick tomorrow and suddenly be gone. A lot of people I know are worried about that. It would be very difficult, maybe impossible, for the Federation to continue growing without Pufang.

Around the same time, an employee of the Beijing city Federation office added his thoughts on the Federation's possible future:

> The two biggest dangers facing the Federation now are a political rupture or Pufang dying. The State Council is really pressuring all government offices to decrease their size and to depend more on local funding. So, without a strong

Figure 9. "Wheelchair-bound Deng Pufang, the son of China's late paramount leader Deng Xiaoping, looks at a large photograph of his father, taken by his sister Deng Lin, at an exhibition in Beijing's Military Museum, Wednesday, February 18, 1998. The exhibition, featuring over 100 photos of Deng Xiaoping taken by the leader's daughter, opened Wednesday to mark the first anniversary of Deng's death Thursday." (AP Photo/Greg Baker)

and capable Pufang, we'd be in a lot of trouble. Without Pufang being active, without him getting out and meeting central government and provincial leaders, without him showing up in newspaper photos sitting in his wheelchair, we would have a hard time keeping our momentum going.

Throughout our conversation in 1998, Deng Pufang came across as very vibrant, intellectually focused, and generally in fine spirits. Beneath his somewhat wrinkled long-sleeve polo shirt, his torso seemed broad and muscular. When he spoke, he regularly gestured with his arms and laughed. His dialogue was filled with ardent expressions of personal commitment, recently memorized statistics, and poignant social observations. And since he struck me as quite hardy, I chose not to question Deng directly about his health or the affiliated issue which was a preoccupation of many others I spoke with that summer: What will happen to the Federation after Deng Pufang declines? I felt that pursuing such a question was unnecessary because, almost certainly, if I raised it, Deng would have deflected it. He would have offered a blanket response that he was in fine health and/or he would have rebutted any assumption that the Federation's future was contingent on his *shenti.*

BURNED

Thinking back on that visit to the central Federation offices in 1998, there is one person's heath that I wish I had learned more about when I had the chance. After my discussion with Deng Pufang and after expressing my gratitude to the staff members who helped orchestrate the meeting, I strolled out of the main building at the central Federation's compound at 44 Beichizi Road and walked across the paved courtyard past the new, large, black Mercedes sedan with high-ranking government plates that was awaiting Deng, making my way toward the compound's front gate. As I passed by the gate room, I spotted the elderly guard, Lao Chen, a man in his sixties who had always greeted me with a warm smile and offers to introduce me to disabled people. He was speaking in a brusque tone to a man and a woman whose backs were to me. Sauntering past toward the road, I heard Chen admonishing the woman to leave the premises and take up her assistance request elsewhere. Lao Chen looked up to acknowledge my departure. The woman turned.

I saw a face of utter devastation. Little was left. A distorted ear. A disfigured eye. A lipless opening for a mouth. Black and red facial skin ravaged by a catastrophic burn that had obviously occurred in the not-too-distant past.

I departed 44 Beichizi the same way as I had come, by taxi. But the ride felt quite different. My mind was filled with a cacophony of sentiments. On the one hand, I felt triumphant that I had finally won an audience with Deng Pufang and had carried off a respectable interview with him, one in which I had asked Deng some fairly forthright questions about problems inherent in his institution. Many people over the years, including more than a few of the mostly male faculty in my Ph.D.-conferring department, had indicated that it would be extremely valuable for me to meet with Deng, even if only for a short visit. My interview that day thus seemed like a perfect coda to years of research and professional maturation. On the other hand, I felt increasingly troubled by this visit, and not just because of what I had seen as I departed 44 Beichizi. Had Deng only granted me the interview because he felt obliged to engage the logics of male authority, biomedical status, and geopolitics: the avuncular advice of his former surgeon and the calculus that having me at 44 Beichizi on that day, during Clinton's China visit, would attest to the central Federation's support of Deng Xiaping's handpicked successor's aim at improving relations between America's and China's statesmen?[5] I likewise wondered to myself, had I actually learned anything of significance from the interview? Did Deng tell me anything that was particularly enlightening? Or was the benefit to me something else? Was

the benefit more a matter of professional credibility, mine and, by extension, that of this book? Clifford Geertz (1988) argues that the authority of
anthropology initially sprang from the fieldwork experiences of a small
group of mostly Euro-American men. And anthropology's ongoing claim to
knowledge and legitimacy, Geertz contends, remains the experience of
"being there," of traversing borders and confronting face-to-face an aptly
chosen, different context (1988, 1–24). Wasn't my interaction with Deng
just another twist in this logic? Wasn't it a claim to ethnographic competence based less on "being there" than on being there with an aptly chosen,
different body—sitting inches from the paraplegic founder of the Federation, shaking hands with Deng Xiaoping's offspring, exchanging verbal
communications with one of China's top princelings for over an hour, and
glimpsing his catheter bag slowly fill near my feet?

As that day came to an end, as I thought about the fact that I had been
able to enter the central Federation compound and meet with Deng Pufang,
as I contemplated the fact that, in that very same time span, the burned
woman had been deterred from entering, my memory also focused on other
moments in my fieldwork—much earlier moments. These were the hours
passed not in Hainan or Beijing, but in Cambridge, Massachusetts, at Harvard University's Health Services Center. In 1993, before I could even start
the dissertation research upon which much of this book is based, before I
could even begin accruing my disciplinary authority of "being there," I had
to receive a year-long Chinese-government-issued student visa. And to receive
that type of visa, I had to provide the China Foreign Ministry not only with
documentation of my academic credentials, proof of a Chinese-government
sponsor, and my passport, but I also had to provide proof that I had recently
passed a complete biomedical exam, including a chest X-ray and tests for
HIV, hepatitis B, and syphilis. In other words, before I could study aspects of
disability in China having to do with medicalization and embodiment, I had
to be examined and certified as having a body that was at once acceptably
"different" (foreign) and "normal" (biomedically healthy). So, I now asked
myself, had the interview with Deng Pufang been nothing more than the
most recent fruits of my earlier experience in Cambridge, Massachusetts,
with international biopolitics? Did not my interview represent simply the
most high-profile product of that invasive exam at the Health Services
Center, that certification not just of my clinical and citizenry status, but also
of biomedicine's preeminence, the Chinese nation-state's sovereignty, and
internationalism's supremacy?

Consumed by these thoughts, I made the decision to return to 44
Beichizi the next day. My goal was not to meet Federation officials. I went
back to talk with the guard, Lao Chen, at the front gate and inquire about
the burned woman. Although willing to talk about the woman, Lao Chen
did not seem eager for me to locate her. Perhaps Chen's previous desire to

introduce me to *canji ren* was now undercut by his ill-at-ease feelings over how he had treated the woman. Whatever the case, Chen said he did not know where the woman and her husband were headed after departing 44 Beichizi, nor did he volunteer their names or that of their community of origin. He only said that the woman had indicated that she was a migrant laborer, that she had suffered a chemical accident while working at a factory in China's northeastern provinces, that she had accrued massive debts to family and friends owing to medical bills and her inability to find new work, that she had unsuccessfully pressed local courts to hear a legal case against the factory, and that she hoped that direct appeal to Federation leaders would galvanize that case. Before I left the guardhouse, Lao Chen also had this to add:

> It's so sad what happened to that woman's face. It's just dreadful. But, alas, she's not that different from many others appearing here: very much in need of assistance. They're all so sad. Thank goodness for Deng Xiaoping's Open Door reforms. Thank goodness for the international disability movement. Thank goodness for the Federation! . . . More and more, every day, people like the burned woman learn something about the Federation, drop by at our offices across the country, and receive some help. That's what they're supposed to do. That's social progress [*shehui fazhan*]. But they're not supposed to be dropping by here. That's why I had to direct that woman back to her local Federation office. We're an administrative center here, not a service facility. That's why we don't have the words "Disabled Persons' Federation" on a sign out front, just that simple "44 Beichizi Road" sign. Otherwise, we'd be mobbed. Even worse, if the sign read "Central Federation" [Zhongyang Canlian] . . . aiya! . . . everyone would be coming here from all over the country asking for Deng Pufang. They'd come here from everywhere and request, "While he still can, couldn't Deng help resolve my problem?"

EXPERIENCES OF DIFFERENCE

What are we to make of Lao Chen's words? What are we to make of his multiple expressions of appreciation? What are we to make of the anxiety his comments betray about the evanescence of Deng Pufang? And what are we to make of how Lao Chen's statement emerged through my own ethnographic trajectory?

If nothing else, Chen's statement attests to the broad themes that animate this book. First, there is biopolitics, a significant yet still underexplored component of what academics have been discussing in recent years under the catch-word globalization. If globalization involves an escalation in the flow of things across national borders—for example, forms of knowledge, commercial goods, institutional frameworks, modes of practice, people, finances— then something that has certainly been at play for decades in such escalation is biopolitics: the conceptualization and management of human life in terms of the biomedical health of individuals and populations. Second, biopolitical expansion has been dependent on and helpful not just for diffuse forms of authority, what some might call transnational discourses and practices of modernity. More concretely, the expansion has been deeply entrenched in national and, to varying degrees, international governance. Third, in many contexts throughout the world, the proliferation of biomedical institutions and professionals has subjected community members to increasing scrutiny and representation in terms of a medically and bureaucratically managed body. Fourth, embodiment has a more complex role in biopolitics than is usually depicted in academic literature. Biopolitical expansion has been contingent on more than just how bodies are understood. So, too, of great importance has been how bodies are used and lived. Fifth, biopolitics has often been highly influenced by and targeted to a specific sphere of bodily authority: masculinity. The projection of manhood, the management of male status, and the care of male health have been issues extremely significant to what we might call biopolitical globalization.

Chen's words also seem to attest to more specific arguments made in this volume. During the 1980s and 1990s, the category of disability was the pivot point for two major sets of activities in China: the genesis of a new nation-wide institution of social assistance and the configuration of *canji* as a notably male field of biomedically conceived Otherness and state-managed palliation. But the genesis of this new institution did not alone cause this field, *canji*, to be configured as such. Nor, for that matter, did the increasing mapping of *canji* as a medicalized, bureaucratized, and gendered realm of difference during the latter part of the twentieth century, in and of itself, cause the Federation to emerge. The interplay was far more complex. That is, as the anthropological refrain goes, multiple processes were at work. Yet, as I have emphasized often, to understand any interplay between institutionalization and medicalization, particularly in a venue like contemporary China, it is vital to look at the generative roles of two domains of sociopolitical process. These domains are the biopolitics of state-building and embodiment.

In the preceding chapters, a welter of detail has been delivered about modes of statecraft and means of bodily objectification, subjectification, and practice. Some of these details have centered around how Deng Pufang's embodiment has unfolded: how his rearing as a son of the polity's hyper-elite incorporated historical contingencies and national/international discourses to generate a governmental initiative to help a newly conceived population within China, and then how that initiative became transformed through further statecraft and embodiment into a biobureacracy, the Federation. That I have heard so many people raise questions about Deng Pufang's longevity in the years since his father's death, one could say, reflects as much as anything else the degree to which Deng's bodiliness (his fusion of the self, soma, and social) has been so central to the Federation's formation and to the configuration of *canji* in contemporary China.

But, it must be said that, while portions of this book chronicle the embodiment of Deng Pufang, a persistent theme here has been the importance of many other persons. The Federation's emergence and *canji*'s definitional framing during the 1980s and 1990s did not occur simply in relation to Deng Pufang. Legions of people were involved. From the very beginning, some of those in the mix were career biocrats: Chinese and non-Chinese epidemiologists, health educators, rehabilitation medicine advocates, welfare functionaries, and social scientists. Others involved were people who—sometimes successfully, sometimes not—strove to be active and regular clients of the Federation, aiming to draw benefits from the institution, but also, to a limited degree, challenging it to take specific kinds of action. Included among those incited to be client-minded were more than a few Beijing mototrikers. Also included were workers like the I.D.-seeking woman Ma Zhun, parents such as Qin Yan striving to enhance the lives of their children, assertive agriculturalists like the Wenchang coconut farmer Guo Li, and no doubt tides of migrants like the burned woman who had been deformed by industrial accidents. But equally in the mix was a vast contingent of people who were far less eager, who had far less direct contact with the Federation, and who were either without or possessed only nascent clientelist aspirations. Of these, many likely resembled the men and women I met while conducting fieldwork in Hainan's Min Song village and Beijing's Xuan Wu district: members of shifting kinship and community networks who fit local notions of a "problematic body" *(shenti you wenti)* but who had deeply ambiguous feelings about self-associating with *canji*.

How have all these people's embodiments come to contribute to the formation of the Federation and the instantiation of disability as a category of Otherness? Some have contributed in very overt ways, others less so. Yet all have done so through what we might call experiences of difference: felt flows of differentiation and, too often, denigration.[6] In China these experiences may be mapped, and increasingly seem to be, through notions of normalcy and alterity that one might associate with internationally informed criteria of disability. But so, too, they may be framed by notions of normalcy and alterity that, before you delved into this book, might have seemed unrelated to any consideration of a category like *canji*. For instance, as I have detailed, gender expectations—about being male, about being female—have been pivotal for the formation of the Federation and *canji*. But no less significant have been other normalizing structures of distinction and domination, nearly all of them, like gender, highly patterned by binaries, for example, urban / rural, citizen / foreigner, fast / slow, lame / non-lame, married / single, competent / incompetent, rich / poor, governmental /

non-governmental, modern / backward. No matter around how many such notions they are framed, though, experiences of difference are often intensely somatosocial and somatopolitical: they involve how one is viewed corporeally, by oneself and others, and they involve how one can utilize that corporeality to access affective and economic resources. And, as such, experiences of difference have, over the years, greatly textured the mutual construction of the Federation and *canji* as emergent elements of a national polity. They have textured, as I have frequently shown, not only who has been understood as disabled in China during recent years, and thus who may be potential beneficiaries of the country's only nationwide disability advocacy organization. They have also textured who may be deemed suitable to serve, represent, manage, and even study the Chinese nation-state, specifically its segment of, what starting sometime in the twentieth century began to be spoken about as, the world's disabled population.

Focusing a conceptual lens on experience at the final stage of this book is further called for because it reminds us again of the depth and breadth of suffering at stake here. In my interview with Deng Pufang, he asserted, in no uncertain terms, that the Federation's genesis and ongoing development are based on not just experience but a collective form of experience: the suffering of China's currently recognized sixty million disabled constituents. How are we to assess that claim? Much of this book has explored aspects of the claim from perspectives of biopolitics and embodiment. These perspectives have helped us see that, since the mid-1980s, Deng Pufang and others within the upper ranks of China's government have used various discursive, epidemiological, and administrative techniques to frame *canji* as an object of institutional intervention and bureaucracy-building. These perspectives have additionally allowed us to glean that the Federation has used many of the same techniques to delimit whose bodies merit the institution's assistance. But most importantly, the perspectives have allowed us to see that there are immensely intimate and personal issues involved here—experiences of difference, denigration, and dispossession—not just for those who have been included under the Federation's tent, but also for many who have been excluded.[7] In other words, the suffering at stake here far exceeds that of reputed *canji ren*.

Paying attention to experience is imperative for one more crucial reason. It compels us to act and agitate. Although experiences of difference cannot be separated from the modes by which we come to know about and make sense of pain and immiseration—what Max Weber called theodicy ([1922] 1963)—such experiences can never be written off as just the products of those modes of knowing. There have been and there continue to be untold numbers of children and adults living within the territorial borders of China and elsewhere who, owing to one injustice or another, struggle daily with unwanted differences and the deprivations, agonies, and humiliations that for them are often the most immediate felt flows of those differences. While such experiences cannot exist without or escape from theodicy, they are not simply generated by it. And whereas few of us can exist without or escape from theodicy, we may not just sit back and offhandedly observe our and others' embeddedness in it and do nothing else. People suffer, and that suffering requires, demands, our response—from numerous directions and from multiple sectors of the social order.

GAZING BACK

The mixture of concern and intrigue one hears expressed these days about Deng Pufang's political and bodily durability, I would argue, reflects a growing sense of anxiety among many in the PRC about the current level of societal response to experiences of difference. It reflects a popular sense that— no matter how oblique and gendered the category of *canji* is, no matter how it is increasingly subject to governmental machination and narrow biostatistical visions of existence—*canji* signifies a piece in a much broader and expanding field of unmet moral responsibility, one that demands far greater attention. Untold multitudes are suffering today worldwide under the weight of difference, whatever its exact form. Quite a large portion of these people, certainly far more than sixty million, live within the territorial boundaries that make up China today. As much as they have been defining it, as much as they have been defined by it, as much as they have been using it to define the nation-state, Deng Pufang and his allies have been responding to one piece of what is a much larger global morass of suffering. And while clearly there have been significant shortcomings in what Deng has been doing, it seems that the feelings among many I have encountered up and down eastern China is that Deng and his institution have comprised one of only a regrettably small array of forces responding to this broad field of unmet moral responsibility—that the Federation has been one of the only players on the field, one of the only organizational forces available in a national climate dominated by party-state intolerance for large-scale, nongovernmental political intervention and in a global context awash with humanitarian discourses yet enamored of political-economic tenets hostile to comprehensive public assistance.

In light of these sentiments, my agenda in writing this book has not been to denigrate, dismiss, or disavow the Federation. Too much is at stake for too many people to take such a stance. Then again, given these stakes, scholars working in China cannot afford to be ethnographic glad-handers, uncritically chronicling networks of social control, such as the party-state and male dominance, that might be driving certain efforts to redress some of China's morass of suffering yet doing so for questionable ends, inequitably, and in ways that often amplify forms of difference and denigration. In short, a middle ground must be struck when representing an institution like the Federation, because when it comes to the "administration of pain," as Veena Das so poignantly states, we are always faced at once with the legitimacy and illegitimacy of the social order (1997, 565).

Striving to strike such a middle ground, I have found it useful to keep a dual focus on biopower and embodiment. And I believe others in the future—not simply just those who happen to work in my chosen disciplinary areas of critical medical anthropology and disability studies—might likewise find it useful to deploy this type of dual focus, what Robert Desjarlais has called a "phenomenology with sharp edges" (2002). This demands, however, that we not be satisfied with a vague understanding that biopower is expansive, that it is becoming omnipresent and multiply layered. Likewise, it demands that we view embodiment not just as shaping the lives of the so-called "afflicted" and "dispossessed." Rather we must recognize that in any given context biopower gets and gives its greatest bounce from specific sociopolitical springboards, and that contrary to Foucault's oft-expressed outlook, this bounce may often involve the inner workings of the nation-state. Furthermore, we must recognize that quite a wide variety of people's embodiments, including those within government, and including some within the academy who write about government, can be implicated in producing the bounce.

If recognizing all this is vital, so too is communicating information about it. Whether through my favored medium of ethnography or through other avenues of agitation, it is imperative that we enhance professional and popular understanding of how biobureaucracies like the Federation and realms of existence like *canji* come to be. For only then can people in places like Beijing and Min Song village not only more fully "claim disability," to borrow a phrase of Simi Linton (1998), but they can also more fully and fairly redress the broader experiential spectrum of difference. Only then can people, as they struggle, from moment to moment, with meanings and practicalities of normalcy and alterity—such as function and dysfunction, health and sickness—redirect the effects of those meanings and practicalities in the ways they find most welcome. And only then can people, as they encounter the complex medical, bureaucratic, and governmental gazes of our age—gazes like disability advocacy—take greater control over how those gazes work, how inclusive they are, and what benefits they actually generate.

NOTES

PREFACE

1. All personal names appearing in this book, save for those of well-known historical figures and widely recognized public officials, are pseudonyms.

2. This and other quotes appearing in the preface were entered into my field notes immediately following the lunchtime meal at the Shandong restaurant. Many quotes in the chapters that follow are also the product of similar information-gathering methods. Inasmuch as it could be argued that recording informants or taking down notes of their statements concurrent with the utterances are likely to produce highly accurate "data," the need to depend frequently on my short-term recall and post-interview notetaking was mandated by an overriding concern about factual authenticity, a concern with which many anthropologists are familiar. While conducting the research upon which much of this book is based, I found that my requests to use a tape recorder or a notebook in an informant's presence often so discomfited the informant that for sometime thereafter s/he would be unwilling to converse or would provide misinformation.

INTRODUCTION

1. As with all Chinese names, the surname Deng appears before the given name Pufang. I will be referring to Deng either by his surname or his full name, especially where his surname alone might cause confusion alongside mention of his father, Deng Xiaoping, and other family members. In some cases, quoted passages will refer to him by his given name of Pufang alone.

2. *Canji ren* can be translated as either "disabled person(s)" or "person(s) with disability."

3. In contemporary China, people just as often couple *shen* with a second ideogram to form words meaning "posture" (*shenduan*), "height" (*shenliang*), or "pregnancy" (*shenyun*, or *shenzi*), as they also do to produce words signifying "political status" (*shenfen*), "family background" (*chushen*), or "social situation" (*shenshi*).

Shenti, a couplet usually translated in recently published dictionaries as "body," has in recent decades been used by people in China to convey notions like "carriage" or "corporal structure" as frequently as it has been used to express such things as "sensibility" or "character" (Brownell 1995, 16; Sun 1983, 20; see also Sivin 1995, 14).

4. For further information about the institutionalization of biomedical sciences in China since the late nineteenth century, see Benedict 1996; Bullock 1980; Goldstein 1998; Henderson 1984, 1989; Lu and Needham 1988; MacPherson 1987; Needham and Lu 2000; and Yip 1995. For more details about biomedicine's relationship to and influence upon "traditional Chinese medicine," see Andrews 1996; Farquhar 1987, 1994; Hsu 1999; Bowers, Hess, and Sivin 1988; Unshuld 1992; and Zhan 2002. For further readings on biomedicine's influence on notions of normalcy and alterity in twentieth-century China, see Dikotter 1992; Henriot 1992; Kleinman and Lin 1981; Lee 1999; Ng 1990; Shapiro 1998; and Wilson et al. 1977.

5. Bourdieu writes extensively about the body via the term "habitus," a Latin term Mauss adopted in his essay, "Les Techniques du Corps" ([1935] 1979) to refer to the culturally patterned body in society. "Habitus," under Bourdieu's pen, constitutes an objectivist-subjectivist bridge: a quasi-bodily involvement in the world—a non-conscious "system of durable, transposable dispositions" (1977, 72)—through which social structures and personal strategies ostensibly make and maintain one another. Some of Bourdieu's most exciting applications of "habitus" occur in his writings on the sentience of socialization—what he calls the "feel for the game" (1990)—and how the aesthetics of taste, posture, and gesture work to maintain power relations (1984).

6. Whereas Foucault often sharply criticized academics for overestimating the role of the state, in at least one instance, that being an analysis he made of racism, Foucault gave considerable weight to the state (see Stoler 1995; 2002, 140–61).

7. For variations on this argument, see Butler 1992; Csordas 1994a; Farquhar 2002a, 3–10; Kleinman 1995, 95–119; and Waquant 1995.

8. There are several anthropological monographs that are now recognized as precursors to the interdisciplinary field of Disability Studies. Examples are Joan Ablon, *Little People in America: The Social Dimension of Dwarfism* (1984); Nora Groce, *Everyone Here Spoke Sign Language: Hereditary Deafness on Martha's Vineyard* (1985); and Robert Murphy, *The Body Silent* (1990). Since the publication of these volumes, a growing number of anthropological works specifically examining disability have been produced. For examples of recent works in this area, as well as bibliographic information, see Kasnitz and Shuttleworth 2001, the special issue of *Public Culture* (vol. 13, no. 3 [2001]), and Ginsburg and Rapp 2005.

9. Prior to the 1980s it was rare for anthropologists to write about male gender issues, which today are increasingly discussed under the terms "manhood," "masculinity," and "male hegemony" (cf. Benedict 1953; Hambly 1931). What attention anthropologists did manage to give to men as men prior to 1980 tended to be subsumed under or placed in dialogue with such issues as initiation rites (Hocart 1935; Moore 1976; Whiting et al. 1958), paternity and lineage (Freedman 1958; Leach 1966; Spiro 1968), or physiology and somatotyping (Rolleston 1888; Sheldon 1954). For a review of recent anthropological writings about manhood and masculinity, see Gutmann 1997.

10. A form of spoken Chinese, Mandarin is the official language of the People's Republic. It is widely spoken throughout Northeast China, including Beijing.

11. For example, over the course of our acquaintance, Ma and I enjoyed many meals together, sometimes with his wife and son, frequently in his Haikou residence. Twice we journeyed by bus to eastern Hainan to stay at his parents' village home, to visit nearby communities, and to attend memorial ceremonies for his then recently diseased father.

12. These two fieldwork stints occurred during the mid-1990s and totaled eighteen months. The first stint began in September 1993 and continued through early summer 1994. It was largely spent in Hainan, living in Min Song village, an agricultural community of Wenchang County. Most of my efforts involved visiting with Min Song community members, interviewing them, and engaging in participant-observation in and around the community. A considerable portion of my energy also involved traveling back and forth between Min Song and other, more cosmopolitan environments (the nearby town, the local county seat, and the provincial capital, Haikou) in order to meet with medical practitioners and government officials. In September 1994 I began conducting extensive research in Beijing, a city where I had been a language student for two years in the late 1980s. During that second lengthy research stint, which lasted eight months, I split most of my time between two research tasks: (1) conducting interviews with Beijing residents and local officials in the capital city's middle-income district of Xuan Wu, located southwest of Tiananmen Square; and (2) investigating the institutional history, elite politics, and national programs undergirding the State's and Deng Pufang's evolving disability agendas. In addition to these lengthy stints of fieldwork, I made preliminary research trips to China in the summers of 1990, 1991, and 1992, and then follow-up trips in 1998 and 2000. Much of my 1992 summer visit involved daily tutorials in Wenchangese at Hainan University. This language study was subsequently complemented by a year's worth of weekly Wenchang tutorials with an older Hainanese woman at the Boston home of her daughter and son-in-law, both computer scientists.

13. The ICIDH's tripartite definition of "impairment, disability, and handicap" reads as follows:

Impairment
In the context of health experience, an impairment is any loss or abnormality of psychological or anatomical structure or function.

Disability
In the context of health experience, a disability is any restriction or lack (resulting from an impairment) of ability to perform an activity in the manner or within the range considered normal for a human being.

Handicap
In the context of health experience, a handicap is a disadvantage for a given individual, resulting from an impairment or a disability, that limits or prevents the fulfillment of a role that is normal (depending on age, sex, and social and cultural factors) for that individual. (WHO 1980)

14. I owe much of my initial insight about international resistance to the ICIDH to personal correspondence with Robert Trotter, Regent's Professor at Northern Ari-

zona University in January 1997. In the 1990s, Trotter worked as a consultant for the WHO group that redesigned the ICIDH into the ICF.

15. The visibility of biomedical reductionism is particularly evident in the "ICF Checklist," released by the WHO in September 2001 (WHO 2001b). The checklist states it is to be used to "elicit and record information on the functioning and disability of an individual." Part 1a centers on "Impairments of Body Functions" and defines "body functions" as "the physiological functions of body systems" (e.g., "functions of the cardiovascular, hematological, immunological, and respiratory systems"); it defines "impairments" as "problems in body function as a significant deviation or loss." Part 1b centers on "Impairments of Body Structures"; "body structures" are defined as "anatomical parts of the body, such as organs, limbs, and their components" (e.g., "structures related to the digestive, metabolism, and endocrine systems"). Moreover, the first page of the checklist requires tabulators to record "medical diagnosis" and to do so by placing in blank boxes the corresponding WHO International Classification of Diseases code numbers.

CHAPTER ONE

1. In the last few decades, an increasing number of ethnographers have recognized that, to understand processes of social change and domination, it is necessary to investigate not only the middle or bottom levels of the social hierarchy, but also the top level (e.g., Allison 1994; Gusterson 1996; Nader 1972; Marcus and Hall 1992; Yanagisako 2000).

2. Anthropologists have often applied these two streams sequentially in their writings, first, discussing how biocrats create biomedical structures, and second, describing how the afflicted have responded to the new structures.

3. To be sure, anthropologists interested in embodiment and social suffering have at times examined groups (e.g., Myerhoff 1978; Jackson 2000) and individuals (e.g., Murphy 1990; Greenhalgh 2001a) that occupy relatively well-off class positions. Yet such studies of elite affliction have been sparse in number and rarely have they given attention to questions pertaining to the building of biobureaucracies.

4. For a discussion of subjectification (*mode d'assujettissement*), see Foucault 1997. In most of his late writings, Foucault used the term "self-formation" to refer to the constitution of personhood (e.g., Foucault 1985, 28). Because throughout this book I frequently make comments about broader issues of sociopolitical and biobureaucratic formation, I have opted, for clarity's sake, to diverge from Foucault's original phrasing and instead use terms such as "self-development" and "subject-making."

5. For instance, Keenan (1995, 424) quotes Foucault as stating: "[One] has to take into account . . . the points where the technologies of domination . . . have recourse to processes by which the individual acts upon himself. And conversely, [one] has to take into account the points where the technologies of the self are integrated into structures of coercion or domination."

6. A number of scholars working in a non-European context have turned to the notion of subjectification in recent years, although not necessarily from the classic Foucauldian perspective of the elite. Examples here include Alter 2000; Bailey 1999; Butler 1997; Fernandez 1980; Kondo 1990; and Stein and Wright 1995. Within U.S.-based China Studies, recent inquiries into the formation of subjectivity, some of

which have not been in direct dialogue with Foucault's notion of subjectification, include Anagnost 1997; Barlow 1991; Farquhar 1998; Hubbert 1999; Kipnis 1997; Ong 1996; Yang 1997; and Zito 1997.

7. Many medical anthropologists hail from elite Euro-American institutions and have therefore been schooled in the Enlightenment vision of personal disclosure and its elevated truth value. As such, many medical anthropologists have easily moved across or down social hierarchies to seek out "informants" to gather information outside the public eye; moreover, they have found it imperative to do so. Yet, when it comes to the project of studying elite embodiment—particularly hyper-elites—anthropologists cannot expect their Euro-American, scholarly subject-positions willy-nilly to facilitate research access (Gusterson 1993). For instance, largely because numerous PRC officials of high rank often see my persona as being a "white U.S. intellectual" and because they frequently read my persona as worrisome and/or lackluster, I found it immensely challenging to arrange an interview with Deng Pufang. In the summer of 1998, with the intervention of Deng Pufang's Canadian surgeon, Federation officials scheduled my only interview with Pufang to date. While this Beijing interview ran for more than twice the time initially allotted, it lasted only ninety minutes. As such, I had to choose my questions carefully during the interview and limit their scope to topics of significance for my long-term research, especially topics about which there was little extant documentary information. So, in fact, that interview provided me little new insight into Deng Pufang's life story.

8. Qin's account of Deng Pufang is the most widely known in China, and for that reason I rely on it the most heavily here. I also draw from accounts produced by Ruan (1992), Wang (n.d.), and Deng (1995). These accounts are fairly consistent in the way they narrate Deng Pufang's life. For more information about the genre of biography and hagiography in modern China, see Di and Shao 1994.

9. I use the phrase "biomythography of statesmanship" to foreground important methodological and analytical issues at play here. These include the public nature of the data examined, their sociopolitical constructedness, and the degree to which this constructedness draws upon a variety of modernist genres to further an agenda that serves the aims of state-building as well as patriarchal claims to authorize the nation. I am also drawn to the term "biomythography" because I find it helpful for highlighting interconnections between biological and biographical production, epistemology, and otherness. For additional applications of "biomythography," see Haraway (1991, 174) and Lorde (1982).

10. For further discussions of the "literature of the wounded," or "scar literature," see Barme and Lee 1979; Honig 1984; and Siu and Stern 1983.

11. Zhuo Lin was born Pu Qiongying. According to official accounts, she changed her name in the late 1930s because, after graduating from Northern Shaanxi College in Yan'an, she began training as a Communist spy inside Japanese-occupied China. In 1938 Zhuo married Deng Xiaoping. She was his third and last wife, according to official accounts. Together they had five children.

12. Chinese naming practices have a long and rich history (Ning 1995, 3). Many are linked to ancient ideas about the social, corporeal, political, and temporal embeddedness of personhood. As such, the decision of what formal personal name to give a newborn often involves several factors, including the perceived "constitu-

tion" of the infant as well as the family's desire to augur a specific future and/or to enshrine certain events (R. Watson 1986, 621–22). Today, as in the past, it is quite common for newborns to be given an informal name. As the child matures, a ceremony is often held at a time of the family's choosing to give the child a formal name.

13. This kind of mimetic merging of Deng Pufang's life and the emergent communist nation-state, Qin Yan indicates, further occurred through the young Pufang's regular visits to the tombs of communist martyrs. In elementary and middle school, Pufang's teachers often took him and his classmates to Baba Mountain in northwest Beijing. Baba Mountain became one of the holiest places in the young People's Republic, a center of remembrance and spiritual sanctification for all Communists. The Communist leadership had a huge stone-and-concrete facility built on Baba Mountain after 1949 for the purpose of memorializing the people who had given "life and limb" for the New China (*xin zhongguo*). On their regular field trips to Baba Mountain, Pufang and his classmates learned the proper technique for holding their adolescent frames in quiet and still respect for the fallen of China's revolutionary patriarchy.

14. Pressing large numbers of people to participate in manual-labor projects was a tactic the party deployed often during the 1950s and 1960s, in the hope of speedily modernizing the nation and instilling in the general population the tenets of selfless obedience to authority and respect for proletarians and peasants.

15. Of the students enrolled in the two classes in the Department of Technophysics during Deng's first year at Beida, only four or five were women (Qin 1992, 153).

16. When Mao's essay was published in English in 1978, the title was translated as "Study of Physical Education" (Mao [1917] 1978). But a more accurate translation, I would suggest, is "Study of Body Training."

17. Over the years the university's physical entrance-exam has prevented untold numbers of Chinese from enjoying the benefits of higher education.

18. This is conveyed in a description of Deng's elementary school: "The students of Bayi were to have a glorious rearing . . . and, through hard work, gradually they were to become the revolutionaries' hardworking successors" (Qin 1992, 114).

19. Over the last decade or so, information of this kind, as well as far more lurid details about the elite CCP leaders' lives, has been circulating in and out of China through a variety of media, including Hong Kong journals, translations of U.S. academic texts, and pirated copies of such books as *The Private Life of Chairman Mao: The Memoirs of Mao's Personal Physician* (Li 1994). More recently, the Internet has also been a medium for such information.

20. A national campaign orchestrated and promoted by Mao, the Great Leap Forward (1958–61), was a set of policies aimed at mobilizing "the masses" and redirecting their energies toward rapid industrialization. Today, the campaign is nearly universally viewed as having been a colossal failure and as the primary cause of a famine that may have taken as many as thirty million lives in the early 1960s (see MacFarquhar 1997; Becker 1996).

21. Beida soon divided the Technophysics Department into the departments of High-Energy Physics and Nuclear Physics. Nuclear physics then became Deng's primary scholarly focus.

22. The Cultural Revolution, a set of sweeping social transformations and political upheavals that took place in China, was aimed at reviving the ardor of the Com-

munist Revolution of 1949 and directing it toward a more political and less techno-cratic path (Meisner 1986; Madsen 1984). Historians usually recognize the Cultural Revolution as starting in 1966 and ending with the death of Mao in 1976. Today, many China scholars see the creation and management of the Cultural Revolution as representing a calculated move by Mao and his followers to reassert their ascendancy over the party-state in the wake of the devastating failure of the Great Leap Forward (e.g., MacFarquhar 1997; Spence 1990).

23. To be sure, one other possible explanation for Deng Pufang's authority needs to be mentioned, and that is that the PRC's party-state has long afforded significant political status to the adult children of its elite personnel. Today, this is evidenced by the large number of children of high-ranking officials who hold high government posts.

24. In April 1976 Maoist leaders once again purged Deng from his government posts. But within the year, Deng, together with his close military allies, choreographed what would be his final return to the apex of the Chinese government system (Evans 1995, 219). In October (a month after Mao's death), elite troops arrested the Gang of Four. In July 1977 Deng was reappointed vice-minister to the Politburo and to the Military Affairs Commission. And between 1977 and 1978 the Deng group gradually pushed through a set of policies that stressed the modernization of China through foreign investment and technology. They also pressed for students to train both overseas and within a revamped Chinese university system, liberalized the economy, and called for the party to "rehabilitate all those wrongly condemned going back to the year 1957" (Spence 1990, 656).

25. In North America the total bill for the kind of treatment MacEwen recommended (including postoperative therapy) could have run to nearly half a million dollars. Because the Deng family did not have such a large sum of money, and because they could not draw on Chinese government funds, the bill would need to be shouldered by others. To that end, MacEwen initially investigated Deng being treated at a U.S. military hospital. But because the Chinese–U.S. détente was still in its infancy and was a political minefield for Chinese and American politicians, such special military accommodations were not possible (Ruan 1992, 4).

26. Owing to the spring 1989 public criticism of Deng Pufang and the Federation, the party-state leadership forced the dismemberment of one of the Federation's largest sources of income, its nationwide trading company, Kanghua. In the preceding years, Kanghua had frequently been the target of muted criticism within the CCP for what in hindsight is known to have been the company's rampant abuse of the special tax- and duty-exempt status it enjoyed as a Deng-family sponsored welfare enterprise.

CHAPTER TWO

1. In fact, over the years quite a few anthropologists, many of them medical anthropologists, have studied the role of statistics in sociopolitical formation (e.g., DiGiacomo 1999; Inhorn 1995; Kleinman 1994; Trostle 1996).

2. See also Cole 2000; Kaviraj 1992; Kooiman 1997; Worton 1998.

3. To be sure, Hacking discusses many people in his writings about statistics. For instance, in his volume *Taming of Chance* (1990), he comments at length on the

works of Condorcet, Durkheim, and Peirce, who were each quite influential in promoting quantification as a key component of European governance and social thought in the nineteenth century. That noted, Hacking gives little attention to the processes of subject-making that these types of figures encountered on a daily basis or to how such processes may have shaped their work.

4. This passage has itself played a key role in shaping people's actions and thinking about bodies at different times in Chinese history. For example, Chang's (1996, 9) grandmother, born at the twilight of the Qing dynasty (1644–1911), relates how she was taught this Confucian passage (what she called "the first lesson of filial piety") early in life, and notes that its prohibition against self-mutilation inhibited her from committing suicide when she suffered great torment as a young woman.

5. Starting as early as the Han dynasty (206 B.C.–220 A.D.), Chinese sovereigns required local magistrates to count people within their assigned administrative regions (Rockhill 1904, 659). Over time, this enumeration came to be called the Yellow Books.

6. This edict also demanded that the Yellow Books stop counting as *ding* the following males: "the aged," "children under ten," "widowers," and "migrants." For more information on this edict, see Ho 1959, 11.

7. Ho translates *jiling* as "odd lot" (1959, 11), yet I believe the terms "fractional" and "refuse" are more apt here. Moreover, I would suggest that the common English-language equivalents for *ji*—that is, "lopsided" and "unbalanced"—betray how Yellow Book enumerators coded *canji* negatively in terms of classical Chinese cosmology's vision of "the moral evil" of imbalance (Schwartz 1985, 270–71).

8. Da Yuan Shengzheng Guochao Dianzhang 31.11b. This edict is also cited in Hansson 1988, 20.

9. According to Hansson, during the Ming and Qing dynasties, "the main categories of mean people were slaves, entertainers (including prostitutes), and government runners. In addition, social groups in certain regions had mean status. These were the musicians' households in Shanxi and Shaanxi, the fallen people in Zhejiang, the beggars' households in southern Jiangsu, the boat people of South China, the fishermen of the nine surnames in Zhejiang, and the hereditary servants in Anhui" (1988, iii).

10. To understand this, one must be aware of a long-standing imperial requirement: those wishing to sit for government exams had first to acquire written approval from their local magistrate. So, after 1391, if a magistrate conducted a Yellow Book enumeration and registered a local man as *canji*, in theory, the magistrate would thereafter be prohibited from providing that man the written approval needed to sit for a government exam (Benjamin Elman, personal communication, January 3, 1996).

11. The 1942 Kunming census involved 1,300 researchers, only a small portion of whom were actually biomedical practitioners. In addition to enumerating *canfei*, the survey produced detailed data on topics as varied as population density, family size, occupation, birth and death rates, marriage, minority populations, life expectancy, educational level, and migration patterns.

12. Tsinghua University was established by the U.S. government in 1910 to prepare Chinese students for advanced studies in America; it was funded with Boxer Rebellion indemnity funds paid to the United States by the Qing government.

13. For a discussion of the "sick man of Asia" concept, see n. 26, this chapter.

14. In the opening section of his census report, Chen takes pains to emphasize the empiricism that distinguishes his study from the earlier Yellow Book approach. Rather than counting mostly men, and a limited array of men at that, the Kunming exercise counted everyone in its target regions, Chen explains. In addition, Chen emphasizes that his study used a more rational (i.e., less expensive, more efficient, and more accurate) mode of analysis than that deployed in the Yellow Books. It used what was called "the slip system for statistical analysis." While opting not to explain exactly how the slip system works, Chen highlights that the system was created by George von Meyer for the Bavarian census in 1871 and that it had been used in British India and in the State of Massachusetts (Chen 1946, 14).

15. William Ogburn joined the University of Chicago's Department of Sociology as a professor in 1927 and went on to become a leading figure in the development of sociological empiricism and statistics during the middle of the twentieth century.

16. This entitlement system was initiated in November 1931 when the Central Committee of the Chinese Communist Party issued a vaguely written regulation calling for the compensation of Red Army soldiers. Who may have received benefits, if any were given, and in what form is unclear for the period before the founding of the People's Republic in 1949. According to Li (1988, 50), such decisions were left to the discretion of military leaders in each "revolutionary district" (jiefang qu).

17. The term geming canfei junren was changed to geming shangcan zhunren in the late 1980s, as part of the Disabled Persons' Federation's attempt to rid government of what the Federation leadership considered to be the particularly derogatory term canfei.

18. Since the 1950s the military has required that all veterans who request disability benefits be examined by biomedical doctors assigned to a hospital; the doctors' assessment reports must then be scrutinized against the criteria by officials of the military's public health system (Li 1988, 53).

19. More recently, Rehabilitation International has dampened its earlier emphasis on biomedicine and biomedical knowledge. In previous decades, R.I. not only promoted biomedically informed ways for defining disability, but also promoted the creation of large, centralized, technologically advanced rehabilitation facilities. Over the last decade or more, R.I.'s programmatic approach has tended to give greater emphasis to social equity perspectives and community-based rehabilitation initiatives.

20. At the end of World War II, after two decades mostly spent coordinating orthopedic medical care for children, members of the National Society for Crippled Children successfully managed to revive and internationalize the organization with the assistance of former U.S. naval orthopedic surgeon and then rehabilitation medicine evangelist Henry Kessler (1968, 160). Their successful revivification of the society was spurred no doubt by the fact that, as was the case following World War I, so in the wake of World War II, there was a pressing desire among national and international organizations to find a clinical means to return war wounded to their previous states of well-being. The legacy of this period is enshrined in the Kessler International Fellowship, awarded annually by Rehabilitation International, which provides an opportunity for non-U.S. residents to learn about physical rehabilitation services, education, and research as practiced in the United States.

21. As Acton explained to me by phone on January 15, 1996, his motivations for this proposal were at least twofold:

> I believed that gathering such household data would help the Chinese to respond to the disabled's medical problems, but more importantly, to address how the disabled could participate more in family and community. And I was convinced, based on talking to people in China, I needed to help them develop political ammunition. Numbers are very important for policymaking and the Chinese needed strong numbers if they were going to get rehabilitation programs off the ground and if they were going to have such programs expand beyond the hospital realm.

22. "Obviously and seriously unhealthy" was loosely defined as (1) seriously congenitally deformed, blind, deaf, and mute, or (2) postnatally disabled (e.g., as a consequence of polio and encephalitis) (Social Statistical Section of the National Statistical Bureau 1985).

23. Examples of the deployment of the 10 percent figure include Wang 1981; Moyes 1981; Doyal 1983, 7–8; and Priestley 2001, 3. In 1992 the office of the U.N. Secretary General drew upon the figure in a large glossy brochure produced to mark the culmination of the Decade of Disabled Persons (Boutros-Ghali 1992, 2). Like the U.N., Rehabilitation International continues to utilize the figure extensively today. A newsletter that R.I. and UNICEF co-publish biannually on "childhood disability in developing countries" is titled "One in Ten." And R.I.'s *Charter for the Third Millennium* states that, "Statistically, at least 10% of any society is born with or acquires a disability" (Henderson and O'Reilly 1999).

24. Not surprisingly, normative authority strongly affected the way in which many governments like China's responded to the U.N. call for national disability surveys. In several countries so strong was the idea of "10 percent" that not only did local statisticians sometimes hide their newly conducted disability surveys whose results did not closely approach 10 percent, but some of these statisticians subsequently took their most up-to-date population figures, applied a 10 percent rate, and published disability statistics based on that equation (U.N. Statistical Office, personal communication, January 28, 1996).

25. Cole 2000; Kaviraj 1992; Kooiman 1997; Worton 1998.

26. The exact source of the concept "sick man of Asia" (*dongya bingfu*, which accurately translates as "East Asia's sick man") is unclear. It is usually associated with the one-hundred-year period following the Opium War (1840), when large sectors of what is now the PRC were controlled by European, North American, and Japanese colonial forces. The concept was built around Social Darwinian notions (common during that period and still latent within much contemporary modernist discourse) that health, racial strength, and modernity co-evolve. After the Opium War, the concept was used by both Chinese and colonial forces to characterize the Chinese people and the then nascent Chinese nation-state as weak, backward, and economically torpid. Nowadays, the concept is still regularly invoked in China, most often by Chinese nationalists, to highlight China's past humiliations and to emphasize recent forms of "progress."

27. For details of the 1987 survey's disability criteria, see Appendix A.

28. The English-language translations provided here are those that are usually provided by the Disabled Persons' Federation's own translators.

29. This information was also conveyed to Drs. Michael Phillips and Veronica Pearson during a formal interview they conducted in the early 1990s with one of the leaders of China's psychiatric community (Michael Phillips, personal communication, March 16, 1995).

30. This revised approach was ultimately approved by China's State Council, making the standards for *canji* adopted by the Disabled Persons' Federation the official government-wide standards. During implementation of the 1987 survey, of course the type of assessment that government-employed biomedical practitioners were expected to carry out when evaluating a person's disability status differed depending upon the category of disability under consideration. In general, however, the move toward a biomechanically based orientation was particularly significant in terms of physical, visual, and hearing disabilities. In the case of *tingli yuyan canji* (hearing and speech disability), for instance, potential candidates for the designation "disabled" were assessed mainly in relation to a decibel system. For *shili canji* (visual disability), candidates were primarily assessed using the radius of visual field as measured in mathematical degrees and the best-corrected visual acuity as measured by the Monoyer's decimal scale. In the case of *zhili canji* (mental disability), potential candidates were assessed mainly in terms of I.Q. as then defined by the WHO, and to a lesser degree in terms of the American Association on Mental Deficiencies Adaptive Behavior Scale (AAMD 1970). For psychiatric disability, candidates were persons understood to have suffered for more than one year from "(1) psychosis associated with organic diseases of brain and body; (2) toxic psychosis including alcohol- and drug-dependencies; (3) schizophrenia; and (4) affective paranoid reactive schizo-affective and periodic psychotic disorders." The 1987 survey literature does not detail what methods were used for diagnosing these forms of mental illnesses. The literature does make clear that, for the purposes of "international comparisons," the WHO's Social Disability Screening Schedule was used to grade mental illnesses as more or less severe (Di 1989, 1474–82).

CHAPTER THREE

1. One justification the proposal writers made for the creation of a state-directed association for the physically disabled was equity with other kinds of disabled people. The proposal writers argued that the Chinese state already had an organization for other kinds of disabled people (i.e., the China Blind, Deaf and Mute Association) and that all they were asking for was equity for the physically disabled.

2. The China Association for the Blind, Deaf and Mute was established in 1960, but its history dates to before the founding of the People's Republic. The association has a great deal to do with early North American educational approaches to visual and auditory limitations. In the years leading up to the 1949 Revolution, there were more than 40 schools for the deaf and the blind in China, many of them founded by American missionaries. Building on this pedagogical foundation, the central government made "special education" for the deaf and blind a part of the PRC's educational system in 1951, and between 1949 and 1959 the state built an additional 19 schools for the blind and 117 for the deaf and mute. Moreover, the state reorga-

nized the previously U.S.-subsidized China Welfare Society for the Blind (*mengmin fuli hui*) in 1953. Three years later, the state created the China Welfare Society for the Deaf and Mute. The two societies were initially placed under the directorship of the Minister of Internal Affairs and the Secretary of the Central Relief Office (*jiuji zong hui*), respectively. Among their various efforts (some of which included building schools, establishing "welfare factories," and organizing sporting events), the societies conducted a statistical survey of fifty-four cities and counties in the late 1950s. The State Council in 1960 fused the two societies into the China Association for the Blind, Deaf and Mute. But before the association had a chance to develop, it became bogged down when leftist radicals in 1962 started depicting as reactionary anything related to the concept of "welfare." During the Cultural Revolution, this sort of thinking resulted in the closure of nearly all association offices, schools, and welfare factories. Moreover, it led to the detention, persecution, injury, and even death of association staff members. In 1978 the State Council formally "rehabilitated" (*huifu*) the association, making it a bureau (*ju*) of the Ministry of Civil Affairs. The association slowly rebuilt during the 1980s, and then, in 1988, it became a part of the Disabled Persons' Federation (Chu et al. 1996, 261–67).

3. For example, members of the club set up a booth on a main Beijing street to provide free bicycle and TV repair during the 1983 "Civic Virtue Month."

4. Poliomyelitis is an acute viral infection with a wide range of manifestations, of which the most well known is a weakening of the leg muscles. In China, polio is usually referred to as *xiaoer mabi zheng* (infantile paralysis). Owing to intensive immunization efforts, the government was able to largely eradicate polio by the mid-1990s, to the point where in 1994 there were only 261 newly reported cases nationally (WHO 1995). It is impossible to know how many people paralyzed to some extent by polio live in China today. Data produced by China's 1987 National Sample Survey of Disabled Persons place the figure in excess of one million (Ministry of Civil Affairs 1993).

5. My use of the term "strategies" stems largely from the work of Pierre Bourdieu (1977; 1990). Bourdieu argues that strategies are not premeditated coherent logics developed by rational maximizing actors, but are more a "feel for the game," to whit, "objectively oriented lines of action which social agents continually construct in and through practice" as a consequence of "the encounter of habitus with the peculiar conjuncture of the field" (Bourdieu and Wacquant 1992, 128–29). While Bourdieu's notion of "strategy" was seemingly originally designed for a "practice theory" largely focused on everyday social actions like gift exchange (1977, 3–9), he became far more interested in the interface of strategy and state formation starting in the late 1980s (see Bourdieu and Wacquant 1992, 110–15).

6. Previous studies of bureaucratic formation in the People's Republic of China are numerous. Some of these to consider, in relation to my discussion of the Federation's formation, include Chan 1993; Cooper 2000; Dixon 1981; Harding 1981; Henderson and Cohen 1984; Lieberthal and Lampton 1992; Lü 2000; Oi 1999; Saich 2001; Townsend 1967; Walder 1986; Whyte 1974; and Zheng 1997. Also of importance is Lü and Perry 1997.

7. Mouzelis (1967, 16–17) describes the other two poles of Weber's tripartite model of domination as follows:

· *Traditional Domination.* The traditional leader is the Master who commands by virtue of his inherited status. His orders are personal and arbitrary but within the limits fixed by custom. His subjects obey out of personal loyalty to him or out of respect of his traditional status. When this type of domination, typical in the patriarchal household, is extended over many people and a wide territory, the ensuing administrative apparatus can ideally take two forms. In the patrimonial form of traditional domination, the officials of the apparatus are personal retainers—servants, relatives, favourites, etc.—usually dependent on their master for remuneration. On the other hand the feudal apparatus has a greater degree of autonomy towards the master. The feudal officials are not personal dependants but allies giving an oath of fealty to their vassal.

· *Legal Domination.* The belief in the rightness of law is the legitimation sustaining this type of domination . . . [The] ruler is considered as a superior who has come to hold a position by legal procedures (appointment, election, etc.). It is by virtue of his position that he exercises power within limits set by legally sanctioned rules. The typical administrative apparatus corresponding to the legal type of domination is called bureaucracy.

8. It is unclear exactly how Weber understood "bodies." He rarely wrote about them directly. Though his outlook seems strongly informed by his engagement with and analyses of religion, particularly Judeo-Christian traditions, as suggested when he characterizes "charisma" as distinguished along the lines of "body and spirit" (see also Turner 1993; Weber 1946, 245).

9. Within anthropology, some of the earliest articulations of these first three critiques were made in the 1950s and 1960s by members of what is now called the Manchester School (see Wright 1994, 10–14). Since then, critiques of this line of thinking have been extended and broadened by scholars in the growing field of "organizational studies" (e.g., Morgan 1986; Mouzelis 1967; Nader 1972; Pettigrew 1985; see also Herzfeld 1992; Heyman 1995). A significant source of intellectual inspiration for a number of these scholars has been Marx's views about bureaucrats and bureaucracy (see Mouzelis 1967, 8–11).

10. In 1990 Deng retired from his last formal leadership post as chair of the State Military Commission. Within the Chinese party-state, the title "paramount leader" (*zuigao lingxiu*) has no official duties or post affiliated with it.

11. During the mid-1990s there were sporadic flurries of news reports about Deng Xiaoping's health. In general, these reports would be initiated by news services located outside of China, in Hong Kong and sometimes elsewhere, and would be followed by reports by Chinese government media or spokespersons. The "foreign" reports regularly quoted anonymous doctors and Deng family contacts, who would describe Deng Xiaoping's "failing health" and his most recent admittance to the 301 Brigade Military Hospital for urgent biomedical care. Chinese central government propagandists responded by regularly stating that Deng was in "good health for a man in his 90s." All of these reports, whatever their accuracy, were nearly always framed in the language of the biosciences. Foreign news services conjectured that Deng was suffering from a variety of biomedical conditions (including cancer,

stroke, advanced Parkinson's disease, Alzheimer's disease, pneumonia, and influenza), whereas PRC sources offered statements that Deng was "in good health at present," or that he was blessed with "a longevity gene" (AFP 1995; *Sing Tao Daily* 1996; *South China Morning Post* 1995; United Press International 1995). Despite their frequent pronouncements of confidence in Deng Xiaoping's durability, the Chinese Communist Party's second-tier leadership in the mid-1990s was greatly concerned about Deng Xiaoping's impending death and actively worked to forestall and manage that event through healthcare techniques. This is indicated by the fact that, in early April 1994, the Central Committee Political Bureau created a leading group under the Central Committee charged with attending to Deng's "health" (BBC 1994).

12. Although I am unaware of Deng Xiaoping having ever publicly made statements in support of Deng Pufang's work, several pieces of evidence indicate that this support was regularly being exercised, just out of the public view. For example, Carter Center documents indicate that during a private Beijing meeting in 1987 Deng Xiaoping and former U.S. President Jimmy Carter discussed, among other things, how a Carter organization, Global 2000, could assist in improving the quality of life of China's disabled population. Also, the September 29, 1993, issue of the *China Daily* reported Deng Pufang as saying that "he felt sure that his father, Deng Xiaoping, would support and promote China's disabled undertaking."

13. By capital, I, of course, do not mean simply money. Like Bourdieu (1977, 178), I understand capital as something socially celebrated that can be exchanged for like or other socially celebrated items. Capital within this framework might be anything from allegiances, prerogatives, skills, knowledge, aesthetic sensibilities, and corporeal beauty, to personal relations, certificates of achievement, real estate, financial items, consumer goods, moral standing, and bureaucratic authority.

14. Originally, the CRRC was slated to have a different name—the China Rehabilitation Research Center for the Physically Handicapped—but as Deng's and his colleagues' understanding of foreign definitions of disability and rehabilitation expanded, they bowed to outside pressure to widen the center's programmatic reach beyond just helping the physically disabled.

15. It bears noting that even before it opened, the China Rehabilitation Research Center was as much a locus of controversy as a source of care. One protracted wrangle revolved around whether resources (Chinese or foreign) could be better spent developing local rehabilitation programs rather than elite, capital-intensive, technology-laden facilities like the CRRC (cf. Henderson 1989; World Bank 1992). The CRRC cost millions of dollars to build and outfit with myriad high-tech instruments, including an MRI scanner, and a fleet of luxury sedans for center administrators. But when compared to other medical facilities of equal or lesser cost in China, the center was acutely underutilized in the 1980s and 1990s and generally benefited only those with the wherewithal to afford its high fees. It was partially owing to the inaccessibility of the center for most of the population in China that in the early 1990s Federation leaders bowed to pressure from outside organizations like the WHO to coordinate with the Ministry of Public Health to develop more decentralized, "low-tech" community-based rehabilitation (CBR). Another conflict was over which institution, the CRRC/Federation or the Ministry of Public Health, should control and dictate the development of rehabilitation medicine in China.

Primarily a battle over resources, the conflict became somewhat contentious in the 1980s and 1990s and involved the Ministry of Public Health denying insurance coverage (*gongfei yiliao*) for many kinds of rehabilitation treatment, sponsoring competing rehabilitation centers and projects, and briefly challenging the Federation's right to co-author documents with institutions of ministerial rank (*buji*) or higher.

16. The Three Target program was launched in the late 1980s and continued on through the 1990s. The targets consisted of (1) cataract surgery, (2) oral-language training for deaf children, and (3) polio-correction surgery. Several high-ranking Federation officials have told me that these targets were initially chosen because Deng Xiaoping's warm ties to the military could guarantee their implementation and because they were perceived as quick and impressive ways for the Federation to assist the disabled (see Chapter 4).

17. No doubt, favors were exchanged, and possibly often. One notable example of reciprocation has to do with the Tiananmen demonstrations of 1989 and the tract of land at 44 Beichizi, which the military had provided to the Welfare Fund for its central offices. The construction of the Fund's 44 Beichizi facility, which is located only 1.5 kilometers from Tiananmen, was nearly finished when the student demonstrations began unfolding in the spring of 1989. And since, by that juncture, Deng Pufang's staff had yet to move into their shiny new compound with its green-tiled buildings, the army's martial law troops were offered the building as their main command center. During the month of June, it was from 44 Beichizi that the military managed much of its bloody suppression of protestors in central Beijing.

18. Because Kanghua employees were increasingly brazen in their money-making tactics, because so many of them were elite cadres or well-known princelings, and because the party-state still justified its ascendance on the grounds that it provided clean socialist government, many people in the Chinese polity became increasingly disgruntled with Kanghua in the mid-1980s (Quan 1994). According to at least one report, intragovernmental irritation at Kanghua was so great that Deng Xiaoping chided his son during this period and directed Deng Pufang to distance himself from the company (*New York Times*, editorial, June 25, 1989). Possibly for this reason, Deng Pufang handed over formal control of Kanghua to the State Council in the summer of 1987, although he officially arranged for Kanghua's profits to still be funneled to the Fund (Deng 1989). As mentioned in Chapter 1, popular disgruntlement toward Kanghua spilled forth quite publicly during the 1989 democracy movement, and this public outcry led to the company being closed down by the State Council not long after the bloody June crackdown. When they began marching through Beijing that spring, a central complaint of student demonstrators—one which significantly galvanized popular support for their movement—was that the party-state was thoroughly befouled by corruption. Not surprisingly, a primary target for the activists was Kanghua. Many of the thousands of posters (*dazibao*) that activists affixed to walls around Beijing and other cities contained biting criticisms of the links between Kanghua, the Deng family, and elite corruption (Han 1990). Following the June crackdown, the State Council ordered Kanghua closed and disbanded.

19. This account of the passage of the Protection Law was explained to me by an official in the Ministry of Public Health, who took part in the law's passage.

20. In actuality, the creation of the journal *Disability in China* was merely a mat-

ter of re-licensing and a change in title. The journal was the successor to a previously established periodical, *Voices of the Blind and the Deaf.*

21. One example of such intragovernment reports comes from a reprint of a somewhat disjointed speech that Deng Pufang gave in the late 1980s to an audience of high-ranking party-state officials:

> In our country, enduring the reforms is a problem. Expanding productivity and conducting reform requires that constant attention be paid to [people's] ability to endure. Within this issue of endurance, one important issue is the popular masses' trust in the Communist Party and the Peoples' Government. By performing real and down-to-earth good deeds for the people, we can raise the Communist Party's and the People's Government's prestige. Earlier practice proves, if we do good deeds, the masses will feel indebted to the Communist Party, and their belief in socialism will rise. In this way, during the processes of reform and productive expansion, the masses will have a relatively high capacity for enduring and the country can develop relatively smoothly. Doing good work for disabled persons is not only a developmental mechanism, it is a stabilizing mechanism, it is many stabilizing mechanisms. Beyond the surface level significance of decreasing societal contradictions and stabilizing society, these stabilizing mechanisms have a deeper importance, that being raising popular trust in our party, socialism, and the People's Government. Through this sort of work, it can be made clear that Chinese society's most outstanding people [*jingying rencai*] are within our government and party, and that these people are sincerely committed to serving the masses. (Deng 1988, 7)

22. When the State Council created the Federation, it granted it administrative status as a *juji*, which in the PRC's governmental hierarchy is an office two notches below the level of Ministry (*shengji*).

23. Pufang and his aides, by the early 1990s, had succeeded in convincing the State Council to issue directives that formally released the Federation from the MCA. They also managed to get the State Council, the central MCA office, and other central government agencies to issue pointed directives (down through China's hierarchy of People's Government offices) that required that local Federation chapters should become self-managing institutions, possessing the same administrative status as the local offices of any ministerial agency.

24. The most famous of these tours was probably that made by Mao in mid-July 1966. This was a tour of China's central coast cities during which Mao set the stage for the Cultural Revolution, striving to reposition himself as the most influential figure in the party-state, a status he had lost a short time earlier owing to policy failures such as the catastrophic effects of his Great Leap Forward initiative (1958). At one point during the tour, the then seventy-three-year-old leader swam in the Yangze River. His propagandists hyped the swim throughout the national media as an example of Mao's extraordinary athleticism and vitality, and over the ensuing months used it to construct the cult of personality that enveloped Mao during the rest of his life.

25. Deng Xiaoping's last public "inspection tour" was to Guangdong Province in

1992. His last known public appearance outside of Beijing was in 1994, during a brief Chinese Lunar New Year visit to Shanghai.

26. Since the late 1970s, post-Mao regimes have publicly celebrated the "separate kitchens" fiscal shift and have characterized it as a hallmark of Deng Xiaoping's authority and managerial prowess. But the source of the shift remains an open debate among scholars. To what degree did the Deng regime initiate and direct the shift in the late 1970s and 1980s? To what degree was the shift already set in motion by the decades of turmoil wrought by the Great Leap Forward, the Cultural Revolution, and by the nascent Deng regime, which needed to cement its authority and legitimacy over a weakened central government in the late 1970s and was thus quick to formalize and extend the shift through policy pronouncements?

27. As Cadre Gao told me shortly before I concluded my research in Wenchang County, East Hainan:

> To be completely honest, I'm not very keen to have our Federation chapter leave the MCA system, and so I haven't worked that hard to get the local finance ministry officials to allocate money for a separate office. There are so many little benefits from being attached to such a big and well-established system like the MCA. The Federation is new and doesn't have much to offer its employees. One of my children got a job working at our local MCA enterprise, the big hotel up the street. He's doing very well. But, if I become a full-time Federation employee, I won't be able to place my other child there.

28. The central Federation office notwithstanding, by the mid-1990s nearly all independent chapters were either in major metropolitan areas, provincial centers, or in the capitals of China's so-called autonomous regions. By 1993, among the 99 percent of all Federation chapters that existed outside of large urban settings (i.e., outside of major metropolitan areas, provincial centers, or the capitals of China's so-called autonomous regions), only 3 percent were what Deng Pufang's staff might call "able-bodied" (Chu et al. 1996, 616–18).

29. That patriarchal forces were at play is also evidenced by the explanations men and women working at such low levels in the Beijing Federation system gave for why slightly greater gender parity existed in their offices, explanations which are indicative of how inequity often seeks materialist justification whatever the sociocultural context. Such employees have said to me repeatedly that the slightly greater gender parity at the bottom of the Federation's urban system is rooted in men's and women's natural differences (*ziran chabie*). They say that the employment of men decreases as one moves down the Federation's urban hierarchy, largely because men's natural preoccupation with status subjects them to stronger feelings of embarrassment whenever they hold subordinate positions within welfare organizations, whereas women's natural capacities for patience, kindness, and nurturance means that they are more suited for care-giving posts.

30. Beijing in the 1990s seems particularly illustrative of these trends. According to a longtime official working in Beijing's Municipality's central Federation office, in 1998 only half of Beijing's eighteen district- and county-level Federation offices employed a *canji* registrant. The total number of *canji* registrants employed in those offices was eleven. Among those *canji* employees, all eleven were male and all were

physically disabled, except for one who was blind. According to the same official, in 1998 Beijing Municipality's central Federation office had more than one hundred employees. Seven were *canji* registrants. Of these, five were physically disabled, one was deaf, and one was blind. All but one was male.

31. Another example comes from Beijing's Municipality's central Federation office. In 1995, of the *canji* employees in the chapter, only two likely met the Federation's 1987 *canji* criteria. The other *canji* employees were recognized by the Federation as *canji* only as a consequence of its reciprocity agreement with the military. (Note: By "employees," here, I mean Executive Council members, as described in Appendix 2.)

CHAPTER FOUR

1. For a discussion of characteristics that scholars have commonly associated with Fordism, see Allen 1996.

2. In his treatise on the subject, Antonio Gramsci argued that Fordism entailed "the biggest collective effort to date to create, with unprecedented speed, and with a consciousness of purpose unmatched in history, a new type of worker and a new type of man" (1971, 279–318). Paralleling the rise of Fordist forms of social organization, Gramsci further held, was the emergence of new modes of "living and thinking and feeling life" (ibid.; also quoted both in Martin 1992, 122; and Harvey 1990, 126). Martin (1994) has extended Gramsci's thinking by examining how transformations wrought by Fordist and post-Fordist modes of production in the United States over the last few decades have coincided with changing bodily precepts.

3. For example, in 500 B.C., Sun Tzu intoned, "Speed is the essence of battle." This quote comes from *The Art of War,* a Chinese classic that Sun Tzu wrote shortly after his feet had been amputated (De Bary 1960, 234).

4. Until the early 1980s one needed fifty coupons to buy a bicycle of choice brand. But work units only issued, on average, five coupons per worker a year. Not surprisingly, a black market existed for coupons.

5. Despite communist doctrine, the paradigm of the modern mobile urbanite has been juxtaposed for most of the twentieth century to a view of the rural laborer as "backward and sedentary." Until recently, so much were farmers seen as being fixed in space, as bound to the earth (lit., "soiled" [*tu*]), that Chinese scholars such as the anthropologist Fei Xiaotong considered it "abnormal" for peasants to migrate from their native communities (Fei 1992, 38–40).

6. Gaubatz, in his discussion of Chinese transportation devices, tells us: "The change from reliance on public bus service in the 1950s and 1960s to the dominance of the bicycle in urban transport started in the late 1970s. Urban residents perceive the bicycle as a faster and more convenient means of transportation than the public buses" (1995, 43).

7. Around half of all Beijing commuters pedaled to work by 1980, and the city had an estimated eight million bicycles by 1996 (Gaubatz 1995, 43; Reuters 1996). The rising numbers of bicycles allowed people to move across the urban landscape at speeds that were far faster than had ever before been collectively achieved in China.

8. Bicycles specifically marketed to females (which lack a horizontal beam

between the seat and handlebars) were produced in China as early as the 1950s. But because of limited supply and because in the 1950s Chinese women began wearing pants, the small but growing number of female riders through the 1960s and 1970s tended to use bicycles with a horizontal crossbar. By the 1990s, bicycle riding was altogether commonplace among females, and many women continued to use bicycles with a horizontal crossbar.

9. Before the twentieth century wheelchairs in China were extremely rare and usually home-built. One classical figure known to have used a wheeled device of unknown design was the warrior-inventor-scholar Zhu Geliang (Giles 1898, 181), who lived during the Three Kingdoms Period (220–280 B.C.). Until very recently, four-wheeled steel wheelchairs were uncommon in China and were generally found only in hospitals. Most of these chairs were imports and thus costly. Another problem was that the chairs were too large for many Chinese homes, particularly in cities.

10. For a detailed explanation of the term *quezi* and its pejorative meaning, see Chapter 6.

11. For insightful commentary on the history of Chinese concepts pertaining to sex/gender and male/female, see Brownell and Wasserstrom 2002.

12. Gramsci also pauses to highlight, however briefly, links between Fordism and an "anti-feminist and 'masculinist' tendency" (1971, 297).

13. China scholars who have explored the relationship between power, gender, and inside/outside distinctions include Gilmartin (1994), Rofel (1992), Watson (1986), and Bray (1997). According to Bray, a synchronicity of gender dimorphism (male/female) and spatial dualism (inside/outside, or *nei-wai*) was particularly acute during the late imperial epoch. As she states: "In late imperial China, all levels of society considered the seclusion of women and the segregation of the sexes inside and outside the house to be not simply a sign of respectability but an essential factor in maintaining public morality. Spatial and social segregation was an expression of a doctrine of separate spheres dating back to classical times. This doctrine was not a simple charter for female subordination; rather it represented the sexes as fulfilling complementary roles of equal dignity (if not equal power). . . . Men and women controlled different domains, into which the other should not intrude. The female domain was the inner, domestic one (although we should beware of presuming absolute coincidence between Chinese and Western meanings of 'domesticity'), and the male domain was the outer one" (1997, 128). For discussions of how anthropologists working outside the China context have explored such issues, see Rosaldo 1974; Dubisch 1986; and Strathern 1988.

14. The use of motorized vehicles to speed up male existence in the late twentieth century was far from harmless to the well-being of men. Vehicular fatalities rocketed in China during the 1980s and 1990s, and most of the people dying from accidents were likely male. According to Chinese government figures, traffic-related deaths jumped 8.6 percent between 1994 and 1995 and 20 percent between 1998 and 1999 (AFP 2000; Reuters 1995).

15. See Mark 1995 for a discussion of contemporary urban Chinese women's emphasis on beauty and bodily perfection.

16. When I posed this question, one concern I had was that my own gender might influence respondents' answers. In order to mitigate such bias, in Hainan, I had my research assistant, a thirty-year-old native Wenchang woman, ask the same

questions in my absence. Consistently, she received similar responses as I did. Because I did not have a research assistant in Beijing, I was not in a position to use the same technique. But I believe that the Xuanwu Federation's registration records clearly support my observations that local Xuanwu residents in the late 1980s and early 1990s tended to associate males more frequently with the category *canji* than they did females.

17. In the survey's Wenchang sample, 6.0 percent of females had a disability, compared to 4.5 percent of males. For Xuanwu, the rates were female 5.3 percent and male 4.8 percent. The aggregate national rates were female 4.9 percent and male 4.8 percent. That the survey-indicated rates among women were consistently higher than among men—in Wenchang, Xuanwu, and nationwide—probably was a reflection, at least in part, of the fact that in 1980s China (like now) women on average lived longer than men and thus were more likely to develop conditions that fit the survey's criteria for disability.

18. During the period of my field work, one reason it took me some time to come to this realization about the paradigmatic portrait of a *canji ren*—as being someone who not only has trouble walking but who is also male—has to do with a woman that the Chinese government has treated as a "model figure" since the early 1980s. She is Zhang Haidi. As her official narrative states, Zhang was born in 1955 in Shandong Province. Following four operations to remove tumors in her spine, she became a paraplegic at the age of five and thereafter never attended school. Through hard work and self-study, she became well read in politics, literature, and medical science, and she established competency in several languages, including English, Japanese, and German. In the early 1980s the combination of her laudatory writings about socialism and her bodily condition brought her to the attention of China's state-run propaganda system. In 1983 she was elevated to the status of model figure by Deng Xiaoping. Inasmuch as she has been regularly invoked by the Federation as an exemplar of the productive *canji ren*, she has been even more often touted by the Chinese Communist Party as an embodiment of exemplary socialist youth. And perhaps it is because of how she has been coded more often as a paragon for China's youth, rather than as a model for the country's disabled, that she has not had greater influence in raising women's overall presence in Federation activities and community understandings of *canji*. This is an observation that Zhang did not dispute when I raised it during my interview with her in the fall of 1995. For more on Zhang Haidi, see Zhang 1999.

19. In the 1980s and 1990s the sales of most new gas-powered vehicles were taxed at rates exceeding 100 percent. During this period, policemen were often present at most major intersections in big cities during the daytime. Furthermore, the procedures for acquiring a driver's license or for licensing a motorized conveyance in a metropolitan area were Byzantine in their complexity. And only a few of the many categories of vehicles found in China then—cars, bicycles, trucks, tractors, vans, buses, jeeps, two-wheeled motorcycles, three-wheeled vans, etc.—were allowed onto streets in big cities, and many of these only during tightly restricted hours. Leaders in certain cities, like Beijing, banned devices such as motorcycles because they considered them too "Third World."

20. In the mid-1990s it was common for motorized tricycle drivers to earn sizable

incomes moving consumer goods and transporting people. This was particularly common in cities where standard motorcycles were banned.

21. Also cited in Zhang 2001.

22. Like nearly all state agencies throughout China during the 1980s and 1990s, Federation chapters received most of their funding from local city, county, and district governments; and chapters were expected to bolster their budgets by pursuing entrepreneurial activities (see Chapter 3). Prices in Beijing for the most popular type of three-wheeler, one produced by the motorcycle manufacturer Jia Ling, hovered around 3,500 yuan in 1995.

23. Not long before I interviewed a senior central Federation official in the mid-1990s, Federation officers conducted an informal assessment of the percentage of owner-operators of three-wheeled motorcycles that would fit the Federation's criteria for disability. Their finding, according to the official, was that at least 70 percent of owner-operators were not *canji*.

24. According to a Central Federation informant, the arguments were loosely the following:

- Market reforms and traditional Chinese attitudes have left most disabled people today unemployed and homebound. Most are too poor to buy motorized tricycles, except as a business investment. Such an investment allows them to both participate in society and have a personal income.

- Banning motorized tricycles will cause additional harm to disabled people. *Canji ren* will have no choice but to protest. Such protest will be worse for the country than the traffic created by their vehicles.

- The Federation apologizes for bothering the Ministry of Public Security, but regulations need to be drafted stipulating that *canji ren* may both operate three-wheelers and use them for financial gain. There is no other recourse until China becomes more developed. When China has jobs enough for disabled people, the Federation will agree to restrict the vehicles, which are admittedly quite hazardous.

25. In Beijing, where city-level regulations began to appear as early as 1989, the barriers included: (1) getting registered as a disabled person, (2) buying a vehicle, (3) getting the vehicle and oneself licensed, (4) registering for commercial status. Each of these steps had numerous substeps, many of which required owner-operators to visit hospitals and government offices to have their bodies scrutinized along a host of axes (e.g., national identity, residential status, age, psychological competency, physical-spatial functionality, biomedically defined impairment level).

26. Oddly, though, campaigns like this one in the 1990s did little to stem the number of illegally operated three-wheelers. The main reason was the cost-benefit ratio. The fines assessed during the campaigns were paltry when compared to the potential earnings for using motorized tricycles illegally. According to several Beijing government acquaintances, fines were kept low in the capital because of the tremendous influence the Federation wielded there.

27. The rise of such unemployment was closely tied to the state's "welfare factories." Created in earlier decades, mostly by the Civil Affairs Ministry, these factories

employed large numbers of people who, once the Federation was created, were rec-ognized by the state as *canji*. That is, the factories employed large numbers of *canji* until the 1990s. Like so many state-run enterprises established during the Mao era, welfare factories were being shut down left and right across China while I was con-ducting my fieldwork. Why? They were closed on the grounds that they were unprofitable.

28. For further discussion of the ways that Chinese citizens in the late twentieth century expected men to be more able than women, see Judd 1994, 1, 224–25.

29. Whether in Beijing or elsewhere, most three-wheeler accidents likely went unreported to traffic authorities because so many of the devices were illegally oper-ated. Nonetheless, according to the police, there were forty motorized tricycle acci-dents in Beijing during 1994, which resulted in thirty-one injuries and seven deaths (Zhang 1995).

30. I never met any disability brothers who did not have Beijing residency permits.

CHAPTER FIVE

1. According to the 1987 National Sample Survey of Disability, 74 percent of people in China who fit the state's *canji* criteria lived in village settings (the rest lived in towns and cities). According to national census data from the same period, 63 percent of China's total population lived in village settings (Guo 1990).

2. Following Hall (1996) and Handler (1994), I treat identity as an ongoing process of becoming, open-ended and multi-threaded, and not as a static aspect of existence by which each person constructs only one identity. This orientation requires us to investigate not identity per se but identity-formation. Such formation is "worked out" within the confluence of, at the very least, normalizing discourses, political economic structures, and desires. And this working out always happens rela-tionally and thus intersubjectively, between people and things, through objectifica-tion and embodiment (see also Butler 1990; Jenkins 1996; Strathern 1988).

3. Social scientists who in recent years have examined health in rural China from sociocultural perspectives include Anson and Sun (2002), Hyde (2000), Jing (2000), Li and Tracy (1999), White (1998; 1999), Wei et al. (1997), and Wong (1995). One of the few attempts to think about the effects of rural health issues at the level of intersubjective processes has been that of Farquhar (1996).

4. A key feature of these associational groups, Rapp says, are that they simulta-neously spring from and serve political agendas, in which those people who are iden-tified similarly (as, say, having Down's syndrome) or who have family members so identified come to imagine themselves as a unifying force and thereby able to act as a wedge for lobbying civil society, the state, and scientific researchers.

5. In other words, it is important for us to recall Rabinow's observation that new kinds of biologically informed labeling always involves a "dissolution of the category of 'the social'" because it always entails a move "away from holistic approaches to the subject or social contextualism" (1996, 99–100). Whether such "dissolution" leads, in turn, to new associational community, and if so, whether such community is par-ticularly beneficial to specifically categorized persons is far less certain.

6. In a recent article, Das and Addlakha (2001) likewise call for greater nuance

in the study of disability, biosociality, and identity. They argue that students of disability have often been too quick to try to locate disability within a "liberal political regime" of salubrious sociality defined in terms of "political mobilizations." Instead of advocating such an approach, Das and Addlakha explore the emergence of a different kind of disabled identity in Delhi, India, one they describe less in terms of political mobilization and more in terms of "notions of publics constituted through voice" (512).

7. According to Feng (1990, 53), by the mid-1970s, more than 95 percent of all Wenchang residents were enrolled in the collective healthcare system.

8. Between 1966 and 1976 villagers were charged very little for health-station treatment. Registration and examination cost five fen; an injection cost five fen; and a house call cost one mao. Likewise, during this period, the community of Min Song paid the village doctor only three yuan a month.

9. This income figure was provided to me by Cadre Chen, who was in charge of filling out income reports for the Min Song government in the early 1990s.

10. When I arrived in Min Song in the fall of 1993, Cadre Chen estimated that the most well-off members of the community enjoyed a per capita income of 2,000 yuan (10,000 yuan for a family of five) and that the least well off had a per capita income of 100 yuan (or 500 yuan for a family of five).

11. Technological advancements played a large part in all this movement of people, goods, and knowledge. During the 1980s Wenchang was flooded with new transportation devices (motorcycles, minibuses, and large three-wheeled jitneys). By 1993 direct-dial long-distance phone service (both domestic and international) was available at the Wenjiao post office. Nearly every Min Song resident watched some TV on the sets located in each hamlet's general goods shop. And Min Song's well-heeled residents owned video players on which they watched pirated movies (some domestic, some foreign, some pornographic) supplied to them by Wenjiao entrepreneurs.

12. From 1977 to 1980 and from 1984 to 1986 county statisticians saw a more than 70 percent rise in infant mortality (Feng 1990, 169). Yet, it must also be noted that, according to the same statisticians, during the late 1970s and throughout the 1980s the prevalence of most communicable diseases in Wenchang continued to decline (Feng 1990, 112–40).

13. For additional data on China's post-Mao healthcare reforms and their effects, see World Bank 1997.

14. Most of these enrollees (four of the six) were, in fact, among the ninety-three villagers that Cadre Chen registered as disabled. But, as Chen explained to me, the overlap between Min Song subsidy recipients and disability registrants was not a matter of bureaucratic design, but rather one prompted by the way in which "bodily defects" (*shenti quedian*), as he often called them, undermined people's life chances. No superiors ever directed Chen to use the state's *canji* criteria to determine who in the community should receive subsidies, nor did he do so on his own.

15. During my time living in Min Song there were several state-directed redistributive schemes through which villagers, in theory, contributed to Wenjiao's three welfare programs, as well as the emergent Federation initiatives. The oldest and most involuntary scheme was an annual per capita welfare tax known as *you fu liang*, which the township government had levied on all residents after the breakup of the Wenjiao commune in 1979. The second scheme, which was developed in the early

1990s, was a 20 yuan tax charged by the township government when it issued marriage licenses. The last scheme came into existence not long after I moved to Min Song. It was titled the Wenjiao Benevolent Foundation and was created by order of and with financial support (5,000 yuan) from the county Civil Affairs office. The foundation was directed by the town's government leaders. According to Wenjiao's mayor, its mission was to raise money from Wenjiao natives (generally, those who had left the township for more lucrative jobs elsewhere) and then, over time, to use the interest on the foundation's assets to assist people within the township who were "destitute, disabled, or elderly and in need." Because of their limited scope, these three schemes were not especially effective at generating money. Nor, it should be said, were they particularly effective in redistributing whatever funds they did generate back to those villagers in greatest need of financial assistance. One of the biggest problems undermining redistribution had to do with the administrative and geographic distance of villagers from the people who had the greatest influence over how funds were disbursed, that is, from the township cadres. (By contrast, during the Maoist period, villagers could turn to and receive aid, usually in the form of grain, from brigade and production team leaders.) The new structural remove fostered bureaucratic indifference on the part of those who controlled welfare funds toward those who needed the funds. It also meant that it was very difficult for anyone in the villages, whether they were cadres or residents, to know anything about the size or management of welfare resources. So, for example, in early 1994 almost no one in Min Song knew that Wenjiao natives living in Haikou had recently pledged sizable sums to enhance the Wenjiao Benevolent Foundation's assets, nor did they know, for that matter, that Wenjiao's mayor was planning to devote a large proportion of those pledges to buy a car for his official use.

16. All of these people, the nursing home director told me in response to my inquiry, fell within the state's parameters for *canji*, and one of them—a woman who was nearly blind—happened to be from one of Min Song's hamlets. But while the director acknowledged a high rate of disablement among the home's handful of inhabitants, she also emphasized that the only official prerequisite for residency was enrollment in the Five Guarantees program.

17. Wenchang Disabled Persons' Federation, personal communication, December 4, 1993.

18. To a sizable degree, Dr. Ma's anger was born of what he characterized as financial impropriety on the part of Min Song's village committee. Supralocal officials responsible for the polio-eradication campaign had distributed a small sum of money in advance to village committees in exchange for local government assistance. But these funds had done little to induce Min Song officials to act. Other than one cadre affixing a poster announcing the campaign to a wall of a village teahouse and another cadre spending about an hour on the campaign's first day helping the township doctor with paperwork, Min Song's village committee was invisible during the campaign.

19. As I accompanied him, it was patently obvious to one and all why parents were avoiding him. Many households had young children whose births they had not reported to government officials, so as to bypass the population control system. When Dr. Ma came upon these unregistered children, not only did he provide them

with vaccine, either at the pro forma fee of one yuan or for free, but he also added their names to the public health system's registry of village children.

20. Wenchang and Beijing officials described to me that the logic for cash collateral had several sources, including Maoism, the Federation's weak infrastructure, and how market reforms were transforming local state authority. They also indicated that their logic was built upon the bureaucratization of family relationships. As a high-ranking Beijing official in the central Federation office, who ran the loan program, explained:

> Probably as a legacy of Maoism, most people think they can treat government loan money as subsidies, just eating it all up, never returning a cent. Because of that, we lost a lot of loan money initially. We therefore had little choice but to come up with policies to stop our loan funds, which are quite limited, from disappearing. As you know, the Federation doesn't have enough staff at the local level to manage carefully each loan. Also, with the demise of the communes, the state has little leverage over local people, say, to repossess a thing put up as collateral. So, what we've found is that the only way for local Federation staff to make sure loan money is properly used by recipients and repaid on time is to demand cash collateral up front, which is easily controlled from above. Where are *canji ren* expected to get cash collateral? Well they could always get it from a family member, you know, someone who the *canji ren* is strongly bound to, but who without government oversight might otherwise feel uneasy providing a personal loan.

21. At the end of the Maoist period, the Hainan government created new land-utilization regulations that allowed rural families in possession of Republican-era deeds or other substantive records to take contractual control over specific kinds of erstwhile family land, including ancestral burial sites.

CHAPTER SIX

1. Aside from liminality, other early approaches developed by social scientists and historians to study disability include deviance (Lemert 1967), stigmatization (Goffman 1963), labeling (Zola 1993), structural-functionalism (Groce 1985), chronicity (Estroff 1993), social stratification (Jenkins 1991), medicalization (Davis 1995; Oliver 1996; Zola 1972), and political economy (Doyal 1983; Stone 1984).

2. Similar findings were produced by China's 1987 National Sample Survey of Disability. According to that study, by age forty-four, only 4 percent of China's general population had never married (Di 1989, 134–37). Because I have been able to acquire only limited background material on either the survey by the National Statistical Bureau or the 1987 National Sample Survey of Disability, I do not know if their designers only recognized as "married" those citizens who had received a formal marriage certificate after fulfilling the proper government procedures for marriage registration. This issue probably did not significantly affect the surveys' findings, however, since in the People's Republic of China, common-law marriage has only recently reemerged, after having been nearly wiped out by Maoism. Also, this

issue is not crucial here since my goal in presenting these data is simply to paint a rough picture, relative to the national population, of the numbers of "never-married" within China's so-called disabled population.

3. One person who has examined the intersection of disability and marriage in post-Mao China is Phillips (1993). Almost no scholarship exists that examines the intersection of marriage, disability, and gender in China; this can be explained to some degree by the fact that, throughout the social sciences, a heightened sensitivity to the gendered body, which emerged in the 1970s, has only recently given way to, if not spawned, greater analytical attention to bodies more generally.

4. To be sure, treating the conjugal unit as a primary social-assistance bulwark was not something invented by the Federation just for the *canji*. China's party-state has long legislated that the family is to be the main source of protection for the aged and infirmed and has forbidden family desertion of the elderly and infirm (Ikels 1993, 307). This is plainly stated in the PRC's constitution (Article 49). And it is strongly articulated in the nation's marriage law:

> Husband and wife shall have the duty to maintain each other. (Article 20, Marriage Law of the PRC)

> Children shall have the duty to support and assist their parents. . . . If children fail to perform their duty, parents who are unable to work or have difficulties in providing for themselves shall have the right to demand support payments from their children. (Article 21, Marriage Law of the PRC)

In 1990, the Federation simply extended this legislative orientation when it established the Disability Protection Law:

> Family members . . . should encourage and assist disabled persons. . . . Mal-treatment and desertion of disabled persons is forbidden. (Article 9, Disability Protection Law of the PRC)

5. China scholars who have observed that men have historically had a harder time finding a spouse than women include Harrell (1985), Li and Lavely (1995), Pasternak (1989), Min and Eades (1995), Seldon (1993), Sommer (2000), and J. Watson (1989). The 1990 National Statistical Bureau survey mentioned above, for instance, found that men in midlife were twenty times more likely to have never married than women (6.0 percent versus 0.3 percent) (National Statistical Bureau 1990, 530–35). According to China Studies literature, there are two overlapping answers to the question "Why are men in China more likely to never marry than women?" First, because people in China have culturally celebrated males more than females, girls have fallen victim to infanticide more frequently or have been provided far fewer vital resources (food, medical care, parental attention, etc.), both of which have led to sharp disparities in neonatal mortality. These facts, together with other amplifying forces (taboos on widow remarriage and male polygamy prior to 1949), have meant that fewer women have been available to marry (see Chiao and Chen 1938, 53; Croll 1987; Greenhalgh and Jiali 1995; Fei 1939, 33–34; Sen 1990; State Statistical Bureau 1996, 72–77). Second, Chinese society has made marrying problematical for men by having their entry into marriage be especially contingent

on social status, primarily defined as access to such economic variables as land and the wherewithal to make marriage payments (Li and Lavely 1995; Telford 1992).

6. Sinologists have not been alone here. In the social sciences overall, the above lacunae are quite common, as Yanagisako and Collier (1987) and, more recently, Borneman (1996) highlight. Yanagisako and Collier point out that kinship studies frequently have ignored bodily differences or have treated them as presocial, natural facts, as things that exist "outside of and beyond culture" (1987, 29). As a corrective, they argue that further attention needs to be placed on marriage as being a set of sociopolitical practices that influence the formation of people's gender identities. Challenging, yet ultimately building upon Yanagisako and Collier's insights, Borneman argues that anthropologists must also examine how marriage regimes contribute to the reification and marginalization of categories of persons—such as "gay" and "HIV positive"—that are not necessarily gender-specific, but that, like all social categories, exist in relation to gender. He additionally argues that, to better understand how marriage contributes to such reification and marginalization, anthropologists must pay closer attention to the inner workings of marriage practices, especially how such practices exclude, how they prevent people who wish to wed from doing so.

7. In the 1980s, owing to such factors as the U.N.'s effort to globalize Euro-American disability advocacy initiatives and to moves taken by Deng Pufang to create a more salubrious environment for China's less-abled citizenry, elements within China's party-state began pressing for the Chinese people to avoid pejorative terminology for bodily differences and to use more neutral, often biomedical, signifiers. As a consequence, China's state-run media in the late 1980s began urging that terms such as "the insane" (*fengzi*) or "the demented" (*sha*) be shunned, and that, instead, people should use terms like "the mentally ill" (*jingshen bingren*) and "the mentally disabled" (*zhili canji*). As part of this campaign, China's veterans affairs bureaucracy did away with the term "revolutionary crippled soldiers" (*geming canfei zhunren*), substituting "revolutionary injured and disabled soldiers" (*geming shangcan zhunren*) instead.

8. See n. 4, ch. 1.

9. For my informants in rural Hainan and Beijing, the desire to marry somebody local was related only nominally to the household registration (*hukou*) system. Having a locally registered spouse was of minimal advantage in rural Hainan, largely because of the province's liberal "special economic zone" policies. Changes in Beijing's *hukou* system for people officially labeled as disabled made for a similar situation there. In the late 1980s the Beijing government created a loophole in the city's household registration regulations, permitting Beijing residents who were officially categorized as disabled to have their spouses' household registration cards transferred to Beijing. With *hukou* less of a problem, there remained at least two reasons why Beijing and Hainan residents, who were often called *quezi*, desired a local spouse. The first was that they felt that a common upbringing was important for facilitating interpersonal communication and, increasingly, for developing "romantic" affection. The second reason was that marrying a local resident would show that one had the ability, the *nengli*, to attract a person of high cultural quality (*wenhua suzhi*) (cf. Lavely 1991, 286). Many Beijing residents, particularly those born and raised in Beijing, considered Beijingers to be the most culturally sophisticated of all Chinese.

Similarly, most Hainanese considered Wenchang County to be one of the most culturally sophisticated areas of the island, and thus local residents placed a high premium on matches between Wenchang families.

10. Dictionaries usually gloss *nengli* as "ability" and, to a lesser degree, "functional force" or "power." At times, Chinese people today define *nengli* as a biologically inherited quality similar to the English word "talent." At times, they view it as an extension of one's parents' authority, as in the phrase, "Her dad is a vice-secretary of the standing council; she's got a lot of *nengli*." Yet, when questioned closely, Chinese speakers are just as likely to describe *nengli* as a "thing" or "things" that are acquired through various spoken and unspoken modes of practice, things that through habitual action gradually become an indistinguishable part of the body-self. At different times in the twentieth century, there has been great debate over what constituted proper ability. Indeed, much of the political turmoil that occurred during Mao's rule was connected to whether *nengli* should be structured around Marxist orthodoxy or technical knowledge (Meisner 1986; Madsen 1984).

11. Kleinman et al. (1995, 1326) found that it was common, when arranging a marriage, for parents to "try to disguise that their child has epilepsy." See also M. Wolf 1972, 107.

12. People (of whatever gender) who were called *quezi* were not the only persons to whom Chinese in the 1990s negatively applied the concepts of *nengli*; there were many others (including children and the very elderly). Moreover, the supposed incompetence of the "lame" varied, depending on the specific Chinese environment in which they lived. For example, I found that Beijing residents often considered *quezi* to be the most capable individuals from among those people in the five government-sanctioned categories of disability (the blind, the deaf, the severely mentally ill, the mentally retarded, and the physically impaired), possibly because the state supplied the urban *que* with three-wheeled motorcycles and assisted many of them in finding jobs or starting small businesses. But in rural China, where bodily movement outside the home has always been crucial to agricultural production and where most roads in the 1990s were made of dirt and thus inaccessible to nearly all mobility aids for the disabled, residents regularly told me that among the government's five categories the most incompetent (*gan bu liao huo*) people were *que* men.

13. According to China's 1990 national census, in Wenchang County there were fifty-two men for every forty-eight women in the 20–44 age group (Hainan Province Census Office 1992, 15–17).

14. *Gnou hui* is a Wenchangese cognate of the Mandarin *sha*, which is a pejorative vernacular term often applied to what today are often called the "mentally ill" and "mentally disabled" by English speakers.

15. Similarly, Phillips found that in some cases schizophrenic patients refuse arranged marriages, "either because they have unrealistic expectations for a spouse or because they have no interest in any form of social interaction" (1993, 295).

16. Guangxi's administrative title is *zizhi qu*, or "autonomous region." Today, the People's Republic of China is comprised of twenty-one provinces and five autonomous regions, the latter being Inner Mongolia, Ningxia, Xinjiang, Guangxi, and Tibet. All of these autonomous regions have been lagging behind China's coastal provinces economically. The economic distance between Guangxi and

Hainan has grown increasingly wide since the mid-1980s, when Beijing granted Hainan "special economic zone" status.

17. The different uses of the word "disposition" by Bourdieu (1977) and Iser (1974) reflect an important sociological tension. Bourdieu uses the word "disposition" to emphasize how the individual's entire being is bound up with collective structures of representation and organization. In contrast, Iser seems to use the word to emphasize the idiosyncratic capacities of persons and to show how these capacities are linked to collective processes. These differences aside, Bourdieu seems quite amenable to a literary-derived approach such as Iser's. As Bourdieu states, "Native membership in a field implies . . . a capacity for practical anticipation of the 'upcoming' future contained in the present. . . . This is exactly the effect produced by the novel" (1990, 66–67). See also Hanks 1996, 240–42.

18. Although I believe Iser's ideas on narrativity offer certain conceptual clarity for exploring the effects of marriage exclusion on identity formation, to use the ideas properly one must be careful to see them as, at best, "translational devices" (Herzfeld 1985, 273). Otherwise, people like the men described in this and previous chapters could easily be misconstrued as readers or texts. And this is obviously not the case. These men, as I try to show here, are socially involved individuals, at one moment co-conspirators with family and friends, and at the next angry agents intensely distressed by others' delegitimizing views of them. They are active members of local communities who, often unsuccessfully, try to shape their and others' expectations.

EPILOGUE

1. Xinhua, the national news service of the People's Republic of China, published the list of names of Deng Xiaoping's Funeral Committee on February 19, 1997. The only significant distinction the Xinhua report makes about the composition of the committee, aside from Jiang Zemin functioning as chairman, is gender. The report states that of the 459 members of the funeral committee, 433 were male and 26 were female (see BBC 1997).

2. If nothing else, the challenge of scheduling an interview with Deng highlights the key methodological and epistemological hurdles of studying elite embodiment. Particularly when studying the hyperelite, anthropologists cannot expect that their scholarly subject-position will facilitate research access (Gusterson 1993). For instance, one meeting I had tentatively scheduled with Deng Pufang, planned for March 1995 in Beijing, was inexplicably canceled. Another tentative meeting, set to occur in Atlanta, Georgia, following the 1996 Paralympics was called off. Federation officials explained that this was because representatives of Coca-Cola and other American corporations interested in developing better ties with Chinese elites had been allowed to overbook Deng Pufang's limited U.S. schedule.

3. After receiving permission from Deng at the start of this interview, I audiotaped our conversation. A Federation notetaker was also present throughout the interview.

4. In the mid-1990s the Disabled Persons' Federation leadership changed their estimate of the number of disabled persons in the PRC from 51 million to "over 60

million." They based this change on updated national census data and on the information that 4.9 percent of China's total population is disabled, a figure that was established by the 1987 National Sample Survey of Disabled Persons (as described in Chapter 2).

5. It was only years later, when I stumbled across a photo (Baker 1998) in the Associate Press archives, that I learned that a few days before my interview with Deng, Jiang Zemin had introduced Bill Clinton to Deng at a formal state function.

6. My invocation of the term "experience" is prompted in part by the frequency with which, during my fieldwork, acquaintances used the terms *jingyan* (which is usually translated as "experience") and *tiyan* (which can be translated as "learning through experience" or, literally, "bodily experience"). Yet, by invoking the concept experience, my aim is not to claim some essential and universal ground for understanding sociopolitical formation, whether biobureaucracy, alterity, or anything else. Thankfully, scholars like Joan Scott (1991), Robert Desjarlais (1997), and Judith Farquhar (2002b) have alerted us to the essentialist and universalist pitfalls of trafficking in the term "experience"—that is, the degree to which, as a concept, experience is always something that is historically and sociopolitically framed from place to place. So, instead, I approach the term "experience" in a way quite similar to its use by the China scholar and medical anthropologist Arthur Kleinman (1995). I understand "experience," and in particular, what I am calling "experiences of difference" to be part of the "intersubjective medium of social transactions" that have framed people's lives in the PRC and have constituted the Chinese nation-state in the last few decades (Kleinman 1995, 96). Experience, as Kleinman suggests, is best understood as "the outcome of cultural categories and social structures interacting with psychophysiological processes such that a mediating world is constituted. Experience is the felt flow of that intersubjective medium" (ibid.).

7. For a further discussion of how attention to "what is at stake" is vital for an anthropology of experience and societal suffering, see Kleinman 1995, 97–102.

The Five Criteria of Disability Used by the 1987 National Sampling Survey of the Disabled

(These criteria were approved by the State Council and issued by the Leading Group of the National Sampling Survey of the Disabled.)

Criteria of Visual Disability

I. Definition

Visual disability refers to a bilateral impairment of visual acuity or contraction of visual field due to various causes that renders the victim unable to accomplish work, study, or other activities of which the common people are capable.

Visual disability includes two categories, i.e., blindness and low vision.

II. Grading of Visual Disability

1. Blindness

Grade-1 Blindness: The best corrected visual acuity of the better eye is below 0.02; or the radius of visual field is less than 5°.
Grade-2 Blindness: The best corrected visual acuity is 0.02 or greater but below 0.05; or the radius of visual field is less than 10°.

2. Low Vision

Grade-1 Low Vision: The best corrected visual acuity of the better eye is 0.05 or greater but below 0.1.
Grade-2 Low Vision: The best corrected visual acuity of the better eye is 0.1 or greater but below 0.3.

Category	Grading	Best Corrected Visual Acuity
Blindness	Grade-1 Blindness	<0.02–no PL; or visual field <5°
	Grade-2 Blindness	<0.05–0.02; or visual field <10°
Low Vision		<0.1–0.05
		<0.3–0.1

Notes

(1) Visual disability refers to both eyes. When visual acuities of the two eyes differ, that of the better eye counts.

(2) When one eye is blind or low-visioned while the other eye has a visual acuity of 0.3 or greater, the subject is not considered to be visually disabled.

(3) The best corrected vision refers to the best visual acuity obtainable with correction lenses or to visual acuity with the pinhole.

Criteria of Hearing and Speech Disability

I. Definition

Hearing disability refers to bilateral loss or impairment of hearing due to various causes which render persons unable to hear or to hear clearly in their surroundings. Speech disability refers to muteness or impairment of speech due to various factors that cause an inability to carry out normal linguistic communication with common people.

Hearing and speech disability include (1) complete loss of hearing and speech ability (deaf mute); (2) loss of hearing accompanied by ability to speak clearly or unclearly (deaf but not mute); (3) sole linguistic disorder including aphasia, aphonia, dysallia, and severe stuttering.

II. Grading of Hearing and Speech Disability

1. Deafness

Grade-1 Deafness: At average linguistic frequency, loss of hearing is greater than 91 dB.
Grade-2 Deafness: At average linguistic frequency, loss of hearing is greater than 71 dB and equal to or less than 90 dB.

2. Hard of Hearing

Grade-1 Hard of Hearing: At average linguistic frequency, the loss of hearing is greater than 56 dB and equal to or less than 70 dB.
Grade-2 Hard of Hearing: At average linguistic frequency, the loss of hearing is greater than 41 dB and equal to or less than 55 dB.

Category	Grading	Loss of Hearing
Deafness	Grade-1 Deafness	>91 dB
	Grade-2 Deafness	90–71 dB
Hard of Hearing	Grade-1	70–56 dB
	Grade-2	55–41 dB

3. Sole speech disability is not graded.

Notes:

(1) The above-mentioned "at average linguistic frequency" refers to the mean of linguistic frequencies 500, 1,000, and 2,000 Hz.

(2) Deafness and hard-of-hearing refer to both ears. When the loss of hearing of the two ears differs, that of the better ear counts.

(3) If there is loss of hearing or hard-of-hearing of one ear while the loss of hearing of the other ear is equal to or less than 40 dB, the subject is not considered to be hearing disabled.

Criteria of Mental Disability

I. Definition

Mentally disabled are those people whose intelligence is significantly below average accompanied by impairment of adaptive behavior.

Mental disability includes: mental retardation which is caused by various harmful factors during the period of mental development (before the age of 18); impairment of intelligence caused by various harmful factors after the period of mental development; and senile dementia.

II. Grading of Mental Disability

The grading of mental disability is based on IQ and on the social-adaptive behavior of the victim with criteria of mental disability worked out by the WHO and AAMD taken for reference so as to make international comparisons possible.

1. Grade-1 Mental Disability (Profound): The person has an IQ below 20–25, poorest adaptive behavior, slow-moving face, and must be taken care of by others for life. Motor and sensory functions are very limited and training may only result in reaction of legs, hands, and chin.

2. Grade-2 Mental Disability (Severe): The IQ value is 20–35 or 25–49 and adaptive behavior is poor. Even if training is provided, the person can hardly take care of himself (or herself) without the help of others. Motor and speech functions and the ability to communicate with other people are minimal.

3. Grade-3 Mental Disability (Moderate): The IQ value is 35–50 or 40–55 and adaptive behavior is incomplete. The person has poor practical skills and is able to take care of himself (or herself) partly and to do simple housework; has primary knowledge about health care and safety but poor ability to read and calculate and is not good at distinguishing surrounding things; is able to communicate with others in a simple way.

4. Grade-4 Mental Disability (Mild): The IQ value is 50–70 or 55–75 and adaptive behavior is below the average level. The person has considerable practical skills so is able to take care of himself (or her-

self); to do some household chores and work but lacks skills and creativity; to adapt to the society with instruction and to read and calculate to a certain extent after special education. The person is able to distinguish surrounding things and to communicate with other people in a proper way.

Grade	Degree	Level below average (SD)	IQ Value	Adaptive Ability
Grade-1	Profound	≥5.01	Below 20–25	Very severe deficiency
Grade-2	Severe	4.01–5	20–35 or 25–40	Severe deficiency
Grade-3	Moderate	3.01–4	35–50 or 40–55	Moderate deficiency
Grade-4	Mild	2.01–3	50–70 or 55–75	Mild deficiency

Notes

(1) Mental retardation is determined according to AAMD's 1983 diagnostic criteria: (1) the person's intelligence is significantly below the average level and the IQ value is more than two SD less than the mean of the population, i.e., below 70 and 75; (2) deficiency of adaptive ability; (3) before the age 18.

(2) IQ = (mental age/actual age) × 100. The IQ value varies with methods of intelligence tests. Nevertheless, diagnosis is based mainly upon social-adaptive behavior.

Criteria of Physical Disability

I. Definition

Physical disability refers to the absence of extremities or paralysis or deformities of extremities and trunk which cause loss of function or dysfunction of motor system in varying degrees.

Physical disability includes: (1) amputation of upper or lower limb due to trauma, lesion, or congenital absence; (2) deformities or dysfunction of upper or lower limb due to trauma, lesion, or abnormal development; (3) deformities or dysfunction of spine due to trauma, lesion, or abnormal development; (4) dysfunction of trunk or extremities caused by trauma, lesion, or abnormal development of central or peripheral nervous system.

II. Grade-1 Physical Disability

The grading of physical disability is based upon a comprehensive consideration of number of locations, level of involvement, and degree of dysfunction, with the latter as the most important.

1. Grade-1 Physical Disability:

A. Quadriplegia, paraplegic without active motion of both; hemiplegia with complete loss of function of unilateral limbs.

B. Amputation or congenital absence of extremities at various levels of amputation or absence of a total upper (or lower) extremity and both shanks (or forearms); amputation or absence of both upper arms and one thigh (or shank); amputation or absence of both upper (or lower) limbs.

C. Severe dysfunction of both upper extremities; severe dysfunction of three extremities.

2. Grade-2 Physical Disability:

A. Hemiplegia or paraplegia with only a very small part of function of the involved limbs.

B. Amputation or absence of both upper limbs (upper arms or forearms), or both thighs; amputation or absence of one total lower limb (or upper limb) and one single upper arm (or thigh); amputation or absence at different levels of three limbs.

C. Severe dysfunction of two limbs; moderate dysfunction of three limbs.

3. Grade-3 Physical Disability:

A. Amputation or absence of two shanks; amputation or absence of one limb at the level of forearm (or thigh) or above.

B. Severe dysfunction of one limb; moderate dysfunction of two limbs.

C. Defect of both thumbs and index (or middle) finger.

4. Grade-4 Physical Disability:

A. Amputation or absence of one shank.

B. Moderate dysfunction of one limb; mild dysfunction of two limbs.

C. Spinal ankylosis (including cervical spine); kyphosis over 70°; scoliosis over 45°.

D. Length discrepancy of legs (more than 5 cm).

E. Defect of one thumb and index (or middle) finger; amputation or absence of four fingers with thumb reserved.

Notes:

The following conditions are not taken as physical disability:

(1) Loss of three fingers with thumb and index (or middle) finger intact.

(2) Loss of forefoot with the heel intact.

(3) Length discrepancy of legs (less than 5 cm).

(4) Kyphosis (less than 70°) or scoliosis (less than 45°).

Total Functional Evaluation of Physically Disabled

The various abilities of the physically disabled to accomplish the activities of daily living (ADL) can be used as a criteria of total evaluation of the person before any rehabilitation measure is adopted.

ADL include eight items of activity, namely, sitting, standing, walking, putting on clothes, washing and mouth-rinsing, eating, passing urine and stool, writing. One point is scored if the victim is able to accomplish one item, while 0.5 points if the item is accomplished with difficulty, and 0 points if the victim is unable to accomplish the task. Based on the points scored, four grades are listed, as follows:

Grade	Degree	Point
Grade-1	Completely unable to accomplish ADL	0–2
Grade-2	Physically unable to accomplish ADL	3–4
Grade-3	Able to accomplish partial ADL	5–6
Grade-4	Able to accomplish basic ADL	7–8

Criteria of Psychiatric Disability

I. Definition

Psychiatric disability refers to those persons who suffer from psychosis and are not cured after more than one year, so that their social ability to perform their role in the family and society is affected to various degrees.

Psychiatric disability includes: (1) psychosis associated with organic diseases of the brain and body; (2) toxic psychosis including alcohol and drug dependencies; (3) schizophrenia; (4) affective, paranoid, reactive, schizo-affective, and periodic psychotic disorders.

Grading of Psychiatric Disability

For international comparisons, the grading of psychiatric disability is based upon scoring of the ten items listed in the "Social Disability Screening Schedule" provided by the WHO.

1. Grade-1 (Profound): "2" is scored for three or more items out of the ten in SDSS.

2. Grade-2 (Severe): "2" is scored for two items out of ten in SDSS.

3. Grade-3 (Moderate): "2" is scored for only one item out of ten in SDSS.

4. Grade-4 (Mild): "1" is scored for two or more items out of ten in SDSS.

Notes:

(1) The mentally ill who have been sick less than one year are not taken to be psychiatrically disabled.

(2) The mentally ill who score "1" for only one item or "0" for all items of the ten items in SDSS are not taken to be psychiatrically disabled.

APPENDIX B

How did the Federation's early design come to structurally inhibit chapter offices from hiring *canji*? One way was through the creation of intra-organizational employment guidelines. To understand these guidelines, one must know something of the Federation's basic administrative structure.

According to the Federation's founding documents, every chapter has the following four branches:

· Executive Council
· National Representative Group
· Chairmanship Group
· Advisory Board

The Federation's original constitution *(zhangcheng)* dictates that the National Representative Group and the Advisory Board (and, to a lesser degree, the Chairmanship Group) should be staffed with large proportions of "disabled" people: two-thirds in the case of the Advisory Board and one-half in the case of the Representative Group.

Although these are high quotas, they were largely meaningless in the 1980s and 1990s for several reasons. First, Federation chapters up to and through the mid-1990s rarely used the administrative services of anyone except Executive Council members. Second, the Federation's founding documents dictated that, in the interests of "simplicity and efficacy," nearly all Federation activity was to be directed and controlled by the Executive Councils (Chu 1996, 468–69). Third, only Executive Council positions were salaried. In other words, the quotas were moot because full-fledged

Federation functionaries were the only employees attached to Executive Councils.

When the Federation was founded, no quota was established for hiring "disabled" Executive Council members. When such a quota was created, three years later, it was pegged at just 10 percent—and it came with specific hiring regulations that made it as much a barrier to employment as a mechanism of "affirmative action." These regulations stated that the 10 percent of jobs were to be filled by only "exceptional" people (Chu 1996, 617) and that such people should be either disabled persons who enjoyed "clearly defined levels of social functionality" or were "the relatives of the mentally retarded or the mentally ill" (Chu 1996, 469).

Such a move—creating barriers against disability employment—was more fully deployed when it came to the posts of greatest authority within Federation chapters: the director and vice-director positions on the Executive Council. Although Federation leaders publicly encouraged the employment of "disabled" people at these upper levels, they created attendant regulations that were so narrow as to make such hiring extremely difficult if not impossible. The regulations stated (Chu 1996, 469) that, for a "disabled" individual to be employed as director or vice-director of a Council, they:

- should be a "duty officer" *(zhuanzhi ganbu)*
- should meet the following "four criteria":
  (a) be "enthusiastic about disability services"
  (b) have "high intellectual standing"
  (c) have "strong social competence"
  (d) be relatively young

Of these criteria, the most restrictive regulation was probably the duty officer requirement. Duty officer status in late-twentieth-century China was a privilege generally reserved for only a fragment of the population—maybe as few as 2–3 percent—most of whom received the title owing to high educational or political achievement and, often, elite parents. But the prevalence of duty officers among the "disabled" was far lower, maybe as low as 0.4 percent according to the 1987 national sample survey, which illustrates better than any statistic how certain bodily differences at that time in China commonly undermined educational, political, or professional advancement.

Statistics on duty officers *(zhuanzhi ganbu)* are difficult to come by. Even more rare are comparable statistics on the numbers of duty officers among China's so-called "able-bodied" and "disabled" populations. The designers of the 1987 China National Sample Survey of Persons with Disabilities did not tabulate for duty officers, but they did tabulate for two categories of persons that would likely include duty officers. These were (1) "state, party, or enterprise leaders" *(guojia jiguan, dangqun, qishiye danwei fuzeren)* and (2) "office clerks or related staff" *(banshi renyuan he youguan renyuan)*. How many of the people sampled—"able-bodied" and "disabled"—fell into these two categories? Among those "able-bodied" who were fifteen years of age or older (1,118,698 individuals), only 2.2 percent (24,755) inhabited the categories "state, party, or enterprise leader" or "office clerk or related staff." Among those "disabled" who were fifteen years of age or older (65,103), just 0.4 percent (288) fit the categories (Di 1989, 866, 874, 930).

REFERENCES

AAMD (American Association on Mental Deficiency). 1970. Adaptive Behavior Scales. Washington, DC: American Association on Mental Deficiency.

Ablon, Joan. 1984. *Little People in America: The Social Dimension of Dwarfism*. New York: Praeger.

Acton, Norman. 1981. Report of Joint UNICEF/Rehabilitation International Mission for a Preliminary Examination of Childhood Disability in the People's Republic of China, March 9th to 21st, 1981. Rehabilitation International.

AFP (Agence France-Presse). 1995. Deng Xiaoping in Good Health, Government Says. April 27.

———. 1998. China Warns Against "Fabricated" Statistics. January 10.

———. 2000. China's Deadly Roads Claim Increasingly More Lives. February 21.

Agamben, Giorgio. 1998. *Homo Sacer: Sovereign Power and Bare Life*. Stanford, CA: Stanford University Press.

Albrecht, Gary L. 1992. *The Disability Business: Rehabilitation in America*. Sage Library of Social Research, vol. 190. Newbury Park, CA: Sage.

Allen, John. 1996. Fordism and Modern Industry. In *Modernity: An Introduction to Modern Societies*, edited by Stuart Hall, David Held, Don Hubert, and Kenneth Thompson, 280–306. Oxford: Blackwell.

Allison, Anne. 1994. *Nightwork: Sexuality, Pleasure, and Corporate Masculinity in a Tokyo Hostess Club*. Chicago: University of Chicago Press.

Alter, Joseph. 2000. *Gandhi's Body: Sex, Diet, and the Politics of Nationalism*. Philadelphia: University of Pennsylvania Press.

Ames, Roger. 1993. The Meaning of Body in Classical Chinese Philosophy. In *Self as Body in Asian Theory and Practice*, edited by Thomas Kasulis, Roger Ames, and Wimal W. Dissanayake, 157–78. Albany: State University of New York Press.

Anagnost, Ann. 1997. *National Past-Times: Narrative, Representation, and Power in Modern China*. Durham, NC: Duke University Press.

Anderson, Benedict. 1991. *Imagined Communities: Reflections on the Origin and Spread of Nationalism*. New York: Verso.

255

Andrews, Bridie. 1996. The Making of Modern Chinese Medicine, 1895–1937. Ph.D. diss., University of Cambridge.

Anson, Ofra, and Shifang Sun. 2002. Gender and Health in Rural China: Evidence from Hebei Province. *Social Science and Medicine* 55 (6): 1039–54.

Appadurai, Arjun. 1986. *The Social Life of Things: Commodities in Cultural Perspective.* New York: Cambridge University Press.

———. 1996. *Modernity at Large: Cultural Dimensions of Globalization.* Minneapolis: University of Minnesota Press.

Bailey, Lucy. 1999. Refracted Selves? A Study of Changes in Self-Identity in the Transition to Motherhood. *Sociology of Sport Journal* 33 (2): 335–52.

Baker, Greg. 1998. *Deng Pufang Meets Bill Clinton.* Associated Press Photo.

Bakhtin, Mikhail. 1981. *The Dialogic Imagination: Four Essays.* Translated by Caryl Emerson Holquist and Michael Holquist. Austin: University of Texas Press.

Barlow, Tani. 1991. Zhishifenzi [Chinese Intellectuals] and Power. *Dialectical Anthropology* 16 (3–4): 209–32.

Barme, Geremie, and Bennett Lee. 1979. *The Wounded: New Stories of the Cultural Revolution.* Hong Kong: Joint Publishing.

Barnes, Colin, Geoff Mercer, and Tom Shakespeare. 1999. *Exploring Disability: A Sociological Introduction.* Malden, MA: Polity Press.

BBC. 1994. Cheng Ming: New Leading Group to Attend to Deng's Health. June 16.

———. 1997. President Jiang Zemin Heads Funeral Committee for Deng Xiaoping. February 21.

Becker, Jasper. 1996. *Hungry Ghosts: Mao's Secret Famine.* New York: The Free Press.

Benedict, Carol. 1996. *Bubonic Plague in Nineteenth-Century China.* Stanford, CA: Stanford University Press.

Benedict, Ruth Fulton. 1953. Male Dominance in Thai Culture. In *Study of Culture at a Distance,* edited by Margaret Mead and Rhoda Métraux, 382–86. Chicago: University of Chicago Press.

Bergère, Marie-Claire, and Janet Lloyd. 1998. *Sun Yat-sen.* Stanford, CA: Stanford University Press.

Bhabha, Homi. 1994. *The Location of Culture.* New York: Routledge.

Bolton, Ralph. 1979. Machisimo in Motion: The Ethos of Peruvian Truckers. *Ethos* 7 (4): 312–42.

Borneman, John. 1996. Until Death Do Us Part: Marriage/Death in Anthropological Discourse. *American Ethnologist* 23 (2): 215–38.

Bourdieu, Pierre. 1977. *Outline of a Theory of Practice.* Translated by Richard Nice. Cambridge: Cambridge University Press.

———. 1984. *Distinction: A Social Critique of the Judgment of Taste.* Cambridge, MA: Harvard University Press.

———. 1990. *The Logic of Practice.* Translated by Richard Nice. Stanford, CA: Stanford University Press.

Bourdieu, Pierre, and Loïc Wacquant. 1992. *An Invitation to Reflexive Sociology.* Chicago: University of Chicago Press.

Bourgois, Philippe. 1995. *In Search of Respect: Selling Crack in El Barrio.* Cambridge: Cambridge University Press.

Bourque, Susan, and Kay B. Warren. 1987. Technology, Gender, and Development: Incorporating Gender in the Study of Development. *Daedalus* 116 (Fall): 173–97.

Bowers, John Z., J. William Hess, and Nathan Sivin. 1988. *Science and Medicine in Twentieth-Century China: Research and Education.* Science, Medicine, and Technology in East Asia, vol. 3. Ann Arbor: University of Michigan Center for Chinese Studies.

Bradley, Jeff. 1984. I Will Probably Never Walk Again—Deng's Son. *South China Morning Post,* June 19.

Bray, Francesca. 1997. *Technology and Gender: Fabrics of Power in Late Imperial China.* Berkeley: University of California Press.

Brown, Wendy. 1995. *States of Injury: Power and Freedom in Late Modernity.* Princeton, NJ: Princeton University Press.

Brownell, Susan. 1995. *Training the Body for China: Sports in the Moral Order of the People's Republic.* Chicago: University of Chicago Press.

Brownell, Susan, and Jeffrey Wasserstrom. 2002. Introduction: Theorizing Femininities and Masculinities. In *Chinese Femininities, Chinese Masculinities,* edited by Susan Brownell and Jeffrey Wasserstrom. Berkeley: University of California Press.

Bruner, Jerome. 1986. *Actual Minds, Possible Worlds.* Cambridge, MA: Harvard University Press.

Bullock, Mary Brown. 1980. *An American Transplant: The Rockefeller Foundation and Peking Union Medical College.* Berkeley: University of California Press.

Butler, Judith. 1990. *Gender Trouble: Feminism and the Subversion of Identity: Thinking Gender.* New York: Routledge.

———. 1992. Contingent Foundations: Feminism and the Question of "Postmodernism." In *Feminists Theorize the Political,* edited by Judith Butler and Joan Scott. New York: Routledge.

Chan, Cecilia. 1993. *The Myth of Neighbourhood Mutual Help: The Contemporary Chinese Community-based Welfare System in Guangzhou.* Hong Kong: Hong Kong University Press.

Chang Hao. 1987. *Chinese Intellectuals in Crisis: Search for Order and Meaning (1890– 1911).* Berkeley: University of California Press.

Chen Da. 1946. *Population in Modern China.* Chicago: University of Chicago Press.

Chiao Chi-ming, Warren S. Thompson, and D. T. Chen. 1938. *An Experiment in the Registration of Vital Statistics in China.* Oxford, OH: Scripps Foundation for Research in Population Problems.

Chu. Shuowei, et al., eds. 1996. *Zhongguo Canjiren Shiye Nianjian (1949–1993)* [China's Disabled Persons Almanac of Efforts (1949–1993)]. Beijing: Hua Xia Publishing House.

Cohen, Lawrence. 1998. *No Aging in India: Alzheimer's, the Bad Family, and Other Modern Things.* Berkeley: University of California Press.

Cohen, Myron. 1976. *House United, House Divided: The Chinese Family in Taiwan.* New York: Columbia University Press.

Comaroff, Jean. 1985. *Body of Power, Spirit of Resistance: The Culture and History of a South African People.* Chicago: University of Chicago Press.

Connell, R. W. 1995. *Masculinities.* Berkeley: University of California Press.

Connerton, Paul. 1989. *How Societies Remember.* Cambridge: Cambridge University Press.

Cooper, Eugene. 2000. *Adventures in Chinese Bureaucracy: A Meta-Anthropological Saga.* Huntington, NY: Nova Science Publishers.

Corker, Mairian, and Tom Shakespeare. 2002. Mapping the Terrain. In *Disability/*

Postmodernity: Embodying Disability Theory, edited by Mairian Corker and Tom Shakespeare, 1–17. New York: Continuum.

Croll, Elisabeth. 1987. New Peasant Family Forms in Rural China. *Journal of Peasant Studies* 14 (4): 469–99.

Csordas, Thomas. 1994a. *The Sacred Self: A Cultural Phenomenology of Charismatic Healing*. Berkeley: University of California Press.

———. 1994b. *Embodiment and Experience: The Existential Ground of Culture and Self*. Cambridge: Cambridge University Press.

Das, Veena. 1997. Sufferings, Theodicies, Disciplinary Practices, Appropriations. *International Social Science Journal* 49 (154): 563–72.

Das, Veena, and Renu Addlakha. 2001. Disability and Domestic Citizenship: Voice, Gender, and the Making of the Subject. *Public Culture* 13 (3): 511–31.

Davis, Lennard. 1995. *Enforcing Normalcy: Disability, Deafness, and the Body*. London: Verso.

De Bary, William Theodore. 1960. *Sources of Chinese Tradition*. New York: Columbia University Press.

Dean, Mitchell. 2001. Demonic Societies: Liberalism, Biopolitics, and Sovereignty. In *States of Imagination: Ethnographic Explorations of the Postcolonial State*, edited by Thomas B. Hansen and Finn Stepputat. Durham, NC: Duke University Press.

Deng Maomao. 1995. *Deng Xiaoping My Father*. New York: Basic Books.

Deng Pufang. 1988. Zhongguo Canlian Zhuxituan Zhuxi, Zhixinglishihui Lishizhang Deng Pufang de Jianghua [Talk Given to the China Disabled Persons' Federation, by Deng Pufang, Chair of the Presidium, Director of the Implementation Council]. *Mang Long Ya Zhiyin* [Voices of the Blind, Deaf, and Mute] 67: 6–8.

———. 1989. Deng Pufang Da Zhongwai Jizhemen [Deng Pufang Responds to Chinese and Foreign Journalists]. *Sanyuefeng* [Spring Breezes] 53: 15–17.

———. 1995. Deng Pufang Tongzhi Zai Dibazi Quan Guo Canlian Gongzuohuiyi Shangde Jianghua [Comrade Deng Pufang's Speech at the 8th National Disabled Persons' Federation Working Conference]. Beijing: China Disabled Persons' Federation.

Desjarlais, Robert. 1992. *Body and Emotion: The Aesthetics of Illness and Healing in the Nepal Himalayas*. Philadelphia: University of Pennsylvania Press.

———. 1997. *Shelter Blues: Sanity and Selfhood among the Homeless: Contemporary Ethnography*. Philadelphia: University of Pennsylvania.

———. 2002. A Phenomenology of Dying: Subjectivity and Death among Nepal's Yolmo Buddhists. Paper read at Ethnografeast, An International Conference on Ethnography for a New Century: Practice, Predicament, Promise, University of California at Berkeley, September 12–14.

Di Feng, and Dongfang Shao. 1994. Life Writing in Mainland China (1949–1993): A General Survey and Bibliographical Essay. *Biography* 17 (1): 32–55.

Di Ya, ed. 1987. *Quanguo Canjiren Qiuyangdiaocha Gongzuoshouce* [Research Manual for the 1987 National Sample Survey of Disabled Persons]. Beijing: Office of the National Sample Survey of Persons with Disabilities.

———. 1989. *Zhongguo 1987 Nian Canjiren Chouyang Diaocha Cailiao* [Data from China's 1987 Sample Survey of Disabled Persons]. Beijing: Office of the National Sample Survey of Persons with Disabilities.

Diamant, Neil J. 2001. Making Love "Legible" in China: Politics and Society during the Enforcement of Civil Marriage Registrations, 1950–66. *Politics and Society* 29 (3): 447–80.

DiGiacomo, Susan M. 1999. Can There Be a "Cultural Epidemiology"? *Medical Anthropology Quarterly*, 13 (4): 436–57.

Dikotter, Frank. 1992. *The Discourse of Race in Modern China.* London: Hurst.

Dixon, John. 1981. *The Chinese Welfare System, 1949–1979.* New York: Praeger.

Douglas, Mary. 1966. *Purity and Danger: An Analysis of the Concepts of Pollution and Taboo.* London: ARK Paperbacks.

Doyal, Lesley. 1983. Poverty and Disability in the Third World: The Crippling Effects of Underdevelopment. Introduction to *A Cry for Health: Poverty and Disability in the Third World,* edited by Oliver Shirley. Frome, Somerset, U.K.: Third World Group for Disabled People.

Dubisch, Jill, ed. 1986. *Gender and Power in Rural Greece.* Princeton, NJ: Princeton University Press.

Ebrey, Patricia. 1993. *The Inner Quarters: Marriage and the Lives of Chinese Women in the Sung Period.* Berkeley: University of California Press.

Elvin, Mark. 1989. Tales of Shen and Xin: Body-Person and Heart-Mind in China during the Last 150 Years. In *Zone: Fragments for a History of the Human Body (Part Two),* edited by Michel Feher, Ramona Naddaff, and Nadia Tazi. Cambridge, MA: MIT Press.

Erwin, Kathleen. 2000. Heart-to-Heart, Phone-to-Phone: Family Values, Sexuality, and the Politics of Shanghai's Advice Hotlines. In *The Consumer Revolution in Urban China,* edited by Deborah S. Davis, 145–70. Berkeley: University of California Press.

Estroff, Sue. 1993. Identity, Disability, and Schizophrenia: The Problem of Chronicity. In *Knowledge, Power, and Practice: The Anthropology of Medicine and Everyday Life,* edited by Shirley Lindenbaum and Margaret Lock. Berkeley: University of California Press.

Evans, Richard. 1995. *Deng Xiaoping and the Making of Modern China.* London: Penguin.

Evans-Pritchard, E. E. 1937. *Witchcraft, Oracles, and Magic among the Azande.* Oxford: Clarendon.

Farnell, Brenda. 1999. Moving Bodies, Acting Selves. *Annual Review of Anthropology* 28: 341–73.

Farquhar, Judith. 1987. Problems of Knowledge in Contemporary Chinese Medical Discourse. *Social Science and Medicine* 24 (12): 1013–21.

———. 1994. *Knowing Practice: The Clinical Encounter of Chinese Medicine.* Boulder, CO: Westview Press.

———. 1996. Market Magic: Getting Rich and Getting Personal in Medicine after Mao. *American Ethnologist* 23 (2): 239–57.

———. 1998. For Your Reading Pleasure: Popular Health Advice and the Globalization of Desire in 1990s Beijing. Paper read at Annual Meeting of the American Anthropological Association, Philadelphia, December 5.

———. 2002a. *Appetites: Food and Sex in Postsocialist China.* Durham, NC: Duke University Press.

———. 2002b. Anthropology (and Historiography) In and Of China. Paper read at

Center for Chinese Studies Annual Symposium, University of California at Berkeley, March 8–9.

Fei Xiaotong. 1939. *Peasant Life in China.* New York: E. P. Dutton.

———. 1992. *From the Soil: The Foundations of Chinese Society.* Berkeley: University of California Press.

Feng Changye, ed. 1990. *Wenchangxian Weisheng Zhi* [Wenchang County Annals of Public Health]. Wencheng, PRC: Wenchang County Publishing House.

Fernandez, James. 1980. Reflections on Looking into Mirrors. *Semiotica* 20 (1–2): 27–39.

Foucault, Michel. 1965. *Civilization and Madness.* New York: Random House.

———. 1971. *The Order of Things: An Archaeology of the Human Sciences.* New York: Pantheon Books.

———. 1973. *The Birth of the Clinic: An Archaeology of Medical Perception.* New York: Pantheon.

———. 1977. *Discipline and Punish: The Birth of the Prison.* New York: Vintage Books.

———. 1980a. *Power/Knowledge: Selected Interviews and Other Writings, 1972–1977.* Edited by Colin Gordon. New York: Pantheon Books.

———. 1980b. Truth and Subjectivity. Paper read for Howison Lecture in Philosophy, University of California, Berkeley.

———. 1984. On the Genealogy of Ethics: An Overview of Work in Progress. In *The Foucault Reader,* edited by Paul Rabinow. New York: Pantheon Books.

———. 1985. *The Use of Pleasure.* New York: Random House.

———. 1991. Governmentality. In *The Foucault Effect: Studies in Governmentality,* edited by Graham Burchell, Colin Gordon, and Peter Miller. Chicago: University of Chicago Press.

———. 1997. On the Genealogy of Ethics: An Overview of Work in Progress. In *Michel Foucault: Ethics, Subjectivity, and Truth,* edited by Paul Rabinow. New York: The New Press.

Fox, Nick. 1997. Is There Life after Foucault? Texts, Frames, and Differends. In *Foucault, Health, and Medicine,* edited by Alan Petersen and Robin Bunton. London: Routledge.

Frank, Arthur. 1991. For a Sociology of the Body: An Analytical Review. In *The Body: Social Process and Cultural Theory,* edited by Mike Featherstone, Mike Hepworth, and Bryan Turner. London: Sage.

Frank, Gelya. 2000. *Venus on Wheels: Two Decades of Dialogue on Disability, Biography, and Being Female in America.* Berkeley: University of California Press.

Franklin, Sarah. 1995. Science as Culture, Cultures of Science. *Annual Review of Anthropology* 24: 163–84.

Freedman, Maurice. 1958. *Lineage Organization in Southeastern China.* London: Athlone.

Gaubatz, Piper Rae. 1995. Urban Transformation in Post-Mao China: Impacts of the Reform Era on China's Urban Form. In *Urban Spaces in Contemporary China: The Potential for Autonomy and Community in Post-Mao China,* edited by Deborah Davis, Richard Kraus, Barry Naughton, and Elizabeth Perry. Washington, DC: Woodrow Wilson Center Press.

Geertz, Clifford. 1973. *The Interpretation of Culture: Selected Essays.* New York: Basic Books.

―――. 1988. *Works and Lives: The Anthropologist as Author.* Stanford, CA: Stanford University Press.

Gennep, Arnold van. [1909] 1960. *The Rites of Passage.* Chicago: University of Chicago Press.

Giddens, Anthony. 1971. *Capitalism and Modern Social Theory: An Analysis of the Writings of Marx, Durkheim, and Max Weber.* Cambridge: Cambridge University Press.

Giles, Herbert. 1898. *A Chinese Biographical Dictionary.* London: Bernard Quaritch.

Gilmartin, Christina. 1994. Gender, Political Culture, and Women's Mobilization in the Chinese Nationalist Revolution, 1924–1927. In *Engendering China: Women, Culture, and the State,* edited by Christina Gilmartin, Gail Hershatter, Lisa Rofel, and Tyrene White. Cambridge, MA: Harvard University Press.

Ginsburg, Faye, and Rayna Rapp. Forthcoming. Anthropology of Visible Disability. *Annual Review of Anthroplogy* 34.

Gladney, Dru. 1991. *Muslim Chinese: Ethnic Nationalism in the People's Republic.* Cambridge, MA: Council on East Asian Studies, Harvard University.

Goffman, Erving. 1963. *Stigma: Notes on the Management of Spoiled Identity.* Englewood Cliffs, NJ: Prentice-Hall.

Goldstein, Joshua. 1998. Scissors, Surveys, and Psycho-Prophylactics: Pre-natal Health Care Campaigns and State Building in China. *Journal of Historical Sociology* 11 (2): 153–84.

Gramsci, Antonio. 1971. *Selections from the Prison Notebooks of Antonio Gramsci.* New York: International Publishers.

Greenblatt, Sidney. 1977. Campaigns and the Manufacture of Deviance in Chinese Society. In *Deviance and Social Control in Chinese Society,* edited by Amy Wilson, Sidney Greenblatt, and Richard Wilson. New York: Praeger.

Greenhalgh, Susan. 2001a. *Under the Medical Gaze: Facts and Fictions of Chronic Pain.* Berkeley: University of California Press.

―――. 2001b. Science, Modernity, and the Making of the One-Child Policy. Paper read at Annual Meeting of the American Anthropological Association, Washington, D.C.

Greenhalgh, Susan, and Li Jiali. 1995. Engendering Reproduction Policy and Practice in Peasant China: For a Feminist Demography of Reproduction. *Signs* 20 (3): 601–41.

Groce, Nora Ellen. 1985. *Everyone Here Spoke Sign Language: Hereditary Deafness on Martha's Vineyard.* Cambridge, MA: Harvard University Press.

Grosz, E. A. 1994. *Volatile Bodies: Toward a Corporeal Feminism: Theories of Representation and Difference.* Bloomington: Indiana University Press.

Guo Ming. 1990. An Account of Disability in China. *Disability and Rehabilitation* (Newsletter of the China Rehabilitation Research Centre) 1: 4.

Gupta, Akhil. 1998. *Postcolonial Developments: Agriculture in the Making of Modern India.* Durham, NC: Duke University Press.

―――. 2001. Governing Population: The Integrated Child Development Services Program in India. In *States of Imagination: Ethnographic Explorations of the Postcolonial State,* edited by Thomas B. Hansen and Finn Stepputat. Durham, NC: Duke University Press.

Gupta, Akhil, and James Ferguson. 1997. *Anthropological Locations: Boundaries and Grounds of a Field Science.* Berkeley: University of California Press.

Gusterson, Hugh. 1993. Exploding Anthropology's Canon in the World of the Bomb: Ethnographic Writing on Militarism. *Journal of Contemporary Ethnography* 22 (1): 59–79.

———. 1996. *Nuclear Rites: A Weapons Laboratory at the End of the Cold War.* Berkeley: University of California Press.

Gutmann, Matthew. 1997. Trafficking in Men: The Anthropology of Masculinity. *Annual Review of Anthropology* 26: 385–409.

Habermas, Jurgen. 1984. *The Theory of Communicative Action.* Vol. 1, *Reason and The Rationalization of Society.* Boston: Beacon Press.

Hacking, Ian. 1986. The Archaeology of Foucault. In *Foucault: A Critical Reader,* edited by David Hoy. New York: Blackwell.

———. 1990. *The Taming of Chance.* Cambridge: Cambridge University Press.

Hainan Province Census Office, ed. 1992. *Tabulation on the 1990 Population Census of Hainan Province.* Haikou, PRC: Hainan Statistics Institution Press.

Hall, Richard. 1980. Closed-System, Open-System, and Contingency-Choice Perspectives. In *A Sociological Reader on Complex Organizations,* edited by Amitai Etzioni and Edward Lehman. New York: Holt.

Hall, Stuart. 1985. Signification, Representation, Ideology: Althusser and the Post-Structuralist Debates. *Critical Studies in Mass Communication* 2 (2): 91–114.

———. 1996. The Question of Cultural Identity. In *Modernity: An Introduction to Modern Societies,* edited by Stuart Hall, David Held, Don Hubert, and Kenneth Thompson, 595–634. Oxford: Blackwell.

Hambly, Wilfrid Dyson. 1931. Ideas of Manhood in West Africa. *Field Museum News* 2 (7): 3.

Han Minzhu, ed. 1990. *Cries for Democracy: Writings and Speeches from the 1989 Chinese Democracy Movement.* Princeton, NJ: Princeton University Press.

Han Suyin. 1984. I Am Just as Good as Anyone Else! *China Daily,* March 15.

Handler, Richard. 1994. Is Identity a Useful Cross-Cultural Concept. In *Commemorations: The Politics of National Identity,* edited by John Gillis. Princeton, NJ: Princeton University Press.

Hanks, William. 1996. *Language and Communicative Practices.* Boulder, CO: Westview Press.

Hanson, Perry. 1984. UNICEF in China, 1947–1951. Unpublished manuscript, United Nations, New York.

Hansson, Harry. 1988. Regional Outcast Groups in Late Imperial China. Ph.D. diss., Department of History and East Asian Languages, Harvard University, Cambridge, MA.

Haraway, Donna. 1991. *Simians, Cyborgs, and Women: The Reinvention of Nature.* New York: Routledge.

Harding, Harry. 1981. *Organizing China: The Problem of Bureaucracy, 1949–1976.* Stanford, CA: Stanford University Press.

Harrell, Stevan. 1985. The Rich Get Children: Segmentation, Stratification, and Population in Three Chekiang Lineages, 1550–1850. In *Family and Population in East Asian History,* edited by Susan Hanley and Arthur Wolf, 81–109. Stanford, CA: Stanford University Press.

Harvey, David. 1990. *The Condition of Postmodernity: An Enquiry into the Origins of Cultural Change.* Cambridge, MA: Blackwell.

Henderson, Gail. 1989. Issues in the Modernization of Medicine in China. In *Science and Technology in Post-Mao China*, edited by Denis Simon and Merle Goldman, 199–221. Cambridge, MA: Harvard University Press.

Henderson, Gail, and Myron S. Cohen. 1984. *The Chinese Hospital: A Socialist Work Unit*. New Haven, CT: Yale University Press.

Henriot, Christian. 1992. Medicine, VD, and Prostitution in Pre-Revolutionary China. *Social History of Medicine* 5: 95–120.

Heper, Metin. 1985. State and Public Bureaucracies: A Comparative and Historical Perspective. *Comparative Studies in Society and History* 27 (1): 86–110.

Hershatter, Gail. 1997. *Dangerous Pleasures: Prostitution and Modernity in Twentieth-Century Shanghai*. Berkeley: University of California Press.

Herzfeld, Michael. 1985. *The Poetics of Manhood: Contest and Identity in a Cretan Mountain Village*. Princeton, NJ: Princeton University Press.

———. 1992. *The Social Production of Indifference: Exploring the Symbolic Roots of Western Bureaucracy*. Chicago: University of Chicago Press.

Heyman, Josiah McC. 1995. Putting Power in the Anthropology of Bureaucracy. *Current Anthropology* 36 (2): 261–87.

Hocart, Arthur Maurice. 1935. Initiation and Manhood. *Man* 35: 20–22.

Honig, Emily. 1984. Private Issues, Public Discourse: The Life and Times of Yu Luojin. *Public Affairs* 57: 252–65.

Horn, David G. 1994. *Social Bodies: Science, Reproduction, and Italian Modernity*. Princeton Studies in Culture/Power/History. Princeton, NJ: Princeton University Press.

Hsu, Elisabeth. 1999. *The Transmission of Chinese Medicine*. Cambridge Studies in Medical Anthropology, no. 7. Cambridge: Cambridge University Press.

Huang Shu-min. 1989. *The Spiral Road: Change in Chinese Village Through the Eyes of a Communist Party Leader*. Boulder, CO: Westview.

Huang Yasheng. 1996. The Statistical Agency in China's Bureaucratic System: A Comparison with the Former Soviet Union. *Communist and Post-Communist Studies* (March): 59–75.

Hubbert, Jennifer. 1999. Generations and Moral Authority among Intellectuals in Contemporary China. Paper read at Annual Meeting of the American Anthropological Association, Chicago, November 17.

Hughes, Bill, and Kevin Paterson. 1997. The Social Model of Disability and the Disappearing Body: Toward a Sociology of Impairment. *Disability and Society* 12 (3): 325–40.

Hyde, Sandra Teresa. 2000. Selling Sex and Sidestepping the State: Prostitutes, Condoms, and HIV/AIDS Prevention in Southwest China. *East Asia: An International Quarterly* 18 (4): 108–36.

Ikels, Charlotte. 1993. Settling Accounts: The Intergenerational Contract in an Age of Reform. In *Chinese Families in the Post-Mao Era*, edited by Deborah Davis and Stevan Harrell, 307–34. Berkeley: University of California Press.

Ingstad, Benedicte. 1997. *Community-based Rehabilitation in Botswana: The Myth of the Hidden Disabled*. Lewiston, ME: Edwin Mellen Press.

Ingstad, Benedicte, and Susan Reynolds Whyte. 1995. Disability and Culture: An Overview. In *Disability and Culture*, edited by Benedicte Ingstad and Susan Reynolds Whyte, 3–32. Berkeley: University of California Press.

Inhorn, Marcia C. 1995. Medical Anthropology and Epidemiology: Divergences or Convergences? *Social Science and Medicine* 40 (3): 285–90.

Institute of Sociology, Chinese Academy of Social Sciences. 1994. The Figures of the First National Random Sampling Investigation of Private Enterprises and Its Analysis. In *A Yearbook of Private Enterprises in China (1978–1993)*, edited by Zhang Xuwu et al. Hong Kong: Hong Kong Economic Herald Press.

Iser, Wolfgang. 1974. *The Implied Reader: Patterns of Communication in Prose Fiction from Bunyan to Beckett*. Baltimore: Johns Hopkins University Press.

Jackson, Jean. 2000. *Camp Pain: Talking with Chronic Pain Patients*. Philadelphia: University of Pennsylvania Press.

Jackson, Michael. 1989. *Paths toward a Clearing: Radical Empiricism and Ethnographic Inquiry*. Bloomington: Indiana University Press.

Jaschok, Maria. 1988. *Concubines and Bondservants: A Social History of a Chinese Custom*. London: Zed Books.

Jenkins, Richard. 1991. Disability and Social Structure. *British Journal of Sociology* 42 (4): 557–80.

———. 1996. *Social Identity*. New York: Routledge.

Jing Jun. 1996. *The Temple of Memories: History, Power, and Morality in a Chinese Village*. Stanford, CA: Stanford University Press.

———. 2000. Food, Nutrition, and Cultural Authority in a Gansu Village. In *Feeding China's Little Emperors: Food, Children, and Social Change*, edited by Jing Jun. Stanford, CA: Stanford University Press.

Judd, Ellen. 1994. *Gender and Power in Rural China*. Stanford, CA: Stanford University Press.

Kasnitz, Devva. 2003. A Sociocultural Model of Impairment-Disability. Paper read at Inaugural Conference of the Disability Studies Association, Lancaster, England, September 4–6.

Kasnitz, Devva, and Russell Shuttleworth. 2001. Introduction: Anthropology in Disability Studies. *Disability Studies Quarterly* 21 (3): 2–17.

Keenan, T. 1995. Foucault on Government. In *Michel Foucault: Critical Assessments*, vol. 4, edited by Barry Smart. New York: Routledge.

Kessler, Henry. 1968. *The Knife Is Not Enough*. New York: W.W. Norton & Co.

Kipnis, Andrew. 1997. *Producing Guanxi: Sentiment, Self, and Subculture in a North China Village*. Durham, NC: Duke University Press.

Kleinman, Arthur. 1978. Concepts and a Model for the Comparison of Medical Systems as Cultural Systems. *Science and Medicine* 12: 85–93.

———. 1994. An Anthropological Perspective on Objectivity: Observation, Categorization, and the Assessment of Suffering. In *Health and Social Change in International Perspective*, edited by Lincoln Chen, Arthur Kleinman, and Norma Ware, 129–38. Boston: Harvard School of Public Health.

———. 1995. *Writing at the Margin: Discourse between Anthropology and Medicine*. Berkeley: University of California Press.

Kleinman, Arthur, and Joan Kleinman. 1991. Human Suffering and Its Professional Transformation: Toward an Ethnography of Interpersonal Experience. *Culture, Medicine, and Psychiatry* 15: 276–301.

Kleinman, Arthur, and Tsung-yi Lin. 1981. *Normal and Abnormal Behavior in Chinese Culture*. Culture, Illness, and Healing, vol. 2. Boston: Kluwer Boston.

Kleinman, Arthur, Wen-zhi Wang, Shi-chuo Li, Xue-ming Cheng, Xiu-ying Dai, Kun-tun Li, and Joan Kleinman. 1995. The Social Course of Epilepsy: Chronic Illness as Social Experience in Interior China. *Social Science and Medicine* 40 (10): 1319–30.

Ko, Dorothy. 1997. The Body as Attire: The Shifting Meanings of Footbinding in Seventeenth-Century China. *Journal of Women's History* 8 (4): 8–27.

Kohrman, Matthew. 1999a. Motorcycles for the Disabled: Mobility, Modernity, and the Transformation of Experience in Urban China. *Culture, Medicine, and Psychiatry* 23 (1): 133–55.

———. 1999b. Grooming Que Zi: Marriage Exclusion and Identity Formation among Disabled Men in Contemporary China. *American Ethnologist* 26 (4): 890–909.

———. 2003a. Authorizing a Disability Agency in Post-Mao China: Deng Pufang's Story as Biomythography. *Cultural Anthropology* 18 (1): 99–131.

———. 2003b. Why Am I Not Disabled? Statistics and Transnational Subject Making in Modern China. *Medical Anthropology Quarterly* 17 (1): 5–24.

Kondo, Dorinne K. 1990. *Crafting Selves: Power, Gender, and Discourses of Identity in a Japanese Workplace.* Chicago: University of Chicago Press.

Kriegel, Leonard. 1991. *Falling Into Life.* San Francisco: North Point Press.

Kuriyama, Shigehisa. 1999. *The Expressiveness of the Body and the Divergence of Greek and Chinese Medicine.* New York: Zone Books.

Lamson, Herbert. 1935. *Social Pathology in China: A Source Book for the Study of Problems of Livelihood, Health, and the Family.* Shanghai: Commercial Press.

Landsman, Gail. 2001. Models of Disability: Agency, Identity, and Mothers of Disabled Children. Paper presented at the Annual Meeting of the American Anthropological Association, Washington, DC.

Langan, Celeste. 2001. Mobility Disability. *Public Culture* 13 (3): 459–84.

Latour, Bruno, and Steve Woolgar. 1979. *Laboratory Life: The Social Construction of Scientific Facts.* Beverly Hills: Sage Publications.

Leach, Edmund. 1966. Virgin Birth. *Proceedings, Anthropological Institute of Great Britain and Ireland,* 39–49. London.

Lee Sing. 1998. Higher Earnings, Bursting Trains, and Exhausted Bodies: The Creation of Traveling Psychosis in Post-Reform China. *Social Science and Medicine* 47 (9): 1247–61.

———. 1999. Diagnosis Postponed: Shenjing Shuairuo and the Transformation of Psychiatry in Post-Mao China. *Culture, Medicine, and Psychiatry* 23 (3): 349–80.

Lemert, Edwin. 1967. *Human Deviance, Social Problems, and Social Control.* Englewood Cliffs, NJ: Prentice-Hall.

Li Bu. [1887] 1989. *Qin ding ke chang tiao li.* Taipei: Wen Hai Press.

Li Hong, and Martin B. Tracy. 1999. Family Support, Financial Needs, and Health Care Needs of Rural Elderly in China: A Field Study. *Journal of Cross-Cultural Gerontology* 14 (4): 357–71.

Li Jianghong, and William Lavely. 1995. Rural Economy and Male Marriage in China: Jurong, Jiangsu, 1933. *Journal of Family History* 20 (3): 289–306.

Li Taoyun. 1995. Canjiche Guizou Zhengdao Le [Disability Vehicles Should Follow the Right Path]. *Jiefang Ribao* [Liberation Daily].

Li Zheng, ed. 1988. *Zhongguo Canjiren Shouce* [Chinese Disabled Persons Handbook]. Beijing: Di Zhen Press.

Li Zhisui. 1994. *The Private Life of Chairman Mao: The Memoirs of Mao's Personal Physician.* New York: Random House.

Lieberthal, Kenneth, and David M. Lampton. 1992. *Bureaucracy, Politics, and Decision Making in Post-Mao China.* Studies on China, no. 14. Berkeley: University of California Press.

Linton, Simi. 1998. *Claiming Disability: Knowledge and Identity.* New York: New York University Press.

Litzinger, Ralph A. 2000. *Other Chinas: The Yao and the Politics of National Belonging.* Durham, NC: Duke University Press.

Liu Xiaocheng. 1995. Wancheng "Bawu" Renwu, Zhiding "Jiuwu" Jihua Quanmian, Tuijin Canjiren Shiye [Completing the "Eighth Five-Year Plan," Setting the "Ninth Five Year Plan," Fully Advancing Efforts on Behalf of Persons with Disabilities]. Beijing: China Disabled Persons' Federation.

Lock, Margaret, and Nancy Scheper-Hughes. 1996. A Critical-Interpretive Approach in Medical Anthropology: Rituals and Routines of Discipline and Dissent. In *Handbook of Medical Anthropology: Contemporary Theory and Method,* edited by Thomas Johnson and Carolyn Sargent, 41–70. Westport, CT: Greenwood Press.

Lock, Margaret M. 1993. *Encounters with Aging: Mythologies of Menopause in Japan and North America.* Berkeley: University of California Press.

Lorde, Audre. 1982. *Zami: A New Spelling of My Name.* Trumansburg, NY: Crossing Press.

Lu Deyang, and Senxinzhao Dao. 1996. *Zhongguo Canjiren Shi* [The History of Persons with Disabilities in China]. Shanghai: Xuelin Press.

Lu Gwei-djen, and Joseph Needham. 1988. A History of Forensic Medicine in China. *Medical History* 32: 357–400.

Lü Xiaobo. 2000. *Cadres and Corruption: The Organizational Involution of the Chinese Communist Party.* Stanford,CA: Stanford University Press.

Lü Xiaobo, and Elizabeth J. Perry, eds. 1997. *Danwei: The Changing Chinese Workplace in Historical and Comparative Perspective.* Armonk, NY: M. E. Sharpe.

Luhrmann, Tanya. 1996. *The Good Parsi: The Fate of a Colonial Elite in a Postcolonial Society.* Cambridge, MA: Harvard University Press.

———. 2000. *Of Two Minds: The Growing Disorder in American Psychiatry.* New York: Knopf.

MacFarquhar, Roderick. 1997. *The Coming of the Cataclysm, 1961–1966.* Oxford: Oxford University Press.

MacPherson, Kerrie. 1987. *A Wilderness of Marshes: The Origins of Public Health in Shanghai, 1843–1893.* Hong Kong: Oxford University Press.

Madsen, Richard. 1984. *Morality and Power in a Chinese Village.* Berkeley: University of California Press.

Maneker, Jerry. 1991. An Extension of Max Weber's Theory of Bureaucracy. In *Max Weber, Critical Assessments 2,* edited by Peter Hamilton, 66–71. London: Routledge.

Mann, Susan. 1991. Grooming a Daughter for Marriage: Brides and Wives in the Mid-Ch'ing Period. In *Marriage and Inequality in Chinese Society,* edited by Rubie Watson and Patricia B. Ebrey, 204–30. Berkeley: University of California Press.

Mao Tse-tung. [1917] 1978. Study of Physical Education, April 1, 1917. In *Collected Works of Mao Tse-tung (1917–1949).* Arlington, VA: Joint Publications Research Service.

Marcus, George. 1998. *Ethnography through Thick and Thin.* Princeton, NJ: Princeton University Press.

Marcus, George, and Peter Dobkin Hall. 1992. *Lives in Trust: The Fortunes of Dynastic Families in Late Twentieth-Century America*. Boulder, CO: Westview.

Mark, Renee. 1995. On the Beauty of Beijing. In *China for Women: Travel and Culture*. New York: The Feminist Press.

Martin, Emily. 1987. *The Woman in the Body: A Cultural Analysis of Reproduction*. Boston, MA: Beacon Press.

———. 1992. The End of the Body? *American Ethnologist* 19: 121–140.

———. 1994. *Flexible Bodies: Tracking Immunity in American Culture from the Days of Polio to the Age of AIDS*. Boston: Beacon Press.

Mauss, Marcel. [1935] 1979. The Notion of Body Techniques [Les Techniques du Corps]. In *Sociology and Psychology*, edited by Marcel Mauss. London: Routledge and Kegan Paul.

McClintock, Anne. 1994. *Imperial Leather: Race, Gender, and Sexuality in the Colonial Conquest*. New York: Routledge.

McGough, James P. 1981. Deviant Marriage Patterns in Chinese Society. In *Normal and Abnormal Behavior in Chinese Culture*, edited by Arthur Kleinman and Tsung-yi Lin, 171–201. Dordrecht, Holland: D. Reidel.

Meisner, Maurice. 1986. *Mao's China and After: A History of the People's Republic*. New York: Free Press.

Merli, M. Giovanna. 1998. Underreporting of Births and Infant Deaths in Rural China: Evidence from Field Research in One County of Northern China. *China Quarterly* 155 (September): 637–55.

Min Han, and J. S. Eades. 1995. Brides, Bachelors, and Brokers: The Marriage Market in Rural Anhui in an Era of Economic Reform. *Modern Asian Studies* 29 (4): 841–69.

Mindes, Jerome. 1991. A Study of Bilateral, Multicultural, and International Voluntary Efforts to Help China Rehabilitate People with Disabilities. New York: World Rehabilitation Fund.

Ministry of Civil Affairs. 1993. *Zhiti Canjiren Cailiao* [Information on the Physically Disabled]. Beijing: Ministry of Civil Affairs Press.

Moore, Sally Falk. 1976. The Secret of the Men: A Fiction of Chagga Initiation and Its Relation to the Logic of Chagga Symbolism. *Africa* 46: 357–70.

Morgan, Gareth. 1986. *Images of Organization*. London: Sage.

Mosse, George. 1985. *Nationalism and Sexuality: Middle-Class Morality and Sexual Norms in Modern Europe*. Madison: University of Wisconsin Press.

Mouzelis, Nicos. 1967. *Organisation and Bureaucracy: An Analysis of Modern Theories*. Chicago: Aldine.

Murphy, Robert. 1990. *The Body Silent*. New York: Norton.

Murphy, Robert, et al. 1988. Physical Disability and Social Liminality: A Study in the Rituals of Adversity. *Social Science and Medicine* 26 (2): 235–42.

Myerhoff, Barbara. 1978. *Number Our Days*. New York: Simon and Schuster.

N. A. 1976. *Da Yuan Sheng Zheng Guo Chao Dian Zhang* [The Laws and Institutions of the Present Dynasty under the Imperial Government of the Great Yuan]. Taipei: National Palace Museum.

Nader, Laura. 1972. Up the Anthropologist—Perspectives from Studying Up. In *Reinventing Anthropology*, edited by Dell Hymes, 284–311. New York: Pantheon.

National Statistical Bureau. 1990. *China Population Statistical Yearbook, 1990*. Beijing: Science and Technology Documents Press.

Needham, Joseph, with the collaboration of Lu Gwei-djen. 2000. Medicine. In *Science and Civilisation in China*, vol. 6, *Biology and Biological Technology*, edited by Joseph Needham and Francesca Bray. Cambridge: Cambridge University Press.

Ng, Vivien W. 1990. *Madness in Late Imperial China: From Illness to Deviance*. Norman: University of Oklahoma Press.

Nicholson, Linda. 1990. *Feminism/Postmodernism: Thinking Gender.* New York: Routledge.

Nietzsche, Friedrich. 1967. *On the Genealogy of Morals*. Translated by Walter Kaufmann. New York: Vintage Books.

Ning Yeh-kao. 1995. *Chinese Personal Names*. Singapore: Federal Publications.

Oi, Jean. 1999. *Rural China Takes Off: Institutional Foundations of Economic Reform*. Berkeley: University of California Press.

Oldenziel, Ruth. 1999. *Making Technology Masculine: Men, Women, and Modern Machines in America, 1870–1945*. Amsterdam: Amsterdam University Press.

Oliver, Michael. 1990. *The Politics of Disablement*. London: Macmillan.

———. 1996. *Understanding Disability: From Theory to Practice*. London: Macmillan.

Ong, Aihwa. 1999. *Flexibly Citizenship: The Cultural Logics of Transnationality*. Durham, NC: Duke University Press.

Ong, Aihwa, and Donald Nonini, eds. 1997. *Ungrounded Empires: The Cultural Politics of Modern Chinese Transnationalism*. New York: Routledge.

Ong, Aiwha. 1996. Cultural Citizenship as Subject-Making: Immigrants Negotiate Racial and Cultural Boundaries in the United States. *Current Anthropology* 37 (5): 737–51.

Ots, Thomas. 1994. The Silenced Body—The Expressive Leib: On the Dialectic of Mind and Life in Chinese Cathartic Healing. In *Embodiment and Experience*, edited by Thomas Csordas. Cambridge: Cambridge University Press.

Pasternak, Burton. 1989. Age at First Marriage in a Taiwanese Locality, 1916–1945. *Journal of Family History* 14 (2): 91–117.

Patterson, Kevin, and Bill Hughes. 1999. Disability Studies and Phenomenolgy: The Carnal Politics of Everyday Life. *Disability and Society* 14 (5): 597–610.

Pettigrew, Andrew. 1985. *The Awakening Giant: Continuity and Change in Imperial Chemical Industries*. Oxford: Blackwell.

Phillips, Michael. 1993. Strategies Used by Chinese Families Coping with Schizophrenia. In *Chinese Families in the Post-Mao Era*, edited by Deborah Davis and Stevan Harrell. Berkeley: University of California Press.

Priestley, Mark. 2001. Introduction: The Global Context of Disability. In *Disability and the Life Course: Global Perspectives*, edited by Mark Priestley. New York: Cambridge University Press.

Qin Yan. 1990. *Mama*. Directed by Zhang Yuan. Xian: Xian Film Studio.

———. 1992. *Deng Pufang De Lu* [The Deng Pufang Road]. Taiyuan: Shuhai Chubanshe.

———. 1997. *Deng Pufang De Lu* [The Deng Pufang Road]. Hong Kong: Kai Yi Press.

Quan Yanchi. 1994. *Deng Pufang Yu "Kang Hua"* [Deng Pufang and "Kang Hua"]. Kunming, PRC: Yunnan People's Publishing House.

Rabinow, Paul. 1984. Introduction. In *The Foucault Reader*, edited by Paul Rabinow. New York: Pantheon Books.

———. 1996. *Essays on the Anthropology of Reason.* Princeton, NJ: Princeton University Press.

Rapp, Rayna. 1999. *Testing Women, Testing the Fetus: The Social Impact of Amniocentesis in America.* New York: Routledge.

Reuters. 1995. Road Death Toll Increases in China. October 23.

———. 1996. Old Peking Hard to Find in Beijing. June 4.

Ricoeur, Paul. 1981. *Hermeneutics and the Human Sciences.* Cambridge: Cambridge University Press.

Rofel, Lisa. 1992. Rethinking Modernity: Space and Factory Discipline in China. *Cultural Anthropology* 7: 93–114.

———. 1999a. *Other Modernities: Gendered Yearnings in China after Socialism.* Berkeley: University of California Press.

———. 1999b. Qualities of Desire: Imagining Gay Identities in China. *Gay and Lesbian Quarterly* 5 (4): 451–75.

Rolleston, H. D. 1888. Description of the Cerebral Hemispheres of an Adult Australian Male. *Journal of the Anthropological Institute of Great Britain and Ireland* 17: 32–42.

Rosaldo, Michelle. 1974. Women, Culture, and Society: A Theoretical Overview. In *Woman, Culture, and Society,* edited by Michelle Z. Rosaldo and Louise Lamphere. Stanford, CA: Stanford University Press.

Ruan Cishan. 1992. Deng Pufang. *Sanyuefeng* [Spring Breezes] 87: 2–6.

Saari, Jon L. 1990. *Legacies of Childhood: Growing Up Chinese in a Time of Crisis, 1890–1920.* Harvard East Asian Monographs, no. 136. Cambridge, MA: Council on East Asian Studies, Harvard University.

Saich, Tony. 2001. *Governance and Politics of China.* New York: Palgrave.

Scharff, Virginia. 1991. *Taking the Wheel: Women and the Coming of the Motor Age.* New York: Free Press.

Schein, Louisa. 2000. *Minority Rules: The Miao and the Feminine in China's Cultural Politics.* Durham, NC: Duke University Press.

Schneider, Laurence. 1989. Learning from Russia: Lysenkoism and the Fate of Genetics in China, 1950–1986. In *Science and Technology in Post-Mao China,* edited by Denis Simon and Merle Goldman, 45–65. Cambridge, MA: Council on East Asian Studies, Harvard University.

Scott, Joan. 1991. The Evidence of Experience. *Critical Inquiry* 17: 773–95.

Seldon, Mark. 1993. Family Strategies and Structures in Rural North China. In *Chinese Families in the Post-Mao Era,* edited by Deborah Davis and Stevan Harrell, 139–64. Berkeley: University of California Press.

Sen, Amartya. 1990. More Than 100 Million Women Are Missing. *New York Review of Books,* December 20, 61–66.

Shapiro, Hugh. 1998. The Puzzle of Spermatorrhea in Republican China. *Positions: East Asia Cultures Critique* 6 (3): 551–96.

Sheldon, William Herbert. 1954. *Atlas of Men: A Guide for Somatotyping the Adult Male at All Ages.* New York: Harper.

Shirk, Susan. 1993. *The Political Logic of Reform in China.* Berkeley: University of California Press.

Shuntermann, M. F. 1996. The International Classification of Impairments, Disabilities, and Handicaps (ICIDH)—Results and Problems. *International Journal of Rehabilitation Research* 19: 1–11.

Si Tuxiang. 1992. *Hainan Dao Lishi Shang Tudi Kaifang Yanjiu* [The History of Hainan Island and the Research of Territorial Opening]. Qionghai, PRC: Hainan Publishing House.

Sing Tao Daily. 1996. Deng Xiaoping Rushed to Hospital. December 31.

Singer, Merrill, Lani Davison, and Gina Gerdes. 1988. Culture, Critical Theory, and Reproductive Illness Behavior in Haiti. *Medical Anthropology Quarterly* 2 (4): 370–85.

Siu, Helen, and Zelda Stern. 1983. *Mao's Harvest: Voices from China's New Generation.* Oxford: Oxford University Press.

Sivin, Nathan. 1995. State, Cosmos, and Body in the Last Three Centuries B.C. *Harvard Journal of Asiatic Studies* 55 (1): 5–37.

Skocpol, Theda. 1992. *Protecting Soldiers and Mothers: The Political Origins of Social Policy in the United States.* Cambridge, MA: Belknap Press of Harvard University Press.

Smart, Barry. 1994. *Michel Foucault: Critical Assessments.* New York: Routledge.

Social Statistical Section of the National Statistical Bureau, ed. 1985. *Zhuo Zhuang Cheng Zhang De Zhong Guo Er Tong: 1983 Nian Quan Guo Er Tong Qiu Yang Diao Cha Cai Liao* [Growing into Sturdiness: Data from the 1983 National Sample Survey of Children]. Beijing: National Statistical Bureau Press.

Sommer, Matthew Harvey. 2000. *Sex, Law, and Society in Late Imperial China.* Stanford, CA: Stanford University Press.

South China Morning Post. 1995. Deng Back in Hospital. Hong Kong. June 26

Spence, Jonathan. 1990. *The Search for Modern China.* New York: Norton.

Spiro, Melford. 1968. Virgin Birth, Parthenogenesis, and Physiological Paternity: An Essay in Cultural Interpretation. *Man* 3 (2): 242–61.

Stacey, Judith. 1983. *Patriarchy and Socialist Revolution in China.* Berkeley: University of California Press.

State Statistical Bureau. 1996. *China Statistical Yearbook.* Beijing: China Statistical Publishing House.

Stein, Dieter, and Susan Wright. 1995. *Subjectivity and Subjectivisation: Linguistic Perspectives.* New York: Cambridge University Press.

Stigler, Stephen M. 1999. *Statistics on the Table: The History of Statistical Concepts and Methods.* Cambridge, MA: Harvard University Press.

Stockard, Janice E. 1989. *Daughters of the Canton Delta: Marriage Patterns and Economic Strategies in South China, 1860–1930.* Stanford, CA: Stanford University Press.

Stoler, Ann. 1991. Carnal Knowledge and Imperial Power: Gender, Race, and Morality in Colonial Asia. In *Gender at the Crossroads of Knowledge: Feminist Anthropology in the Postmodern Era,* edited by Micaela di Leonardo. Berkeley: University of California Press.

———. 1995. *Race and the Education of Desire: Foucault's History of Sexuality and the Colonial Order of Things.* Durham, NC: Duke University Press.

———. 2002. *Carnal Knowledge and Imperial Power: Race and the Intimate in Colonial Rule.* Berkeley: University of California Press.

Stone, Deborah. 1984. *The Disabled State.* Philadelphia: Temple University Press.

Strathern, Andrew. 1996. *Body Thoughts.* Ann Arbor: University of Michigan Press.

Strathern, Marilyn. 1988. *The Gender of the Gift.* Berkeley: University of California Press.

Sun Lung-kee. 1983. *Zhongguo Wenhua De "Shenceng Jiegou"* [The "Deep Structure" of Chinese Culture]. Hong Kong: Ji Xian Press.

Telford, Ted A. 1992. Covariates of Men's Age at First Marriage: The Historical Demography of Chinese Lineages. *Population Studies* 46 (1): 19–35.

Terry, Jennifer, and Jacqueline Urla. 1995. *Deviant Bodies: Critical Perspectives on Difference in Science and Popular Culture.* Bloomington: Indiana University Press.

Tien, H. Yuan. 1973. *China's Population Struggle: Demographic Decisions of the People's Republic, 1949–1969.* Columbus: Ohio State University Press.

———. 1991. *China's Strategic Demographic Initiative.* New York: Praeger.

Townsend, James R. 1967. *Political Participation in Communist China.* Berkeley: University of California Press.

Tremain, Shelley. 2002. On the Subject of Impairment. In *Disability/Postmodernity: Embodying Disability Theory,* edited by Mairian Corker and Tom Shakespeare, 32–47. New York: Continuum.

Trostle, James A. 1996. Medical Anthropology and Epidemiology. *Annual Review of Anthropology* 25: 253–74.

Turner, Bryan. 1992. *Regulating Bodies: Essays in Medical Sociology.* New York: Routledge.

———. 1993. *Max Weber: From History to Modernity.* New York: Routledge.

Turner, Terence. 1994. Bodies and Anti-Bodies: Flesh and Fetish in Contemporary Social Theory. In *Embodiment and Experience,* edited by Thomas Csordas, 27–47. Cambridge: Cambridge University Press.

———. 1995. Social Body and Embodied Subject: Bodiliness, Subjectivity, and Sociality among the Kayapo. *Cultural Anthropology* 10 (2): 143–70.

Turner, Victor. 1969. *The Ritual Process: Structure and Anti-Structure.* Lewis Henry Morgan Lectures, 1966. Chicago: Aldine.

United Nations. 1990. Disability Statistics Compendium. *Statistics on Special Population Groups. Series Y* (4).

United Press International. 1995. Deng Marks 91st Birthday. August 21.

Unschuld, Paul. 1992. Epistemological Issues and Changing Legitimation: Traditional Chinese Medicine in the Twentieth Century. In *Paths to Asian Medical Systems,* edited by Charles Leslie and Allan Young, 44–61. Berkeley: University of California Press.

Üstün, T. Bedirhan. n.d. WHO Family of International Classifications, ICIDH-2: Toward International Standards to Report Functioning, Disability, and Health. Geneva: World Health Organization Classification Assessment Surveys and Terminology Group.

Wacquant, Loïc. 1995. Pugs at Work: Bodily Capital and Bodily Labour among Professional Boxers. *Body and Society* 1 (1): 65–93.

Walder, Andrew. 1986. *Communist Neo-Traditionalism: Work and Authority in Chinese Industry.* Berkeley: University of California Press.

Wang Minpei, ed. n.d. Xinwei De Huigu [Relieving Memories]. Beijing: Zhongguo Kangfu Yanzhou Zhongxin [China Rehabilitation Research Centre].

Watson, James L. 1989. Self Defense Corps: Violence and the Bachelor Sub-culture in South China: Two Case Studies. In *Proceedings on the Second International Conference of Sinology.* Taipei: Academia Sinica.

Watson, Rubie. 1986. The Named and the Nameless: Gender and Person in Chinese Society. *American Ethnologist* 13 (4): 619–31.

———. 1991. Wives, Concubines, and Maids: Servitude and Kinship in the Hong Kong Region, 1900–1940. In *Marriage and Inequality in Chinese Society*, edited by Rubie Watson and Patricia B. Ebrey, 231–55. Berkeley: University of California Press.

Watson, Rubie, and Patricia Buckley Ebrey. 1991. *Marriage and Inequality in Chinese Society*. Studies on China, no. 12. Berkeley: University of California Press.

Weber, Max. 1946. *From Max Weber: Essays in Sociology*. Translated and Edited by Hans H. Gerth and C. Wright Mills. New York: Oxford University Press.

———. 1963. *The Sociology of Religion*. Boston: Beacon Press.

———. 1978. *Economy and Society: An Outline of Interpretive Sociology*. Berkeley: University of California Press.

Wei Deng, Andreas Wilkes, and Gerald Bloom. 1997. Village Health Services in Rural China. *IDS Bulletin* 28 (1): 32–38.

Weston, Timothy. 2004. *The Power of Position: Beijing University Intellectuals, and Chinese Political Culture, 1898–1929*. Berkeley: University of California Press.

White, Sydney. 1998. From "Barefoot Doctor" to "Village Doctor" in Tiger Springs Village: A Case Study of Rural Health Care Transformations in Socialist China. *Human Organization* 57 (4): 480–90.

———. 1999. Deciphering "Integrated Chinese and Western Medicine" in the Rural Lijiang Basin: State Policy and Local Practice(s) in Socialist China. *Social Science and Medicine* 49 (10): 1333–47.

Whiting, John Wesley Mayhew, Richard Kluckhorn, and Albert Anthony. 1958. The Function of Male Initiation Ceremonies at Puberty. *Readings in Social Psychology*, 3rd ed., 359–70.

WHO. 1995. *Information System: Expanded Programme on Immunization*. WHO/EPI/CEIS/95.2. Geneva: World Health Organization.

———. 2001a. WHO Publishes New Guidelines to Measure Health. Geneva: Information Office.

———. 2001b. ICF Checklist. Press Release. WHO/48. Geneva: WHO.

Whyte, Martin King. 1974. *Small Groups and Political Rituals in China*. Michigan Studies on China, 267–92. Berkeley: University of California Press.

Wilson, Amy Auerbacher, Sidney L. Greenblatt, and Richard W. Wilson. 1977. *Deviance and Social Control in Chinese Society*. New York: Praeger.

Wolf, Arthur, and Chieh-shan Huang. 1980. *Marriage and Adoption in China, 1845–1945*. Stanford, CA: Stanford University Press.

Wolf, Arthur P. 1986. The Preeminent Role of Government Intervention in China's Family Revolution. *Population and Development Review* 12 (1): 101–16.

Wolf, Margery. 1972. *Women and the Family in Rural Taiwan*. Stanford, CA: Stanford University Press.

Wong, Glenn C. 1995. Seeking Women's Voices: Setting the Context for Women's Health Interventions in Two Rural Counties in Yunnan, China. *Social Science and Medicine* 41 (8): 1147–57.

World Bank. 1992. *China: Long-Term Issues and Options in the Health Transition*. Washington, DC: World Bank.

Wright, Susan. 1994. Culture in Anthropology and Organizational Studies. In *Anthropology of Organizations*, edited by Susan Wright. London: Routledge.

Xiong Zhennan, ed. 1995. *Women and Men in China: Facts and Figures.* Beijing: China Statistical Publishing House.

Yanagisako, Sylvia. 2000. Patriarchal Desire: Law and Sentiments of Succession in Italian Capitalist Families. In *Elites: Choice, Leadership, and Succession,* edited by João de Pina-Cabral and Antónia Pedroso de Lima, 53–72. Oxford: Berg.

Yanagisako, Sylvia, and Jane Fishburne Collier. 1987. Toward a Unified Analysis of Gender and Kinship. In *Gender and Kinship: Essays toward a Unified Analysis,* edited by Jane F. Collier and Sylvia J. Yanagisako. Stanford, CA: Stanford University Press.

Yang, Mayfair. 1997. Mass Media and Transnational Subjectivity in Shanghai: Notes on (Re)Cosmopolitanism in a Chinese Metropolis. In *Ungrounded Empires: The Cultural Politics of Modern Chinese Transnationalism,* edited by Aihwa Ong and Donald Nonini, 25–54. New York: Routledge.

Yeh Wen-hsin. 1990. *The Alienated Academy: Culture and Politics in Republican China, 1919–1937.* Harvard East Asian Monographs, no. 148. Cambridge, MA: Council on East Asian Studies, Harvard University.

Yip Ka-che. 1995. *Health and National Reconstruction in Nationalist China: The Development of Modern Health Services, 1928–1937.* Ann Arbor, MI: Association for Asian Studies.

Young, Iris Marion. 1990. *Justice and the Politics of Difference.* Princeton, NJ: Princeton University Press.

Yuan Fang, and Quan Weitian. 1981. Sociologist Chen Da. *Chinese Sociology and Anthropology* 13 (3): 59–74.

Zhan Mei. 2002. The Worlding of Traditional Chinese Medicine: A Translocal Study of Knowledge, Identity, and Cultural Politics in China and the United States. Ph.D. diss., Cultural and Social Anthropology, Stanford University, Stanford, CA.

Zhang, Everett. 2001. *Goudui* and the State: Constructing Entrepreneurial Masculinity in Two Cosmopolitan Areas of Post-Socialist China. In *Gendered Modernities: Ethnographic Perspectives,* edited by Dorothy Hodgson, 235–65. New York: Palgrave.

Zhang Li. 2001. *Strangers in the City: Reconfigurations of Space, Power, and Social Networks within China's Floating Population.* Stanford, CA: Stanford University Press.

Zhang Mei. 1999. From Lei Feng to Zhang Haidi: Changing Media Images of Model Youth in the Post-Mao Reform Era. In *Civic Discourse, Civil Society, and Chinese Communities,* edited by Randy Kluver and John H. Powers, 111–23. Westport, CT: Ablex Publishing.

Zhang Yang. 1995. Zhengdun Jidong Sanlun Weizhang [Reorganizing Illegal Motorized Three Wheelers]. *Beijing Wanbao* [Beijing Evening News], February 21.

Zheng Shiping. 1997. *Party vs. State in Post-1949 China: The Institutional Dilemma.* Cambridge: Cambridge University Press.

Zhong Mei. 1999. Same Language, Yet Different: News Coverage of Clinton's China Visit by Two Prominent Newspapers. In *Civic Discourse, Civil Society, and Chinese Communities,* edited by Randy Kluver and John H. Powers, 153–66. Westport, CT: Ablex Publishing.

Zito, Angela. 1997. *Of Body and Brush: Grand Sacrifice as Text/Performance in Eighteenth-Century China.* Chicago: University of Chicago Press.

Zola, Irving. 1972. Medicine as an Institution of Social Control. *Sociological Review* 20 (4): 487–504.

———. 1981. *Missing Pieces: A Chronicle of Living with a Disability.* Philadelphia: Temple University Press.

———. 1993. Self, Identity, and the Naming Question: Reflections on the Language of Disability. *Social Science and Medicine* 36 (2): 167–73.

INDEX

"abominations of the body" (Goffman), 62
activities of daily living, 249–50
Acton, Norman, 72–73, 74, 224n21
Addlakha, Renu, 236–37n6
administrative directives, 99–100
Agamben, Giorgio, *Homo Sacer* by, 82
Ah Bo, 182, 183, 186–91, 192
alterity, 29, 176–77, 191; definitions of, xi, 58
American Association on Mental Deficiencies, 247, 248, 225n30
amputation, 249
Anagnost, Ann, 36–37, 42, 50, 54
ancestor worship, 150–51, 156, 169–70
ancestral burial sites, 169, 239n21
Annual Day of Disabled Persons, 203
anonymity, 196, 215n1
anthropology: body in, 5; medical, 11, 35, 213, 219n7, 221n1; mentioned, xii, 207; narrative approaches in, 184, 191; and statistics, 58–59, 61, 176, 221n1; study of disability, 10–11, 216n8; study of elite, 34, 218n3, 243n2; study of gender, 11, 216n9, 233n13. *See also* disability studies
Appadurai, Arjun, 137
Armstrong, Gordon, 52, 53, 201
arthritis, 18, 30
Association of Neurology and Psychiatry, 77
autonomous regions, 242–43n16

Baba Mountain, 220n13

backwardness, 71, 73, 98, 155, 224n26
barefoot doctors, 152, 154, 162
Bayi primary school, 39–40, 220n18
Beichizi Street. *See* China Disabled Persons' Federation, administrative center
Beihai park, 83
Beijing: and cultural sophistication, 241n9; Federation office, 86, 93; motorized tricycles in, 114, 131, 132, 137; Xuan Wu district, 57–58, 126, 217n12, 234n16
Beijing Medical College hospital, 1, 47
Beijing University (Beida), 1, 31, 41, 42–44, 220n15, 220n17, 220n21
bicycles, 117–19, 122, 232nn4,6,7, 232–33n8
binaries, 29, 108–9, 194, 210–11
Bingcan Qingnian Julebu (Disabled Youths Club), 83–87, 109, 111, 119, 148
biobureaucracy, 3, 7–8, 22, 34, 35, 37, 218nn2–3. *See also* biopolitics; biopower
biomedical institution-building, 33–34, 50, 65. *See also* medicalization
biomythography of statesmanship, 36, 54, 219n9
biopolitical globalization, 209
biopolitics, 6, 7, 21, 148, 208–9. *See also* biobureaucracy; biopower
biopower: Foucault's view of, 8–9, 23–24, 213; and the state, 9, 24, 60–61, 82, 147–48, 153, 213
biosociality, 148, 237n6
blind: assistance for, 84, 129, 225–26n2;

and development of China Disabled
Persons' Federation, 26–27, 87–88;
and marriage, 182, 241n6; and state-
building, 209, 213. *See also* bodiliness;
Deng Pufang
emperor, 103
employment, 109–12, 135–36, 186, 232n31.
See also China Disabled Persons' Federation; entrepreneurship
"entrepreneurial masculinity" (Zhang), 131
entrepreneurship, 12–13, 131, 138, 167, 178
epidemiology, 65
eugenics, 67, 68
experiences of difference, 210–12, 213,
244n6

"face," 73, 74, 167
family: filial piety and ancestor worship,
150–51, 156, 169–70; and marriage,
158–59, 193–94, 195–96, 197; as
protection for the aged, 170, 240n4;
sociality based on, 149, 155–56, 166,
168, 169
Far East and South Pacific Games for the
Disabled (FESPIC), 113, 140
Farquhar, Judith, 236n3
feiji ("useless/diseased"), 61–62, 63–64
fei ren (social outcasts), 31
Fei Xiaotong, 232n5
Feng family of Min Song, 169
fenzao chifan (eating in separate kitchens),
103, 104, 231n26
Ferguson, James, 115
FESPIC (Far East and South Pacific Games
for the Disabled), 113, 140
fieldwork: information-gathering methods,
215n2; sites of, 15, 217n12
filial piety, 150
fingers, loss of, 249
fiscal decentralization, 103–4, 231n26
Five Guarantees Households, 160, 164,
238n16
foot, conditions of, 58, 79, 249
Ford, Henry, 116
Fordism, 115–16, 126–27, 130, 141,
232n1, 232n2
foreigners, xii, xiii
Foucault, Michel: on biopower, 6, 8–9, 61,
82; critiques of, 9, 23, 24, 25; ideas on
"subjectification," 34–35, 55, 218nn4–5;
mentioned, 175; and role of the state, 9,

24, 213, 216n6; "technologies of
domination," 183
Four Cleanups, 43
Fourteenth Automatic Tricycle Rectification
Campaign, 134

ganbu (cadres), 2, 42, 151. *See also* duty
officers
Gang of Four, 44, 51
Gao Xiaoqi, 103–4, 177–78, 179, 180–81,
231n27
gaogan zinu (children of high-ranking
officials), 38, 91–92
Gaubatz, Piper Rae, 232n6
Geertz, Clifford, 207
gender: bicycles and, 117–18; in Chinese
history, 233n11, 233n13; of Deng Xiaoping's funeral committee, 200, 243n1;
and independent entrepreneurship, 131;
inequality, 106, 107–8, 110, 134–35,
136, 166, 231n29; and marriage, 180,
240–41n5, 241n6; and mobility, 122–
24, 185–86; and physical disability, 124;
and study of *canji*, 10, 210; and study of
men, 11, 216n9; use of the term, 122–
23. See also *canji*, association with
maleness
Geng Bailu, 105
Geng La, 193–94, 197
Gennep, Arnold van, 173
Germany, 94
Ginsburg, Faye, 216n8
Global 2000, 228n12
global disability-advocacy movement, 28, 70,
71, 72, 73, 241n7
globalization, 22, 24, 198, 208–9
gnou hui (mentally ill), 188, 242n14
Goffman, Irving, "abominations of the
body," 62
Good, Byron, 191
Gramsci, Antonio, 232n2, 233n12
Great Leap Forward, 43, 220n20, 221n22,
230n24, 231n26
Guangxi Province, 190, 242–43n16
guanxi (connections), 46–47, 106–7
Guo Li, 167–70, 210
Gupta, Akhil, 115

"habitus" (Bourdieu), 8, 216n5
Hacking, Ian, 60–61, 67, 70, 221–22n3;
Taming of Chance by, 221–22n3

Compositor:	BookMatters, Berkeley
Indexer:	Susan Stone
Text:	10/12 Baskerville
Display:	Baskerville
Printer and binder:	Thomson-Shore, Inc.